W9-CAP-231

ALICE JAMES

JEAN STROUSE is the author of *Morgan, American Financier* as well as *Alice James*, which won the Bancroft Prize. Her essays and reviews have appeared in *The New York Review of Books*, *The New Yorker*, *The New York Times*, *Newsweek*, *Architectural Digest*, and *Slate*. She is currently the Sue Ann and John Weinberg Director of the Dorothy and Lewis B. Cullman Center for Scholars and Writers at the New York Public Library.

COLM TÓIBÍN is the author of six novels, including *The Master* (a novel based on the life of Henry James) and *Brooklyn*, and two collections of stories, *Mothers and Sons* and *The Empty Family*. He has been a visiting writer at Stanford, the University of Texas at Austin, and Princeton, and is now Mellon Professor in the Humanities at Columbia University.

ALICE JAMES

A Biography

JEAN STROUSE

Preface by
COLM TÓIBÍN

NEW YORK REVIEW BOOKS

New York

THIS IS A NEW YORK REVIEW BOOK
PUBLISHED BY THE NEW YORK REVIEW OF BOOKS
435 Hudson Street, New York, NY 10014
www.nyrb.com

Library of Congress Cataloging-in-Publication Data
Strouse, Jean.
  Alice James : a biography / by Jean Strouse ; preface by Colm Tóibín.
    p. cm. — (New York review books classics)
  Originally published: Boston : Houghton Mifflin, c1980.
  Includes bibliographical references and index.
  ISBN 978-1-59017-453-1 (alk. paper)
  1. James, Alice, 1848-1892. 2. United States—Biography. 3. James family. I.
Title.
  CT275.J29S77 2011
  973.7092—dc22
  [B]

                    2011012585

ISBN 978-1-59017-453-1

Printed in the United States of America on acid-free paper.
10 9 8 7 6 5 4 3 2 1

CONTENTS

Preface · vii

Introduction · xiii

PART I: AN ACCIDENTAL CHILD

Chapter One: Divine Maternity And a Calvinist God · 3

Chapter Two: Natives of the Family · 22

Chapter Three: A Sensuous Education · 37

Chapter Four: Civil War · 60

PART II: A FEMININE AGE

Chapter Five: Bostonians · 85

Chapter Six: "Nerves" · 97

Chapter Seven: Breakdown · 117

Chapter Eight: "Trying To Idle" · 132

Chapter Nine: A Grand Tour · 144

Chapter Ten: Love and Work · 161

Chapter Eleven: Dark Waters · 177

Chapter Twelve: Gains and Losses · 191

Chapter Thirteen: Alone · 214

PART III: THE WIDER SPHERE OF REFERENCE

Chapter Fourteen: "Peculiar Intense and Interesting
    Affections" · 233
Chapter Fifteen: A London Life · 253
Chapter Sixteen: A Voice of One's Own · 273
Chapter Seventeen: Divine Cessation · 296

Afterword: The Diary · 319
Notes · 329
Acknowledgments · 355
Illustrations · 327
Index · 357

Preface

Like the James family, the Yeats family produced two brothers who specialized in finishing everything they started. While their father found it difficult to complete an oil painting or write a whole book, W. B. Yeats, the poet, and his brother Jack, the painter, produced a large quantity of work; they remained single-minded and dedicated throughout their lives partly as a response to their untidy upbringing and their father's fondness for distraction.

In both the Yeats and the James families, there was also a talented, clever sister who did not marry and lived all her life in her brothers' orbit, whose letters remain fascinating for their sharpness, wit, and intelligence. Lily Yeats and Alice James did not write novels or poems or make paintings, but for all that, their personalities emerge from the past with considerable gnarled energy. Their lives were lived within limits—and how they managed within those limits tells us much about the fate of clever women in the second half of the nineteenth century. Yet in another sense, the limits left these two women free to be nothing but themselves. That ambiguous position is what makes them so fascinating, and it is why they had as much force and individuality as their famous brothers, and at times even more.

Jean Strouse's biography succeeds in giving Alice James her full due, allowing a long-submerged figure to shine as a brilliant individual, while also making clear that her unusual and unhappy fate was the result both of the rules and restrictions of society and of the eccentricities of a particular family. Alice appears as a woman caught between the demands of her own fierce intelligence and the dullness of the domestic sphere occupied by her mother and aunt. Strouse makes ingenious use of her letters and diaries, but is also superb in her examination of the milieu in which Alice was raised. Alice's parents, brothers, and friends are all brought vividly before us. If the world of Alice James was circumscribed, the limits were, as she herself was well aware, of the highest and most interesting sort.

Strouse is a connoisseur of tone. She can read a letter from Alice with full knowledge of its nineteenth-century context. She can also analyze the peculiar fears, neuroses, and delusions which lie between the words. She depicts Alice's longings and sense of panic and inadequacy with subtlety and care. She moves through the years making clear the significant influences, the moments of change, the sudden shifts and turns in Alice's psyche—her responses to life and illness, and her family's responses to her. But Strouse is not prepared to offer a reductive interpretation or a blanket explanation. She is not a biographer who begins with a theory and sets about proving it; her version of this complex life is judicious and detailed. Alice James is allowed her proper strangeness.

Alice was clearly subject to damaging historical and family circumstances, but she was also in some ways heroic. She suffered for much of her life, and Strouse shows us how real and intense that suffering was. We see Alice's struggle against her mysterious invalidism, and yet we also see her wallowing in it, needing it. In addition to telling a story of conflict within a woman of intelligence and sensitivity, this biography sheds considerable light on the history of nineteenth-century medicine. Strouse manages an evenness of tone in her accounts of the theories about what was wrong with Alice and the efforts made to cure her. Some of the treatments she endured, viewed from almost a century and a half later, seem like pure quackery. Strouse understands, however, that the field of medicine was groping to understand "nervous" disorders, and that myriad, useless "cures" were new and seemed credible at the time.

It was Alice's mother and father, and, less directly, her brother William— in the sense that he teased her, flirted with her, and insisted on pitying her, which she hated—who did much to crush her spirit. We can see the developing dynamics of destruction because what happened within the James family is unusually richly documented. Not only do we have letters which give a picture of ordinary life, of the context for the dramas and the crises; we also have Alice's diaries, and the novels of Henry, which reveal a great deal about his own preoccupations and preconceptions. And finally we have William's writings on psychology, which throw a strange light on his sister's dilemma. Strouse sifts through this extraordinary mass and variety of source material with the skill of a literary critic, and also with remarkable sympathy and flair.

Thus her book is not only a life of the youngest of the five James children, and the only girl among them, but a portrait of the inner workings of the entire family. It shows how differently each one of them was treated by the parents and what a distinct creature each one of them became. The biography is deeply disturbing in its clear delineation of the essentially neurotic character of the search for power and space within the James family and household. Out of this neurosis, as if by right, grew two American geniuses. And out of it also emerged the wounded figure of Alice.

By treating the family as a unit, Strouse also gives each of them a pure individuality, whether as a striving artist or scientist, or a struggling patient (the family members wrote constantly to each other about illnesses real and imaginary)—a pure individuality, that is, within the genteel prison created for them by their parents. The story of their lives is the story of how they each sought to be released from this prison with various levels of success.

What Alice and her two oldest brothers shared—what sets them apart and makes their lives of such continuing interest—was the quality and intensity of their self-consciousness. These were lives deeply examined by the subjects themselves, and yet the very subtlety and acuteness of their self-awareness makes them highly unreliable as witnesses; what they left were clues or evasions or half-truths, versions that are hardly to be trusted. The Jameses need and can bear endless scrutinizing. Alice's letters and diaries, her command of vocabulary, her savage wit, her indiscretion, her brittle lack of self-pity, her interest in the political world, her gift for friendship make her a character of extraordinary interest.

In her final years in England, Alice became ever more of what Henry might have called "a case." Her taking to her bed and her intense relationship to her friend Katharine Loring, not to speak of her relationships with the doctors who treated her and the servants who looked after her, tempt us to feel that we are following a story which is either vastly comic or utterly tragic. It is a credit to Strouse's sympathy and forensic patience that we are allowed the luxury of neither extreme. She approaches this most complex psychology with remarkable wisdom. She doesn't gloss over difficulties; she doesn't seek to simplify. She gives us a masterly portrait of a brilliant mind placed under the greatest pressure, of an extraordinary family that was expert at doing damage to its members, and of a social and intellectual world in which William and Henry James were able to thrive while their sister moved willfully or bravely into shadows which become, in these pages, substantial and haunting.

—COLM TÓIBÍN

ALICE JAMES

Introduction

Why Alice James?

W HEN I AM GONE," Alice James wrote to her brother William as she was dying, "pray don't think of me simply as a creature who might have been something else, had neurotic science been born."

By neurotic science she meant the science of nervous disorders, since her existence had long been dominated by mysterious illnesses for which no organic cause could be discovered and no cure found. Her prescient plea to William insisted that her life be judged on its own terms, without apology or excuse. At the same time, it recognized the temptation her friends and posterity would feel to explain her somehow, to imagine what she might have been. And in recognizing that temptation, Alice acknowledged that her life appeared to have been a failure.

By conventional measures, it was. Alice James did not produce any significant body of work. She never married. She did not have children. She was not socially useful, particularly virtuous, or even happy. Her interests and talents might have led her to become the "something else" she referred to in her letter to William — perhaps (to ignore her injunction for a moment) a historian, or a writer on politics, a pioneer in women's education, or the leader of a radical movement. Instead, she became an invalid. Like a great many other nineteenth-century women, she was "delicate," "high-strung," "nervous," and given to prostrations. She had her first breakdown at the age of nineteen, and her condition was called, at various points in her life, neurasthenia, hysteria, rheumatic gout, suppressed gout, cardiac complication, spinal neurosis, nervous hyperesthesia, and spiritual crisis. "Try not to be ill," wrote her brother Henry in 1883, " — that is all; for in that there is a failure."*

Alice would have liked to put her mind to use in ways the world could recognize. She knew she was intelligent. When she was not incapacitated, she held salons in Boston and London and taught correspondence courses in history to women all over the United States. She had considerable power as a writer, though it was undisciplined: all her life she wrote lively, detailed letters to relatives and friends, and her diary, published after she died, presents a wide range of original reflections on society, politics, literature, history, and the people she knew. An avid reader and an energetic thinker, she formulated a radical philosophy that helped her bear a difficult life and meet an early death with remarkable courage. But these activities were private. They marked no worldly success.

Success, however, had unconventional measures within the James family. And though Alice's life can be seen in several contexts — including the history of nineteenth-century women, the science of nervous disorders, and the literature of private life — it was in the family group that she lived with greatest intensity. The Jameses, isolated during her childhood by money, travel, and the particular chemistry of their personalities, constituted a self-consciously "special case," self-enclosed and self-referring. William was, in a sense, describing them all when he told Alice in 1889 that Henry Jr. was really "a native of the James family, and has no other country."

Two of Alice's brothers possessed real genius, and their work met with tremendous public acclaim during her lifetime. William, the eldest, a physician by training, is probably the most important psychologist in American history and one of its most interesting philosophers. Her second brother, Henry, ranks among the greatest novelists in the English language. Their father, too — Henry James, Sr. — achieved renown as a writer and lecturer on religion, although his ideas did not earn him a place in the pantheon of history's thinkers.

Henry Sr. adored his two brilliant oldest sons and took great pride in

---

* "HJ wrote 'future' but fairly obviously meant failure," writes Leon Edel in a note to this letter as published in his *Henry James Letters*. It is also possible that James meant "there is no future," but the meaning would be the same. James's mistake did contain a certain truth, however, for within the James family there *was*, oddly enough, a "future" in illness. But that is getting ahead of the story.

their accomplishments, but he did not equate writing novels and teaching at Harvard with success. He urged on all five of his children a strenuous individualism that stressed *being extraordinary* no matter what one chose actually to do. In fact, he encouraged them not to make narrowing career choices, but "just to *be* something," recalled Henry Jr. in his autobiography, "something unconnected with specific doing, something free and uncommitted, something finer in short than being *that,* whatever it was, might consist of." Success in this rather murky scheme had nothing to do with the temporal rewards of laurels, lucre, and fame. Its indices were internal. "I am not sure indeed," continues Henry Jr.'s autobiography, "that the kind of personal history most appealing to my father would not have been some kind that should fairly proceed by mistakes, mistakes more human, more associational, less angular, less hard for others, that is less exemplary for them (since righteousness, as most understood, was in our parent's view, I think, the cruellest thing in the world) than straight and smug and declared felicities." In the eyes of this novel parent, an interesting failure seemed far more worthy of appreciation than any "too obvious success."

James encouraged his children to "convert and convert" the raw data of experience into interesting forms of communication (explained Henry Jr.), "success — in the general air — or no success; and simply everything that should happen to us, every contact, every impression and every experience we should know, were to form our soluble stuff . . . the moral of all of which was that we need never fear not to be good enough if we were only social enough: a splendid meaning indeed being attached to the latter term."

If the moral of all of that seems somewhat obscure, it is not more so in Henry's account than it was in real life. The indirection that serves as the hallmark of Henry's late style (he was nearly seventy when he wrote his autobiography) has parallels in the opacity of what all the Jameses had to say about their past. Henry's "moral" pointed toward perception and the conversion of perception into articulate communication as the principal ingredients of a Jamesian success.

These preoccupations fostered in some of the Jameses a highly articulate self-awareness. But there were, inevitably, great holes in what they could see about the experiences that shaped their lives — particularly about the nature and dynamics of the family itself. Most families generate myths about themselves, but few place the kind of premium the

Jameses did on simultaneously reinforcing the myths and presenting private perceptions of truth for public consumption. More often than not, myth and perception conflicted, and the James children grew adept at giving eloquently ambiguous voice to the way things were supposed to be: they learned to see and not see, say and not say, reveal and conceal, all at the same time.

The notion that communication ranked as the ultimate value in human experience grew out of a painful awareness of all one could *not* share. The intense, close-knit family group bred within itself a profound sense of individual solitude. "Perhaps the greatest breach in nature," wrote William in 1890, is "the breach from one mind to another." He went on to describe two brothers waking up in the same bed, each reaching back into the stream of his last conscious thoughts before sleep, each unable to enter the other's consciousness except by being told. Peter cannot *feel* Paul's last drowsy state of mind; he can only imagine or hear about it. Only through words can the brothers cross that breach in nature. Words marked the intersection of pubic and private experience.

Not all the James children excelled in the lessons of this unusual catechism. William, Henry, and Alice learned — at different times and in very different ways — to pay acute attention to their perceptions and convert this "soluble stuff" into words. The two middle boys, Garth Wilkinson and Robertson, never mastered the alchemical art; both felt they had missed out on the family genius, and Robertson once said he thought he was a foundling.

Henry Jr. put the principles of conversion to their fullest imaginative use, adapting them, in the process, to his own larger definitions of what it meant to "succeed" at the private business of life. In the world of his novels, moral vision counts for far more than action. Everything depends not on what a character does, but on how much he (or, more often, she) *sees* in life, other people, tradition, art, nature, the possibilities of the absorbing, reflecting mind. James's great theme was the confrontation of two worlds — American and European — one, innocent, fresh, unabashed, energetic, relatively simple; the other, rich, dense, knowing, intricately subtle and complex. The novels' protagonists, who start out in relative innocence, slowly take in the full breadth, range, and depth of experiences larger than anything they could have previously imagined. It was the process and consequences of learning to see that fascinated James, and it was the ability to open out one's imaginative vision as far as

possible — to take in all the simpler dichotomies of good and evil, innocence and knowledge, new world and old — that constituted, for him,
living in the largest sense.

William, too, though by nature of a more practical and scientific bent
than Henry, adapted these family themes to his own professional ends.
He spent long years unable to work, struggling with questions about the
nature of good and evil in the universe and his own soul. Later, his psychological and philosophical work asked, in effect, what exactly one can
know about good and evil, the mind and the body, feeling, perception,
expression, religious faith, the process of thought itself. He conducted
exhaustive examinations of these questions, never hesitating to experiment on himself, and wrote up his ideas in straightforward, energetic
prose.

To "succeed" as a person, then, in the broadest Jamesian interpretation, meant to achieve a complex identity forged out of all these ideas
about morality, consciousness, perception, and communication — a sense
of self that had to do with a quality of being and the ability to see life
steadily (as Matthew Arnold put it) and see it whole. Of the five, Henry
appears to have gone the farthest toward living out this ideal — it is virtually, in fact, his definition. William made forays, asked questions, had
flashes of insight, but he stopped at the borders of psychology and religion — he did not push on to the profound understanding of himself
and others exacted by this description of success; he might not even have
agreed with it.

And Alice? How did she measure up to a recondite standard in which
interesting failure had more value than too-obvious success? That is the
principal question to be kept in mind throughout the course of her story,
and it has no simple answer. "In our family group," wrote her novelist
brother, "girls seem scarcely to have had a chance." There was only one
girl in the family, which made her a particular kind of "special case"
within the rarefied circle. Her father viewed women as personifications of
virtue, innocent purity, holy self-sacrifice. Boys had to learn to be good,
through suffering and the interesting uses of perception, but girls were
good by nature and could dispense with interesting ideas. To be a James
and a girl, then, was a contradiction in terms. And it is Alice's struggle to
resolve that essential contradiction, her attempt to find something whole
and authentic in her own experience, that gives her life its real stature
and interest.

Virginia Woolf wondered, in *A Room of One's Own,* what would have happened if Shakespeare had had a "wonderfully gifted sister . . . as adventurous, as imaginative, as agog to see the world as he was." The girl would not, guesses Woolf, have been sent to school, or given a chance to learn grammar, logic, Horace, and Virgil. She would have "picked up a book now and then, one of her brother's perhaps, and read a few pages." But then her parents would have come in and told her to do something practical "and not moon about with books and papers. They would have spoken sharply but kindly, for they were substantial people who knew the conditions of life for a woman and loved their daughter — indeed, more likely than not she was the apple of her father's eye. Perhaps she scribbled some pages up in an apple loft on the sly, but was careful to hide them or set fire to them." Eventually, however, the time came for her to marry, and to avoid that "hateful" fate she ran away to London, to the stage door, where the actor-manager finally took pity on her. Soon "she found herself with child by that gentleman" and in the end killed herself one dark winter's night.

That, surmises Woolf, is how the story might have gone, since "any woman born with a great gift in the sixteenth century would certainly have gone crazed, shot herself, or ended her days in some lonely cottage outside the village, half witch, half wizard, feared and mocked at."

William and Henry James did have a sister gifted with fine intelligence, and through her it is possible to look closely at the scenario Woolf imagined. Although Alice James lived a good 300 years after the hypothetical "Judith" Shakespeare, her intellectual life was bound by many of the same strictures. The moral and philosophical questions that Henry wrote up as fiction and William as science, Alice simply lived. Her private quest for a sense of her life's integrity offers a special, personal angle of vision on the past. Not the past of great men and historical events, nor the past of the unknown masses who left no record of their thoughts, but the past of a sentient, articulate person whose particular history makes vivid the ideas, personalities, and social conditions of her time.

Alice James is not a representative figure in any obvious sense. She was too much a part of the peculiar Jamesian universe to "stand for" something larger than her own experience. Still, the general outlines of her life parallel those of a great many other women of her period and social class. Mysterious nervous ailments, ranging from occasional "sick headaches" and a becoming Victorian delicacy to screaming hysterics and bizarre psychotic episodes, dominated the lives of vast numbers of American women. Taken all together, these illnesses, with their distinct personal origins, can be seen as a collective response to the changing shape of late nineteenth-century American life, in particular to the changing social positions and functions of women. Industrialization had altered the nature of housework, for example, leaving some women with leisure time to use their minds and others with a heightened commitment to motherhood as a perfectable science and the apotheosis of femininity; the Civil War proved that women could do men's jobs if necessary, and abolitionism intensified agitation for women's right to vote; the increasing democratization of education in the postwar years included new possibilities for the education of women. Some women addressed themselves to these changes directly, trying to encourage or thwart them. Others turned inward, making their private lives the battleground for what Woolf called their "own contrary instincts."

Alice took the latter route, registering social change and personal conflict in the dramatic wars that raged through her body and mind. She did not see it that way. She made no claim to have carried on an exemplary struggle or to have achieved anything beyond the private measure of her own experience. To make her into a heroine (or victim-as-heroine) now would be seriously to misconstrue her sufferings and her aims. Nonetheless, her experience has a unique value, and it is no sacrifice to take her at her word and not dwell on who she might have been. Because she fought to define for herself what it meant to be Alice James, she gave posterity a way to think about who she was.

Part I

An Accidental Childhood

How grateful we ought to be that our excellent parents had threshed out all the ignoble superstitions, and did not feel it to be their duty to fill our minds with the dry husks, leaving them *tabulae rasae* to receive whatever stamp our individual experience was to give them, so that we had not the bore of wasting our energy in raking over and sweeping out the rubbish.

— Alice James, *Diary,* December 31, 1890

What enrichment of mind and memory can children have without continuity and if they are torn up by the roots every little while as we were! Of all things don't make the mistake which brought about our rootless and accidental childhood. Leave Europe for them until they are old eno' to have *the* Grand Emotion, undiluted by vague memories.

— Alice James to William James, November 4, 1888

Chapter One

Divine Maternity
and a Calvinist God

INTERESTING PERCEPTIONS are preferable to marketable achievements only when there is enough money to go around. The money that paid for the unusual freedom of the James family had been earned long before Alice's parents were married.

On both sides, her forebears had been Calvinist for several generations. Her mother's maternal grandfather, Alexander Robertson, brought a strong Scottish strain into a lineage that was otherwise Irish. He came to New York City from Reading Parish, Palmont, Sterling County, Scotland, in 1761, at the age of twenty-eight. Two years later he married a Philadelphian, Mary Smith, whose father was also Scottish. They had eleven children before Mary died. In 1890, one of Alice's cousins told her that the Robertson descent could be traced back to Robert Bruce, King of Scotland. "I asked how," reported Alice. " 'Oh, why Robert*son*, son of Robert — er, er, — Bruce!' She showed me the coat-of-arms, but whether it was of the house of Robertson, Bruce, or 'Er — er,' I couldn't clearly make out." Whether or not there was royal blood in Alexander Robertson's veins, he appears to have been a wealthy man even before he emigrated, and by the 1780s he was a highly successful merchant in New York.

His tenth child, Alice James's grandmother Elizabeth, was born in 1781. At the age of twenty-five, she married James Walsh, a young tobacco and cotton merchant, the oldest son of her father's Irish friend

Hugh Walsh. Her new father-in-law had come to Philadelphia from Kil-lingsley, on the west shore of Strangford Lough, County Down, in 1764. During the Revolutionary War he furnished the American army with supplies, and when the war was won he bought land up the Hudson River near Newburgh, New York, and set up a general merchandise and freighting business, operating sloops between Newburgh, Albany, and New York City. He also established one of the first paper mills in New York State, and left a substantial fortune when he died in 1817, at the age of seventy-two. His wife, Catharine Armstrong, was a small, delicate woman who gave birth to nine children, was something of an invalid, and died sixteen years before her husband, at the age of forty-six.

James, Hugh and Catharine's third child, married Elizabeth Robertson on November 18, 1806. The young couple settled on John Street in lower Manhattan to be near Walsh's merchant offices, at 66 South Street. By 1815 they had six children — Alexander Robertson, Mary Robertson, Catharine, John, Hugh, and James — and had moved to a larger house, at 49 Warren Street. James Walsh was away from home much of the time on business, leaving Elizabeth to manage on her own. One morning in March of 1820, he was found dead of apoplexy in his bed in Rich-mond, Virginia.

Elizabeth remained in deep mourning for several years. She withdrew inside a small circle of relatives and old friends, worshiped her Presbyte-rian God, and continued to raise her children by herself. Although she had ample income from the estates of her husband, father, and father-in-law, she refused to spend it on cultural pleasures. Her children did not go to New York's opera, theater, museums, or concert halls; they lived quietly together at home. As they reached young adulthood, some of the sons were sent uptown to Columbia College, and several of the young Walshes were seized with a passionate Presbyterian piety. Mary, Cath-arine, and two of the boys joined the Murray Street Presbyterian Church.

Young Hugh Walsh soon decided to be trained for the Presbyterian ministry and enrolled at the Princeton Theological Seminary. There, in 1835, he met a fellow student, from Albany, called Henry James. The two had a great deal in common — including prosperous fathers and Presbyterian catechisms — and quickly became friends. Together they ar-gued over the teachings of the seminary, found them unsatisfactory, and in 1837 both young men abandoned their studies at Princeton. Walsh returned to his family in New York to take up the study of medicine. Henry James, after a summer trip to the home of his ancestors in Ireland, also went to New York, but with no clear plan for further study or a career. He read widely on religion, politics, and philosophy, and he spent a great deal of time with the family of his friend Hugh, now at 19 Washington Square, where Elizabeth Walsh had had a house built for herself and those of her children who remained at home. Hugh's sisters, Mary and Catharine, were captivated by the intensity and originality of their brother's friend. Mrs. Walsh, too, was intrigued by this energetic young talker who argued so good-heartedly against her religious beliefs that she grew fond of him, though she remained unconverted. Her daughters, however, were convinced. In the comfortable parlor of Washington Square the young women listened quietly to Henry James's denunciations of Presbyterian theology, and they soon withdrew from the Murray Street Church.

Mrs. Walsh, described by her friends as prudent rather than generous, had raised her daughters carefully in her own image. Mary and Catharine were serious, practical women. They were not young — Mary was thirty in 1840, and Catharine twenty-eight. They ought to have married. Neither had artistic or intellectual aspirations: their talents and interests were entirely domestic. Both were charmed by the young man from Albany who paced their drawing room as he argued, and when Mary agreed to marry him in 1840, her decision came as no surprise to her family.

Many years later, Henry James, Sr., described his wife to their novelist son: ". . . She was not to me 'a liberal education,' intellectually speaking, as some one has said of his wife, but she really did arouse my heart, early in our married life, from its selfish torpor, and so enabled me to become a man. And this she did altogether unconsciously, without the most cursory thought of doing so, but solely by the presentation of her womanly sweetness and purity, which she herself had no recognition of."

Mary, for her part, found in Henry James a tender man who needed her love and ministrations; "intellectually speaking," she endorsed his ideas without question. She wrote to him, thirty years after their wedding, when she was away from home with Alice and he was ill, "My heart melts with tenderness toward you my precious one, but my prayer is that we may both be saved from the great folly and wickedness of anxiety about each other — Your loving wify." And to her mother-in-law she gave an account of one of her husband's books (probably *The Church of Christ Not an Ecclesiasticism*, 1854): "It is addressed to the church and meets so rationally and satisfactorily so many of the difficulties, that every one in the church, who is not a mere formalist must sometimes have felt in many of its teaching [sic], that I am sure you will read it with interest. It fills too with new meaning and beauty, so many of the old Scriptures, which we have all been taught to revere, by giving them their true spiritual significance that no one I think can read it attentively without going with new delight to their Bible."

Mary had so far accepted the unorthodox sentiments of her future husband that she agreed to a civil ceremony. On July 28, 1840, wearing India muslin and a gold headband, she was married to Henry James in her mother's parlor at 19 Washington Square by the mayor of New York, Isaac Leggett Varian.

•

Henry James was twenty-nine years old when he married Mary Walsh. He had been born in Albany on June 2, 1811, the son of William and Catharine Barber James. His childhood had been exuberant and active. In a fragment of autobiography disguised as fiction, he described himself as "an ardent angler and gunner" who loved nature, laughter, and play: "I lived in every fibre of my body. The dawn always found me on my feet; and I can still vividly recall the divine rapture which filled my blood as I pursued under the magical light of morning the sports of the river, the wood, or the field." For as long as he could remember, however, the young Henry had been in conflict over these natural delights, for the stern God of his father frowned on them. "My headlong eagerness in pursuit of pleasure plunged me incessantly into perturbations and disturbances of conscience, which had the effect often to convert God's chronic apathy or indifference into a sentiment of acute personal hostility." To this sensitive small boy who stammered slightly, the idea of a cold, alien God was intensely real: "I doubt whether any lad had ever just so thorough and pervading a belief in God's existence as an outside and contrarious force to humanity, as I had. The conviction of his supernatural being and attributes was burnt into me as with a red-hot iron, and I am sure no childish sinews were ever more strained than mine were in wrestling with the subtle terror of his name. This insane terror pervaded my consciousness more or less. It turned every hour of unallowed pleasure I enjoyed into an actual boon wrung from his forbearance; made me loath at night to lose myself in sleep, lest his dread hand should clip my thread of life without time for a parting sob of penitence, and grovel at morning dawn with an abject slavish gratitude that the sweet sights and sounds of nature and of man were still around me."

He was taught that man, fallen with Adam, could be redeemed only through grace and good works, but all his "insane terror" did not blight him into virtue. Whenever his debts to the neighborhood confectioner mounted up, he helped himself to silver from his father's drawer. He took books, food, and liquor from home to share with the older, glamorously tougher sons of the local shoemaker. And at the shoemaker's shop the ten-year-old Henry got into the habit of having a drink of raw gin or brandy twice a day on his way to school, morning and afternoon. His exploits exposed him so often to serious physical danger that his parents lived in "perpetual dread" that he would one day be brought home disabled or dead.

God's "chronic apathy or indifference" had an equivalent in Henry's father. William James had emigrated from County Cavan, Ireland, in 1789, at the age of eighteen, with a little money, a Latin grammar, and a desire to see a Revolutionary battlefield. He soon settled in Albany, and from a job as clerk had risen through merchandising, commerce, banking, real estate, and public utilities to become one of the richest men in New York State. At his death, in 1832, he left an estate worth $3 million. William James had three wives and fourteen children, took part in the opening of the Erie Canal, was a trustee and benefactor of Union College in Schenectady, and an active parishioner in the Presbyterian Church. He was a shrewd, practical man with a great deal of energy and full confidence in the Calvinist doctrine of election.

Henry recalls having little contact with his father except at family prayers and meals, "for he was always occupied during the day with business; and even in the frank domestic intercourse of the evening, when he was fond of hearing his children read to him, and would frequently exercise them in their studies, I cannot recollect that he ever questioned me about my out-of-door occupations, or about my companions, or showed an extreme solicitude about my standing in school." Throughout his fragment of autobiography, Henry James, Sr., expresses a polite fondness for this "easy parent" and takes pains to say that he never suffered from "any particularly stringent administration of the family bond . . . strive as I may, I cannot remember anything but a most infrequent exhibition of authority towards us on my father's part."

Nonetheless, he described himself as "never so happy at home as away from it." And since most of his autobiography is an indictment of punitive Calvinism ("I cannot imagine anything more damaging to the infant mind than to desecrate its natural delights, or impose upon it an ascetic regimen"), the "easy parent" who imposed this Puritanical God comes in for a share of indirect condemnation: "The parent, or whoso occupies the parent's place, should be the only authorized medium of the Divine communion with the child; and if the parent repugn this function, he is by so much disqualified as parent."

The paternal intimacy Henry longed for seemed possible only under special conditions. When one of the children fell ill, William James became "weakly, nay painfully, sensitive" to "claims upon his sympathy" — a fact young Henry learned in a dramatic way. His adventures ended abruptly one day when he was seventeen. He had been playing fireball with friends in a park across from his Albany school — a game in which balls of tow soaked in turpentine were used to fly paper balloons. The boys ignited the highly flammable tow under the balloons, which rose into the air as they heated. Once a balloon caught fire, the ball of tow dropped to the ground, to be kicked about like a flaming soccer ball. On this particular day, Henry's pants had got splashed with turpentine. When a ball of flaming tow fell through an open stable window, Henry rushed to help stamp out the fire. His pants were set instantly aflame, severely burning one of his legs. For weeks he was confined to bed in acute pain. The leg would not heal properly. Finally, on May 6, 1828, his brother Augustus wrote to their elder brother, the Reverend William James:

Dear Brother,

I take my pen, just as the mail is closing, to inform you that our brother Henry's leg was this morning amputated. You may have heard about three weeks since that several black spots had appeared on his leg which it was feared were the forerunners of *mortification*. These were subdued for the time, but it was thought by Doctrs. McNaughton, Bay, & James, that should they reappear in the course of the summer, that *Death* would be inevitable. Therefore after mature deliberation on their part, and indeed of us all, it was concluded to perform the operation this day at twelve o'clock. It was cut off some distance above the knee. The operation lasted (that is severing) about six minutes, but the most painful part was the securing the arterys, tendons, cords, &c.

He is now thank God safely through it, and in a sound sleep, with every appearance of doing well —

It was a distressing operation, to be sure, but if it had been procrastinated, we would have been in dreadfull anxiety through the summer because had these symptoms then reappeared, amputation would have been out of the question. He bore it much better than we expected . . .

In haste
Your affectionate brother,
Augustus James

Henry's protracted illness established a new emotional connection with his father. Throughout the boy's long confinement, his father's tenderness "showed itself so assiduous and indeed extreme as to give me an exalted sense of his affection." There were, of course, no anaesthetics in 1828, and when the doctors performed the excruciatingly painful amputation, Henry noted his father's sympathy as "so excessive that my mother had the greatest possible difficulty in imposing due prudence upon his expression of it."

William James had disapproved of his son's daredeviltry, but this injury was so extreme a punishment for boyish high spirits that the elder James may have wanted to make it up to Henry somehow. Perhaps he perceived the boy's impulsive, rebellious temperament, responsible for the disaster, as a reaction against his own self-righteousness; perhaps, too, he found a mutilated son easier to love than a rebel.

Whatever the reasons, Henry's account makes clear that through this experience he gained his father's affection in a way he might never otherwise have done. He had seen his "headlong eagerness in the pursuit of pleasure" as converting God's indifference to hostility; now that same force had turned his father's indifference to tenderness — at a terrible price. He came to the conclusion that selfish pleasure incurred punishment, and that suffering brought love. And he passed both those notions along to his own children.

Henry's joyful rambles in the woods and fields and his participation in the rough games of male adolescence were over. Now the ardent nature that had set him roving before dawn could find expression only in his emotions and mind. His inner life proved to be as intense and turbulent as his brief life of physical activity had been — the characteristic strain in all his adult writing is a roaming, passionate energy.

•

Henry's mother, too, had hovered by his sickbed. He recalls her sleep-walking to his room during the night, with a candle in her hand, to cover his shoulders and adjust the pillows just as if she were awake. She was "maternity itself in form," he wrote, "a good wife and mother, nothing else — save, to be sure, a kindly friend and neighbor."

Catharine Barber, the Albany grandmother of Alice James's childhood, had married William James in 1803 at the age of twenty-one; he was thirty-two. She was his third wife, and bore ten of his fourteen children. She came from Protestant Irish stock, the second generation to be born in the United States. Her parents, John and Janet Rhea Barber, spent their old age with the James family, and their grandson Henry never failed to contrast the "soft flexibility and sweetness" of Janet Barber's demeanor with the "stoicism" of her husband's, and "early noted the signal difference between the rich spontaneous favor we children enjoyed at her hands, and the purely voluntary or polite attentions we received from him." Henry made certain not to repeat within his own family that division in which spontaneity, softness, flexibility, feeling, and love were associated with women, and men were stoical, cold, exacting, respectable, and boring.

His mother, like his father, never brandished authority, he reported. "She made her own personal welfare or dignity of so little account in her habitual dealings with us as to constitute herself for the most part a law only to our affections." She ruled, in other words, by self-sacrifice. Henry found the subtler coercions of emotional indebtedness preferable to the stern rules traditionally associated with paternity. All his life, in private and in print, he exalted female devotion and tried to imitate it in his own relations with his children. What he failed to see was that the law of affections is still a law. And in his own life he was not prepared to make the kind of sacrifice he worshiped in women. When he described Catharine James as a good wife and mother, he added that she was "nothing else." With that qualification he implied the existence of something more, and though he married just such a woman, his adoring worship concealed an obscure judgment about these strong, virtuously selfless females: they were somewhat less than whole.

Henry James the novelist added in *his* autobiography to the portrait of Catharine Barber James. She had a passion for the "fiction of the day" — novels by Mrs. Trollope, Mrs. Gore, Mrs. Marsh, Mrs. Hubback,* Miss Kavanagh, Miss Aguilar. And she had a habit of disappearing from a

* Catherine Austen Hubback was Jane Austen's niece.

room full of grandchildren into a corner with her novel to sit, bent forward at her table, with the book held out at a distance and a candle placed directly between it and her farsighted eyes.

Henry Jr. points up the connection between female selflessness and power in describing his grandmother as a "fond votary of the finest faith in the vivifying and characterizing force of mothers." He recalled his childhood visits to Catharine James's Albany house, populated with relatives and servants, with its gardens full of peaches and its sense of ample leisure: "the very air of long summer afternoons — occasions tasting . . . above all of a big much-shaded savoury house in which a softly-sighing widowed grandmother, Catharine Barber by birth, whose attitude was a resigned consciousness of complications and accretions, dispensed an hospitality seemingly as joyless as it was certainly boundless." She was a "dear gentle lady of many cares and anxieties," his "gently-groaning — ever so gently and dryly — Albany grandmother."

In a daguerreotype taken at about this time, Catharine Barber James appears determined, stately, and tired. Her gentle groans and sighs were undoubtedly signs of age and fatigue; but perhaps her self-sacrifice — the joyless hospitality and resigned consciousness noted by Henry Jr. — had as much to do with duty and stoicism as with the bountiful generosity of divine maternity. Maternal force and emotional parsimony characterize the female lineage of the James family, from Catharine Barber James and Elizabeth Robertson Walsh to Mary Walsh James.

•

Henry James's troubles were not over when he got out of bed at last with only one leg. For one thing, he was addicted to alcohol. The habit that had begun at the shoemaker's shop on the way to school had been reinforced during his long illness as parents, doctors, and nurses plied him with "all manner of stimulants." He went off to Union College, in 1829, "hopelessly addicted to the vice." Also, his relations with his father deteriorated after he got well. William James wanted Henry to study law at Union, but instead, the young man treated himself to liquor, fine clothes, expensive books, "segars," and oysters — paid for with drafts on his father's account. Furious, the elder James refused to pay, and predicted that his son's vices would land him in prison. Henry left Union, fell in with professional gamblers, "scarcely ever went to bed sober, and lost my self-respect almost utterly." He finally returned to graduate from Union College in 1830, cured of alcoholism but not of religious doubt, and the peace he re-established with his father on returning to college was an uneasy one.

In 1832 William James died. His will, documenting his moral rigidity, decreed that none of his estate was to be distributed until the youngest then-living grandchild turned twenty-one, because of the "lamentable consequences" of inherited wealth on young people. To "discourage prodigality and vice and to furnish an incentive to economy and usefulness," James gave his trustees the power to exclude any of his heirs who led a "grossly immoral, idle or dishonorable life" and urged the trustees to carry out his posthumous orders with "rigid impartiality, sternness and inflexibility." He himself cut off his rebel sons, Henry and William, with small annuities. His children — including Henry and William — brought suit, and on June 24, 1833, much of the will was declared void; the $3 million estate was divided equally among James's many surviving heirs. Whatever compunction the sons and daughters may have felt in breaking their father's will was not recorded. None of them followed in his prosperous footsteps. "The rupture with my grandfather's tradition and attitude was complete," wrote Henry the novelist; "we were never in a single case, I think, for two generations, guilty of a stroke of business."

Henry James, Sr., came out of the fray with property yielding an annual income of $10,000. During his entire adult life he never worked a day at a conventional job. He used his money much as his father had feared he would, to support his pursuit of religious truth and to cultivate his family's intellect and taste. He was as devoted to the life of the mind as his father had been to the dollar, and he aimed to be as strenuously loving and present a parent as he had felt his father to be remote and indifferent.

•

Though Henry James rejected many of the tenets of Calvinism, he did not reject religion itself or even very much of the Puritan spirit. On the contrary, in an age that was becoming increasingly secular he struggled with his own doubts until he found — or, rather, invented — a system of belief that satisfied him, and then devoted himself to explaining his convictions to a world that didn't listen.

The doubts that caused his departure, with Hugh Walsh, from the Princeton Theological Seminary in 1837 were temporarily allayed by his marriage to Hugh's sister in 1840. His faith in female love and "the marriage sentiment" saved him throughout his life from a private hell of "envy, hatred, contempt of others, ill-will, lasciviousness, memories, unchaste nay unclean desires." Men alone were capable of sin — rage, lust, selfishness, doubt. Women knew nothing of temptation or skepticism. When all the "clanging rookery" of hell was let loose in him, he later wrote to his youngest son, he would "run to the bosom of your mother, the home of all truth and purity, and deafen my ears to everything but her spotless worth till the pitiless inflowing infamy had spent itself."

But the peace he found in the worship of his wife's "moral unstainedness" did not answer his questions about God and evil. These continued to plague him as his young family began to take shape. Fruitlessly, he sought help from his friend Ralph Waldo Emerson, whom he scolded for being a "man without a handle," elaborating, "You don't look upon Calvinism as a fact at all, wherein you are to my mind philosophically infirm, and impaired as to your universality." Emerson introduced him to Thoreau (who reported back after three hours' talk that meeting Henry James made "humanity seem more erect") and to Bronson Alcott. When Alcott claimed that he was one with Pythagoras and Jesus in never having sinned, James asked: "You say you and Jesus are one. Have you ever said, 'I am the resurrection and the life'?" "Yes, often," came the reply. "And has anyone ever believed you?" James rejoined, abruptly terminating the conversation.

In 1843, James took his wife, his sister-in-law, and his two young sons, William and Henry, off to live in England. Emerson wrote of his "selfish alarm" at losing his friend's affectionate antagonism, and gave James a letter of introduction to Thomas Carlyle. As soon as his family was settled in England, James called on Carlyle, Tennyson, John Stuart Mill, and George Henry Lewes, and was disappointed in most of them. Carlyle, he told Emerson, was "still the same old sausage, fizzing and sputtering in his own grease," and years later, on the occasion of Carlyle's death, James wrote in the *Atlantic,* "Thomas Carlyle is incontestably dead at last, by the acknowledgment of all newspapers. I had, however, the pleasure of an intimate intercourse with him when he was an infinitely deader man than he is now." Carlyle, like Emerson, held out no spiritual solace to James, and after a few months of visits in Chelsea and travel to Paris, James settled his young family in a cottage in Windsor near the Great Park and began to work alone on the questions that plagued him.

One day in May 1844, having finished a comfortable dinner with his family, he remained sitting at the table after the others had dispersed, watching the embers sift and glow in the grate, thinking about nothing in particular, feeling the pleasant effects of a good meal. Then something happened that changed the course of his life and thought. "Suddenly," he later wrote, "in a lightning-flash as it were — 'fear came upon me, and trembling, which made all my bones to shake.' To all appearance it was a perfectly insane and abject terror, without ostensible cause . . ." What he felt was "some damnèd shape squatting invisible to me within the precincts of the room, and raying out from his fetid personality influences fatal to life. The thing had not lasted ten seconds before I felt myself a wreck; that is, reduced from a state of firm, vigorous, joyful manhood to one of almost helpless infancy. The only self-control I was capable of exerting was to keep my seat. I felt the greatest desire to run incontinently to the foot of the stairs and shout for help to my wife, — to run to the roadside even, and appeal to the public to protect me; but by an immense effort I controlled these frenzied impulses, and determined not to budge from my chair till I had recovered my lost self-possession." For about an hour he managed to hold still in his chair, "beat upon meanwhile by an ever-growing tempest of doubt, anxiety, and despair, with absolutely no relief from any truth I had ever encountered save a most pale and distant glimmer of the divine existence, when I resolved to abandon the vain struggle, and communicate without more ado what seemed my sudden burst of inmost, implacable unrest to my wife."

His distress did not subside, and he sought help from doctors: they prescribed rest, fresh air, and water cures. He found a degree of comfort in the English countryside, but could not reconcile himself to the evil symbolized in that "damnèd shape."

At an English watering place, James met a Mrs. Chichester, who told him that he had undergone what the Swedish mystic Emanuel Swedenborg called a "vastation." James went immediately to London to find Swedenborg's books, and devoured them, against doctors' orders. In these books, which he would carry with him for the rest of his life, he found the answers he had been seeking for so long. What he found was not what other people found in Swedenborg: his friend Dr. J. J. Garth Wilkinson* later commented that there was nothing in common be-

---

* Wilkinson was an English doctor of medicine and an editor and translator of Swedenborg. When James met him, he was also interested in mesmerism, hypnotism, spiritualism, and mystical healing, and in the social philosophy of Charles Fourier. Later, in the 1850s, he became so involved in homeopathy that his Swedenborgian work was temporarily suspended. He was an ideal intellectual companion for Henry

tween Swedenborg and James except the phrase "Divine Natural Humanity." What James made of Swedenborg, in brief, was that evil is part of God's plan. God is not an alien, hostile tyrant but infinite love and creation. Out of nothing, God created Nature and Man, and without Him they are nothing. In antithesis to infinite, loving God, man is finite and selfish. All human misery stems from this antithesis, but so does the possibility of salvation. If man was not free to be selfish and evil, he could not freely choose goodness and God. Only when men voluntarily abolish their natural selfishness can they know and love each other as God knows and loves. And only then will the world be saved in the synthesis of God and man that Swedenborg called Divine Natural Humanity.

James came to see his vastation, then, as a stage in his regeneration: he had had to touch bottom, to apprehend evil itself; he had had to give up his strivings toward the truth in order to awake to a world transformed by his faith in God's love. With this faith, he could countenance evil in the universe and in himself as part of a progress toward good. In effect, his new vision absolved him of responsibility for his sins: to the degree that he was bad, God had made him that way for a purpose and would not condemn him. Once he perceived his struggles as the workings of Divine Providence, James could see evil itself as good.

This system of belief was as optimistic as the Calvinism of James's childhood had been pessimistic. With it, he erased the terrifying specter of hostility that had dominated his youth and substituted pure benevolence: his loving God combined the forgiving tenderness of an ideal father and the infinite selflessness of a perfect mother. Yet in many respects his ideas did not depart radically from Calvinism. Calvinism, too, holds that evil exists in the universe so that man may be free to choose good; the necessary condition for salvation in both systems is despair; and faith, under both sets of belief, is the means of approach to God. It was in his social formulations that James stood orthodox Calvinism on its head. In Calvinism, men fall collectively with Adam and are saved individually — elected, distinguished by their faith and good works. For James, man's

---

Sr., and the two remained friends in spite of intellectual differences. Emerson described Wilkinson in terms that might also apply to Henry Sr., noting his "native vigor . . . catholic perception of relations . . . and a rhetoric like the armoury of the invincible knights of old. There is in the action of his mind a long Atlantic roll not known except in deepest waters, and only lacking what ought to accompany any such powers, a manifest centrality. . . ."

sense of a superior self accounts for the fall; the child, born in innocence, becomes sinful only through inevitable assertions of self. Progress toward salvation begins with the destruction of selfishness, and the solidarity of mankind is the means and the goal of redemption.

The family, in James's view, became "literally the seminary of the race ... the sole Divine seed out of which the social consciousness of man ultimately flowers." But the family in isolation — and he cited his own childhood as an example — was antithetical to man's destiny, for it concentrated only on itself and the worth of its members. It would achieve its true spiritual significance only when the bonds of parental authority relaxed so that the natural instincts of childhood could serve as "divinely endowed educational forces" for mankind. In the ultimate "demoralization of the parental bond" he saw "pregnant evidence of ... an expanding *social* consciousness among men, which will erelong exalt them out of the mire and slime of their frivolous and obscene private personality, into a chaste and dignified natural manhood." The authority that had for centuries been paternal and tyrannical, he wrote, was in his own time fast becoming maternal, characterized by "the utmost relaxation, indulgence, and even servility." Now, he concluded, intelligent, conscientious parents would cheerfully subordinate themselves to the welfare of their children, rather than insist on their own prerogatives.*

---

* James put his ideas about the changing nature of the family (in the shift from patriarchal authority to more maternal and egalitarian bonds) to idiosyncratic use, but his perception of the change at midcentury was acute. A recent book about another influential nineteenth-century American family, the Beechers (Marie Caskey, *Chariot of Fire, Religion and the Beecher Family,* New Haven: Yale, 1978), makes the point that the "sanctified" life of Lyman Beecher's first wife, Roxana Foote, gave their children (who included Henry Ward Beecher, Catharine Beecher, and Harriet Beecher Stowe) a sense of religious authority that was as much maternal and feminine as patriarchal and masculine in the traditional Calvinist sense. In a review of that book, George M. Fredrickson writes:

> What Caskey fails to explore ... is the extent to which the intense family ties of the Beechers may have reflected changes in the conception of the family in American society as a whole. Social historians have shown that the traditional ideal of unquestioning obedience to patriarchal authority began to be displaced in the early nineteenth century by the more egalitarian image of the family as held together primarily by mutual affection. It is at least arguable that the Christian view of the relationship between man and God had always been closely correlated with prevailing conceptions of parenthood and that what was new was not so much the presence of God "by the hearth" as a transformed notion of parental authority that made the remote and severe patriarch of earlier times an inappropriate symbol for divinity in an age that exalted a more affectionate and consensual style of family life.

James spent the rest of his life lecturing and writing about Divine Natural Humanity, but for all the intensity of his devotion and vigor of his prose, he never managed to deliver his message to the world as he would have liked. As the titles indicate — *The Nature of Evil, Christianity the Logic of Creation, The Social Significance of Our Institutions, Society the Redeemed Form of Man* — his books tackle large topics and repeat in various contexts his perception of the true relation between man and God. Yet William noted in his introduction to his father's literary remains, "With all the richness of style, the ideas are singularly unvaried and few. Probably few authors have so devoted their entire lives to the monotonous elaboration of one single bundle of truths." Henry Sr. was theological and monistic in a secular, pluralist age; his mind leaped constantly from the individual to the general, and his readers were unwilling or unable to follow. William Dean Howells remarked, on reading James's *Secret of Swedenborg* (1869), that James had "kept it." And in 1863, when James was about to publish a book called *Substance and Shadow; or Morality and Religion in Their Relation to Life: An Essay on the Physics of Creation,* his son William, aged twenty-one, designed for the title page a woodcut of a man beating a dead horse.

•

"Father's ideas," though abstract and often vague, had profound effects on James family life. Henry Sr. turned his household into an impromptu laboratory for experiments in child-rearing and moral philosophy — with results his children found beneficial, confusing, painful, and diverting by turns. Henry Jr. was later bemused by his childhood discomfort over his father's unconventional career. He had been impressed, he wrote, with other boys who could casually announce the nature of their fathers' work. "*We* had no note of that sort to produce, and I perfectly recover the effect of my own repeated appeal to our parent for some presentable account of him that would prove us respectable." He asked constantly, "What shall we tell them that you *are,* don't you see?" And his father, greatly amused, would reply, "Say I'm a philosopher, say I'm a seeker for truth, say I'm a lover of my kind, say I'm an author of books if you like; or, best of all, just say I'm a Student." Young Henry found this answer less than satisfying — *abject,* he called it — and looked with envious admiration on a friend who told him "crushingly . . . that the author of *his* being . . . was in the business of a stevedore."

The elder James wanted to be everything to his children — father, mother, teacher, fellow pupil, intimate friend. Of them, he asked only that they be good. "I desire my child," he wrote in 1855, "to become an upright man, a man in whom goodness shall be induced not by mercenary motives as brute goodness is induced, but by love for it or a sympathetic delight in it. And inasmuch as I know that this character or disposition cannot be forcibly imposed upon him, but must be freely assumed, I surround him as far as possible with an atmosphere of freedom." Where he had had to memorize and recite, he wanted his children to absorb and consider; where he had been told what was good, he wanted them to find out for themselves. His educational ideas mirrored his religious philosophy: as God leaves man free to choose evil so that he may freely choose good, a parent leaves his child free to choose among the entire range of moral and intellectual experience so that he may freely choose virtue.

This system did not foster quite the freedom James thought it would, and it contained a great many contradictions. Though he based his entire philosophy on the personal confrontation of evil, he did his loving best to protect his offspring from all knowledge of sin, to prolong their innocence and develop their spontaneous natural goodness. Evil, acknowledged in the abstract, had no place at the family hearth. That basic contradiction, between what their father espoused (man finds God only after directly experiencing the evil in his own nature) and what he practiced (evil does not exist), fostered in each of the children a preoccupation with morality and a tendency to dichotomize. To be innocent and good meant *not to know* the darker sides of one's own nature. To love and be loved, then, required the renunciation of certain kinds of knowledge and feeling.

In their relative freedom from parental tyranny, the only right the James children did not have (as F. W. Dupee observed in his book about the novelist), was the right to be unhappy. "Ah!" exclaimed Alice in her diary in 1889, "those strange people who have the courage to be unhappy! *Are* they unhappy, by-the-way?" Her ignorance was unfeigned. For all his avowals of altruism, her father steadfastly refused to acknowledge the reality of his children's pain. He was so absorbed in his own feelings that he once told Emerson he "wished sometimes the lightning would strike his wife and children out of existence, and he should suffer no more from loving them." And to his novelist son he wrote in 1873:

My paternal feeling grows so much ... as I grow older, becomes so much more intense and absorbing, that I am compelled in self-defense to keep it under, lest its pains (so inevitable in the present disjoined social state) should come to exceed its pleasures ... Your long sickness, and Alice's, and now Willy's have been an immense discipline for me, in gradually teaching me to universalize my sympathies. It was dreadful to see those you love so tenderly exposed to so much wearing suffering, and I fought against the conviction that it was inevitable. But when I gained a truer perception of the case, and saw that it was a zeal chiefly on behalf of my own children that animated my rebellion and that I should perhaps scarcely suffer at all, if other people's children alone were in question, and mine were left to enjoy their wonted health and peace, I grew ashamed of myself, and consented to ask for the amelioration of their lot only as a part of the common lot. This is what we want, and this alone, for God's eternal Sabbath in our nature, the reconciliation of the individual and the universal interest in humanity.*

None of his children found God's eternal Sabbath in his or her own nature. Alice bestowed characteristically ambiguous praise on the touted freedom of the past as she looked back on her childhood from England in her diary in 1890: "How grateful we ought to be that our excellent parents had threshed out all the ignoble superstitions, and did not feel it to

---

* Robertson, more than any of the others, kept trying to find meaning and a connection with his father in the teachings of Swedenborg. A sad (undated) letter he wrote to William some years after their father's death shows him still yearning for this spiritual and intellectual bond. He was living by this time (probably the 1890s, which would put him in his fifties) in Concord, Massachusetts.

My interest in life is becoming nearly wholly absorbed in studying Swedenborg. I should like to perform some *visible* use in life — but I can't yet see what that is ... I have begun to read extracts (carefully selected) to half a dozen ladies here — from father's books ... His books are becoming nothing less than a heaven to me and I am now getting so thoroughly familiar with his thought that I am able to read between the lines ... it gives me the utmost delight to meet these people and endeavor to impart to them even a faint echo of the truth which it seemed to me father found in Swedenborg. He seems very near to me most of the time. I don't doubt he is. I know my thought and affection must be now touching his thought and affection (i.e. himself). Somewhere ... I say I feel his nearness because I am subject to these inexplicable moods of an utter and incommunicable sadness the very core of which is a holy delight and peace ... this dumb aching of the heart which feels itself breaking because it is alone and then suddenly flooded to repletion by the answering sense of that want in some other heart. So deep and real was his presence with me yesterday in that answer from his heart to mine that I know I can never be alone in time to come. How divine are these tears which come up unashamed in the broad face of day washing away as they seem to for awhile at least the dirty conceits and egotisms which are always acting as a barrier against the deliverance from ourselves which all are craving for ...

be their duty to fill our minds with the dry husks, leaving them *tabulae rasae* to receive whatever stamp our individual experience was to give them, so that we had not the bore of wasting our energy in raking over and sweeping out the rubbish." Perhaps her sense that she "ought to be" grateful concealed a desire for clearer guidelines, more tangible propositions, and the real liberty to thresh out answers for herself.

Alice neither accepted nor rejected her father's ideas. Ten years after his death, in the privacy of her diary, she covered up a hint of criticism by making it a mock sacrilege: "In a rash moment, panting to rise out of the trivial and draw a breath of *life,* I read one of Father's letters to a friend, it fell perfectly flat — Ah, what a wilted moment was that! I felt as if I had committed a desecration." And in the same entry she related a story from Herbert Spencer's *Autobiography*: "H.S. one day in talking to Huxley said that the only thing to hope for was to make a little mark before one died, to which Huxley — 'Oh, no matter about the mark, if one only gives a shove.' At first it makes Huxley seem the bigger animal of the two, which he is, no doubt, but surely Herbert restores the balance by repeating it to his own harm, if he doesn't make it tip a little thro' the superior weight of voluntary virtue over spontaneous." Then, carated in as an afterthought: "Shade of my Father visit me not if that heresy fall upon thine ear!"

Heretical she was, though her irreverence echoed her father's. "The impish passion displayed by that 'Unknowable Reality behind Phenomena,'" she wrote in 1890, "for making the creature self-destructive, the very quantities which make him strong before his fellows insidiously eating into his own vitals, is delightsome to watch from a sofa for an unsentimental spinster. Can it be, perhaps, that the *Unknowable Reality* simply jokes with Phenomena? as they say that the American public does with all the serious things of life — or is it only that mankind is so dense that it cannot perceive all the cowardices, follies and self-love unless they are carried to the limits of the grotesque?"

Instead of assessing the substance of her father's philosophy (William alone, of the five, tried to meet him on his own ground), Alice admired his intellectual energy, adopted his excoriative tone, and loved him unconditionally. "A week before Father died," she wrote, "I asked him one day, whether he had thought what he should like to have done about his funeral. He was immediately very much interested, not having apparently thought of it before; he reflected for some time, and then said, with the greatest solemnity and looking so majestic: 'Tell him to say only this, "here lies a man who has thought all his life, that the ceremonies attending birth, marriage and death were all damned nonsense," don't let him say a word more.' But there was no Unitarian, even elastic enough for this: what a washed out, cowering mess humanity seems beside a creature such as that."

Chapter Two

Natives of the Family

A LICE was the only one of the five James children not named for a relative or family friend. In later years, there would be other Alice Jameses: her brother Wilky named his daughter Alice; another brother, William, married a woman named Alice, and so did *their* son William. But in her childhood and adolescence, Alice was singular.

William, born in New York on January 11, 1842, was the grandson, great-grandson, and nephew of men named William James. Henry Jr., born fifteen months later, on April 15, 1843, was called Harry by his family but never liked sharing his father's name; he protested when William named his second son William in 1882 (the first was another Henry), and dropped the "unfortunate *mere* junior," after forty years, with a practically audible sigh of relief as soon as his father died. When a third James son came into the world on July 21, 1845, his parents named him Garth Wilkinson, after their English Swedenborgian friend, Dr. J. J. Garth Wilkinson. And the following year in Albany a fourth boy was called Robertson for Mary James's maternal grandfather, Alexander Robertson. (The unwieldy surnames given to the third and fourth boys were shortened in daily family usage to "Wilky" — sometimes spelled "Wilkie" — and "Rob" or "Bob.")

Shortly before Alice's birth on August 7, 1848, her family moved to 58 West 14 Street in New York City. The neighborhood, then known as "uptown," was the finest residential area in the city. It turned on the axis of Fifth Avenue — still unpaved north of 23 Street. Manhattan's business center flourished downtown, and horse-drawn streetcars ferried people along Sixth Avenue between business, shopping, and home. The James house stood on the south side of poplar-lined 14 Street between Fifth Avenue and Sixth. With three floors and an attic, a sunny library, and two parlors, front and back, it comfortably accommodated five children under the age of six, their parents, Mrs. James's sister, Kate, and several servants. But there was no room to spare. Two-year-old Robertson was put to bed with Aunt Kate when Alice was born.

As a small child, Alice had curly, light-brown hair, high coloring, and a playful, energetic disposition. The only young James not forcibly evicted from the nursery, and the only girl, she was treated to prolonged tenure as the "delicious infant" of the family. Some of her later remarks suggest that this position had its drawbacks. She protested frequently in her adult diary and letters against large families. What she emphasized was not poverty, hunger, or church opposition to birth control, but "how feeble and diluted, of necessity, must the parental instinct be, trickling down ... Just as the mind refuses to enjoy or to suffer save within limits, so does the heart refuse to love." The family she was referring to had twenty-five children, but she found a less spectacular array of progeny no less disturbing: when her neighbors in England had a new baby in 1889, she wrote in her diary, "This is No. 5 ... — one more tiny voice to swell the vast human wail rising perpetually to the skies!" In the "multiplication of the species" she saw something that "fairly haunts me, something irresistible and overwhelming like the tides of the sea or the Connemaugh flood, a mighty horde to sweep over the face of the earth." She herself came fifth, of course, and what haunted her in this wasteland vision may have had to do with a sense of deprivation, of there not being enough love in her own family to go around.

Mary James's ideas about child-rearing contrasted sharply with Henry Sr.'s, but since she did not articulate them as a philosophy or argue with her husband's intellectual assumptions, the disparity in parental approaches caused no overt conflict. Besides, Henry Sr. interested himself in the moral and aesthetic education of children who could talk, read, and think; infancy, in his view, was the province of mothers.

The paternal attitudes Mary James did not share included her husband's reverence for children's "divinely endowed natural instincts" and his purported desire to be subservient to his offspring. Firm and authoritative, she wanted to foster strength of body and character in her brood. She did not believe in letting the "little tyrants" rule too soon — they should not disturb their mother's sleep at night. And maternal self-sacrifice had limits: Mary held the help of servants and relatives essential, for a mother ought to "husband all her strength and vigor, to nourish her baby, and not exhaust herself by taking sole care of it." When her first grandchild was born, she told the infant's parents: "If he has such broad shoulders and deep chest, let him bawl a good bit, that is if you are sure that his stomach is full and there is no pin running in him." And asked for advice about this baby's constipation, Mary dismissed it as a common trouble with strong infants, saying "the less fine specimens" were apt to be "troubled the other way — so this is not a weak, but a strong point in the little man — Everything evinces his great superiority."

When her own fourth son, Robertson, was born in 1846, Mary wrote approvingly to an English friend that little Wilky had "come out for himself" since his brother's birth. ". . . Seeing that he was about to be shoved off [he] concluded to let us see how well he could take care of himself. He began to walk when the baby was two weeks old, took at once into his own hand the redress of his grievances which he seems to think are manifold, and has become emphatically the *ruling* spirit in the nursery. Poor little soul! my pity I believe would be more strongly excited for him were he less able or ready to take his own part, but as his strength of arm or of will seldom fails him, he is too often left to fight his own battles."

Robertson commented later on having been "shoved off" to the care of Aunt Kate when Alice was born. He still, after fifty years, carried with him the hurt he had then felt at his aunt's "mandatory ways. A mother does wrong to confide her offspring recklessly to others than herself." And he wondered if he had really been "as little appreciated as I fully remember feeling at that time. I never see infants now without discerning in their usually solemn countenances a conviction that they are on their guard in a more or less hostile surrounding."*

Mary James, accustomed to managing everyone around her, continued to supervise the emotional lives of her children long after they were grown. When William was struggling with poor physical and psychological health at the age of thirty-two, in 1874, his mother wrote to Henry Jr. that "the trouble" with William was "that he *must express* every fluc-

---

* Elsewhere, however, Robertson (like his sister) painted his childhood in rosy tints, contradicting his indictments by calling his early years "full of indulgence and light and color and hardly a craving unsatisfied."

tuation of feeling, and especially every unfavorable symptom"; she called his temperament "morbidly hopeless." By contrast, to William she praised Henry's "angelic patience" in *his* periods of ill health, and underlined her point: "Happily, that side of his character is always in relief, and does not need great occasions (as it does with some of us) to bring it to view."

William commended in his mother the physical strength and stoical self-sacrifice he felt lacking in himself. He wrote to Alice in 1866 that "Mother is recovering from one of her indispositions, which she bears like an angel, doing any amount of work at the same time, putting up cornices and raking out the garret-room like a little buffalo." He felt keenly her disapproval of his "morbidly hopeless" temperament.

Even Mary's "angel," Henry, got no exemption from her supervisory admonitions. When he was traveling abroad in the 1870s, she wrote anxious, hovering questions: Was he eating well, getting sufficient sleep? Was he spending too much money, or not enough? She missed him sorely, and longed to "throw around you the mantle of the family affection, and fold you in my own tenderest embrace. — It seems to me darling Harry that your life must need this succulent, fattening element more than you know yourself." She worried that the life of his affections was languishing far from the "moisture and sunshine" of home, and she had in mind a solution: "I know only one thing that would solve the difficulty, and harmonize the discordant elements in your life — You would make dear Harry according to my estimate, the most loving and loveable and happiest of husbands. I wish I could see you in a favorable attitude of heart towards the divine institution of marriage."

She half-apologized for this intrusion, saying, "I see so much in favor of your staying abroad, and I *feel* so much in favor of your coming home, that I am blindly feeling about, for some way of reconciling the difficulty." Henry quietly ignored her advice. He answered lightly, "If you will provide the wife, the fortune, and the 'inclination' I will take them all." She could not, needless to say, provide the inclination, though she may well have been tempted to arrange for the wife and the fortune; in fact, the complicated folds of her "own tenderest embrace" may have had a great deal to do with her favorite son's lifelong disinclination.

To the adult Robertson, too, Mary James "explained" her unsolicited advice with dubious logic: "Don't think I am meddling with your affairs in the advice I have given for I can't help giving it."

She would brook no criticism of the mothering she described to Henry as a "succulent, fattening element." Robertson once reproached her for not writing often enough, and she sent back a sharp rebuke. When he replied that he had meant only he was longing for more communication from home, she described herself as "heartily ashamed of my childish sensitiveness ... How could I have ... resented [your words] in such a childish way ... So forgive and forget dear Bob all that has passed, and promise to love me more than ever, after this exhibition of my infirmity."

Mary James had learned in her own childhood — and her husband's ideas on the subject daily reinforced the lesson — that a woman gets what she wants not by assertion but by selflessness. Like her mother, her mother-in-law, and countless other women throughout history, Mary James governed her family by means of self-sacrifice. And her husband and children idealized this practice. Almost ten years after Mary James's death, Alice reread her parents' letters and found "Mother's words breathing her extraordinary selfless devotion as if she simply embodied the unconscious essence of wife and motherhood." Then, the following year, she wrote, "Ever since the night that Mother died, and the depth of filial tenderness was revealed to me, all personal claim upon her vanished, and she has dwelt in my mind as a beautiful illumined memory, the essence of divine maternity from which I was to learn great things, give all, but ask nothing."

An interesting ambiguity lies in Alice's use of that predicative infinitive "I was to learn." It can be read as a statement of fact, made in the past about a future that has now also become the past — the sense being "from which I did learn." Or it can be read as a subjunctive infinitive of arrangement, expressing a command, the sense then being "from which I was supposed to learn" and containing the possibility that in fact she did not. She described what she did or did not learn from her mother as "Give all but ask nothing" — *but*, not *and*. With *and*, the giving might sound freer, more natural and easy; the *but* calls special attention to the self-sacrifice involved — it seems determined and willed, demanding recognition.

Henry Jr. also extolled his mother's saintly disinterestedness after she died: "She was patience, she was wisdom, she was exquisite maternity ... one can feel, forever, the inextinguishable vibration of her devotion ... It was a perfect mother's life — the life of a perfect wife. To bring her children into the world — to expend herself, for years, for their happiness and welfare — then, when they had reached a full maturity and were absorbed in the world and in their own interests — to lay herself down in her ebbing strength and yield up her pure soul to the celestial power that had given her this divine commission."

The mothers in Henry's novels, however, bear no resemblance to this portrait of exquisite maternity. As Leon Edel has pointed out, James's fictional mothers are grasping, selfish, demanding, and often terrifying. Some, like Mrs. Brookenham in *The Awkward Age* and Mrs. Beale and Mrs. Farange in *What Maisie Knew,* resemble vultures or vampires feeding on their innocent children. Madame de Bellegarde, in *The American,* has murdered her husband, and by preventing her daughter from marrying the American, Mr. Newman, she virtually kills her as well. Others, such as Mrs. Touchett in *The Portrait of a Lady* and Mrs. Newsome in *The Ambassadors,* are so selfish and removed from what goes on between people as to be irrelevant except as obstructions.* Even the obtuse, hapless, hypochondriacal mother in *Daisy Miller* exerts a negative influence on her daughter's fate through her self-absorbed failure to notice what is happening to Daisy. That Henry James never created in fiction a mother imbued with anything like the selflessness he ascribed to his own mother suggests that he recognized aspects of her character that were more complex than perfection.

Though Mary James devoted her entire life to others, her pure disinterestedness was a myth. By giving all but asking nothing, she placed everyone else squarely in her debt. They owed her nothing less than everything.

•

Fifty-eight West 14 Street had no indoor playroom, and when the three oldest boys wanted diversion, they looked to find it in the neighborhood. While they were out during the day, at school or exploring lower Manhattan, Alice shared the quiet nursery with Rob. Under the watchful eye

---

* Many of James's major characters do not, conveniently, have mothers: Milly Theale and Kate Croy in *The Wings of the Dove,* Maggie Verver and Charlotte Stant in *The Golden Bowl,* Isabel Archer in *Portrait,* Catherine Sloper in *Washington Square,* Christopher Newman in *The American,* Paul and Rosie Muniment in *The Princess Casamassima.* The illegitimate Hyacinth Robinson in *The Princess* has one of the few good mothers in James's fiction — and she dies, impoverished, in prison, when he is a child.

of a large Irish nurse, the youngest Jameses played for hours, pretending they were married, calling each other "Henry" and "Mary." They got the measles together, and scarlet fever. Sometimes they accompanied their mother down Sixth Avenue to the Washington Market, carrying her empty basket or trailing behind with their fists knotted in the end of her shawl. And they waited eagerly for the clatter of dropped books, slammed doors, and disputing voices that signaled their older brothers' return at the end of the day.

Robertson, older and stronger, exacted a quotient of revenge by teasing and mildly torturing the small sister who had forced his relegation to the care of Aunt Kate in 1848. But whatever pains it entailed, the nursery served for a time as a miniature world in which brother and sister could roughhouse, tease, and explore, unaware of their disparate destinies. When Rob left to join the other boys outside, Alice stayed behind — at first because she was the youngest, and then, forever apparently, because she was a girl.*

William had already become something of an explorer and "motor," as he later called himself. He loved to draw, and spent long afternoons working in the back-parlor lamplight, finishing off sketch after sketch; more often, however, he went out for adventures with the neighborhood boys. When Henry wanted to join in, William breezily dismissed the re-

---

* In *Literary Women,* Ellen Moers observes:

Every reader of Dickens knows the importance of a sister to a brother struggling to resolve the extreme Victorian separation between the purity and the desirability of womanhood. But to Victorian women the sister-brother relationship seems to have had a different and perhaps even greater significance — especially to those women, so commonplace in the intellectual middle class, who in a sexual sense never lived to full maturity. The rough-and-tumble sexuality of the nursery loomed large for sisters: it was the *only* heterosexual world that Victorian literary spinsters were ever freely and physically to explore. Thus the brothers of their childhood retained in their fantasy life a prominent place somewhat different in kind from that of the father figures who dominated them all.

Little sisters were briefly and tantalizingly the equals of little brothers, sharers of infant pains and pleasures that boys quickly grew out of, but that girls — as Maggie Tulliver bitterly tells us — clung to despairingly at an inappropriate age. Women authors of Gothic fantasies appear to testify that the physical teasing they received from their brothers — the pinching, mauling, and scratching we dismiss as the most unimportant of children's games — took on outsize proportions and powerful erotic overtones in their adult imaginations. (Again, the poverty of their physical experience may have caused these disproportions, for it was not only sexual play but *any* kind of physical play for middle-class women that fell under the Victorian ban.)

quest, declaring, "*I* play with boys who curse and swear!" In childhood and throughout his life, Henry accepted William's primogeniture, his "occupying a place in the world to which I couldn't at all aspire." William forged ahead, always "round the corner and out of sight," while Henry "hung inveterately and woefully back," interested not in doing things but in being somewhere, anywhere, "gaping" (as he put it) — taking in the impressions and sensations he would eventually put to creative use. William, not quite as sanguine about their tacit division of the universe, often repeated the theme of "*I* play with boys who curse and swear!" throughout their lives.* But Henry always maintained an attitude of graceful inadequacy: "Humility had nothing to do with it — as little even as envy would have had; I was below humility, just as we were together outside of competition, mutually '*hors concours.*'" William's competitions were with "others — in which how wasn't he, how could he not be, successful? while mine were with nobody, or nobody's with me, which came to the same thing, as heaven knows I neither braved them nor missed them."

The family interdiction against competition, against the greedy assertions of self that marked man's sinful nature in Henry Sr.'s philosophy, held strong. Yet competition inevitably reared its unwelcome head in this group of extraordinary minds, strong characters, and high ambitions. Inexorable distinctions *were* made — between first, second, fifth; the quick and the dull; favorite and failure; active and receptive; older and younger; male and female. The raw fight for a place in the family sun had to be masked, not just from the outside world but from the self. "I never dreamed of competing," wrote Henry Jr., "— a business having in it at the best for my temper, a displeasing ferocity. If competing was bad, snatching was therefore still worse, and jealousy was a sort of spiritual snatching."

The figure of Wilky is more obscure during this period than those of

---

* Both brothers were elected to the National Institute of Arts and Letters when it was founded in 1898. Seven years later, the institute set up the more limited Academy of Arts and Letters. Henry was chosen by a select committee on the second ballot, in February 1905; William was elected in May of that year, on the fourth ballot. In an extraordinary letter explaining why he would not accept membership in the academy, William gave among his reasons his brother's presence: "I am the more encouraged to this course by the fact that my younger and shallower and vainer brother is already in the Academy and that if I were there too, the other families represented might think the James influence too rank and strong."

the older boys. Physically strong, sociable, affectionate, he grew accustomed to being teased as "plump and corpusculous." A little later he emerged as the only one of the James children who did not love — who, in fact, hated — to read. How little Wilky read, and how much he slept, became the subject of frequent jokes.

Family activities included weekly excursions down Fifth Avenue to Grandmother Walsh's house at Washington Square, a neighborhood somewhat less busy and even more stylish than 14 Street at midcentury. On Saturdays Aunt Kate escorted the children to appointments with a "tremendously respectable" old dentist on Fulton Street, who was so purple and polite in his stock, dress coat, and glossy wig that he reminded the young Henry of Phiz's illustrations to Dickens. After the dentist came a treat: ice cream, "deemed sovereign for sore mouths, deemed sovereign in fact all through our infancy, for everything." And though Kate was at the helm for the painful portions of these Saturdays, Henry Sr. took over for the pleasure: he would have nothing to do with dental agony, but took (or manufactured) every opportunity to treat his brood to ice cream.

He also delighted in providing them with more cerebral pleasures. He communicated to all his children, except Wilky, his love of books, and their young imaginative lives were peopled with the characters of Dickens, Hawthorne, Poe, and Harriet Beecher Stowe, as well as with figures from contemporary magazines and serials, and Rodolphe Toepffer's *Voyages en Zigzag.* He took his small aesthetes to art exhibits, especially when the artist was European, and to the theater, interested for himself only in the plays he thought the children would enjoy: the Jameses saw so many versions of *Uncle Tom's Cabin* that they became connoisseurs of its message and aesthetic merits.* They knew nothing of the "paralytic Sunday routine" that had blighted Henry Sr.'s youth. He and his wife did not attend church, though they left the children free to do so if they wished; none did.

Encouraged to be seen and heard, the children participated in the dinner table talk whether or not there was company. "Company" often meant their father's friends, including Emerson, Charles Henry Dana, George Ripley, Horace Greeley, William Cullen Bryant. At other times,

* One night in the early 1850s they saw Emily Mestayer play Eliza at the National Theatre on the Lower East Side. Henry reported years later, "I am not sure I wasn't . . . more interested in the pulse of our party, under my tiny recording thumb, than in the beat of the drama and the shock of its opposed forces."

the guests' chairs at the dinner table were filled by relatives: Catharine Barber James came down from Albany for long visits, wearing silk dresses and lace mittens and keeping an inexhaustible fund of peppermints in her pockets; and Uncle William, passing from the Albany train to some business or other on lower Broadway, would toss a bundle of nightclothes and personal effects to the surprised servant on the steps, shouting, "Tell Henry and Mary" (that he had arrived, presumably), his voice drowned in the rumble of wheels on cobblestone as he headed downtown.

The Jameses took frequent trips upstate to visit Grandmother James and the Albany cousins, at first by steamboat and then, after the Hudson River Railroad was completed in 1851, by train. And they spent summers out of the hot city, sometimes at a huge Greek temple of a hotel called the Pavillion at New Brighton on Staten Island, sometimes traveling to a "vast caravansery" called the Hamilton House, near Fort Hamilton on the south shore of Long Island.

As early as 1849, when Alice was a year old, Henry Sr. had begun to think about taking his young family to Europe again. In the summer of '49 he wrote to Emerson that his brood had grown so large, he felt obliged to expand the 14 Street house and go to the country for the summer. He wondered, he wrote, looking with pity and dismay "upon our four stout boys, who have no playroom within doors, and import shocking bad manners from the street," whether it might not be better to go abroad for a few years. In Europe, couldn't the children "absorb French and German, and get a better sensuous education than they are likely to get here?" Abroad, his children could immerse themselves in art, literature, music, drama, and could see for themselves the beauty and history of a world older than America. James was merely thinking it over, he told Emerson, and he did nothing more than think about it for six years, except try to provide as "sensuous" an education for his children as he thought New York's theaters, art galleries, and libraries could offer.

But in 1855 he determined to try the experiment of Europe. He booked passage to England for himself, his wife, the "four stout boys," Alice, aged six, and his sister-in-law Kate.

•

Neither Henry's nor Alice's recollections of their mother's virtues took into account that all her life Mary James had someone on hand to share her work and leisure. Her sister, Kate, had been at her side all through their childhood and had managed to remain there even after Mary's marriage to Henry James. From a habit of years, each sister knew what the other wanted or needed without having to be told. They referred to each other in the terms used by the children, Catharine calling Mary "Mother" and Mary calling Catharine "Aunt Kate." They worked out a division of labor that suited their differing personalities. Kate, with her frequent bouts of ill health and occasional "nervous" troubles, had more sympathy and patience with suffering than her sister, and her services as nurse in the illness-prone James household were invaluable. She lived with her sister's family for most of the first twelve years of Alice's life. Later, after Kate moved to her own residence, she came back to the Jameses' whenever there was trouble with Alice's head, William's eyes, Henry's back.

Unlike Mary, Kate had political opinions: she was, for instance, a partisan of Lajos Kossuth, the Hungarian nationalist who had fought for Hungary's independence in 1848 and was working to keep the resistance alive from abroad when he visited America in 1852. She often disagreed with Henry Sr. (who thought Kossuth's United States tour would gain him "nothing . . . but private sympathy"). William wrote to Robertson in 1870 that "the sort of sub-antagonism that used to prevail between her and father seems to have no tendency to show itself as it used to and I hope they have got into a new groove with respect to each other." William (probably echoing his father) dismissed Kate's opinions as "intellectual foibles" but admired the "total absence of any stagnant, lazy, sensual or selfish element in her, everything being so bright and clear with the energy of her active will."

Like many other single women of her time, Kate devoted her life to other people's families. But her life had one brief, colorful episode of its own.

In the fall of 1852, she left the James house on 14 Street to take care of her brother John, who lived on Eighth Street and had fallen ill. Henry Sr. reported himself lonely without her, though her absence made more room in the house for his immediate family and she seemed happy taking care of her brother. She had begun to spend evenings with a rich widower, Captain Charles H. Marshall. From a rugged beginning as a cabin boy on whaling expeditions, Marshall had ended up commanding several ships on the Black Ball Line, or "Old Line," the first to provide regular service crossing the Atlantic under private auspices. The success of the line had had a great deal to do with the rise of the port of New York, and in 1834 Marshall had come ashore to manage the shipping concern from the city. He eventually bought the entire company, and had amassed about $150,000 by the early 1850s. In 1852, he was living just across Fifth Avenue from the Jameses, at 38 East 14 Street, and the two families (Marshall had several children) knew each other casually.

Henry Sr., writing to a friend in Europe in September 1852, mentioned that Kate and "the Captain were in here last evening." Reading over his letter, Mary James found its description suggestive of "wrong impressions" and made her husband add that Kate's meeting Captain Marshall at their house was accidental. Robertson, however, knew more than his parents — or more than they were willing to let on — for he later reported having been a witness to Marshall's wooing of Aunt Kate. Rob was still in her care much of the time, sharing her bed in fact, but since he was only six, she and her suitor supposed him unaware of their courtship.

By early 1853, Henry Sr. was writing to his friend of the approaching wedding: "Captain Marshall's assiduities this winter were boundless, and although Aunt Kate began by the old story of total and permanent insensibility, she finally 'give out,' as they say in Rutland and Danbury, about a fortnight since, and has been doing an immense millinery and mantlemaking business ever since." Standing in his library sometimes with the door open, watching the "steady stream of skirt and chemisette setting in towards the third story," he felt as if he ought to "go up and speak to the Captain about the dimensions of Mrs. M's dressing room. He is rich, however, and can make alterations."

Of the captain himself, James drew a friendly, humorous sketch: he was "faithful, truthful, and an early riser," especially the latter. He "rises at five winter and summer, musters first-mate (or second-mate as the case may be) and crew, takes a look at the weather and a pull at the newspaper, opens all the hatches, examines the condition of the hencoop and larder, and finally brings himself to anchor at the breakfast table with every sail of his appetite sharp-set and helm fast-down."

But then, though still in a jocular vein, he wrote of what losing Aunt Kate would mean: "Hang the old hunks, moreover, for taking away dear good Aunt Kate from us! I hope she will make him spend all his income ... Aunt Kate ... has always been a most loving and provident husband to Mary, a most considerate and devoted wife to me, and an incomparable father and mother to our children. She has paid all the servants' wages over again by her invariable good humour and kindness, and been both sun and stars to us whenever our skies have been overcast by dread, or the night of any great sorrow has threatened to shut us in. God bless her in her new home, and make it as friendly to her as the old one!"

Catharine Walsh was married to Captain Charles H. Marshall on a Friday morning, February 18, 1853, by the Reverend Dr. Bellows in New York. The entire James family attended the ceremony.

But her brother-in-law's wish that Kate's new home be as friendly as the old one was not fulfilled. There is no more news of the marriage in the Jameses' letters until 1855, when the family was getting ready to sail for Europe and Henry Sr. wrote to Emerson that "Mrs. Marshall" was going with them. She had made a "frightful mistake," he told his friend, in marrying a man whose "character hid itself from an intimacy of years, and only disclosed itself in the penetralia of home, as made of all the grinding littlenesses and coldnesses that are effectual in wearing out the human heart." From James's florid account it is difficult to get a sense of what went wrong: it was not Marshall's morality; Kate's high-minded brother-in-law found no fault there. But he described Marshall as having a "spiritual isolation and iciness which left no green thing alive ... and ... banished smiles and tears, laughter and all human sympathies to the opposite hemisphere." The situation proved so untenable that Kate "might have died, were not death too sacred a thing to be disbursed on so base a requisition," and when Marshall suggested a separation "in the way of menace," his wife seized the opportunity to return to her old home, "to be our sweet and stainless 'Aunt Kate' again, the refuge of all hearts, and the solace of every weary hour." This strange, brief marriage excited gossip, and Kate welcomed the opportunity to leave the country for a while with her sister's family shortly after she left her husband.

Marshall's side of their story has not survived. He lived on for ten years after their separation, ran for Congress (and lost) in 1854, was strongly antislavery and active in the Union Defence Committee during the Civil War, and when he died in 1865 an odd obituary appeared in the New York *Herald*:

Captain Marshall was distinguished for his firmness, decision of character, perseverance and manly independence. Like many men, who have from early life been engaged in nautical pursuits, and accustomed to command only to be obeyed, he had an air of sternness about him that was somewhat repulsive to strangers; but to those who knew him best he displayed in his intercourse all the amenities and attributes of a perfect gentleman.

Marshall's cold, "somewhat repulsive" manner may have accounted to some extent for Kate's disaffection. No doubt Marshall, too, had in the "penetralia of home" some complaints about his second wife; perhaps he did not like her "mandatory" nature any more than the infant Robertson had. And perhaps he found Kate's involvement with her sister's family interfering with the commitment he wanted his wife to make to himself and his own children. Kate was forty and he sixty when they married; both were presumably set in their ways — and hers, as her brother-in-law testified, had become an integral part of the James household routine. Kate had no special calling or talent, and marriage seemed — as it nearly always has to most women — the only feasible "career" open to her. The failure of her late marriage disappointed her, but she did have another family, and almost another marriage, to fall back upon. After leaving the captain, she took back her maiden name, appending "Mrs." to the front of it. She was known for the rest of her life as Mrs. Catharine Walsh.

•

The James family, accompanied by Kate and a French maid, Annette Godefroi, sailed for England on the *Atlantic* on June 27, 1855. They had a long, rough voyage, with cold weather and stormy seas nearly all the way. Most of the group got sick, but Kate and Mlle. Godefroi were well enough to nurse the others. Only Robertson and Henry Sr. kept up their full strength, enjoying the journey and dining (copiously, in Rob's case) at the captain's table. They arrived at Liverpool on Saturday, July 7, spent Sunday at the Queen's Hotel there, and on Monday traveled up to London, where they took rooms at the Euston Hotel. They spent a few days visiting with the Wilkinsons and seeing London's sights, then headed south, toward Paris and Geneva.

This trip was Alice's first experience abroad. When her family arrived in Paris, she stood with her brothers, leaning out over the balcony of their hotel high above the Rue de la Paix. She listened to people speaking the beautiful, strange language she was about to learn, and, though she knew nothing of history, literature, or art, she took in the pageantry of the Second Empire and heard Henry and William talk of Napoleon, the Louvre, the Luxembourg Palace; of the bookstalls and print shops along the Left Bank; of Delacroix and Victor Hugo. Years later she remembered her first impressions: the smell of French cupboards, a blue shawl worn by a lady in the Champs Elysées, "when in the golden summer sunshine my soul was in a moment flooded by a sense of the throbbing Union, the mystery and the pain of which has never since been silenced." The sensuous education had begun.

Chapter Three

A Sensuous Education

I N LONDON, Henry Jr. had come down with malarial chills and fever, and his family proceeded slowly toward Geneva so as not to tax what little strength he had. They left Paris at the beginning of July, improvising a stretcher out of a board, a mattress, and several cushions, for a romantic carriage-crossing of the Alps. The troupe, in two carriages piled high with luggage and trunks (no railroad connected Lyon and Geneva in 1855), now included a costumed, black-mustached postillion and an Italian courier who had joined them in Paris, in addition to the blond, rosy-cheeked "bonne Lorraine," Mlle. Godefroi.

Geneva in July seemed as delightful to young American sensibilities as Paris. Its clear, crisp air, sparkling lake, and gaily colored flowers and fabrics welcomed the travelers prepared to look on it for a while as home. The Jameses stopped first with friends on the shore of the lake, and then in August settled into an old villa called the Campagne Gerebsoff, just on the edge of town. The large, solid villa was set on ample grounds and surrounded by great spreading trees that kept its huge rooms cool and dark during hot summer days. Balconies and terraces afforded generous views of the city; nearby, the river Arve flowed into the Rhône; off in the distance stood Mont Blanc, majestic in the brilliant summer light. Here, on August 7, the James family celebrated Alice's seventh birthday.

A governess was engaged to tutor Henry, who was still ill, and Alice, while the other boys went out to boarding school, the Pensionnat Roediger, at Châtelaine. Henry recalled the young Swiss governess, Mlle. Amélie Cusin, as a "remarkably erect person" whose presence he found "quite sharply extrusive but on the whole exhilarating." She was the first in a long series of governesses who tended the James children at home — always Alice, and whichever of the boys happened not to be away at school, either by virtue of illness or parental decree.

On Sundays, Alice and Henry went with their parents to visit William, Wilky, and Rob at the Pensionnat Roediger. Scarcely a month after the boys had been established at school, however, their father was writing home to his mother that Swiss schools were "greatly overrated." The boys seemed happy enough, but their parents could not bear having them away from home. Mrs. James never saw them, reported her husband, "without feeling how much they need her personal care, and how little they get in exchange for that lack." And so in September of 1855 he concluded that home tuition would be best for all the children, and less expensive as well; Mlle. Cusin could teach them all.

"We had fared across the sea under the glamour of the Swiss school in the abstract," wrote Henry Jr., "but the Swiss school in the concrete soon turned stale on our hands." Now that the first educational experiment had failed, Henry Sr. saw no need to stay in Switzerland, and began to think of moving on. He was bored, restless, and disturbed by Geneva's north wind, the *bise,* which (he wrote to his mother) "stirs up a perpetual tooth ache." In early October the Jameses packed up and headed back over the Alps, this time accompanied by Mlle. Cusin. They traveled by mail coach, stopped briefly in Paris, and arrived late one evening in London at the Gloucester Hotel, on the corner of Piccadilly and Berkeley Street. There, exhausted and hungry, they had an English supper of cold roast beef, bread, cheese, and ale, and Henry Sr. expressed his pleasure at being back in England with an exhalation of relief and excitement: "There's nothing like it after all!" By Christmas they had moved into a furnished house, with a garden and view of an archery range, near the Wilkinsons in St. John's Wood, at 10 Marlborough Place.

At Christmas in 1855, the Jameses celebrated being back in London with everyone under one roof, near good friends, and settled in a house of their own. Christmas depends on secrets, however, and Henry James, Sr., in his headlong eagerness to share pleasure with his children, could no more keep secrets from them in 1855 than in any other year. For all his aspirations to selflessness, his performances at Christmastime show him once again deeply absorbed in the pursuit of his own satisfaction. He and his wife conspired about presents and hid them away in high closets;

but then this childlike father would hint and tease and encourage guesses — out of the range of his wife's hearing — until the children coaxed the hiding place out of his willingly unsealed lips. He "used to spoil our Christmases so faithfully for us," wrote Alice later in her diary, "by stealing in with us, when Mother was out, to the forbidden closet and giving up a peep the week or so before. I can't remember whether he used to confess to Mother after, or not, the dear, dear creature! What an ungrateful wretch I was, and how I used to wish he hadn't done it!"

Responsibility for the linguistic aspect of the sensuous education, now that the Jameses were in London, lay with Mlle. Cusin. All the children received daily lessons and practice in French. For the boys, Henry Sr. hired a young Scottish tutor named Robert Thomson (who later tutored Robert Louis Stevenson). Alice's brothers spent their morning studying Latin and "the ordinary branches of an English education" with Thomson, and in the afternoons the young Scot took them out to pitch ball and take long walks around the London of Dickens and Thackeray, to visit museums and the Tower, Westminster Abbey, St. Paul's, Madame Tussaud's, and the Zoological Gardens. Alice was left either in the company of her parents and Aunt Kate, or in the care of Mlle. Cusin.

The "requirements of our small sister were for long modest enough," reflected Henry Jr. later in his autobiography, and he described the procession of governesses hired to act as guides and teachers as an endless stream of rather unprepared young ladies. Alice's requirements did not include the study of Latin or English history; in the mornings she practiced French, and later in the day took long walks with her governess.

On one of these walks, in the gray dusk of a London afternoon, Alice and her chaperon discovered a milliner in the Edgeware Road. After repeated visits they declared him an *artiste,* and determined to order a bonnet for Mlle. Cusin. Mademoiselle had definite ideas of what a bonnet should look like, and so, needless to say, did the milliner. To Alice, aged seven, fell the task of reconciling "the millinery point of view of Neufchâtel and that of the Edgeware Road." When the agreed-upon creation was finally produced, "it came forth green shirred silk and pink roses and I can remember how my infant soul shivered, even then, at the sad crudity of its tone."

Aesthetic discrimination played a leading role in the James family education, whether it had to do with hats, books, art, or theater. In later years, two other adventures stood out for Alice about "that winter [in St. John's Wood] all draped in December densities." Both took place in the theater. The group from Marlborough Place regularly made its way through damp, foggy winter nights to sample the dramatic offerings of the West End. They saw Sheridan's *Critic,* French comedies, and a Christmas production starring Frederick Robson; they heard Fanny Kemble read *A Midsummer Night's Dream.* But the high point for Alice (and the rest of the family as well) was Charles Kean in *Henry VIII.* When the long-awaited evening finally arrived, Aunt Kate was ill and Alice's "joy . . . was somewhat obscured by the anguish of Aunt Kate's not being able to go. No greater misery ever befell a creature of woman born than that, thought I!" But as soon as the family had taken its seats and the lights of the Princess's Theatre began to dim, Alice forgot all about Aunt Kate. She was enthralled, and all her life remembered Cardinal Wolsey on his way to execution. For weeks after the performance the young Jameses painted watercolors of Queen Katharine's dream-vision of the "blessed troop" of angels bringing garlands, and re-enacted Wolsey's final speech to Cromwell, accepting his fall and death.

The second momentous evening occurred at the Olympic Theatre, where Alfred Wigan played John Mildmay in Tom Taylor's *Still Waters Run Deep.* The plot turns on the emerging character of Mildmay, who has been acting the part of dull, remote husband in a household ruled by his wife's tyrannical aunt, Mrs. Sternhold. As Mildmay gradually asserts his intelligence and authority, his father-in-law, Mrs. Sternhold's brother, keeps repeating, "My sister — she's a most superior woman." That was the line Alice James remembered over thirty years later, misquoting it slightly in her diary: " 'My sister is a most remarkable woman!' "

•

By the spring of 1856, Henry Sr. had grown tired of England, finding its citizens stolid and indifferent. He bore no ill will to "brother Bull" and "sister Cow," he wrote to a friend, but he was ready to move to Paris. Back across the Channel his family went, settling temporarily on the Champs Elysées, between the Rond Point and the Rue du Colisée. A new tutor was found for the boys, and a new governess, Augustine Danse, who reminded Henry of Becky Sharp: her smiling green eyes seemed to know everything. More sophisticated than her Vaudoise predecessor, Mlle. Danse introduced her young charges (her favorite was "l'ingénieux petit Robertson," and she found William somewhat bearish) to Paris.

They prowled the Champs Elysées, exploring side streets and coming on hidden gardens, hotels, cafés. The Arc, the young Empress Eugénie riding up and down in her coach on display with the baby Prince Imperial, the prince's baptism at Notre Dame, the fête of Saint-Napoléon — these impressions etched themselves forever into the James children's memories of the French capital.

In August they moved again, to a "wide-faced" apartment in what was then the Rue d'Angoulême–St. Honoré (it later became the Rue La Boëtie). Henry Jr., composing the past into perfect small scenes, recalls the baker's shop at the corner that was the source of "softly-crusty" croissants to enhance the café au lait at breakfast; a small crémerie, "white picked out with blue," that served meals to white- and blue-frocked workingmen and uniformed cab drivers; an oyster lady, "she and her paraphernalia fitted into their interstice much as the mollusc itself into its shell"; a *marchand de bois* packed tightly into his tiny shop with stacks of neatly bundled faggots and chopped logs.

Mary James took an intense dislike to Paris. She resented the high cost of living (they paid $2200 a year in rent, though they were getting only $1400 for their New York house) and French hostility to strangers (on whom the "grossest deception is practiced at every turn"). She found French servants in every way inferior to American ones. Their general brusqueness "shames our republican ideas," she told her mother-in-law, adding that it had been almost impossible to find a large enough apartment since the French made provision only for small families: "The means the French adopt to keep their families small is, I am told, sending their infants away into the country to be nursed, where eight out of ten die, or if they live, to send them to boarding schools."

That neither she nor her husband spoke French may partly account for her displeasure. It was difficult enough without a language barrier to manage servants, children, husband, shopping, packing up, and moving. And although Mary saw the advantages of Paris — the boys had good teachers, the new governess was "most sensible and ladylike," and Wilky, Bob, and Alice had begun to study music "with a good deal of enthusiasm" — nonetheless, she infinitely preferred America and its "vast superiority . . . to this degenerate land."

Alice, unlike her mother, took to the French immediately, and for the rest of her life had a fondness for "that wittiest and most infinitely perceptive of races." At the age of eight she was becoming bilingual: her governess and brothers addressed her only in French, and a copybook that she inscribed *"Offert à papa, maman et ma tante, le 24 December, 1856"* records her first forays into French literature. She copied out several fables of La Fontaine ("Les deux pigeons," "Le nid de fauvettes," "La brebis et le chien") and lessons in grammar and math. Another relic of her early French education, a bound volume containing the first fifty-two issues of the periodical *La Semaine des Enfants,* is inscribed, "Alice James, from her loving father, April 1, '58, Boulogne s/mer." Each issue contained a story from French history, as well as short sketches and dramas (about Sinbad, Midas, Ali Baba) and a series of "Variétés" — *"Merveilles de la création et curiosités de l'industrie; petite chronique, etc."* The weekly was designed for children in the interval between their learning to read and their beginning serious study; it aimed to be short, simple, and amusing — *"mais, en même temps tout sera instructif et surtout moral, et tendra à faire pénétrer insensiblement dans les jeunes coeurs l'amour de la religion et de la vertu."*

After the inevitable dismissal of her brothers' latest tutor, Alice shared her governess with Rob while the three older boys were installed at a Phalanstery called the Institution Fezandié in the Rue Balzac. The school, modeled on the utopian socialist ideas of Charles Fourier, was run by an ex-Fourierist ("I think there were only ex-Fourierists by that time," wrote Henry Jr.). The community bore no resemblance to the "strenuous" American Brook Farm, on which Hawthorne had based his *Blithedale Romance*; the three day boys took *dictées* and read aloud from French classics in the company of the institution's pensioners of all ages, both sexes, and several nationalities. By this time fluent in French, they listened in amusement to the syllabic murder practiced by their Anglo-Saxon fellows. The Institution Fezandié provided Henry with his first long look at the Americans abroad who would appear in so many of his novels, and gave William an early overdose of the French and British characters he would always find less congenial than the American.

•

Henry James, Sr.'s restless, optimistic idealism kept his family in a state of perpetual uprootedness. Each new educational experiment turned out less well than he had hoped; precisely what he wanted these schools to provide was not clear, but one after another they failed to prove as interesting as the intellectual fare of his imagination. As a result, the James children never stayed in one place long enough to establish friendships or a sense of continuity with anything beyond the family itself. They were, recalls Henry Jr., "hotel children," and when the adult William bought a house in New Hampshire years later for his own large family, his sister waxed fervent in praise of a stable family home: "What enrichment of mind and memory can children have without continuity & if they are torn up by the roots every little while as we were! Of all things don't make the mistake which brought about our rootless & accidental childhood. Leave Europe for them until they are old eno' to have *the* Grand Emotion, undiluted by vague memories."

But the uprooting alone did not account for Alice's sense that her childhood was "accidental." *Her* schooling had not been a factor in the deliberations that kept the family scurrying across Europe in pursuit of an ideal education that existed only in her father's mind. The "requirements of our small sister" had seemed "modest enough," Henry observed. Clever and quick, adept at languages and fond of reading, physically and intellectually energetic, Alice participated in all the family experiences that made the James children into a "special case" distinct from their peers; but being a girl set her apart even from her brothers.

While the boys studied and devised projects, went away to school, and roamed the streets of New York, Geneva, London, and Paris, Alice stayed at home with her parents and aunt. She read, practiced French and music, accompanied the women on shopping trips, and could not go out by herself. The boys had no interest in having her trail along after them. Even Henry, the most empathic of her brothers, recalled the degrading fact of having to be at school with "girls . . . even though we drew the line at playing with them and at knowing them." And in Paris he felt somewhat embarrassed at meeting his dashing French schoolmates on the Champs Elysées while "walking sedately . . . with my sister and her governess."

Girls of the middle and upper classes were seen, in the nineteenth century, as emotional and sensible, not intellectual or aesthetic; they were supposed to be "accomplished" — able to sew, dance, sing or play music, read French, discuss certain novels, perhaps draw or paint — but not learned.* Alice had no consistent educational stimulation, and no access

---

* To take an example from outside the James family, Henry Adams wrote of his engagement to Alice's friend Clover Hooper in 1872, "One of my congratulatory letters . . . describes my 'fiancée' to me as 'a charming blue' . . . She reads German — also Latin — also, I fear, a little Greek, but very little. She talks garrulously, but on the

to friends among her own sex who might have helped her feel less bored and excluded.

Observations made by family friends a few years later highlight the contrast between the worlds of the male and female Jameses. Lilla Cabot, who married Henry's boyhoood friend Thomas Sergeant Perry, recalled the "poky banality of the James house ruled by Mrs. James where HJ's father used to limp in and out and never seemed really to 'belong' to his wife or Miss Walsh, large florid stupid seeming ladies, or to his clever but coldly self-absorbed daughter who was his youngest child." Mrs. Perry continued, reporting to Van Wyck Brooks that her own husband "of course saw more of the sons than of the women folk and though I know he knew much of what Harry's mother was like he would be too well-bred to tell you! . . . James's mother (even to my own perception as a child) was the very incarnation of *banality* and his aunt Miss Walsh who lived with them was not much better. His father always seemed to me genial and delightful . . . but he seemed to me out of place in that stiff stupid house in Cambridge."

Of the male Jameses, E. L. Godkin, visiting just before the Civil War, observed, "There could not be a more entertaining treat than a dinner at the James house, when all the young people were at home. They were full of stories of the oddest kind, and discussed questions of morals or taste or literature with a vociferous vigor so great as sometimes to lead the young men to leave their seats and gesticulate on the floor. I remember, in some of these heated discussions, it was not unusual for the sons

---

whole pretty sensibly. She is very open to instruction. *We* shall improve her." And a few weeks later: ". . . It *is* rather droll to examine women's minds. They are a queer mixture of odds and ends, poorly mastered and utterly unconnected. But to a young man they are perhaps all the more attractive on that account."

And Alice's favorite George Eliot heroine, "the immortal Maggie" Tulliver, asking her brother's tutor whether she couldn't do Euclid, " 'and all Tom's lessons, if you were to teach me instead of him?' " learns her bitter truth:

" 'No, you couldn't,' said Tom indignantly. 'Girls can't do Euclid, can they sir?'

" 'They can pick up a little of everything, I daresay,' said Mr. Stelling. 'They've a great deal of superficial cleverness, but they couldn't go far into anything. They're quick and shallow.'

"Tom, delighted with this verdict, telegraphed his triumph by wagging his head at Maggie behind Mr. Stelling's chair. As for Maggie, she had hardly ever been so mortified. She had been so proud to be called 'quick' all her little life, and now it appeared that this quickness was the brand of inferiority. It would have been better to be slow, like Tom."

to invoke humorous curses on their parent, one of which was, that 'his mashed potatoes might always have lumps in them!' "

In Europe and in America, life for Alice held more charm when the boys were at home than when they were not. But her pleasure at having them around was not unalloyed, for she could not participate fully in their world. For all his originality on the subject of education, in the schoolroom and out, Alice's father was interested only in the education of boys. It was not simply for semantic convenience that he used the masculine noun when he wrote, "I desire my child to become an upright man." He firmly believed that girls were moral by nature, whereas boys had to learn how to be good.

In 1853 he published an article called "Woman and the 'Woman's Movement' " in *Putnam's Monthly* magazine:

The very virtue of woman, her practical sense, which leaves her indifferent to past and future alike, and keeps her the busy blessing of the present hour, disqualifies her for all didactic dignity. Learning and wisdom do not become her. Even the ten commandments seem unamiable and superfluous on her lips, so much should her own pure pleasure form the best outward law for man. We say to her, "Do not tell me, beautiful doctor, I pray you, what one ought or ought not to do; any musty old professor in the next college is quite competent to that: tell me only what I shall do to please you, and it shall be done, though the heavens fall!"

He did not claim that "woman" was incapable of learning and wisdom, but that they did not "become" her: as man's spiritual superior, she should consent to rule him by letting him please her. But she was *not* man's intellectual equal, and needed him to tell her (as Henry Sr. does in this article) about her true nature and duty. In her attempt to enter the masculine worlds of politics and law, doctoring and finance, woman was betraying nature's laws. According to an "absolute decree of nature," wrote James in 1853, "woman is . . . inferior to man . . . She is his inferior in passion, his inferior in intellect, and his inferior in physical strength." It was precisely this inequality that made, in his eyes, for woman's exalted function. She embodied everything man was not — "nature's revelation to man of his own God-given and indefeasible self." She was above all a "form of personal affection . . . Her aim in life is . . . simply to love and bless man."*

* Just as, in Calvinism, mankind's mission is to "glorify" God.

Imagining the offspring of a union in which the man and woman were equals, James recoiled in elaborate mock horror:

Alack! alack! what litany would be long enough to recite their abominations! A sprinkling of girls — what could be called girls, perhaps, great muscular jades as agile as wildcats, and yet more mischievous and fierce — might slip into the first generation, but every successive one, as an Irishman might say, would be boys alone, boys of both sexes.

The impact of these ideas on Alice was direct and indirect, overt and covert, affecting her deepest feelings about herself, other women, and men throughout her life. Her father's conception of women was at once flattering and humiliating — and it took no more account of flesh-and-blood females than his ideas about child-rearing took into account the personalities of his children. He made Woman into the abstraction he needed her to be, endowing her with a nature antithetical to his own sinful, selfish, aggressive one, and refused to see anything that did not fit this conception. Perhaps beneath his insistence on women's selflessness lay a certain fear: if women became men's equals, he conjectured, girls would not only turn into "great muscular jades," more fierce than wildcats — they would turn into boys. There may have lurked behind this dire forecast a sense that the distinctions between the sexes were not quite clear enough. The spiritual superiority with which James endowed women may have been a way of reinforcing the boundary — woman differed absolutely from man, and he could never take on either her moral purity or her physical and intellectual handicaps. James wanted to triumph over his own selfishness by loving his children the way a mother would; but a mother did it by nature, not by choice. She was at once all virtue and no virtue, since she did not have to struggle to be good. Struggle, the essence of manhood, marked the path to divinity. Woman, therefore — mindless, selfless, naturally virtuous — was of no real account.

As a child, Alice accepted these ideas. Her adored father was as extravagant in his gestures of love as Mary James was parsimonious, and if Alice felt emotionally undernourished by her mother and excluded from her father's attention to the boys' education, she would please her father by being and letting him please his "darling girl." Henry Sr.'s own pleasure dominated this arrangement, and neither he nor Alice saw how little she gained from it. A letter he wrote her from a New York shopping spree shows him proclaiming his loving generosity while delivering nothing. He had picked up (he wrote) a "half-hundred" foreign photographs for William, "But they are too dear to permit me to buy any fancy ones for you ... I shall go into Stewart's this morning to enquire for that style of ribbon for you. If I had *only* brought a little more money with me! I went into Arnold's for a scarf for you, but the clerks were so rapid with me, I couldn't buy & bought two pairs of gloves for myself, one of which turns out too small for me but will suit Harry ... Goodbye, darling daughter, and be sure that never was daughter so beloved ... Keep my letters and believe me ever your lovingest Daddy."

For all his opposition to female intellect, James delighted in the quickness of his daughter's mind. He addressed her as "heiress of the paternal wit and of the maternal worth." He encouraged her to think, and they spent long hours together in his study, reading, joking, trading opinions and insults. Her early education, then, was a haphazard mixture of encouragement and slight: her father and eldest brothers enjoyed sharing knowledge with her piecemeal, but more as a pleasant way to pass time than as a serious effort to train her mind. Ambiguity characterized Alice's lifelong estimations of the female sex and her own intellectual capacity. Toward the end of her life she wondered wryly whether "if I had had any education, I should be more, or less, of a fool than I am." She then went on to contradict, by example, that assertion of foolishness, for the modesty and irony of her remarks present a clear contrast to her father's solemn, inflated rhetoric on the subject of female "didactic dignity": education, she wrote, "would have deprived me surely of those exquisite moments of mental flatulence which every now and then inflate the cerebral vacuum with a delicious sense of latent possibilities — of stretching oneself to cosmic limits, and who would ever give up the reality of dreams for relative knowledge?"

The sensuous education had what Henry Jr. called its *funesti* (fatal) consequences for each of the children. Their father, "delighting ever in the truth while generously contemptuous of the facts," gave them an education in which the "literal played ... as small a part as it perhaps ever played in any, and we wholesomely breathed inconsistencies and ate and drank contradictions." The presence of bright paradox, as Henry called it, proved more wholesome for some than for others. It may have best suited the future novelist, for it provided him early with direct experience of human nature's complexity and with a capacity for aesthetic appreciation that deepened at each subsequent addition and comparison. William, however, deplored his own lack of training in disciplined thought, and, like Alice, complained of his early education that he "never had any."

•

In spite of the Jameses' isolation from the rest of the world, their physical proximity to each other, and the emphasis on closeness, incidents of real communication between any two members of the family occurred rarely. Alice recalled a moment she shared with Henry in France as one of the most important in her life — the "first time I was conscious of a purely intellectual process."

In the summer of 1857 her family had left Paris for Boulogne-sur-Mer, a popular vacation spot on the coast of northern France, just across the English Channel from Brighton. They had a new governess; Mlle. Danse had been dismissed in a mysterious series of events that left the James children with a baffled sense that she was an "adventuress" (and Henry with the impression that "for the adventuress there might on occasion be much to be said"). The new governess, Marie Boningue, came from the outskirts of Boulogne, where her family had a *campagne,* and the four younger James children were invited to spend a summer day with her there.

Alice remembered: "A large and shabby calèche came for us into which we were packed, save Wm; all I can remember of the drive was a never-ending ribbon of dust stretching in front and the anguish greater even than usual of Wilky's and Bob's heels grinding into my shins." After the midday country dinner, the children were "turned into the garden to play, a sandy or rather dusty expanse with nothing in it, as I remember, but two or three scrubby apple-trees, from one of which hung a swing. As time went on Wilky and Bob disappeared, not to my grief, and the Boningues. Harry was sitting in the swing and I came up and stood near by as the sun began to slant over the desolate expanse, as the dreary hrs, with that endlessness which they have for infancy, passed, when Harry suddenly exclaimed: 'This might certainly be called pleasure under difficulties!' "

In that simple remark Henry acknowledged the truth and converted the hot, tiresome afternoon into a shared consciousness of detachment, irony, and humor. This moment of intellectual initiation had a powerful impact on nine-year-old Alice: "The stir of my whole being in response to the substance and exquisite, *original* form of this remark almost makes my heart beat now with the sisterly pride which was then awakened and it came to me in a flash, the higher nature of this appeal to the mind, as compared to the rudimentary solicitations which usually produced my childish explosions of laughter." And recalling the experience thirty-three years later she could still feel "distinctly the sense of self-satisfaction in that I could not only perceive, but appreciate this subtlety, as if I had acquired a new sense, a sense whereby to measure intellectual things, wit as distinguished from giggling, for example."

Alice and Henry shared throughout their lives a deeper intellectual and spiritual kinship than either felt with any other member of the family. Within the family group the second son and only daughter were more isolated than any of the others. William, in "eldest superiority," looked to his father and the world outside the family for instruction and companionship. Wilky and Bob formed a unit as soon as Bob left the nursery, and they remained paired in all the major activities of their lives. They shared as well a sense that they lacked the special qualities of mind that seemed to distinguish their elder brothers — Bob recalled the Collège Municipale at Boulogne-sur-Mer "where Wilkie and I went and failed to take prizes . . . I see yet the fortunate scholars ascend the steps of [the mayor's] throne, kneel at his feet, and receive crown or rosettes, or some symbol of merit which *we* did not get. The luck had begun to break early!"

What bound Henry and Alice together was a different kind of exclusion, and a profound mutual understanding. Henry had withdrawn early from the competitive masculine fray to a safe inner world, taking the part of the docile, easy, "good" James child. Henry Sr. wrote to his namesake in 1873 that "Mother loves you more than all her other progeny." After she died, he fell heir to her preference: "I can't help feeling that you are the one that has cost us the least trouble, and given us always the most delight," he told his second son. The novelist, then, took the place that might have been filled by the only girl in another family. His mother's "angel," the watcher in the family drama, he freed himself to see and learn, pre-empting the role of creative receptor often occupied in the nineteenth century by women to whom avenues for other kinds of activity were closed.

Leon Edel traces the complex motives and subtle workings-out of this self-definition throughout his five-volume life of the novelist. James practiced what Edel has seen as a "spiritual transvestitism": he protected his sense of masculine integrity by assuming a feminine guise, making himself safe both from the assaults and seductions of women and from the risks of competition with men.* In James's fiction, Edel points out, boys are in greater danger than girls: Miles in *The Turn of the Screw* is killed, as are Dolcino in "The Author of Beltraffio" and Owen Wingrave in the story of that name. Girls, however, from Miles's sister Flora to Maisie Farange and Nanda Brookenham, manage not only to survive but usually to learn and grow from their experience, however painful it proves. "In James's world," writes Edel, "it was safer to be a little girl. They usually endured."

Throughout his life, Henry James, Jr., gravitated toward intelligent, powerful women. He "seemed to look at women rather as women look at them," wrote a London friend. "Women look at women as persons; men look at them as women. The quality of sex in women, which is their first and chief attraction to most men, was not their chief attraction to James." And the novelist reversed his father's conviction that knowledge and women were incompatible: James's fictional women are far more capable of seeing into life than his men are. He placed women at the center of his novels' consciousness. In their freedom from the material and professional constraints of the masculine world, they represented the dilemmas of choice, imagination, and knowledge that James saw as the essence of human experience. He acknowledged that his imaginative vision transformed the ordinary experience of being female into art. "Millions of presumptuous girls," he wrote in the preface to *The Portrait of a Lady*, "intelligent or not intelligent, daily affront their destiny, and what is it open to their destiny to be, at the most, that we should make an ado about it?" He added, "The novel is of its very nature an ado." and then gave George Eliot's answer to his question: "In these frail vessels is borne onward through the ages the treasure of human affection."

* All his life, writes Edel, Henry James harbored within "the house of the novelist's inner world the spirit of a young adult female, worldly-wise and curious, possessing a treasure of unassailable virginity and innocence and able to yield to the masculine active world-searching side of James an ever-fresh and exquisite vision of feminine youth and innocence. For this was the androgynous nature of the creator and the drama of his novels: innocence and worldliness, the paradisical America and the cruel and corrupt Europe — or in other variations, youthful ignorant America and wise and civilized Europe."

His sister did not — much as she might have liked to — see herself as a frail vessel bearing the treasure of human affection through the ages. The "female" province that Henry found so useful, both for what it provided and what it averted, held few attractions for Alice. It bored her, made her restless. She met her novelist brother at a kind of intersection between masculinity and femininity, each participating imaginatively in aspects of what the other possessed by nature and social decree. Where Henry's temperament was reticent and absorbent, Alice's was forthright and energetic. Like him, she renounced overt strife — but in very different terms. "I am not rebellious by temperament," she wrote at the age of forty-two, "and trampled down as much as possible all boresome insurrections, having fortunately perceived that the figure of abortive rebel lent itself much more to the comic than the heroic in the eye of the cold-blooded observer, and that for practical purposes surrender, smiling if possible, is the only attainable surface which gives no hold to the scurvy tricks of Fortune." This willed renunciation belied her claim that she was not rebellious: she learned not to be, because it seemed futile and dangerous. Safety from ridicule and "the scurvy tricks of Fortune" lay in a mocking patience — a simultaneous acceptance and transcendence of privation. Her ostensible passivity, like Henry's, created and defended a safe place within which her mind could be active and free. But whereas Henry described his choice as natural and inevitable, Alice presented hers as the lesser of evils.

•

Alone among the male Jameses, Henry treated Alice as a person rather than as a girl. Teasing was a favorite form of social exchange in the James household, and the teasing Alice experienced at the hands of the other boys, her father, and some of his friends had primarily to do with her female sex. Their jokes underlined her fundamental difference from themselves and kept it a subject of playful mockery.

In the spring of 1857, shortly before the excursion to the country at Boulogne, the James family had a familiar guest at their Paris dinner table: Henry Sr.'s friend William Makepeace Thackeray. Alice sat quietly next to Mr. Thackeray at the table, her hair neatly coiled in a braid around her head, dressed "after the fashion of the period and place," recalled Henry Jr. — probably as in the picture following p. 80, with full petticoats swelling out the light skirt that came midway down her calves. Suddenly, in the middle of dinner (according to Henry), Mr. Thackeray

turned to Alice, "laid his hand on her little flounced person and exclaimed with ludicrous horror: 'Crinoline? — I was suspecting it! So
young and so depraved!' "

Eight-year-old Alice may not have known what "depraved" meant, but
she certainly knew she was being made fun of, and that the joke (which
"lingered long" in the family repertoire) had something to do with her
sex.

Alice did not like this sort of humor, but she had grown used to it.
Within her family, the teasing came in several forms. Wilky and Bob inflicted corporal punishment on their sister — the "anguish" of their heels
grinding into her shins on the day of the Boulogne excursion was
"greater even than usual," and they had mastered the studied exclusivity
a pair of boys can parade before a solitary girl. As she grew older and the
physical torments decreased, Alice found she did not particularly want to
be included in Wilky and Bob's activities, but the early prohibition left
its marks. Years later, in her diary, she expressed heartfelt sympathy on
hearing of the teasing to which William's daughter, Peggy, was sub-
jected by her brothers. Peggy was four and her brother Billy, nine, when
Alice wrote this passage: "Billy it seems teases little Peggy dreadfully; she
bears it usually serenely, but every now and then her indignation breaks
forth. The other day she said to her mother, 'When I speak so to Billy, it
makes my stomach tremble.' Heaven forbid," commented Alice, thinking of her own past, "that this should be a portent of heredity, and that
her innocent framework should be destined to enclose within its depths a
cave of emotional borborygmous, as has been known!"

William teased his sister more subtly and affectionately than Wilky
and Bob did — and his jokes were more overtly sexual. He addressed
courtly, playful letters to her as "You lovely babe," "Charmante Jeune
Fille," "Perfidious child!" and "Chérie Charmante de Bal." He referred
constantly to her physical attributes, and drew verbal portraits of her sensual, untutored, indulged feminine nature. In Paris he imagined "Alice
the widow, with her eyes fixed on her novel, eating some rich fruit which
Father has just brought in for her from the Palais Royal." And "the
sweet lovely delicious little grey-eyed Alice must be locked up alone on
the day after the receipt of this with paper and envelope to write a letter
unassisted, uncorrected and unpunctuated to her loving brothers who
would send her novels and plums if they could . . ." Then, "thousand
thanks to the cherry lipped apricot nosed double chinned little Bal for

her strongly dashed off letter, which inflamed the hearts of her lonely brothers with an intense longing to kiss and slap her celestial cheeks."

One night in 1859 William composed a "sonnate" in honor of Alice and invited the family into the parlor to hear him sing it:

> The moon was mildly beaming
> Upon the summer sea,
> I lay entranced and dreaming
> My Alice sweet, of thee.
> Upon the sea-shore lying
> Upon the yellow sand
> The foaming waves replying
> I vowed to ask thy hand.
> I swore to ask thy hand, my love
> I vowed to ask thy hand.
> I wished to join myself to thee
> By matrimonial band.
>
> So very proud, but yet so fair
> The look you on me threw
> You told me I must never dare
> To hope for love from you.
>
> Your childlike form, your golden hair
> I never more may see,
> But goaded on by dire despair
> I'll drown within the sea.
>
> Adieu to love! adieu to life!
> Since I may not have thee,
> My Alice sweet, to be my wife,
> I'll drown me in the sea!
> I'll drown me in the sea, my love
> I'll drown — me in — the sea!

"Alice took it very cooly [sic]," William reported the next day to his father, who was away in London, and Wilky wrote that the song "excited a good deal of laughter among the audience assembled."

Though Alice had learned to take William's gallant flourishes coolly, it was exciting to be singled out for this flirtatious attention, to be appreciatively catalogued and cast as proud fair lady pursued by an ardent admirer. It was also confusing and embarrassing. Was William complimenting or making fun of her? Did the idea of sweet little Alice as a desirable woman seem ridiculous? Did only boys have inflamed hearts? Did brothers marry sisters? The poem celebrates an Alice who is the object of male dreams, a fatal child-woman whose refusal of her entranced suitor-brother condemns him to suicide. Were girls supposed to be cool and superior to desire and despair?

Alice quickly learned to tease back. A bantering tone characterized all her relations with William, and when he went away from home he wrote of missing her chaffing. Still, his advances titillated and frightened her. They put her on display before the family audience like a bright ornament, calling attention to her female body with mocking praise.

Sex was not a topic of discussion in the James household. William disliked the word all his life. He rarely mentioned sex in all his work on psychology and religious experience, but in the chapter "Instinct" in the second volume of *The Principles of Psychology,* he posited, under the heading "Love," an *"anti-sexual instinct"* (his italics), "the instinct of personal isolation, the actual repulsiveness to us of the idea of intimate contact with most of the persons we meet, especially those of our own sex." ("To most of us," he added in a footnote, "it is even unpleasant to sit down in a chair still warm from occupancy by another person's body ...") He suspected that the sexual impulse, "this strongest passion of all, so far from being the most 'irresistible,' may, on the contrary, be the hardest one to give rein to ..."*

In Henry's novels, sex, though unnamed, often occupies a central place in the characters' preoccupations and actions. It becomes more explicit in his later work (*The Wings of the Dove, The Golden Bowl, The Ambassadors*), but early and late it is nearly always associated with destruction, cruelty, corruption. Sex as a metaphor for knowledge and experience (and knowledge and experience as a metaphor for sex) is what James's innocent (usually American) characters have to come to terms with (usually abroad). His plots turn on the consequences of this kind of

---

* The fondness in other cultures ("ancients and ... modern Orientals") for "forms of unnatural vice, of which the notion affects us with horror, is probably a mere case of the way in which this [antisexual] instinct may be inhibited by habit." After two paragraphs on this topic, William apologized, concluding: "These details are a little unpleasant to discuss, but they show so beautifully the correctness of the general principles in the light of which our review has been made, that it was impossible to pass them over unremarked."

knowledge: Milly Theale dies; Maggie Verver orchestrates her own elaborate triumph; Lambert Strether renounces.

As the only girl in the James family, Alice was inevitably an object of fraternal curiosity, and yet William's playful references to her body were probably the only kind that could be made. She grew up like a rare, fragile tropical plant, in the close quarters of brothers, parents, governesses, and aunt, fed on special preparations of solicitude and indifference. The overstimulations of this heated atmosphere had no natural means of release. Alice kept her reactions inside, in the "cave of emotional borborygmous" she feared for little Peggy. She shared in the family amusement at William's carryings-on, watching herself as object and learning to detach from the flushed confusions involved in also being the subject of the diversion.

•

When William wrote his "sonnate on Alice" in December 1859, the James family was once again established in Geneva. The little group had recrossed the Atlantic twice since the summer in Boulogne. In December of 1857, Henry Sr. had begun to feel "home pulling at his heart," and by August had settled his family at Newport, Rhode Island, for its first brief experience of New England. Soon he was writing to a friend, "Young America male and female is so confoundedly fast, the little people rule the big people so unmistakeably, that we began to tremble for our well established empire over our posterity, and to foresee all manner of dangers to their modest and orderly development." He had said, in another context, that the "big people" ought cheerfully to subordinate themselves to the welfare of the "little," and he alone saw his children's development as modest and orderly. Nonetheless, in October 1859, his family left Newport, sailed from New York to Le Havre on the S.S. *Vanderbilt,* and went directly to Geneva. There they settled at the Hôtel de l'Ecu on the Rhône. The two younger boys were enrolled in another boarding school just outside town, the Pensionnat Maquelin. William and Henry went to schools in Geneva and lived at the hotel with their parents, aunt, and sister.

In December, their father left for Paris and London, where he could read, think, write, and discuss his ideas with other intellectuals. Once having separated himself from his wife and children, he longed for them clamorously. Alice recalled in her diary that he would — "the delicious infant!" — leave for a fortnight and return suddenly at the end of thirty-six hours, "with Mother beside him holding his hand and we five children pressing close round him 'as if he had just been saved from drowning,' and he pouring out, as he alone could, the agonies of desolation thro' which he had come." This time, however, he was to stay away for several months.

Alice wrote to him in March. Penciled in at the end of her letter — the first extant — is the information (in William's handwriting) that it was "All Alice's own composition except the first sentence. She wanted to be started." Her "composition" shows William still playing with the idea of men dying for women:

Sunday, March 11th

My dear Father.

We have had two dear letters from you, and find you are the same dear old good-for-nothing home-sick papa as ever.

Willie is in a very extraordinary state of mind, composing odes to all the family. A warlike one he addressed to Aunt Kate, in which the hero is her husband and dies for her, and he says: "The idea of any one dying for her"!! And he wants mother to take them in to Mrs. Thomas and Mrs. Osbourn [other Americans staying at the Hôtel de l'Ecu] to be read and admired by them.

We have all come to the conclusion that he is fit to go to the lunatic asylum, so make haste home before such an unhappy event takes place.

We are all very well except Mrs. Thomas who was not down to dinner yesterday.

We have given up our play as it is not a pretty one and is too hard. Good bye. I will try and be good and sweet till you come back, and merit the daisy curtains, and get a chance at your dear old pate again.

Your affect. daughter
Alice James

While Alice was trying to be good and sweet, two of her brothers were beginning to try their hands at the work that would occupy the rest of their lives. From Boulogne in October 1857, Henry Sr. had written his mother a state-of-the-family letter, describing the interests and pursuits of his flock, aged, respectively, fifteen, fourteen, twelve, eleven, and nine: "Willy is very devoted to scientific pursuits, and I hope will turn out a most respectable scholar." One of William's professors at the Collège Imperial in Boulogne had told Henry Sr. that William was " 'an admirable student, and that all the advantages of a first-rate scientific education which Paris affords ought to be accorded him.' He is however," continued the father, "much dearer to my heart for his moral worth than for his intellectual. I never knew a child of so much principle, and at the same time of a perfectly generous and conciliatory demeanour towards his younger brothers, always disposed to help them and never to oppress.

"Harry," he went on, "is not so fond of study, properly so called, as of reading. He is a devourer of libraries, and an immense writer of novels and dramas. He has considerable talent as a writer, but I am at a loss to know whether he will ever accomplish much. Wilky is more heart than head, but has a talent for languages, and speaks French they say with a perfect accent. They all speak very fluently indeed, but Wilky & Bob (who is very clever and promising, having ten times the go-ahead of all the rest) are particularly forward in it. Alice also speaks very well, and I presume that this winter will greatly accomplish them."

And in another letter from this period, he joked about Alice's lofty intellectual fate. "Our Alice," he wrote, "is still under discipline, preparing to fulfill some high destiny or other in the future by reducing decimal fractions to their least possible rate of subsistence."

Many years later, living in England, Alice read over the letters her father had written during her childhood, and reported her retrospective reaction to having been excluded from serious consideration. She told William in 1890 that in one of these early letters from Europe, "Father announces ... that none of the children 'save Wm.' show any intellectual taste* — 'Just fancy that now!' and *me* among the group — who all unconscious, constantly give birth to the profoundest subtleties and am 'so *very* clever!' If you could only hear what small coin produces that desirable result amidst this grateful public you *wd.* laugh ..." And then she warned her eldest brother to "arm yourself against my dawn, which may at any moment cast you and Harry into obscurity."

•

When the James boys began, in Europe and at Newport, to find the areas in which they had a more than passing interest, their expansive parent

---

* When Henry Sr. contemplated returning to Newport so that William could study painting, he wrote to Edmund Tweedy of "the other youngsters" from Bonn on July 18 [1860], "They are none of them cut out for intellectual labors."

did what he could to coax them off the mark, to keep before them all the interesting possibilities they might be giving up in settling too soon. Yet for all his opposition to "narrowing" choices, he did have some specific notions as to what they shouldn't be. He dreaded aimlessness as much as he worshiped versatility. His own father's Calvinist fears about prodigality and vice had been realized in most of Henry's brothers: the Albany uncles constituted a roster of "dissipation" — aimlessness, alcoholism, uninteresting failure. To the grandchildren of William James of Albany fell the difficult task of finding something to do that fitted a crypto-Calvinist conception of usefulness and at the same time filled the Jamesian prescription for universality.

Henry Sr. wanted William to pursue a scientific career. However, he did not follow the French professor's advice about first-rate training in Paris. For reasons that remain unclear (except that he found this son dearer for his moral worth than his intellectual), he instead took his children back to the United States in 1857 and installed the boys at Mr. William C. Leverett's Berkeley Institute in Newport. There they studied English, classics, and French. William and Henry occasionally dropped in to visit their friend John La Farge, who was studying painting with William Morris Hunt, and tried their amateur hands at sketching. William, who did have talent, wanted to join La Farge at his labors in Hunt's studio, but his father now determined that William should study science, not art. The family went back to Europe in 1858 chiefly (Henry Sr. wrote later to a friend) because "Willy . . . felt we thought a little too much attraction to painting — as I supposed from the contiguity to Mr. Hunt; let us break that up we said, at all events . . . I thought and still think that the true bent of his genius was towards the acquisition of knowledge: and to give up this hope without a struggle, and allow him to tumble down into a mere painter, was impossible. Let us go abroad then we said, and bring him into contact with books and teachers."

William dutifully studied science at the academy that later became the University of Geneva, and went in the summer of 1860 to Bonn to learn German, along with Henry and Wilky. But his interest in painting did not abate. Before leaving he told his father that since he felt so strongly drawn to painting, no more time or money should be spent on his scientific education. Henry Sr. met in William a persuasive intellectual match, and he agreed that summer to let his eldest son give painting a fuller trial. He wrote to his Newport friend Edmund Tweedy that William's desire to study with Hunt was a "Providential indication" to return to America. Justifying yet another 180° turn, he wrote of his idea that "something was to be found" in Europe "better for boys than at home": "... We go home profoundly persuaded that no wilder hallucination exists, at least in reference to boys who are destined to grow up into American men. America is 'the lost Paradise restored' to boys and girls both, and it is only our own paltry cowardice & absurd ducking to old world conventionalities, that hinder their realizing it as such at once." Apart from William, he went on, the "other boys have been all along perfectly starved on their social side, and not the least battered on their intellectual ..." And "they are getting to an age, Harry & Wilky especially, when the heart craves a little wider expansion than is furnished it by the domestic affections. They want friends among their own sex, and sweethearts in the other; and my hope for their own salvation, temporal & spiritual, is that they may go it strongly in both lines when they get home."

He concluded, then, that the educational experiment in Europe had for the most part failed. It had been conceived for the benefit of the boys, and its negative results were felt most keenly by Alice. When Henry Sr. made the decision to return to Newport, he added to Edmund Tweedy: "One chief disappointment also on this side of the water has been in regard to Alice, who intellectually, socially, and physically has been at a great disadvantage compared with home." In the fall of 1860 the James family turned its back on the European sensuous education and headed home.

Chapter Four

Civil War

NEWPORT, a tiny New England town on the sea, with magnificent high cliffs and clear blue skies, was a pastoral haven for wealthy Americans at the beginning of the 1860s. The great villas and mansions built by new money in the later nineteenth century had not yet begun to appear; the ocean drives had not been paved; the local plant- and wildlife grew in unchecked profusion. Later, Alice characterized Newport as "artificial and sophisticated," and Henry called it a "witless dream of the rich." But in the late fifties and early sixties, its scale was small and its tone subdued.

Summer vacationers came from New York, Boston, and Philadelphia. But the year-round community was made up, noted Henry in *The American Scene*, of "a handful of ... delightfully mild cosmopolites, united by three common circumstances, that of their having for the most part more or less lived in Europe, that of their sacrificing openly to the ivory idol whose name is leisure, and that, not least, of a formed critical habit."

It made a perfect refuge for the worldly young Jameses, fresh from the Continent, with their sensibilities attuned to the uses of leisure and the applications of critical habit. Among the other "cosmopolites" they befriended at Newport numbered the families of Samuel Gray Ward, Charles Eliot Norton, Julia Ward Howe, Longfellow, George Bancroft, and William Wetmore (who eventually built one of the most lavish houses — the Château-sur-Mer — on Bellevue Avenue, and whose son became governor of Rhode Island). Thomas Sergeant Perry, descended from Benjamin Franklin and both commodores, became a lifelong friend of the James boys, and his sister Margaret married another of their New-port friends, John La Farge.

But the principal social attraction of Newport, both for the isolated year 1858–1859 and the longer residence beginning in 1860, was the Temple and Tweedy clan. Edmund and Mary Temple Tweedy were re-lated to Henry James, Sr., by marriage. Mrs. Tweedy's brother, Colonel Robert Temple, had married James's sister, Catharine Margaret. When Colonel Temple and his wife died four months apart, of consumption, in 1854, the Tweedys became the guardians of their six children — Robert, William, Katharine (Kitty), Mary (Minny), Ellen, and Henrietta. The Tweedys lived on Bellevue Avenue, and the Jameses rented a house nearby, at 13 Kay Street, just off the end of the avenue and conveniently near Newport's Palladian Redwood Library. The James and Temple chil-dren had known each other before, in New York and Albany, but the Newport years established a more sustained intimacy. As orphans, these cousins had about them an aura of glamour that impressed young Henry; "parentally bereft cousins were somehow more thrilling than parentally provided ones."

For Alice, especially, Newport afforded a dramatic liberation after the cloistered routines of European city life. In the summer she and her brothers went riding, swimming, and sailing; and both summer and win-ter they indulged in the ultimate Newport pastime — walking. Along the miles of cliffs, down to a favorite pond or beach, along the broad ave-nue they wandered, visiting (recalled Henry) "a thousand delicate secret places, dear to the disinterested rambler, small, mild 'points' and prom-ontories, far away little lonely, sandy coves, rock-set, lily-sheeted ponds, almost hidden, and shallow Arcadian summer-haunted valleys, with the sea just over some stony shoulder: a whole world that called out to the long afternoons of youth ..."

During 1858–1859, the Newport year off from the European experi-ment, Alice had gone to a girls' school, called Miss Hunter's, on Church Street. Miss Rebecca Hunter and her widowed mother ran the little school in their home, an old Newport house of two stories with a gam-brel roof, central chimney, and fine old paneling and balusters of wood. It was considered the best girls' school in Newport, and a schoolmate of Alice's named Mary Powel described it in an unpublished memoir: "Miss Hunter used to sit behind a little table — and looked so fresh and pleas-ant. Her teeth were very white and her hair so smooth. She was not beautiful but she was so intelligent that even to a child she was attractive. She kept the same order as did her mother. Everybody behaved. I do not remember a single instance of an unruly child. When not correcting exercises or hearing recitations Miss Hunter's fingers were employed in knitting bright worsteds — star-stitch shawls, sontags in block patterns, & hoods with loop borders were some of the articles that she made . . . It was certainly a school of great refinement, although rudimentary in tuition at that time, owing to the tender years of most of the pupils."

Miss Hunter committed suicide in 1888. Alice, then living in England, wrote to William, "Tell me when you next write whether the Miss Rebecca Hunter who threw herself off the 40 steps was my Becky! . . . if so, how shocking!" The local newspaper reported that Miss Hunter had died "most probably by venturing too near the sea while taking the sea air along the cliffs where the waves run high and irregularly, and she was drowned." Her obituary summarized the midcentury ideal of female education: "Hers was the genious [sic], and the powers possessed by comparatively few, of gently infusing the highest sentiments to her pupils, and of impressing them not only in the educational, but in all the elevated thoughts, conduct, and duties of life."*

---

* Alice's future friend Katharine Peabody Loring drew a picture of another kind of female education during this period in a letter she wrote to her parents in 1861. Katharine, then eleven, was taking lessons from a governess, probably with her sister and cousins, at a little schoolhouse her family owned near their home at Prides Crossing in Beverly, Massachusetts. Her letter ran:

> My dear Mamma and papa,
> Our Teacher wishes me to let you know what I have studied during the past three months.
> In English
> I have learned the Geography of Europe and part of Asia; I have committed to memory 478 lines of Poetry, I have read in Dicken's History of England from Elizabeth, through James the second. Also 3 chapters in Gray's Botany. [Asa Gray was Katharine's uncle, married to her father's sister, Jane.]
> In French
> I have learned Phrases and Translated two stories, "M. le Chevalier," and "Madame Croque Mitaine," by Madame Guzot. I can recite 52 lines of la Fontaine's Fables, I wrote each day English or French from dictation; added to this I had a frequent writing and drawing lesson, and learned to sing 14 French hymns.
> Hoping you will find I have made a good use of my Time and opportunities. I am
>
> your affectionate daughter
Kittie P. Loring
>
> Saturday September 6th 1861
> Beverly Farms

Alice's informal education during these years featured that staple of the middle-class female diet, *Godey's Lady's Book*. She first came upon it at the Perrys', and thirty years later recalled the "namby pamby tales I used to read in infancy" by Mary V. Terhune, who wrote fiction under the pseudonym Marion Harland. *Godey's*, with a circulation of 150,000 in 1860 (by which time it was in its decline), was a compendium of fashion, piety, entertainment, and advice. An issue Alice might have found at the Perrys', for January 1859, contained the "Snow-Drop Waltz" for pianoforte, lessons in broad line drawing, a passage on history by Samuel Johnson, an article on the formation of dew, charades, enigmas, acrostics and riddles, prayers, poetry and fiction, recipes (receipts), fashion pictures, embroidery patterns, a design for a Tudor cottage, and advice about arrangement of the hair, about health ("Shall we use tea and coffee?" The answer was no), etiquette, curling pins, Marie Antoinette fichu, exercise, sleep, gardening, and how to make a wedding breakfast for forty. A column called the "Editor's Table" defined the magazine's aims: to provide moral and mental food for women's enjoyment and improvement, since the woman with an "elevated" mind could "inspire her son with noble aims and pure principles of conduct and taste . . . No woman, no mother can lay the foundation of a great character in her child, if she be absorbed in frivolous amusements." She must "love the good and do good, or true greatness, always founded on goodness, will perish from our land . . . Happy the woman whose temper has been usefully restrained in infancy — whose childhood has been guided to diligence and truthfulness — whose youth has been guarded from indiscretion. She will, as a mother, be the honor and glory of a family . . . The poet Wordsworth has most feelingly described this 'perfect woman' which it has been our aim to develop and inspire: — 'She was a phantom of delight . . .' "

Godey's editor, Sarah Josepha Hale, had no interest in educating women on the important political issues of the nineteenth century. Her magazine gave no space to public discussion of the Civil War, for instance, although romantic stories about nurses and wounded soldiers turned up in its fiction. The kind of power available to most middle-class women was the power of influence at home, and *Godey's* for over half a century urged them to use it. This doctrine of feminine influence (which Ann Douglas has characterized as "decorous deviousness") was not something Mary James had to read about; she had already put it into efficient practice. Alice, however, had left the United States at the age of six and returned five years later, full of curiosity about the lives of American girls and women. *Godey's,* with its sentimental homilies and practical advice, exposed her to the popular culture of her contemporaries.

•

Through their old friends in Concord, the Emersons, the Jameses learned of a school that had been started there by a young abolitionist from Harvard named Franklin B. Sanborn. Henry Sr., unable to resist another educational and moral experiment, soon enrolled his two younger boys. But though the institution was coeducational, he appears never to have considered sending Alice. For one thing, he wanted her at home. For another, he was somewhat uneasy at the idea of coeducation. After leaving Wilky and Bob at Sanborn's in the fall of 1860, he wrote to a friend, "I buried two of my children yesterday — at Concord, Mass., and feel so heart-broken this morning that I shall need to adopt two more instantly to supply their place . . . [There were] three or four other school-boarders, one of them a daughter of John Brown — tall, erect, long-haired and freckled, as John Brown's daughter has a right to be. I kissed her (inwardly) between the eyes, and inwardly heard the martyred Johannes chuckle over the fat inheritance of love and tenderness he had after all bequeathed to his children in all good men's minds. An arch little Miss Plumley also lives there, with eyes full of laughter and a mouth like a bed of lilies bordered with roses. How it is going to be possible for my two boys to pursue their studies in the midst of that bewilderment I don't clearly see."

Bob and Wilky often visited the Emersons, with whom John Brown's daughters were living, but neither there nor at Sanborn's did the temptations of coeducation prove inordinately bewildering. One day, when Wilky stopped by the Emerson house after school, he found Emerson and his old friend and Harvard classmate George Partridge Bradford* discussing a school Bradford had opened in Newport. The conversation turned to Wilky's sister. Emerson asked Bradford, "And what sort of a girl is Alice?"

---

* When Bradford died in 1890, Alice wrote, "Dear old George Bradford is dead, aged 83 — *the* flower of New England maidenly bachelorhood, the very last, I fancy, of his very special kind. May all tender, benignant thoughts go with him."

"She has a highly moral nature," replied Bradford.

"How in the world," exclaimed the amused Emerson, "does her father get on with her?"

Reporting this conversation years later in her diary, Alice rejoined, "But who shall relate that long alliance, made on one side of all tender affection, solicitous sympathy and paternal indulgence!"

What her own side of that long alliance was made of, she doesn't say, but hints that it did not balance with his. Her solicitous father could be critical on occasion, and in this same diary passage Alice recalls a protest he made against her "highly moral" nature: "I can hear, as of yesterday, the ring of Father's voice, as he anathematized some short-comings of mine in Newport one day: 'Oh, Alice, how hard you are!' and I can remember how permeated I was, not for the first time, but often, with the truth of it, and saw the repulsion his nature with its ripe kernel of human benignancy felt — alas!"

Henry James, Sr., also had a highly moral nature, but kept it well hidden. Alice ascribed to him the power to permeate her whole being with his remarks, and contrasted his perfect loving nature with her own flawed one. But his ripe benignancy was withheld from her, in this instance, as she saw the "repulsion" he felt when he anathematized her faults. Her account shows a little girl accused by her motherly father of being too much like his own "highly moral" and rigid father — of not being soft, nurturing, ideally feminine. Alice here endorsed, as she did throughout her life, another's negative assessment of her, turning the force of her own moral condemnation against herself while attributing to her accuser benign motives, clear purposes, and a disinterested regard for the truth.

•

Emerson's son, Edward, who came home from Sanborn's with Wilky and Bob for spring vacation in 1861, provided glimpses of James family life at Newport. Aunt Kate had moved back to New York, and young Emerson sketched in the remaining cast of characters:

"The adipose and affectionate Wilky," as his father called him, would say something and be instantly corrected by the little cock-sparrow Bob, the youngest, but good-naturedly defend his statement, and then Henry (Junior) would emerge from his silence in defence of Wilkie. Then Bob would be more impertinently insistent, and Mr. James would advance as Moderator, and William, the eldest, join in. The voice of the Moderator presently would be drowned by the combatants and he soon came down vigorously into the arena, and when, in the excited argument, the dinner knives might not be absent from eagerly gesticulating hands, dear Mrs. James, more conventional, but bright as well as motherly, would look at me, laughingly reassuring, saying "Don't be disturbed, Edward; they won't stab each other. This is usual when the boys come home." And the quiet little sister ate her dinner, smiling, close to the combatants.

One night William returned from a visit to Boston while the rest of the family were at dinner. He told, recalled Edward Emerson, how he had been "beset" in town by an eager Boston lady. Emerson calls her "Jane Smith," but she was, in fact, Hawthorne's sister-in-law Elizabeth Peabody, the sweet, foggy Boston reformer whose spectacles were perpetually falling forward onto the bridge of her nose. This time Miss Peabody had "got hold of a really good thing," related Emerson, and had "button-holed William and insisted that he must attend the wonderful lectures on Art Anatomy of Dr. William Rimmer. At this point Mr. James broke in with violence — 'The man's a fraud! It's impossible he should be anything else if Jane Smith believes in him!' Then, stammering with zeal, he went on — 'Wh-wh-why! J-Jane Smith — she's one of the most d-d-dissolute old creatures that walks the earth!' " At this, reported Emerson, the family "shouted with joy, though knowing well the saintly, if too optimistic character of the lady, at the Jamesian felicity of the adjective. For they saw, in memory, the gray hair falling down under the bonnet askew, the spectacles slipping down with resulting upturned radiant face, the nondescript garments and general dissolving effect, symbolizing the loose reasoning and the charity falling all abroad — yes, in a sense a dissolute personality."

Alice appears in the background of these vignettes, if she appears at all. She knew exactly what it felt like to be at the center of scrutiny in this bright circle, and she did not fail to observe the mockery made of earnest reforming ladies like Miss Peabody.

•

Through the renewal of the James family ties with Emerson and Concord, the James and Emerson females began to become friends. Edward Emerson had two older sisters: Ellen, twenty-one in late 1860, and Edith, nineteen. Both had attended Sanborn's school with Edward, Wilky, and Bob, and had earlier been pupils at Elizabeth Cary Agassiz's school in Cambridge.* Ellen preferred coeducation to all-girls schools. What she learned at Sanborn's was better, she thought, more thorough and broader, than what she had been taught at Mrs. Agassiz's; and though even at Sanborn's the boys and girls did not play together, she recalled long years later, at least there the girls could watch the boys play.†

When Edward Emerson returned from visits to the Jameses at Newport in the early 1860s, his sisters pressed him eagerly for details about the interesting new group on their social horizon. William, writing to Newport from Cambridge in December of 1861, ended a description of his hectic social life with a message for his sister: "Tell Alice that I saw the Emerson girls and that they were perfectly wild, crazy, to have her come to Concord. She could very well divide a week between them and Bet Ward [daughter of Anna Barker and Samuel Gray Ward] and me I should think, I would take splendid care of her, and would take most lofty pride in promenading the streets of Boston with her the observed of all observers for manly strength and beauty and for feminine grace and gentility . . . She could come on with Robby very well when he comes to Concord, or have the combined attentions of him, Harry & Sargy if those two yong [sic] Lochinvars pay me a visit."

A few days later, Ellen Emerson invited Alice to visit her in Concord. A letter from Alice's father to Mr. Emerson contains the answer. When the invitation arrived, wrote Henry Sr., he "gave the palpitating Alice carte blanche to go at any expense of health, and got her expectations so

* In 1855, the future first president of Radcliffe founded a private girls' school in her home on Quincy Street in order to bring in some extra money for her family. Unlike the heads of other schools for girls, which concentrated on the humanities and literature, Mrs. Agassiz and her husband, Louis, Harvard's renowned professor of zoology and geology, included the "masculine" sciences of geography, natural history, mathematics, and botany in their curriculum. The school attracted girls from Cambridge, Boston, Brookline, and Concord; Professors Agassiz, Felton, Child, and Peirce of Harvard gave occasional lectures and lessons. This successful educational experiment lasted nine years and brought in an estimated $19,000.

† Henry reported several years later to Alice a story about Ellen and Emersonian innocence that became a James family favorite. A friend of his had traveled by steamer from Nice to Genoa with Ellen and her father in 1872, and had objected to a breach of fairness on the part of one of the ship's functionaries, remarking to Ellen, "The thing itself is small, but I do hate injustice." To which Ellen replied, "I don't know that I have ever known injustice. Father, have we ever known injustice?"

exalted, that her more affectionate and truly long-suffering Mama found it one of the trials of her life to reduce her to the ordinary domestic routine. All I know is I am hopelessly wicked, and cheerfully postpone myself to the world-after-next for amendment. I tell Alice by way of make-up of the delights of heaven, and say that the Emerson house is only a foretaste of that festivity, the Emerson girls being what they are only by an interior most unconscious and unsuspected contact with benignities and generosities and sincerities that she shall there see one day, poor child, in beautiful human form. I think however the tears still trickle in solitude."*

This sad little story shows for the first time a family concern about Alice's health. Her father, who characterized her as "palpitating," urged the visit at "any expense of health" — hardly an encouraging notion — but Mary James appears to have found the expense of excitement too great: Alice was not allowed to go, and Mary had to calm her down. James blamed himself for the upset, contrasting his "comparative infernality" to his wife's "more affectionate and truly long-suffering" nature, yet he looked cheerfully forward to repair in the hereafter. Perhaps he sensed that he had set his daughter vibrating with his own energy and then left his disciplinarian wife to handle the resulting emotional havoc without him, though his remorse seems cursory. His assurances about the future delights of heaven made small recompense to Alice for the loss of the longed-for visit. She drew two lessons from this painful experience: that emotional extremes were dangerous, and that being delicate and high-strung rendered her unable to leave home.

Her family's return to Newport marked the beginning of her adolescence — she turned twelve in 1860 — and other references to her increasing "nervous" susceptibility now begin to appear. From Cambridge in 1862 William wrote to his "Charmante Jeune Fille: . . . The Tappans ex-

* The sage of Concord's second wife, Lidian, the mother of Ellen, Edith, and Edward, suffered throughout her life from "little fevers" and nervous prostrations. (Her name before marriage was Lydia Jackson, but her husband changed it to Lidian because he knew Bostonians would insert an *r* between the vowels that ended her first and began her new last name, making her "Lydiar Emerson.") She became something of an amateur homeopath and was interested in mesmerism, phrenology, astrology, séances, and spiritual healing of all kinds. In her adolescence she often sat up alone in the cold most of the night, sleeping only three or four hours, and she starved herself for long periods, believing that food was poison and that what she did not eat did her more good than what she ate.

pected me to bring you along and were much disappointed that I came without you . . . I hope your neuralgia or whatever you made believe the thing was has gone and you are going to school instead of languishing and lolling about the house."

The middle and upper classes in the nineteenth century generally saw female adolescents as prone to "dangerous" extremes of excitement and lassitude. Throughout America and England in the mid-Victorian decades, these young girls (and the heroines of the novels they surreptitiously read) were urged to learn patience and moderation, to shun the excitements of novels, study, coffee, and gay parties, to cultivate modesty and self-control. Medical science at the time, viewing the human organism as a precarious balance between body and mind, nature and civilization, confirmed society's assumption that the balance was even more unstable in women than in men. The female body seemed a fine, frail mechanism that could easily fall victim to excessive mental activity.

A familial example of high-strung female nervousness arrived at the Jamesian doorstep in 1861, in the person of Alice's cousin Kitty, the daughter of Henry Sr.'s older brother, the Reverend William James. Katharine Barber James was twenty-seven when she visited her cousins at Newport. She had spent the previous year, 1860, at the Northampton (Massachusetts) Hospital for the Insane, where she had fallen in love with her physician, a widower named William Henry Prince. While Kitty stayed with the Jameses, Prince was making up his mind to marry her, and did so in October of 1861. Her life took a different outward form from her younger cousin's — she found a man to take care of her, and was quite spectacularly unstable, in and out of mental hospitals all her life. But like Alice and countless other nineteenth-century women, Kitty spent much of her time seeking to avoid excitement of any kind, and trying endless remedies that involved rest, quiet, and patience. She wrote from Newport in 1861 to her brother-in-law, Julius Seelye, the president of Amherst College, that the James boys were "full of intelligence and quickness . . . each one of them having a strongly marked individuality & being very different from the others . . . & little Alice is a very sweet little girl."

•

From its special vantage point at the edge of the continental United States, the Newport community had "its opera glass turned forever across the sea," wrote Henry Jr. But it could not fail to notice the increasingly apparent signs of trouble at home. In April 1861, the first shots of the Civil War were fired at Fort Sumter.

Slavery was only one of the issues driving the regions apart, and not, in the early sixties, the main one. At the beginning of the war both politicians and populace considered the preservation of the Union, the question of free trade versus protectionism, and the extension of slavery into free-soil areas more important than slavery itself. Henry James, Sr., espoused abolitionism long before many of his fellow intellectuals in the North, but his interest in politics had little to do with issues of state and everything to do with his fervent millennialism. On July 4, 1861, he delivered an oration at Newport, "The Social Significance of Our Institutions," in which he expressed his faith in the common rights of humanity, in "every man's joint and equal dependence with every other man upon the association of his kind for all that he himself is or enjoys." He saw America as "nothing less than a broad human society or brotherhood," and declared that "our very Constitution binds us ... the very breath of our political nostrils binds us, to disown all distinctions among men," to do away with privilege and make laws only for the common good rather than for "those accidents of birth or wealth or culture, which spiritually individualize man from his kind."

The privilege of independent means did not isolate patrician Newport from the war effort. Lincoln called the country to arms on April 15, 1861 — not to fight against slavery, but to quell the southern rebellion. In Newport, the young men from the North began to enlist in the Union Army, the older men to support it according to their politics and pocketbooks, and the women to make blankets, shirts, bandages, and bullets for the soldiers.

Henry Sr.'s abolitionism advocated mystical union and opposed spiritual slavery; he did not at first want to contribute any of his sons to a fight that was to be waged on more narrow political grounds. He wrote to a friend that "affectionate old papas like me are scudding all over the country to apprehend their patriotic offspring, and restore them to the harmless embraces of their mamas." He had had for three days a "firm grasp ... upon the coat tails of my Willy & Harry, who both vituperate me beyond measure because I won't let them go. The coats are a very staunch material, or the tails must have been off two days ago, the scamps pull so hard." He justified his refusal to let them go by saying that "no existing government, nor indeed any now possible government, is worth an honest human life and a clean one like theirs, especially if that government is like ours in danger of bringing back slavery again under one banner: than which consummation I would rather see chaos itself come again." And he went on to say that he thought no young American should be put in the path of death until he had experienced some of the good of life — "until he has found some charming conjugal Elizabeth or other to whisper his devotion to, and assume the task if need be of keeping his memory green."

This report by their affectionate old papa presents the only existing evidence that William or Henry ever wanted to join the army during the Civil War. Neither was physically strong. William, after six months of studying painting with Hunt, had decided that art was not, after all, his calling. Just why he gave up the path he had fought so hard to be able to follow remains unclear, but his eyes had begun to trouble him (as they would for the rest of his life), and he had started to have problems of "nervous weakness" in his stomach. In the opening months of the war, he turned decisively toward science, though his interest in the visual as well as the psychological aspects of perception persisted throughout his career, and he drew pictures all his life with clear, vivid prose. He decided to enter the Lawrence Scientific School at Harvard in the fall of 1861. In turning back to science, he embraced the vocation his father preferred for him; but the decision, far from resolving his difficulties, marked the beginning of a period of emotional turmoil that kept him in a state of almost constant pain for the next seventeen years.

William had grown from an active, curious, energetic boy into a tense, indecisive, and hypochondriacal young man. As the war continued and most of his friends and two of his brothers joined up to fight for the things he believed in, William agonized over his lack of participation. When Wilky was convalescing at home in 1863 from a wound he had received at Fort Wagner, William wrote to Kitty Prince that this younger brother was "the best abolitionist you ever saw, and makes a common one, such as we are, feel very small and shabby."

Fighting was the patriotic, masculine thing to do, and while William floundered through the war years his sense of inadequacy as a man increased. Seeing himself as unfit for a life of action, he grew convinced (and, he claimed, "reconciled to the notion") that he was "one of the very lightest of featherweights ... The grit and energy of some men are called forth by the resistance of the world. But as for myself, I seem to have no spirit whatever of that kind, no pride which makes me ashamed to say, 'I can't do that.' "

He did not suffer this moral lethargy forever — though he thought he might — and much of his later work has its roots in this prolonged crisis. He developed his strenuous mind in so many directions that there was almost nothing he could not, mentally, "do." He became an energetic hiker and intrepid mountain climber, and his philosophy was predicated on an act of will, a conquering assertion that would subdue the chaos of self-doubt.

Henry, too, abstained from participation in the Civil War for reasons of health and temperamental unfitness. His lack of participation seems less surprising than William's, because he was from the first less interested in living up to an ideal of manliness. In his autobiography, he fused an unspecified physical injury that he called his "obscure hurt" with the outbreak of the war in the "soft spring" of 1861, though Leon Edel has placed it later, in the following fall. This injury, like Henry Sr.'s leg wound over thirty years before, was inflicted in an attempt to extinguish a fire, but Henry Jr. concealed the nature of his hurt. He described it in the autobiography as a "passage of personal history," "a private catastrophe . . . bristling with embarrassments." The twenty "odious" minutes during which he received the wound established him during the war years "and for long afterward" in a relation to history "at once extraordinarily intimate and quite awkwardly irrelevant." Trying, with friends, to start up an old water engine to put out a "shabby conflagration," he had been "jammed into the acute angle between two high fences" and had "done myself . . . a horrid even if an obscure hurt."

James's biographers and critics have devoted a great deal of speculation to the nature of this "hurt." Henry's language intimates that it was sexual, and several commentators have assumed it was a groin injury, in their rather mechanical attempts to explain the writer's identification with women, his celibacy, and his literary indirection with regard to sex. Leon Edel argues convincingly, however, that the injury was done to Henry's back. Whatever its nature, the obscure hurt served to confirm Henry's sense of physical inadequacy in relation to other young men — particularly fighting soldiers — and to exempt him from the masculine requirements of his generation. He was ordered to rest, which left him free to read and write.

Henry's yoking of the injury and the war in his recollections reveals a degree of unease at his exemption, though what comes through in his later writing about the war is not guilt or embarrassment but a sense of having missed something interesting. He envied Wilky his "romantic chances" and mastery of "such mysteries, such engines, such arts." War offered so much to *see*, for a young man who lived primarily through his eyes, and in the *"appreciation of the thing seen"* he had to live vicariously through his younger brothers' experience — relegated, as always, to "seeing, sharing, envying, applauding, pitying, all from too far-off."

•

In the spring of 1862 the Jameses moved to a two-story house at the corner of Spring Street and Lee Avenue in Newport. The house, covered with ivy and surrounded by a lawn, Austrian pines, and several large willows, was larger and stood farther from the center of town than the Kay Street house. Henry Sr. added a third floor for more space and an enhanced view of the sea. (The solid stone structure has been converted to a funeral parlor in a thickly settled part of twentieth-century Newport.)

With more room, the family could accommodate visitors more easily, and in the summer of 1862 Ellen and Edith Emerson came to Newport for three weeks, staying first with Sarah Clarke* and then with the Jameses. Ellen's letters home to Concord picture clearly the tangential relation to the war in which most middle- and upper-class girls found themselves. Once the sisters got settled and unpacked, they joined their friends in taking long walks along the Newport cliffs, playing croquet, attending parties, browsing in the Redwood Library, listening to the band on the green, watching barouches full of handsome ladies and gentlemen glide up and down Bellevue Avenue, and talking with convalescing soldiers in the military hospital that had been set up nearby at Portsmouth Grove. They went swimming with Alice and Wilky James, Ellen Temple, and Tom and Bessy Ward. "The water was warm and we went out beyond the surf and had the best time that I almost ever did have in the water," Ellen wrote to Concord. "Edith won't go in and I don't wonder much for it is a trial even to me to lose all the shine of my hair and have a two hours' piece of work with it after every bath, and her

* Sarah Freeman Clarke (1808–1896), the sister of James Freeman Clarke and one of the first women in New England to become a professional artist. She was a close friend of the Emersons, Margaret Fuller, and a number of other leading transcendentalists.

hair is twice as bad as mine . . . Mr. James is very charming all the time and I am in love with Mrs. James, Alice, and all the boys."

One Sunday, Wilky and Henry Sr. called at Miss Clarke's and invited the Emerson girls to go sailing the next day for a picnic on Julia Ward Howe's property at Lawton's Valley, in nearby Portsmouth. At nine the next morning, Bob James appeared in his little sailboat called the *Alice*. With him came Wilky as crew and "the real Alice as passenger," wrote Ellen. The Emersons, Miss Clarke, two other girls, and the three Jameses made up a party of eight setting out for the day. They reached Lawton's Valley at about eleven o'clock and had their picnic under a great ash tree near a brook between two waterfalls. Mrs. Howe had gone to Boston, and her eldest daughter, Julia, was too unwell for visitors; but the younger girls, Flossy and Maud,* came down, and the little group pulled lint (the soft scrapings of linen cloth were used to dress soldiers' wounds) and talked about soldiers until it was time to go.

By then a fierce wind had come up, and the two boys, after half an hour of nautical experiments, announced that the girls would get thoroughly wet and sick if they traveled home by boat. Accordingly, Wilky and Bob set off alone, and the girls wandered over to the soldiers' tents at Portsmouth Grove while they waited for a ferry to take them back to Newport.

The six girls "walked round and round" the convalescing soldiers, reported Ellen, and at last sat down on a piazza. "Everywhere soldiers, everywhere good and interesting faces, everywhere all we wanted to know and no means natural and proper of getting it. 'Water, water everywhere and not a drop to drink.' At last I begged the girls to go round with me to the side of the house nearest to the shed looking carefully at every one in it. But in vain." She was looking for some soldiers she had talked with the week before. Late in the afternoon she spotted a man she recognized, "but I wouldn't go near him. I'm sorry now." At five-thirty another man came up to ask them for a needle. They gave him one, and were sitting talking with him when at last "My sergeant" appeared, wrote Ellen. She questioned the young man shyly but persistently about the war, his background, his friends, thoughts, and feelings. His conversation delighted them all, she reported: "Once he quite carried us away, and though I meant to be very quiet I couldn't help shouting. It was a beautiful story about his horse . . ."

---

* Florence Howe Hull (1845–1922) and Maud Howe Elliott (1854–1948).

Twenty-two-year-old Ellen's little saga of shy advances and precipitate retreats, of curiosity and concern about the "natural and proper" means for getting what she wanted, reads like a Victorian sexual drama. What she wanted was simply knowledge of this male experience, which seemed so foreign and interesting. ("War feels to me an oblique place," wrote Emily Dickinson to Thomas Wentworth Higginson that fall.) Ellen persisted, surmounting her agitation to satisfy her curiosity, getting "carried away" to the point of shouting uncontrollably. The other girls hung back, listening and occasionally laughing, but letting Ellen do the interrogating, until at last the ferry arrived to take them back to town.

Alice, about to turn fourteen at the time of this excursion, plays only a cameo role in Ellen's account. When Ellen returned to Concord she added one more detail in summing up her visit: she described each James to a friend, concluding that "Alice is a dear little creature and of course cannot be happy a minute without her brothers."

•

The two younger James brothers did the conventionally manly thing by joining up to fight in the Civil War. In the fall of 1862, Wilky enlisted in the 44th Massachusetts Regiment from Boston. In 1863 he became an adjutant with the 54th Massachusetts, the first black regiment of the war, under the leadership of Colonel Robert Gould Shaw. The 54th Massachusetts, made up of free black men from all over the country, had been recruited by Governor John Andrew in the belief that black soldiers should be allowed to fight alongside whites for the freedom of their race. Liberal Northerners hoped the regiment's success would dispel all doubts about the Negro character and blacks' ability to assume the responsibilities of free men. The regiment was commanded by white officers, "laughing, welcoming, sunburnt young men," who seemed to Henry Jr. "to bristle with Boston genealogies" and who were only less handsome than their "tawny-bearded Colonel," Shaw, whose pure blue New England blood gave an unassailable dignity to the radical venture.

Henry Sr. wrote proudly to Elizabeth Peabody of Wilky's new virtues and selflessness as a soldier, and published one of the boy's letters from the field in the *Newport News*. In July 1863, Robertson, aged seventeen, enlisted with another black regiment, the 55th Massachusetts. His father wrote Miss Peabody that, though it "cost me a heart-break to part with one so young on a service so hard, I cannot but adore the great Providence which is thus lifting our young men out of indolence and vanity, into some free sympathy with His own deathless life. I seem never to have loved the dear boy before, now that he is clad with such an aureole of Divine beauty and innocence; and though the flesh was weak I still had the courage, spiritually, to bid him put all his heart in his living or dying."

In the two years since 1861, the nature of the war and the political climate of the country had changed, and these factors partly account for James's shift from firmly grasping the coattails of Harry and Willy to blessing the departure of his younger sons. In addition, the older boys were, in their father's eyes, cut out for higher things than war, and Wilky and Rob showed no such intellectual leanings. On the contrary, Henry Sr.'s letter to Miss Peabody suggests that he thought they needed "lifting out of indolence and vanity"; he hoped they might find in war the strength of character he felt they lacked.

In May 1863, the 54th Massachusetts, under Shaw, sailed from Boston while cheering crowds and occasional insults heralded their departure. "Two months after marching through Boston, / half the regiment was dead," wrote Robert Lowell almost a hundred years later, in "For the Union Dead." The black troops had been ordered to lead the attack on a Confederate stronghold, Fort Wagner, near Charleston, South Carolina, on July 18, 1863. Henry James, Sr., pronounced it suicidal to place a black regiment in the front of the charge, "knowing the fury it would provoke." The troops were not trained for heavy fighting, and the attack had been poorly planned. At the beginning of the battle, young Shaw led several of his officers (including Wilky) up a rise to call his troops to battle. He was shot and killed instantly.

Wilky, standing at his side, was hit as well. A canister ball entered his ankle and shattered the bone; it had to be removed aboard an army ship eight days later. And a fragment of shell hit him in the back, making a painful little pocket under the skin near his spine. Sent home to recuperate, Wilky was welcomed as a hero. His father described him as "manly and exalted in the tone of his mind . . . It is really quite incomprehensible to me to see so much manhood so suddenly achieved."

Bob, however, was having emotional trouble. He felt homesick, and was tempted to resign from the army. His father's letters from this period urged him to stay where he was and fight against "a temptation [homesickness] which your manhood is called upon to resist . . . You would not be [home] a month without being back again at all the ennui &

idleness of old times." If Bob yielded to this weakness, he would "regret all your days having done so, provided of course your aspiration towards a manly character be genuine." And then Henry Sr. offered a remarkable piece of fatherly interpretation: "A certain tone recently about your letters suggests to me, my dear Bob, that your conduct may not have been irreproachable of late in your own eyes, and that the softer feelings which are now germinating in your bosom are merely the effort which your better nature is making to restore you to self-respect ... You ought to know the physiology of this experience ... so I will tell you all about it ... Our entire moral life — i.e. our will and affections — is dependent every moment upon a balance of good and evil in the spiritual world." James was giving his son a moral rather than a physiological explanation of the guilty feelings he read between the lines of Bob's letters, and he counseled a "manly" resistance to self-condemnation.

Throughout the summer of 1864 he reiterated these injunctions to his youngest son to be a man: the temptation to resign was a mere "passing effeminacy," "an unmanly project"; "I hope you will not be so insane. I conjure you to be a man and force yourself like a man to do your whole duty."

Poor Bob found little solace in this advice. He wrote home, that fall, comparing himself with his older brothers, who seemed able effortlessly to do good. His father's reply displays the singular enthusiasm with which James responded to his children's sufferings, here making Bob the Prodigal Son:

My darling Bobbins,

Your letter of the 2nd inst. has just come in, and I lose no time in telling you how full of comfort it is in that you are looking at things so seriously. Don't be troubled; you were never so well off as you are now when your opinion of yourself is at the lowest. Certainly you were never so near and dear to your father's & mother's heart as you are at this moment. Be very sure of that.

Our three boys at home, as you say, are very good boys, and we appreciate their goodness very highly; but don't you remember the parable of the Prodigal Son, how the fatted calf is killed, and music and dancing inaugurated, not to celebrate the virtue that never falters, but that which having faltered, picks itself up again? ... It is only the repentant bosom that is really softened to the access of the highest things, and there is nothing accordingly so full of hope and joy to me as to see my children giving way to humiliation. You mistake if you suppose any of the boys have a perfectly good conscience: they all sin and all repent just as you do: though their sins perhaps being of not so conventional or public a quality as yours, their repentence is not quite so profound.

The crucial thing, stressed Henry Sr., was not to do good for the sake of worldly success, but to hate evil, to feel disgust at it, and to turn from sinfulness to God's perfect love.

There — I believe I have now met every demand of your letter, open or tacit, and I close by repeating how joyful your letter has made me — made Mama & me both. We have killed and eaten the fatted calf of our hearts over it, and our souls are full of music and dancing. Keep up your courage then darling child — keep steady to your duties and all will be more than well with you. All the family send their love, bushels full pressed down and running over, and we shall write often.

·

The crises of masculinity experienced in the nation and the James family during the Civil War served to increase Alice's sense of isolation and irrelevance. With William and Henry, she watched the younger boys go off to war. Then William left for Harvard and Henry disappeared into his room to write, until he, too, departed for Cambridge and Harvard — leaving Alice, again, at home with her parents and little to do.

William's letters from Cambridge called constant attention to Alice's inactivity. "Have you got the 2nd part of [*Les Miserables*] yet & is it good? I hope you study more than when I was at home." Scolding her for not writing, he reminded her that she had nothing better to do: "Perfidious child! Que ne m'écris tu, cruelle que tu es, qui te bouches les oreilles & me laisses crier! Toi qui n'as guère autre chose à faire!" In writing to his mother about his own struggles with career choice and the exigencies of finance, he referred to "that idle and useless young female, Alice, too, whom we shall have to feed and clothe." And when homesick, he wrote, "Dearest child, — ... I am quite sick and feverish tonight, and sit under my lamp wrapped in my overcoat writing *à la seule que j'aime* and wishing for nothing so much as an hour or two of her voluble and senseless, though soothing and pleasing, talk. Her transparent eyes, soft step, and gentle hands, her genial voice and mood, never seemed to me more desirable or lovable than now."

If Alice had been poor, she would have had to work in a factory or on a farm, to teach, sew, or do whatever she could to take the wage-earning place of a brother who had gone to fight. If she had been older, she might have volunteered for nursing or relief work in army hospitals,* or involved herself in the newly formed United States Sanitary Commission. She did help cut out shirts, sew, and roll bandages for the Newport Women's Aid Society, organized in April 1861. (Frederick Law Olmsted, secretary of the Sanitary Commission, acknowledged receipt of the commission's first cases of supplies, sent by the women of Newport; and during the winter of 1861–1862, the society arranged for the families of volunteers to make 75,000 flannel army shirts under contract to the quartermaster general in Washington.†) But through most of the war, Alice fit William's description of her as an "idle and useless young female."

Other middle- and upper-class girls were equally peripheral. In nearby Cambridge, Massachusetts, young men (wrote one of Alice's friends) were marching into battle in a "passionate fire of patriotism . . . Their little sisters, full of wonder and only half understanding the darkness of the cloud that had come across the sky, were moved to help as their elders were doing." These "little sisters" formed a sewing group, called the Banks Brigade, to make bandages and soldiers' clothes; Alice joined it when her family moved to Cambridge a few years later. Whenever they saw a United States flag, the members of the brigade would stop and salute it "like true soldiers," continued Alice's friend. "We sometimes passed the old arsenal which stood on the corner of Garden and Follen Streets . . . There we would stop and peer through the fence to watch the evolutions of the Harvard students who lived there in squads and were armed by the State and were regularly drilled. They formed a guard for

* Louisa May Alcott, aged thirty, volunteered for nursing duty in Washington, confiding to her journal that she *"must* let out my pent-up energy in some new way . . . I want new experiences and am sure to get 'em if I go." Although Louisa came down with typhoid fever and had to go home after three months, she had found a way to take part in the central experience of her time: "A most interesting journey into a new world full of stirring sights and sounds, new adventures, and an ever-growing sense of the great task I had undertaken.

"I said my prayers as I went rushing through the country white with tents, all alive with patriotism, and already red with blood.

"A solemn time, but I'm glad to live in it; and am sure it will do me good whether I come out alive or dead."

† Organizations such as the Women's Aid Societies, nursing corps, and the Sanitary Commission did more than help the war effort; they provided a sense of social usefulness for people who were excluded from active participation in the war by virtue of age, sex, leisured status, or all three.

the arsenal. Our brothers and cousins were there and might some day become full-fledged soldiers."

The only record of Alice's thoughts on the War Between the States is her diary, written almost thirty years later in England. There, in 1890, she recorded the remarks of an English peer who had been justifying the cruelty of European wars by reminding the readers of the *Pall Mall Gazette* that "in America the most savage war of modern times — in which thousands of helpless prisoners were starved to death on one side, and wounded men crawling from the field of battle were shot in cold blood on the other — was relentlessly waged between men of one race and one speech!" Did he think, Alice countered, "that the war was waged with no object save as a vent for savagery? or is the freeing of millions of human beings from bondage a cause unworthy to lift up the hearts of wives to send forth their husbands and mothers their sons into battle?" In Alice's impassioned rejoinder, it was the action to which women were inspired — the sacrifice of husbands and sons — that proved the nobility of the cause. (As she had never been wife or mother, she excluded herself even from this form of heroism.)

At the age of thirteen, Alice could only watch, with Henry and William. But watch she did, in true Jamesian fashion: later, again in England, she put the Civil War experience to use in reflecting on the difficulty of understanding "foreign" situations. She was reading the *Memoirs* of "the intelligent and most sympathetic" Massimo d'Azeglio.* Alice endorsed his observation that democracy differed from autocracy in being "a many headed tyrant, a despotism from below instead of from on high," but she took issue with his example: he compared Russia and the United States during the latter's Rebellion, writing, "I am constrained in justice to ask pardon of the Russian despotism for placing it in the same balance with American despotism, for whilst Alexander Romanoff breaks the chains of his slaves Abraham Lincoln only breaks the chains of his enemies' slaves." Alice commented, "The impression given by this, of that embodied benignancy, poor old tragic Lincoln freeing slaves only, *quâ enemy's* slaves with a preserve, perhaps, of his own in the background at the White House shows the marvellous possibilities of non-apprehension."

•

---

* Massimo Taparelli, Marchese d'Azeglio (1798–1866), was an Italian statesman and writer of historical novels. He led the Italian movement for national liberation in 1845 and was premier (under King Victor Emmanuel II) from 1849 to 1852.

ALICE JAMES, June 1870

CATHARINE BARBER JAMES
(from a daguerreotype)

WILLIAM JAMES of Albany

MARY WALSH JAMES

HENRY JAMES, SR., in middle age

CATHARINE WALSH ("Aunt Kate")

ALICE JAMES IN PARIS, about 1857

ALICE JAMES AT NEWPORT, 1862

WILLIAM JAMES, about 1867

HENRY JAMES, JR., at Newport, 1863

GARTH WILKINSON JAMES,
1861 or 1862

ROBERTSON JAMES AT NEWPORT,
April 1862

ALICE JAMES, sketched by Henry James, Jr., at Chester, 1872

SKETCHES BY WILLIAM JAMES (probably of Alice, the 1860s)

WILLIAM JAMES, SELF-PORTRAIT, 1866. Alice tucked the sketch between the pages of a book, where Katharine Loring found it after Alice's death. Miss Loring sent it to Henry, who wrote, "I *dimly* remember William's (quite casually) doing it, before a mirror, on which you see his eye is fixed."

HENRY JAMES, JR., in 1859 or 1860

SARA SEDGWICK (Mrs. William Erasmus Darwin)

SUSAN SEDGWICK (Mrs. Charles Eliot Norton)

Ellen Emerson and Kitty Prince described Alice at Newport as a dear little creature and a very sweet girl. Their scant accounts, though probably
accurate as far as they went, leave almost everything unsaid. Alice herself
provided, much later, a closer look at her experience during these years.
In 1890, surveying the Newport period, she found herself glad that the
"ancient superstition" as to youth's being the happiest time of life was
"pretty well exploded," since for her it had been the most difficult. She
was relieved to have reached middle life, "when serene and sure of our
direction all the simple incidents of daily life and human complication
explain and enrich themselves as they are linked and fitted to the wealth
of past experience." To this serenity she contrasted "the blank youthful
mind, ignorant of catastrophe," standing "crushed and bewildered before
the perpetual postponement of its hopes, things promised in the dawn
that the sunset ne'er fulfills."

As an innocent child, she had looked trustingly toward the bright
vistas of the future. Instead of the fulfillments of her youthful longings,
however, she found herself in adolescence "crushed and bewildered," for
everything she had been promised still hovered tantalizingly beyond her
reach: the paternal promise of happiness perpetually postponed, in Europe, at Newport, back in Europe and back to Newport, at school, in the
celebrated home, with brothers, parents, friends; the promised but postponed visit to the Emersons; the promise of womanhood's rewards, and
the permanent postponements of self they entailed; the eternal, elusive
promise of enough love as a reward for enough virtue.

Alice used powerful but impersonal imagery to describe the catastrophe awaiting the ignorant youthful mind. In the very next sentence,
however, she turned autobiographical and gave an extraordinary account
of her own early adolescence and what she really meant by catastrophe.
She recalled the "low, grey Newport sky in that winter of 62–3 as I used
to wander about over the cliffs, my young soul struggling out of its
swaddling-clothes as the knowledge crystallized within me of what Life
meant for me . . ." At the age of fourteen, she had concluded that life for
her meant renunciation, a sort of spiritual suicide: "Owing to muscular
circumstances my youth was not of the most ardent, but I had to peg
away pretty hard between 12 and 24, 'killing myself,' as some one calls
it — absorbing into the bone that the better part is to clothe oneself in
neutral tints, walk by still waters, and possess one's soul in silence."

Though written in the retrospective light of middle age, and not nec-
essarily an accurate transcript of Alice's fourteen-year-old feelings, this

strong, even shocking, statement does describe the self-strangulation that took place during her adolescence. Instead of moving forward from childhood to meet the tasks and pleasures of adult femininity, Alice in a sense stopped. Like many of the major characters in Henry's novels (and, in fact, like Henry himself), she renounced full participation in life.

She described this process in physical terms: she was "absorbing into the bone" that she should be still, neutral, sexless, silent. Her youth would have been "ardent,"* she implied, if she had not been ill — the victim of peculiar "muscular circumstances"; even so, she had had to "peg away pretty hard"† to stifle her active nature. She acknowledged the perpetual postponement that met her youthful hopes. The changes in her adolescent body forecast further promises to be fulfilled or postponed — of men's love, childbearing, a life independent of her present family. She could not control her altering body, but she could ignore it, and she could suppress her hopes. Since any kind of excitement proved too stimulating — from her family's teasing to Ellen Emerson's invitation to Concord — since promises made could not be fulfilled, and since eager desires led only to catastrophic disappointment, then she had better not want anything; she had better adopt the pose and attributes of a nun.

Though her soul in 1862 was struggling out of its swaddling clothes, it celebrated no new-found freedom. "One feels that she doffed her swaddling-clothes but to don a spiritual straitjacket," observed Leon Edel in his biography of her brother. Alice could not simply renounce life or remove herself to a convent. She was growing up into a world in which she still seemed to have no place, and her spirit rebelled against the enforced uselessness of a female adolescence that coincided with the greatest national crisis of the century. Since her nature *was* ardent, she had to struggle constantly to quench its unruly assertions. It was the struggle of a lifetime. She determined in her solitary adolescence that "the only thing which survives is the resistance we bring to life and not the strain life brings to us."

---

* Her father used the word *ardent* to describe his own exuberantly active youth in his fragmentary autobiography. Alice had read this account of his youth, for William had published it in *The Literary Remains of the Late Henry James* in 1884.

† Perhaps her use of the word *peg* here also connects her experience with her father's youth and adolescent crisis, for his accident resulted in his lifelong use of a wooden or peg leg.

Part II

A Feminine Age

The whole generation is womanized, the masculine
tone is passing out of the world; it's a feminine, a nervous, hysterical, chattering, canting age, an age of
hollow phrases and false delicacy and exaggerated so-
licitudes and coddled sensibilities, which, if we don't
soon look out, will usher in the reign of mediocrity,
of the feeblest and flattest and the most pretentious
that has ever been.

— Basil Ransom in Henry James, *The Bostonians*

I wish you could know Katharine Loring, she is a
most wonderful being. She has all the mere brute superiority which distinguishes man from woman combined with all the distinctively feminine virtues.
There is nothing she cannot do from hewing wood &
drawing water to driving run-away horses & educating all the women in North America.

— Alice James to Sara Darwin, August 9, 1879

Chapter Five

Bostonians

THE JAMES FAMILY finally ended its wanderings by settling in the Boston area in 1864, at first on Beacon Hill, at 13 Ashburton Place, and then permanently in Cambridge. The difference between Cambridge and the rest of the world was the subject of a story Henry Sr. related to Alice a few years later. A visitor to Cambridge one day mentioned "chignons" in the presence of Helen Child, the small daughter of Harvard English professor Francis J. Child. When Helen asked what chignons were, the visitor exclaimed, "Why — don't you know?"

"No," said Helen. "I never heard of them before as I know."

"Do you know," asked the lady, "what the rings of Saturn are?"

"Oh yes," replied Helen. "I know all about the rings of Saturn."

"There," said the lady, "tell me there is no difference between Cambridge and the rest of the world when a growing girl there knows all about the rings of Saturn, and has never heard of chignons!"

Both William and Henry Jr. were living in Cambridge in 1864, and the primary motive for the James family's migration from Newport to Boston appears to have been proximity to the two older boys. When their parents moved to Ashburton Place, Henry and William gave up their boardinghouse rooms to live again at home — and at home they stayed until Henry moved to Europe in 1875 and William got married in 1878. A further reason for the move was that the stimulations of a city rich in intellectual and social life had begun to seem more attractive to Henry Sr. than the pastoral pleasures of Newport.

In Boston, the Jameses entered a number of new social worlds. They visited familiar Concord — the Emersons, Alcotts, Channings, Hawthornes, and Sanborn. They saw old Cambridge friends and made new ones, including the editor of the *North American Review,* Charles Eliot Norton, and his family at Shady Hill; Norton's in-laws, the Arthur Sedgwicks; Francis Child; William Dean Howells; James Russell Lowell; Louis and Elizabeth Cary Agassiz. The editor of the *Atlantic,* James T. Fields, lived with his wife, Annie, on the other side of Beacon Hill from Ashburton Place, at 148 Charles Street. And in the Back Bay, on Beacon Hill, and in outlying towns and suburbs, there were the Brahmins. Henry Sr. greatly enjoyed this varied, genteel, interesting society, with its high-minded idealism and commitment to social responsibility, but he could not resist tweaking its sense of virtue when he described a group of eminent Bostonians to Howells as "simmering in their own fat and putting a nice brown on each other."

Of all the James children, only William took wholeheartedly to the Boston area, making Cambridge his permanent home, but even he appreciated it most when he was 3000 miles away, in Europe or California. The younger boys moved away from home as soon as they could — first to the South and then to the Midwest. Henry always felt bored and restless in the "Puritan capital." He criticized the city's character and spirit in his 1886 novel, *The Bostonians;* and in *The American* (1877), Christopher Newman thinks that a fit punishment for an American in Europe who speaks ill of the United States is to "be carried home in irons and compelled to live in Boston." Henry left for a tour of Europe in 1869 and settled in England for good a few years later. Alice, who eventually followed him to London, was less of an Anglophile, and fonder of America's comparatively simple virtues, but she often found Boston queer and stifling. One night when she had been invited to dinner by her friend Ida Agassiz Higginson, along with two other close friends, Nina Lowell and Frances Rollins Morse, she made fun (not for the first time) of the "stupidity and want of imagination of the Bostonians, whose highest idea of doing a pleasant thing for you is to ask you to meet someone you see every day."

•

In the early part of the nineteenth century, Boston's elite had been in the forefront of American political, cultural, and financial life. But in the decades before the Civil War, the energetic forces of the country's population had begun to shift from New England toward New York and the West, and the enormous fortunes amassed in the early nineteenth century by Boston's first families, with their Harvard educations, democratic ideals, and traditions of political leadership, were beginning to be overshadowed by newer and ever larger accumulations of wealth. The forces of industrialization, immigration, big labor unions, large competing cities such as New York and Chicago, and the new politics of influence and money, were combining to set Boston's Brahmins on the sidelines of midcentury American life.

Many of New England's aristocratic young men in the 1850s had found themselves, like William James, in crises of indecision. They were not attracted to Brahmin tradition or to destinies in their fathers' law firms and counting rooms; they did not have to make new fortunes; the blue life-blood seemed to be thinning in their veins. As George Fredrickson has described in *The Inner Civil War,* the exigencies of war provided these young men, at least temporarily, with something to do. War demanded courage, self-sacrifice, and action in the name of patriotic humanitarianism, and Robert Gould Shaw became a symbol not simply of the abolitionists' cause but of the rediscovered masculinity of America's northern elite.

The war postponed but did not solve the crisis of exhaustion in the North. In the middle 1860s many young men returned to face the problem of career choice, and New England as a whole had to come to terms with its position in a rapidly changing nation. Several of its finest young men, like Shaw and his brother-in-law, Charles Russell Lowell, were killed in the war. Many others, before and after the war, went west, looking for new lives, broader horizons, greater fortunes.

This decimation of the male population left a large surplus of women in the East. In 1850 there were nearly 20,000 more women than men in Massachusetts; by 1870, although there was a surplus of men in the West, the number of "extra" women in Massachusetts was up to 50,000; and by 1880 it had reached 66,000. As the numbers of available men decreased in the East, many women found themselves without the economic security of marriage. The censuses for 1850 and 1860 show a marked drop in the marriage figures in New England, and of the small percentage of women in American history who never married, the proportion is highest for women born in the last four decades of the nineteenth century.

Some of these unmarried women had the time — and many, the economic necessity — to find something else to do besides traditional "women's work" at home. But there were not many choices: teaching, nursing, mill or factory work, or, for a privileged few, art, medicine, writing. When Alice James's friend Elizabeth Boott went to study painting with Thomas Couture in Paris in 1876, Alice wrote to another friend, "I wish that her work wd. come to more than it does . . . Feminine art as long as it only remains a resource is very good but when it is an end its rather a broken reed. Matrimony seems the only successful occupation that a woman can undertake."

Throughout the East the surplus of women created considerable anxiety about spinsters and an amused celebration of what Theodore Parker, noted Unitarian minister, called "the glorious phalanx of old maids." Across the Charles River from Boston, the glorious phalanx was known as "the Cambridge ladies, who seldom marry and never die."*

The postwar years in New England came to be known as an age of strong-minded women. The movement for women's rights in the United States (officially born in the same year as Alice James: the first Woman's Rights Convention was held at Seneca Falls, New York, in 1848) had been reinforced by abolitionist ideals, and by the early 1860s it had begun to develop a real following. In May 1866, the American Equal Rights Association was formed to advance the rights of black people and women; its first meetings in Boston and New York were attended by a number of prominent New England reformers. Julia Ward Howe, William Lloyd

---

* Even the women who did marry saw the accepted terms of feminine identity giving way. In the middle decades of the nineteenth century, middle-class young wives in the northeastern United States found themselves oddly without a function. Earlier, families had constituted small units of communal production under the supervision of mothers. Children, husbands, collateral relatives had joined in the work, and the household under the mother's direction was a functioning economic unit. As food and cloth and educated children began increasingly to be produced outside the home, and as water and steam power increasingly took over women's work in the home, the role of wife-and-mother changed from quintessential to superfluous. The female producer of goods and services became the consumer. Her sense of having an economic place in the family and social world vanished, and her value came to be defined as biological and spiritual. Lucy Washburn, a friend of Alice's who considered becoming a doctor but eventually married one instead, noted succinctly, "I know little about the rights of women in Primitive History, but I have a suspicion that we shall have to work hard to be as valuable a part of society now as they were then."

Garrison, Thomas Wentworth Higginson, John Greenleaf Whittier, James Freeman Clarke, and Louisa May Alcott numbered among the Boston supporters of women's rights in the late 1860s, and in 1870 Bronson Alcott and Frank Sanborn joined them to help form the Massachusetts Woman Suffrage Association.

The James family knew most of the prominent supporters of women's rights in the Northeast, but Henry Sr., his wife, and his sister-in-law did not support this new cause. Mary James wielded all the power she wanted at home and saw no need for the ballot. Her husband never supported reform movements, preferring to mock zealotry of all kinds while pursuing his own idiosyncratic meditations. Besides, as his 1850s' writing showed, he heartily disapproved of equality for women in intellectual and political life. Woman had her own hallowed sphere; any encroachment on man's constituted a violation of the laws of nature.

But regardless of what the Jameses thought and wrote, women in the 1860s were beginning to enter what had until then been male territory. For instance, they got elected to the Boston School Committee. In 1868, Julia Ward Howe and several other Boston women founded the New England Women's Club, modeled on the social clubs of Boston men — the Transcendental Club, the Radical Club, the Saturday Club. The women's club functioned as an intellectual focal point, an "organized social center for united thought and action," and served, like the men's clubs, as a quiet place for meeting, reading, resting in town, "for the comfort and convenience of its members."

Harriet Beecher Stowe's overwhelmingly successful *Uncle Tom's Cabin* had encouraged large numbers of women writers to submit their work for publication, and new magazine and book publishers eagerly bought up their highly marketable "feminine" fiction. The postwar reading public was predominantly female. Many commentators saw nothing but decay in this new cultural climate: the era of Thoreau, Hawthorne, Emerson, Longfellow, Poe, Whittier, Melville, and Whitman had ended, and the hegemony of "masculine" standards in literature was a thing of the past. Longfellow complained in 1873 of "the decline of interest in literature and in the taste for it," and Charles Eliot Norton, reporting Longfellow's remark to Carlyle, added, "This generation is given over to the making and spending of money, and is losing the capacity of thought. It wants to be amused, and the magazines amuse it." Francis Parkman deplored what others would call the "feminization" of American literature, and noted that "flatulent writing" had replaced "pregnant writing."* Even the best male writers in Boston, William Dean Howells and Henry James, wrote novels in which women had the greater strength of character. The young men conceived by both novelists "seemed to be waiting for a breeze," observed Van Wyck Brooks; "their sails were flapping, and the women supplied the breeze, for, with all their 'tastes,' the men seldom had any masculine force or motive. In both these writers, the masculine sex appeared to exist, even in England, in order to fall in love with American girls."

Those characters in James who do embody male forcefulness, such as Caspar Goodwood in *The Portrait of a Lady* and Basil Ransom in *The Bostonians,* do not perceive the cultural and moral distinctions that so interested James and his heroines. The rare men who do see all the implications of culture and moral sensibility in James are either sickly (Ralph Touchett in *Portrait*) or old and beyond the sphere of action (Lambert Strether in *The Ambassadors*). James highlighted the split in postwar American society between femininity, sickliness, and the appreciation of cultural refinement, on the one hand, and a self-assertive masculine tradition blind to the subtleties of imaginative vision on the other.

•

In Boston in the 1860s Alice began for the first time to make close friends among the members of her own sex. She engaged with these young women in the exchanges of visits that were the standard form of female social intercourse in nineteenth-century Boston. She would go for a few days to stay with a friend at Brookline, Milton, or Beverly, and her friend would be invited to stay for a return visit with the Jameses at Ashburton Place.

---

* In religion, the erosion of old certainties led to a parallel flurry of activity: mesmerists, nostrum-mongers, mediums, and zealots of all persuasions moved in to take advantage of the Church's weakening hold over the population. Ann Douglas discusses the causes and effects of the simultaneous disestablishment of women and clergy in nineteenth-century American life, and of the increasing sentimentalism in American writing and religion, in *The Feminization of American Culture* (New York: Alfred Knopf, 1977).

Alice's new friends, the daughters of Boston's first families, occupied a highly regular, close-knit social world. Their fathers — doctors, lawyers, professors, judges, philanthropists — devoted portions of their considerable incomes and energies to charitable organizations and to cultural institutions like the Boston Symphony Orchestra, founded in 1882 by financier Henry Lee Higginson. They spent the winter in town, in comfortable houses with terraced lawns and exquisitely kept gardens; in the summer they went to Maine, Vermont, New Hampshire, the North Shore, the Adirondacks, Cape Cod, or the Elizabeth Islands.

In this cohesive, rarefied world of independent means and shared assumptions, relatives often stayed closer to each other than they ever became with anyone from "outside," and the genealogies show numerous cousins who married each other, widowers who married their deceased wives' sisters, and women who appear to have preferred the familiar company of parents and siblings to life with a stranger.* A favorite summer retreat was the Putnam camp in the Adirondacks, where Miss Elizabeth Putnam followed a rule, in making up a house party of twenty or thirty people, that "no one should be invited whom you would not want your son or daughter to marry." Testifying to her success are the lists of young women visitors from the Lyman, Cabot, Putnam, Jackson, and Lee families who married young men of the Lyman, Cabot, Putnam, Jackson, and Lee families.

Alice met Frances Rollins Morse, her first intimate friend, at the school they attended together in Boston, Miss Clapp's. Alice described Miss Clapp, who had taught in the 1850s at Elizabeth Agassiz's school in Cambridge, as a sweet, pretty lady who "cocked her little head on one side & smiled just like a little bird." Classes, held at Miss Clapp's house in downtown Boston, were conducted by a Miss Ireland, who remained a friend of Alice's for years after their instructor-student relationship had ended.

Fanny Morse was two years younger than Alice James, and through the

---

* Alice's friend Fanny Morse told a story about her great-uncle Judge Charles Jackson, whose first wife, Amelia Lee, died in 1809: Amelia's cousin Frances Cabot had been a childhood playmate of Charles Jackson's, but Mr. Jackson did not see Miss Cabot during the year following his wife's death. One day, however, he drove up to her father's house as she sat on the porch shelling peas, proposed to her, and was accepted. Years later, asked by her daughter-in-law how she could have made up her mind so quickly, the former Frances Cabot replied, "My dear! not marry Mr. Jackson!"

hours they shared in the schoolroom, the two girls became friends for
life. Fanny was descended from Patrick Tracy Jackson, one of the found-
ers of the Lowell Textile Mills and treasurer of the Boston & Lowell Railroad. Her parents, Harriet Jackson Lee and Samuel Torrey Morse, spent
winters on Chauncy Street near Bedford Place, and summers in Brookline. Often during the hot summer months, Alice visited the Morses at
Brookline, where she made friends with Fanny's mother and
younger sister, Mary. The entire James family grew fond of Fanny, who
eventually became a prominent figure in the work of the Associated
Charities of Boston and a founder of the Simmons School of Social
Work. William corresponded with her all his life.

One Sunday, a few days after a brief visit from Fanny, Alice wrote:

My dear Fanny —

I just want to send you a few lines, for no purpose, except to tell you how
glad I was to see you the other day and how much I wish I could see you oftener — in short that I love you very much. I hope you won't mind my telling
you so, I know you wd. not if you knew how true it was. I feel myself to be a
more respectable human being when I consider that I have you for a friend, &
I have you, haven't I, notwithstanding all my sins? You seemed so sweet the
other day that my heart has been full of you ever since.

I am scribbling this in the most improper way on my knee in the midst of
doing up my hair for the night — so that I mustn't write another line, but
with a God bless you, wish you good night my darling Fanny —

                              Yrs. always,
                              Alice James

In this friendship Alice invested all the affection that had until then
found no suitable object outside her family. And as she was to do
throughout her life with everyone she loved, she idealized Fanny and dis-
paraged herself by comparison.

In 1866, Fanny went to Europe with her parents. Alice felt the loss
acutely. She wrote her friend constantly, contrasting Fanny's virtues to
her own drawbacks: "I intend to turn over a new leaf & write to my dear
little girl oftener than I have done heretofore, for I think she deserves it
if any one does for the virtuous way in which she writes to me, but you
know my dear you were always a much better child than I . . . I wish I
did not write such horrid stupid letters. I am perfectly ashamed to send
them, but I am going to be awfully good this summer, so that when you
come back I shall not be afraid of seeing you." And again, "You are the

best and dearest little girl in the world to write to me so often when you have so many other people who are so much more deserving of your goodness . . . This seems such a poor little letter to send to you after your delightful ones so full of all you are doing, but you must make allowances for us poor humdrum people who stay at home & don't see any beautiful views or pictures."

She mocked her own writing and limited experience, but was quite in earnest when she wrote,

I have discovered that either one's friends or oneself change, I don't know which it is, at any rate one or the other does. By the above remark (which I very much doubt whether you will understand) I wish to impress on your young mind that you must not change your small self in any way for you cannot be any nicer, any better, any sweeter, or any dearer to

Your loving friend,
Alice James

Alice's opaque remark about change reflected her conviction that something was bound to go wrong. For all her father's insistence that love was pure innocent goodness, Alice appears to have seen the whole business of loving and being loved as fraught with danger. Her sense of herself was at stake: having Fanny as a friend made her feel "more respectable," and she needed reassurance that "I have you, haven't I, notwithstanding all my sins?" Convinced that love was not freely given but had to be earned by being good (although the paternal philosophy read otherwise), Alice viewed the ultimate emotional reward of love as out of reach, since she knew at heart that she was *not* all innocent purity. In the Jamesian system of moral absolutes, anyone who was not all good was all bad. She did not deserve Fanny's love, she wrote — it was a charity that her friend had the power to give or withhold. Alice could only try to be good — and hope.*

•

* Alice's letters to Fanny Morse express deeply personal fears and quandaries. Their tone, however, and what they suggest about the importance of female friendship, have echoes in the letters other nineteenth-century women addressed to each other in their virginal adolescences and throughout their married or single lives. (See Caroll Smith-Rosenberg, "The Female World of Love and Ritual: Relations Between Women in Nineteenth-Century America," *Signs,* vol. I, no. 1, Autumn 1975). Intense love between women constituted an integral part of social life in a world that kept men and women in separate spheres until marriage. And marrying someone from the alien, masculine world often seemed so much like marrying a stranger that many women

A different kind of love from that between friends now also made its appearance on the horizon of Alice's life. She turned eighteen in 1866, and her friends had begun to pair off. She, too, was expected to do "the usual thing" (as Dr. Sloper says of his daughter, Catherine, in Henry's novel *Washington Square*) — to marry.

In March of 1865, Emerson's second daughter, Edith, had announced her engagement to William Hathaway Forbes, the oldest son of John Murray Forbes (who had made a fortune earlier in the century in the China trade and railroads). Henry James, Sr., wrote Emerson a letter of hearty congratulation: "Marriage is a sacrament which women interpret in so much more celestial a sense than men,* that it is somewhat to a father to find his daughter coveted by a man who doesn't deserve to be shot outright for his presumption. How great your felicity then in being able to bestow your rose-bud upon so sincere and manly a bosom as Willy Forbes! Happy father, first in the possession of such children, and now above all in the clear foresight of his child's happiness! Ah well! perhaps my poor little bird will find as tender a nest."

His poor little bird wrote her friend Fanny about the celestial sacrament of marriage: "I suppose you have heard of Jenny Watson's engagement to Ned Perkins. Is it not funny, he is more than five years younger; can you possibly imagine marrying a boy [the word *man* was crossed out] so much younger than yourself? It would not be so strange if Ned Perkins were not so very immature, but he always seemed to me a perfect infant."

If marrying younger men seemed questionable, older ones were no better. A few months later, Alice wrote to Fanny about General Francis

---

even in marriage maintained the primacy of their female friendships. A visiting friend or sister would sometimes displace a husband from the conjugal bed so that the two women could be together all night, sharing stored-up confidences and affection. Alice's closeness with Henry crossed the nineteenth century's sexual frontier in many ways, but it consisted primarily of intellectual and abstract sympathies, not of the traded secrets and shared domestic activities that made up the fabric of intimate friendships between girls. Female friendships provided women with networks and ties that revolved around their own spheres of interest — books, marriage, health, work, travel. When Fanny traveled, Alice took up with her cousin as a means of maintaining the connection. When Alice went away, Fanny would come to the James house with her sewing to sit with Mrs. James, talking and working — and then both Fanny and Mrs. James would write to Alice about their time together.

* It is difficult to imagine anyone interpreting marriage in a more celestial sense than Henry James, Sr., did.

Barlow's engagement to Nelly Shaw, sister of Robert Gould Shaw and Josephine Shaw Lowell: "It gives one a shiver, does it not? Do you know General Barlow? I don't, but I have a sort of prejudice against him, it does not seem to be nice for a sweet young girl like Nelly to marry a widower does it?"

A photograph from this period shows Alice (see picture following page 80) as a serious, plain-featured young woman with a clear, intent gaze. She was not beautiful, and her face shows none of the then-fashionable delicacy that had begun to mar her health. Her hair, pulled straight back to coil around her head in a braid, reveals a high, broad, Jamesian brow. She looks older than her years, bearing a strong resemblance to her mother and Henry Jr.

Of her own social life, she reported to Fanny, "I have been to one or two parties since you left but nothing very exciting. The Wards have been in town for the last fortnight, staying at Mrs. Dorr's. She had one of the Ladies Social Clubs, to which she asked me I suppose on Bessy's account. Mr. Dorr and Mrs. Hunt acted a charade that was rather funny, but as Mr. Dwight* had asked me to go the opera to hear Fidelio with him, & as I had to go to Mrs. Dorr's instead, the charade perhaps did not seem as funny to me as it might otherwise have done."

Since Mr. Dwight was fifty-three, Alice was probably annoyed at missing the pleasure of his distinguished company and the opportunity to hear *Fidelio* — not at missing a romantic encounter. Besides, her letters to Fanny show her devoting greater interest to women during this period than to men. She had recently met Clover Hooper (the future Mrs. Henry Adams, whose Christian name was Marian) and her sister, Ellen, and wrote to Fanny in June:

Now my dear I am going to tell you something pretty fine. Miss Ellen Hooper is going to ask Mary and me to spend next Sunday with her at Beverly. Did you ever hear anything quite so splendid as that?

You see, Miss, that although we poor folks don't go to Europe and see pictures and climb mountains and sich like, we do have a little amusement as we go along. If you crow too much when you get back I shall begin to talk of my

---

* John Sullivan Dwight (1813–1893), a former Brook Farmer and contributor to *The Harbinger* and *The Dial,* and Boston's foremost music critic. He ran the Harvard Music Association, published the *Journal of Music,* and established the first professorship of music at Harvard. His wife had died in 1860.

dear delightful and intimate friend Miss Hooper. But my dear Fanny if you only come back soon you may crow all day and all night and you may tell me that I have never even seen Miss Hooper if it should give you any pleasure. Your mother implied but did not say that you would be home early in the winter; if you don't make your appearance then I shall send a constable after you.

Chapter Six

"Nerves"

I N THE FALL of 1866, Henry James, Sr., rented a house at 20 Quincy Street in Cambridge. Here, at last, his family made its permanent home. Quincy Street runs along the eastern side of Harvard Yard, beginning at Kirkland Street and ending at Massachusetts Avenue. Number 20, which the Jameses eventually bought in 1870, stood on a small hillock that sloped down toward the Charles River to the south and to swampy lands near Broadway and Harvard's Memorial Church at the north; westward, the slope declined toward what is now Widener Library. The building the Jameses lived in is no longer there — the Harvard Faculty Club occupies the site — but a friend of Alice's remembered it as "a good, square house of simple proportions, with the best fence in Cambridge for children to walk on."

Henry Jr. described it as "about as lively as an inner sepulchre." The junior members of the family at home — William, Henry, and Alice — all suffered nervous crises there in the 1860s. Wilky and Bob, too, were racked by emotional storms, but they were living away from home. Each of the five now faced troubling decisions about what to do in life.

At eighteen, in Cambridge, Alice had to come to new terms with the question — of "what Life meant for me" — that she had glimpsed at Newport when she resolved to clothe herself in neutral tints and possess her soul in silence. She made no mention of "nervous" crises in her letters to Fanny Morse, for, unlike William, she rarely discussed her own illness. But her trouble had not abated. William, on an expedition in Brazil with Professor and Mrs. Louis Agassiz, wrote, in 1865, sending "love to dear old Aunt Kate, Harry, and Alice. Does the latter continue to wish she was dead? Mille baisers to her." And Henry Sr. explained in a letter to Alice's friend Annie Ashburner that his daughter felt too exhausted to accompany Annie to the Museum of Fine Arts: "She is not able even to write to you to say how 'awfully' sorry she is to be forced to disappoint your hospitable intentions once more. 'What a mysterious world it is, she cries, where one's force is never equal to their good-will, or their good-will (which is worse) never equal to their force!' I think with a little more discipline from your kind hand, she will turn out quite a philosopher, don't you?"

Shortly after her family moved to the "inner sepulchre" on Quincy Street in the fall of 1866, Alice wrote to Fanny of "my sad fate for the winter." She was about to leave for New York, where an orthopedic surgeon named Charles Fayette Taylor would treat her maladies. "Is it not dreadful?" Alice asked Fanny. "Don't you suppose you may go to New York during the winter? I don't know what will become of me, but I suppose I will survive it, at any rate, I must try to."

•

Alice left Cambridge for New York to undergo Dr. Taylor's treatments in November 1866. As surgeons often did in the middle of the nineteenth century, Dr. Taylor kept a number of rooms in his own house for patients. Alice and Aunt Kate moved directly into Taylor's house, at 1303 Broadway, near 35 Street. Next door stood his New York Orthopaedic Dispensary, opened the month before. The dispensary provided mechanical and surgical treatment for the deformed children of the poor, especially those with spine and hip-joint diseases. Though the dispensary treated children, most of Dr. Taylor's private patients were apparently old, for William wrote to Wilky that he thought Alice's being secluded "with all those defunct and aged people" would lead either to "an unnatural demureness" or an "open revolution of some kind."

The family in Cambridge staggered their letters so that Alice got one nearly every day. Once a week, her father sent her *The Nation* and *The Illustrated News,* and to Aunt Kate the *Spectator* and *The Saturday Review.* William wrote of his sister's *"delightful"* letters from New York, and Henry of the "shower" she lavished on everyone but him; but not one of her letters from this period has survived. The family correspondence never discussed her illness — only her progress and the trials of separation.

William: "I am glad you think you are doing well and are managing to live comfortably. I little thought you would be able to do so without me and my pills." Teasing still dominated his communications, for at Christmas he mourned, "Alas that at this jocund time we shd. be separated. That we shd. come down each one morose & silent to his separate breakfast & have nothing to say to each other of a pleasant nature after the mechanical & forced salutation of the day. Whereas if Aunt Kate were here with her buoyant nature & thou who art always so overflowing with good humour & merriment in the early morning, things wd. be widely different. The quip, the krank, the merry joke, the flash of poetry, the tinge of pathos, the gleam of love would all be there, where now they are not."

Henry Jr.: "I am charmed, beloved child, to hear accounts of your improvement & of the lovely manner in which you submit to this cruel separation from your family. May it soon cease: yet not however before you are completely restored to health & symmetry." The Temple girls were visiting in Cambridge, continued Harry. "A hundred times a day they cry out how they miss you & then our tears break out afresh & we all sob & tear our hair together." He recommended that Alice read (if she hadn't already) a story in the *Atlantic* called "Lago Maggiore" — " 'T is by a Mr. Howells who lives here, and is a very nice gentleman" — and Dr. Holmes's novel, *The Guardian Angel.*

Mary James wrote approvingly that a cousin had seen Alice in New York "looking as fat as butter." She filled her weekly letters with social news: Minny Temple had apparently taken a liking to young Wendell Holmes, the future Supreme Court justice, but early in 1867 Mary wrote to Alice that she thought Minny "quite disenchanted, and evidently [she] looks at Holmes with very different eyes from what she did; that is she sees him as others do, talks of his thinness and ugliness and pinchedness, as well as of his beautiful eyes — and seems to see his egotism."

Henry Sr.'s letters lovingly foster his exiled daughter's remorse at being away from home. They are, like William's, at one self-absorbed and seductive, teasing about Alice's competitors for her father's affection. Just after she left, he wrote, "Almost any morning an elderly gentleman . . . may be seen wandering about Cambridge, & looking very much as if he missed something very precious to his heart. The townspeople are evidently interested in his apparition, so touched as it is with a tender grace, and pause, ere they go on, to remark upon the mingled wisdom & sweetness that beam from his countenance. Sometimes a lively curiosity is aroused to know the name of the distinguished visitor; and when the inquiry is answered you might feel a responsive thrill — provided only your heart and mind were suitably attuned — all the way to 1303 Broadway. I say no more . . . Such a lovely young lady I met yesterday . . . with such an unconscious grace! . . . I shall possibly adopt her as a daughter unless my legitimate one comes back soon." And the next month, "My darling precious child: It is a 'bitter cold' morning, but my fingers cannot resist the impulsion of my 'sweet warm' heart to flood you with tenderness . . . I have a great deal of attention from the young ladies — here in Cambridge: but I could desire a little — there is large room in my heart for a little — from a certain young lady elsewhere who shall be nameless in this letter for fear that my wish might come to her ear, & so deprive her of freedom of action."

•

The symptoms that led Alice to seek treatment from Dr. Taylor were never mentioned. Certainly she was "delicate" — easily excited, highstrung, "nervous." But that was the way middle-class Victorian young ladies were supposed to be. With its range of meanings, from refined, sensitive, subtle, and gentle to sickly and frail, the word *delicate** described the mid-Victorian ideal of beauty: a graceful languor, pallor, and

---

* William Empson, in *The Structure of Complex Words,* traces the derivations of *delicate* from its original sense:

> apparently that of "giving pleasure" . . . For the English word, the N.E.D. gives a first group of meanings, now all obsolete, mostly extending from the sixteenth to the middle eighteenth century; "delightful," "voluptuous," "self-indulgent," "innocent," "effeminate," "fastidious." Its other two main groups are "not coarse, not robust," etc., and "endowed with fineness of appreciation or execution"; these are equally old but have survived. No doubt the human race has always been moral about delicacy, indeed my other word *refined,* as Dr. Johnson remarks somewhere, also carries a hint of weakness though not so much of it. But it seems fair to say that our two senses of *delicate,* "refined" and "sickly," are implications from the idea of pleasure which were at some point promoted to Senses; they proceed from the two equations "persons devoted to pleasure improve their taste but lose their health" . . . If a trifle baffling, the word was not more so than it was intended to be, and the arrangement had an air of great stability.

vulnerability — even to the point of illness — were seen as enhancing the female form. "Refinement" drew attention away from the base, ordinary body; illness delicately drew it back. Romantic ladies in the literature and art of the period often had pale cheeks, sunken, glittering eyes, painfully thin limbs, and nameless, vaguely glamorous diseases. The refined female spirit inhabited a feverish realm of keen perception and subtle response far above the plane of the body. Abstinence is the mirror image of indulgence, and this kind of nervous illness and denial of the body were intimately linked with sensual pleasure.

Illness, then, made a woman ethereal and interesting. Henry James commented in his preface to *The Wings of the Dove* on the idea of making his protagonist "sick" (Milly Theale slowly dies through the course of the novel), "as if to be menaced with death or danger hadn't been from time immemorial, for heroine or hero, the very shortest of all cuts to the interesting state." Milly's disease, though never named, appears to be tuberculosis, and "consumption" served as the nineteenth century's major example of this "interesting" wasting away of the body while the mind burned on alone.*

The Jameses' cousin Minny Temple, one of the models for Milly Theale (others, according to Leon Edel, were Alice and the novelist Constance Fenimore Woolson, a friend of Henry's), died of consumption early in 1870, at the age of twenty-four. Henry concluded his autobiographical memoir "Notes of a Son and Brother" with an affecting tribute to Minny, quoting long passages from the letters she wrote during her

---

* Susan Sontag has examined the metaphor closely in *Illness as Metaphor,* pointing out the ways in which tuberculosis was seen to spiritualize life, making the body ethereal and death itself noble and beautiful. The disease was "the sign of a superior nature . . . a becoming frailty." Sontag quotes Thoreau aestheticizing death: " 'Death and disease are often beautiful, like . . . the hectic glow of consumption.' " And she observes that "fever in TB was a sign of an inward burning: the tubercular is someone 'consumed' by ardor, that ardor leading to the dissolution of the body." She continues, "Like all really successful metaphors, the metaphor of TB was rich enough to provide for two contradictory applications. It described the death of someone (like a child) thought to be too 'good' to be sexual: the assertion of an angelic psychology. It was also a way of describing sexual feelings — while lifting the responsibility for libertinism, which is blamed on a state of objective, physiological decadence or deliquescence. It was both a way of describing sensuality and promoting the claims of passion and a way of describing repression and advertising the claims of sublimation, the disease inducing both a 'numbness of spirit' (Robert Louis Stevenson's words) and a suffusion of higher feelings. Above all, it was a way of affirming the value of being more conscious, more complex psychologically. Health becomes banal, even vulgar."

final year. Of all the cousins, she was William and Henry's favorite, and Henry called her "incomparably the most interesting." She was, he wrote, "absolutely afraid of nothing she might come to by living with enough sincerity and enough wonder; and I think it is because one was to see her launched on that adventure in such bedimmed, such almost tragically compromised conditions that one is caught by her title to the heroic and pathetic mark." He admired her "restlessness of spirit, the finest reckless impatience," and saw nothing else as "up to her terrible young standard of the interesting." Her letters do show her remarkable brave intelligence and spirit, but in Henry's eyes her beauty was indissolubly linked to her illness: "I . . . see her again . . . ever so erectly slight and so more than needfully, so transparently, fair (I fatuously took this for 'becoming') . . . the impression was to come back to me as of a child struggling with her ignorance in a sort of pathless desert of the genial and the casual."

In Minny Temple and Milly Theale, James highlighted the appealing innocence in the death of a woman who seemed too pure for sexuality. In *The Wings of the Dove,* when Milly learns that the man she loves and her trusted friend are lovers, she "turns her face to the wall" and dies. In the face of terrible knowledge — of sexuality and deep betrayal — Milly renounces not only love but life itself. James implies that her mysterious illness might have been cured if she had found honest love and sexual fulfillment: it is her thwarted passion, turned inward, that kills her. He also suggests, however, that her absolute innocence dooms her: she can know only goodness, and adult sexual love is not innocent. The betrayal counterweighs her virtue exactly. Once she sees it, once she *knows,* the knowledge consumes her and kills her innocent soul.

Like consumption, the non-life-threatening nineteenth-century ailments attributed to delicate nerves reflected the conflicting claims of sexuality and suppression, of the human body at war with "civilized" Victorian society. Nervousness, like a becoming consumptive frailty, was seen as a sign of complexity and sensitivity; it marked intelligence, subtlety, a finely tuned nature.

Extreme nervousness, however, went beyond fashionable high-strung refinement and presented postwar America and its medical community with puzzling problems. Individuals with functional nervous disorders (ailments that could not be traced to organic causes) included men and women, primarily in the upper and middle classes. They did not appear to belong in the insane asylums superintended by psychiatric "alienists," who saw mental illness as essentially untreatable and served primarily as caretakers. But no science of psychology existed to explain the complex connections between body and mind (though William James would be among the first to look into them in America). The task of treating the strange, protean symptoms of nervous disorders fell to the young science of neurology.* Three young neurologists in particular — George M. Beard in New York, Silas Weir Mitchell in Philadelphia, and James Jackson Putnam in Boston — took a special interest in these diseases of the nervous system: they saw in them a combined medical and "moral" problem related to the demands of civilized life.

In 1868, George Beard gave a name — "neurasthenia" (literally, lack of nerve strength, or nervous exhaustion) — to the wide range of unexplained symptoms that were appearing with increasing frequency among medical complaints. Beard and his fellow practitioners conceived of the nervous system as organized rather like a bank account: it contained a limited amount of energy, and if too much was drawn off in one di-

---

* Nathan G. Hale, Jr., writes:
   Neurology grew out of general medicine and psychiatry between the 1850s and the 1870s. In America the Civil War brought rich experience with wounds to the brain and nervous system, malingering, and exhaustion. Many American neurologists had begun as general physicians or professors of anatomy or physiology . . .
   Neurologists first specialized in somatic disorders of the nervous system as well as those illnesses that occupied the borderline between normality and insanity — morbid fears and compulsions, insomnia, fixed ideas, impotence, epilepsy, hypochondria, hysteria, nervous exhaustion. These disorders, neurologists argued, had been ignored or misunderstood. Alienists mistook them for types of madness. General physicians regarded them as gross physical diseases, as purely imaginary or as malingering. Only the most scientific diagnosis could establish their existence and lay the basis for sound treatment. By explaining all of them as somatic in origin, neurologists drew them within the medical model of involuntary sickness.
And according to historian Barbara Sicherman:
   . . . The emphasis on weakness of the nerves coincided with the rise of neurology as a medical specialty in the years after the Civil War. Knowledge of the brain and nervous system advanced rapidly in Europe after 1860 as experimental physiologists demonstrated that fixed parts of the brain controlled specific motor activities. Important clinical advances, especially J. Hughlings Jackson's work on epilepsy and Jean-Martin Charcot's delineations of several classic neurological disorders, followed. By the late 1860s, important teaching and hospital positions in neurology had been established in England, France, and the German-speaking world, a sign that the specialty had come of age.

rection, not enough would remain to cover the expenditures of ordinary life. Beard listed over fifty symptoms of neurasthenia, including fainting spells, headaches, muscle spasms, morbid fears, impotence, menstrual irregularities, neuralgias, dilated pupils, tooth decay, irascibility, paralysis, weariness, constipation, insomnia, dyspepsia, lack of appetite, vomiting, laughing and crying fits, inability to concentrate, temporary blindness, a sense of hopelessness, and convulsions. He observed that neurasthenia appeared most often in "civilized intellectual communities" and concluded that it was "a part of the compensation for our progress and refinement." He isolated five factors as measures of civilization — steam power, the telegraph, science, the press, and an increase of mental activity among women — and observed that America had advanced further along these lines than any other nation. The resultant stress accounted (according to Beard) for the rise of neurasthenia. The new theory of evolution played an important part in his formulations. The most highly refined "brain-workers" in modern society seemed to have more sensitive nervous systems than their laboring brothers, and therein lay the difference between "the nervous civilized man and the hardy barbarian." Neurasthenia, then, was the price of advancing civilization, and susceptibility to nervous disorders distinguished a highly evolved nature.

Neurasthenia differed from hysteria, though the distinctions often blurred and both terms served as catch-pails for a wide variety of ills. Weir Mitchell called hysteria (from the Greek *hustera,* womb) "the nosological limbo of all unnamed female maladies. It were as well called mysteria." The hysteric exhibited emotional volatility and violent behavior, and often had hallucinations, trance states, and fits; the neurasthenic languished in civilized debility. Freud wrote in 1895 that the hysteric "seemed intelligent and mentally normal and bore her troubles, which interfered with her social life and pleasures, with a cheerful air"; he called this attitude the *belle indifférence* of hysteria. The neurasthenic, by contrast, took a great interest in his condition, "clearly of opinion that language is too poor to find words for his sensations and that those sensations are something unique and previously unknown, of which it would be quite impossible to give an exhaustive account. For this reason he never tires of constantly adding fresh details." The use of masculine and feminine pronouns in Freud's descriptions is significant: in the America of the 1860s, as in the Europe of the 1890s, hysteria was seen as primarily characteristic of women, whereas neurasthenia affected men as well (and in men was often called hypochondria).

Some nineteenth-century doctors, faced with nervous women whose symptoms they could neither diagnose nor cure, were provoked to ask difficult questions about the relations between mind and body, individual and society. Others found the failure of the medical diagnostic model frustrating and frightening; it testified to their professional inadequacy and often constituted a sexual threat, as well.* Nervous women who took to their beds with fainting spells instead of doing the housework and bearing children were, in fact, opting out of the roles society had prescribed for them. And their "refusal" to have their bodies cured by science was seen as a challenge to the superiority of the masculine mind. Both the physicians who were stimulated to ask new questions and those who were frustrated and angered by female malaise often looked past the physical to the moral and social dimensions of women's lives to explain these illnesses.

Though the terms neurasthenia and hysteria were inexact, and though the treatments Beard and Mitchell devised often failed to cure, these men pioneered in recognizing that what is now called neurosis was a clinical entity that did not require treatment in a mental hospital, and that their patients were neither malingerers nor madwomen but people who were in intense pain. They had no insight into the intrapsychic conflicts Freud would soon discover, and their treatments reinforced then-predominant assumptions about femininity.† But in tracing the etiology of nervous

---

* For more information on the social history of doctor-female patient relations, see Ann Douglas Wood, "The Fashionable Diseases," *Journal of Interdisciplinary History,* vol. IV, no. 1 (1973), pages 25–52; Caroll Smith-Rosenberg, "The Hysterical Woman," *Social Research,* vol. 39, no. 4 (1972); John S. Haller, Jr., and Robin Haller, *The Physician and Sexuality in Victorian America* (Urbana: University of Illinois Press, 1974); and Barbara Sicherman, "The Uses of Diagnosis: Doctors, Patients, and Neurasthenia," *Journal of the History of Medicine and Allied Sciences,* vol. XXXII, no. 1 (January 1977).

† Mitchell's rest cure removed the patient from her family and put her to bed. There, she was fed (often to excess), massaged, read to, and helped to sit up, turn over, bathe, and urinate. Under this infantilizing regime, Mitchell's patients generally gained weight and lost their neurasthenic pallor. But the Philadelphian stressed the "moral" rather than the physical efficacy of his cure: the masculine "force of character" of the physician brought about the cure of women who had lapsed from their feminine duties into the selfishness of invalidism. He described malingerers, who enjoyed lounging in bed with a little reading and sewing, forced to their feet by the bitter regime of two tedious months of mandatory rest. Those who took a "morbid delight" in rest had to be met with stronger measures. One biography of Mitchell describes a young woman who refused to get out of bed when the doctor asked her to: "After considerable persuasion he threatened, 'If you are not out of bed in five minutes — I'll get into it with you!' He removed his coat, then his vest, but the patient did not move. When he started to take off his trousers, a very angry woman leaped out of bed."

problems to social change, Beard did have a significant insight: men like
William James, trying to resolve in their own lives the conflicting demands of science and religion, and women like Alice, trying to balance
the claims of traditional femininity with those of an independent self,
were struggling in solitude with issues that reached across a wide swath
of American society. Beard's and Mitchell's descriptions of the "com-
monest nervous disorders of women and men" (observed Nathan G.
Hale, Jr., in *Freud and the Americans*) "emphasized conflicts within individuals who could not fulfil social norms, yet, because they had internal-
ized them, could not consciously reject them. Hysteria sabotaged the
'civilized' norm of refinement in two ways, by 'fits,' outbursts of emotion
that directly violated it, or by incapacitating physical symptoms, which,
because they made a woman helpless, caricatured the very delicacy and
softness she and American men had been taught to reverence."*

Weir Mitchell became something of a celebrity in the 1870s with his
rest cure. He viewed diseases of the nervous system as closely related to
deformities of the body, and the Orthopaedic Hospital with which he
was affiliated in Philadelphia changed its name, in the 1870s, to the
Orthopaedic Hospital and Infirmary for Nervous Diseases. In New York,
Dr. Charles Fayette Taylor shared Mitchell's belief in the connections between orthopedics and neurology. An orthopedic surgeon with a particular interest in nervous disorders and the diseases of women, Taylor had
devised a "motorpathic" treatment that Alice James came to try in the
fall of 1866.

•

Charles Fayette Taylor had studied the therapeutic exercises of a Swedish
physiologist named Peter Henrik Ling in London, after getting his M.D.
from the University of Vermont in 1856. In 1861, as Ling's leading
spokesman in the United States, he published a book entitled *Theory and
Practice of the Movement Cure*. Aunt Kate sent it to William from New
York in 1866, and he reported to Alice that he had read it with much
interest and found Taylor "a very original and ingenious man." The book
described Taylor's treatments, which consisted of physical exercises, "mechanical orthopaedics," and a dose of therapeutic philosophy.

The last chapter in *Movement Cure* is called "Derangements of the Ner-

* For a fuller account of Beard and his work, see Charles E. Rosenberg, "The Place
of George M. Beard in Nineteenth-Century Psychiatry," *Bulletin of the History of Medicine*, 1962, and Barbara Sicherman, "The Uses of Diagnosis," cited above.

vous System." Like Beard and his colleagues, Taylor saw a finite amount of energy in the human bank account: the nervous system, drawing to itself too much energy, became "exalted" ("by exaltation is not meant actual strength, but a use and waste of power which otherwise might be converted into nervous strength or endurance") while other bodily functions became "depressed."

The most common illustration of this problem, reported Taylor, could be found in cases of "bed-ridden women, which are such a trial to professional skill." Girls exposed too early to too much intellectual and emotional stimulation, he hypothesized, had the capacities of their nervous systems "perverted from tissue-making, and absorbed, as it were, in the sensational life. The body is literally *starved,* while the nervous system is stimulated to the highest degree."

To cure functional disorders of this kind, he aimed to reverse the energy flow, directing it back from the nervous system toward the body. He had worked out a system of stimulating the muscles — by massage, stretching, and limited exercises — to "accelerate the nutritive processes and cause muscular development, without taxing the nervous system." If a patient was so thoroughly bedridden that exercise was impossible, he would begin with making her bend the toes of one foot and work slowly upward, adding the other foot, then the ankles, flexing of knees, and so on, until she gained control of her extremities. Above all, Taylor advised, "the patient should be impressed with the idea that she must not regard her symptoms, be they temporarily pleasant or unpleasant; but should ignore them as much as possible, taking a course to secure ultimate immunity from them." Taylor, then, viewed the body as a dumb creature gone out of control (as well as the frail victim of mental excess); it had to be mastered, restored to its proper relation to mind.

Several years after he treated Alice James, Dr. Taylor wrote an article called "Emotional Prodigality," providing exactly the sort of moral and social commentary many of these doctors felt called upon to offer. In this paper, read before the New York Odontological Society in 1879, Dr. Taylor countered the prevalent belief that *thinking* caused excessive mental strain and breakdown: "It is not the *thinking* which breaks people down, but it is an excess — often an unnecessary excess — of other mental activities which works the bodily injury; and by 'other mental activities' I would especially include the *emotions* as the most exhausting of all mental attributes." Excited emotions, which could drain the body's energy and power in men and women, were least likely to wreak havoc in people of cool and even temperaments, with disciplined living and working habits. The calm man could engage in a great deal of intellectual activity without harming his body, but "excitable temperaments" were more likely to suffer bodily injury, and women were naturally excitable. "Women are emotional as a class of human beings," continued Taylor. "Characterized as a sex with less manifestation of independent thinking, whether from a feebler endowment of reasoning powers, or whether because the intellect is so habitually subordinated to simple feeling, it is not necessary to discuss . . . While education in men makes them self-controlling, steady, deliberate, calculating, thinking out every problem, the intellectual being the preponderating force, the so-called 'higher education' for women seems to produce the contrary effect on them . . . While men are calmed, women are excited by the education they receive . . ." Woman's tendencies to emotionality, "which would only harmonize her being to her position and destiny under favoring conditions," were exaggerated by education until "the woman of our modern civilization becomes the bundle of nerves which she is — almost incapable of reasoning under the tyranny of paramount emotions; some are wholly incapable of becoming the mothers of rightly organized children." And Dr. Taylor declared his approbation of a different kind of woman: "For patience, for reliability, for real judgment in carrying out directions, for self-control, give me the little woman who has not been 'educated' too much, and whose only ambition is to be a good wife and mother . . . Such women are capable of being the mothers of men."

The assumptions of this approach — that women ought to stay healthy in order to be the mothers of men, to raise "rightly organized" children — reached far in an age that believed in child-rearing as an increasingly perfectable science and in motherhood as the sanctifying purpose of femininity. Women like Alice James who became "bundles of nerves," unable to maintain the delicate balance, found themselves confronted not only with massive batteries of diagnoses and treatments, but with large doses of moral opprobrium as well, from doctors, family, and friends. Taylor's article on emotional prodigality could have been written by Mary James, had she been more intellectual, less well balanced. And though Henry Sr. showed more overt sympathy than his wife did with their daughter's nervous troubles, he too, in his writing, his choice of a wife, and a thousand small daily judgments, voted for the little woman whose only ambition was to be a good wife and mother.

As antediluvian as Dr. Taylor's ideas sound to the twentieth-century ear, they contained a measure of common sense. He did see that the women he treated had been bred for a life of functionlessness: "Cunningly devised means for exciting feeling only, begun at the cradle, are continued through child-life up to the very verge of womanhood. The aesthetic alone, or almost alone, seems to be the sole idea of female mental existence." When Taylor met these "products of civilization" at adolescence he found them "excitable, with wide-open eyes and ears for every sight and sound which can excite feeling, rapid and intense in mental activity, with thin limbs, narrow chests, and ungainly back." Even his diagnosis of education as the root of the problem had a certain logic: these delicate flowers of Victorian American civilization *were* highly "excitable" and prone to dissatisfaction with their obsolescent place in a rapidly moving society. Reading books gave them ideas — about what else they might be doing, about the disjunction between the interesting panorama of history and their own dull lives, about people who managed to become Joan of Arc, Jane Austen, Queen Elizabeth, or, closer to home, Margaret Fuller, Harriet Beecher Stowe, Louisa May Alcott. Reading novels, especially, was guaranteed to stir up romantic-sexual yearnings in young girls languishing in feminine refinement. Even the sanitized tales of chaste courting, popular in magazines and cheap novels, were bound to tap some of the repressed sexuality beneath the surface of these good-girl lives, to upset their carefully maintained balance. If Taylor went awry in blaming the fact of education rather than its impact on physically and emotionally impoverished lives, he was not wrong in his impression that these girls had been virtually starved, nor in thinking that some form of activity — physical exercise, any kind of release from brooding self-absorption — might alleviate the condition, however slightly.

•

Alice's "cure" at Dr. Taylor's took longer than anyone had counted on. In January 1867 Mary James wrote that she heard "such fine accounts of your blooming appearance that I shall expect to hear from the Dr. that the good work of restoration is almost completed." In February, Mary and Henry Sr. visited their daughter in New York. William reported on their return: "They . . . gave a 'graphic' account of you well fitted to tranquilize anxiety & annul pity but not to kindle enthusiasm or excite envy (a good sentence). The best thing you can do is to come home as quickly as you can. I thought all along you were coming the 1st of March, but lo!

they tell me 'tis the 1st of May. I think that if Dr. T. don't bring you out right by the former date you had better quit him & come to me and those pills wh. if you had but taken them last summer you wd. not be where you now are, but at home sitting on the sofa, with my arm around your waste [sic] & the rich tones of my voice lingering in your ear." In closing he notes, "By the way Mother speaks of certain *curls, grey curls,* in a tone which implies — can it be that — but no! — 't were too absurd."

William too had been suffering mentally and physically all winter, though he made light of his own troubles in his letters to Alice. Later, he wrote to his friend Tom Ward that he had been that year "on the continual verge of suicide." He was attending classes at medical school, arguing philosophy late into the night with young Wendell Holmes, having trouble with insomnia, his back, his digestion, and his eyes; he had begun to doubt whether he was cut out for medicine after all. Restless and depressed, he could neither resolve his conflicts nor ignore them. At twenty-five, he urged his nineteen-year-old sister to return to his arms, joked with her about his flirtations with the young women of Cambridge, and invited her to provide him with a partner: "I wish you to find out some handsome, spirited & romantic creature whom I can fall in love with in a desperate fashion. The humdrumness of my life is very tiresome. Find her & bring her on."

In the spring William determined to give up his medical work for a year in Germany, where he could devote his energies to getting well, studying experimental physiology, and learning German. Once he had decided to go, he was eager to set off immediately. He booked passage on the *Great Eastern* for April 16, which meant he would be leaving home before Alice returned. Mary James, writing to her daughter of this plan, anticipated Alice's disappointment and prescribed acceptance in words that by this time had the familiarity of a litany: "There is no wisdom in indulging your selfish regrets in the matter, but accept cheerfully the fact, that life is made up of changes and separations from those we love."

Alice had learned her lessons well. Aunt Kate wrote from New York that she was a "most remarkable girl" who had displayed "all sorts of ultra-spiritual qualities" in this trial of illness. Alice decided to stay at Dr. Taylor's until the first of May to "clinch" her cure, and when she did come home with Kate in May she appeared for a time to thrive. She resumed her Cambridge rounds, visiting with old friends, attending dinner parties, meeting the recent "acquisitions" to her family's social circle. "Alice seems very bright," wrote her mother to William, "and is an immense joy to us. Her presence is a perfect sunbeam to Father."

At the "inner sepulchre" on Quincy Street, Henry had been having his share of troubles, as well. He had tried various remedies for his back pains and constipation, including massage ("He eats capitally," reported their father to Alice, "and has an Hibernian Rubber who attends him every day from 5 to 6") and ice therapy. After Alice's return, Henry wrote to William that he had given up the ice treatments as "pernicious" and planned to go to New York "to get a *corset* from Taylor." (Taylor, whose primary interest was in spinal disease, had devised what he called a "spinal assistant," a brace designed to take pressure off whatever part of the back was under strain.)

Wilky and Bob had bought a plantation in Florida and were employing Negro labor to prove to the North and South that freed black men could work as well as whites. The venture proved expensive — they borrowed money from their father and a number of Boston friends — and difficult. In 1867 Wilky came home with a high fever, anxious and depressed about the farm. Bob had just left for Wisconsin, where he had a job as a railroad clerk. Mary James wrote to William, "I am very doubtful about the wisdom of his going to live in so severe a climate, on acct of his catarrhal trouble which seems to trouble him very much — but there seems no help for it. He is perfectly wretched at home, and makes us all very uncomfortable — so we fitted him out once more and bade him God speed. Poor Wilk will have to struggle on alone in Florida which if he can only keep his health will not be a bad thing for him. Bob was a sore trial to him on account of his temperament, and he thinks we [probably she meant "he"] will be happier without him."

Parallel to the nineteenth-century bank account conception of an exhaustible fund of energy ran a Jamesian notion about a constant level of family health and pleasure. One member, when sick, might feel that he or she was making a sacrifice so that the others could remain healthy — or, less positively, that he or she was forced to pay the family "tax" in suffering while the others got off free. Henry, struggling with ill health in Europe in 1869, wrote home, "I have invented for my comfort a theory that this degenerescence of mine is the result of Alice and Willy getting better and locating some of their diseases on me — so as to propitiate the fates by not turning the poor homeless infirmities out of the family. Isn't it so? I forgive them and bless them."*

It did seem as though Henry and William were for years on opposite ends of a scale: when one was healthy and productive, the other floundered in illness and a sense of uselessness. William, failing to get well with the European water cures in 1868 and deploring his worthlessness, wrote to Alice, "I somehow feel as if I were cheating Harry of his *birthright* by staying here all this time but he wd. not come abroad if I shld go home now, so that is an unreasonable notion. I authorize you if ever you feel any compassion or the like nonsense on account of my back, to let it express itself in renewed and increased attentions and benefits to that 'Angel,' who needs & deserves it more than I do." And he wished he "had the inclination to write or anything to write about as Harry has. I feel ashamed of fattening on the common purse when all the other boys are working, but writing seems for me next to impossible."

Meanwhile, from Florida, Wilky wrote, "If I only had in my staunch body, full of strength and health half the delicate and moral force which either one of you afflicted brethren and inmates of Quincy Street possess, I could not only be a great comfort to myself, but I could be of great material comfort to all of you." And throughout her life Alice joked about competing with her brothers and "explained" her intellectual poverty as accounting for their riches. If the family unit had not enough health to go around, it also had only a finite amount of intellect.

Suffering, then, paid for someone else's well-being, and being well might cost someone else pain. In addition, everyone in the James family claimed to suffer so intensely with and for the others that ill health seemed almost contagious (though happiness was not). William and Alice in particular were said when sick to have such "morbid sympathy" with suffering that they were not told about the ailments of others, as the news would have been too much to bear.

---

* This same idea appears, in more elaborate form, in his 1901 novel, *The Sacred Fount*. There, the narrator (unnamed) is struck during a weekend country-house visit by certain dramatic changes in people: Mrs. Brissenden, having married someone much younger than she, seems to have grown suddenly young while her husband has visibly aged. Another guest, the formerly rather dull Mr. Long, has now become animated, witty, and quite bright. The narrator wonders about the "sacred fount" from whom Mr. Long must be draining his new life force — rather like an incubus — and guesses that she is May Server (always the perfect Jamesian name), a pale, broken relic of a formerly lovely, intelligent woman.

•

Alice did not remain "a perfect sunbeam" for long. Early in June 1867, she went to Brookline for a visit of a few days with Fanny Morse. Suddenly, on a Sunday, she had a nervous "attack." She reported soon afterward to William that "the admirable mother" had been "summoned to my bed of sickness" and had brought her home in a carriage. Several days went by before Alice could declare herself "sufficiently recovered in mind and body" to ask for William's latest letter, but was told it had been sent on to Florida: "As the letter was addressed to me I thought this proceeding *cool indeed!!*"

Mary offered William a vague diagnosis: "Alice I am sorry to say, from a little overexertion, has had one of her old attacks; and a very bad one. She will have dear child to live with the extremest care." Mrs. James then filled William in on news about the ailments of all the Quincy Street inhabitants, and concluded, "So dear Willy you have a full account of our invalids. The poor old Mater wears well I am happy to say; strong in the back, strong in the nerves, and strong in the eyes so far, and equal to her day."

Everyone credited Mary (who after all had not been born a James) with superior strength in the nerves, back, and eyes. But there were other kinds of superiority, and Alice readily aligned herself with the forces of higher intelligence and finer perception. Her letters to William in the late 1860s make fun of her mother's placid insensitivity to subtleties of language and other people's feelings. "The other evening," she wrote in the summer of 1867, "father and mother and I were sitting on the piazza together when Mr. Howells made his appearance. He sat talking a little while when father asked how a certain Mr. Nichols looked. Mr. H. who was sitting all doubled up in a deep armed-chair looking smaller, if possible, than ever, said 'he is about my size, with white beard, black eyes, etc.' when mother ups and says in her inimitable way, 'Ah, then he is a *small* man.' Mr. Howells for about five minutes was quite invisible, in fact mother was for some time the only person in existence; by degrees we one by one recovered ourselves."*

---

* And on another occasion: "I read to mother the other day out of the 'In General' column of the Advertiser that there was a paper printed in Paris on some sort of material that could be eaten after read, consequently the contents would be well digested. Whereupon mother remarks in her charming way, 'Why, that's very true, isn't it?' She was also heard to say the other day that love-letters were meant for one eye, whereupon father said that he supposed that the other eye winked at them. The mother constantly makes these delightful remarks, but I forget them all."

Alice's attacks were becoming increasingly severe, and she did now have to live with the "extremest care," but her letters to William rarely mentioned her health. In spite of his own ailments, William maintained his characteristic spontaneity and forthrightness in his letters home (he reserved his complaints for private notes to Henry), and Alice answered in an energetic vein of her own. In 1867 she regaled him with stories about her activities, her reading, family antics, and social life in Cambridge. She created whole comic scenarios from the family drama (in which Mary and Kate play the role of straight man):

The scene is laid in the dining room, time, dinner:

Harry to the mother. "May I have some of those brown rolls that were left this morning at breakfast?"

M[other]. "Yes, certainly, but do you wish to eat them with your soup?"

H. "You can't certainly expect me to minutely explain what I intend to do with them."

Laughter from the family . . .

H. "I was coming over the bridge this afternoon and stopped a run-away horse."

You may imagine the shouts of the family at this.

A[unt] K[ate]. "I hope you did not try and stop him by the bridle."

H. "Would you prefer to have me take hold of his legs?"

A.K. "But you should not run after horses and stop them."

H. "Would you rather have me run before them?"

You must let your imagination supply the manner of this Harry, a good deal of eyebrow nostril and shoulder affectation.

In the fall of 1867, Alice told William that she had been invited by a group of young Cambridge women to join the sewing bee they had started during the Civil War. "Have you the faintest idea of what the 'Bee' consists? I suppose not. It is a sewing society formed at the beginning of the war by the girls and kept up now for the poor. Miss Susy Dixwell is the head of it and all the Cambridge young misses go, so I shall have plenty of gossip to tell you."

And in August, trying to cheer up her ailing eldest brother, Alice gave him a long draft of her Cambridge life:

Cambridge   August 6 [1867]

My darling Willy

Your letter was most gratefully received the other day ... Father has deso-
lated me this morning by telling me about your back. How perfectly dreadful
it is to think of your having to go through with all poor Harry has suffered.
But how delightful it is to hear that you are already feeling better. I hide my
head in shame when I think how I used to tease you when sick. Do be careful! ...

Mr. [Samuel Gray] Ward said that he liked Harry's story exceedingly;* in
fact every one seems to think it capital. Wilky says that there is a perfect *furore*
in Lenox among the young ladies to see the young author. But Harry with his
high calm alabaster brow maintains his usual indifference to all their [word
indecipherable].

We had a little visit a short time since from Minny [Temple] on her way to
Conway from New Rochelle where she had been staying at the Emmetts. She
is not nearly as interesting as she used to be, she is so much influenced by the
last person she has been with and taken a fancy to that one never knows where
to find her. She was looking very pretty and her manner is certainly perfectly
fascinating ...

Harry and I made a visit on Mrs. Charles Peirce† the other evening. Her
husband was not visible but we saw one of her sisters who seemed an amiable
maid but had rather a Philistine way of talking ... Mrs. P. is a nice woman,
she seems very intelligent and energetic, if she would only refrain from
throwing up her head and glaring at one like a wild horse on the prairies. She
inquired enthusiastically and affectionately after "Willy." Harry's health seems
very fair considering how much he is usually run down by warm weather ...

You need not give us any of your theatre experiences as [if] we were deprived of the same delights. Did not Harry and I go to the Museum the other
night and see Uncle Tom's Cabin acted with the most touching and dramatic
effects? It was so touching in fact that we had to leave shortly.

You must excuse the frivolity of this letter if you condescend to read it, on
account of the frivolity and want of intelligence of the writer. You must remember that this mental baseness is not her own fault, and that as she is your
sister her having so little mind may account for your having so much. With

---

* "Poor Richard," serialized in the *Atlantic* in the summer of 1867.

† Melusina Fay Peirce (1836–1923) described herself as a "pioneer advocate of the
organization of women among themselves." She wrote about cooperative housekeeping, to relieve women of housework and encourage their financial independence, in
the *Atlantic Monthly* in 1868, and formed the Cambridge Co-operative Housekeeping
Society in 1869. She divorced Charles Sanders Peirce in 1883.

heaps of love from every one in the family and out of it, believe me my dearest
Willy

> Your loving *idiotoid* sister,
> Alice James

Alice endorsed the bank-account theory of family intelligence in this
closing, and indirectly underlined her sense that she must be intellectually incompetent, for if "her having so little mind may account for
your having so much," the opposite might also hold true — her having a
mind of her own might rob someone else of his.

The letters of this *"idiotoid* sister" show an energetic if self-depreciating
spirit and a lively mind at work on its limited surroundings. Only occasional references in the letters of others and her own retrospective commentary years later in the diary show the struggle being played out in the
background drama of "Alice's nerves."

Chapter Seven

Breakdown

THE DRAMA OF NERVES came to a climax early in 1868: Alice collapsed. She was nineteen years old. No first-person account written at the time survives. But Alice did describe this breakdown over twenty years later in her diary. It is the first picture — and one of the only ones — she drew of what was going on behind her fainting spells, mysterious pains, attacks, and nervous prostrations. When she did look beneath this surface, momentarily putting aside endurance and self-mockery, she gave a vivid account of the forces at war within her.

She had been reading in 1890 an essay by William called "The Hidden Self," in which he discussed hysteria, hypnosis, and the splitting of human consciousness into discrete parts, or "personages." William described Pierre Janet's work with hysterical patients in France, and the *"contractions of the field of consciousness"* the French philosopher had observed in the hysteric mind. One part of the body or mind splits off from normal consciousness, reported William, and is virtually abandoned; an entire leg, for instance, becomes anaesthetized, and loses not only all sensation, but all memory of past sensation, as well. In her diary on October 26, 1890, Alice endorsed William's description of this process: he used (she wrote) an "excellent expression" in saying that the nervous victim " 'abandons' certain portions of his consciousness. It may be the word commonly used by his kind. It is just the right one at any rate, altho' I have never unfortunately been able to abandon my consciousness and get five minutes rest."

Her imagination captured by this formulation, she turned to survey her own psychological history:

I have passed thro' an infinite succession of conscious abandonments and in looking back now I see how it began in my childhood, altho' I wasn't conscious of the necessity until '67 or '68 when I broke down first, acutely, and had violent turns of hysteria. As I lay prostrate after the storm with my mind luminous and active and susceptible of the clearest, strongest impressions, I saw so distinctly that it was a fight simply between my body and my will, a battle in which the former was to be triumphant to the end. Owing to some physical weakness, excess of nervous susceptibility, the moral power *pauses,* as it were for a moment, and refuses to maintain muscular sanity, worn out with the strain of its constabulary functions. As I used to sit immovable reading in the library with waves of violent inclination suddenly invading my muscles taking some one of their myriad forms such as throwing myself out of the window, or knocking off the head of the benignant pater as he sat with his silver locks, writing at his table, it used to seem to me that the only difference between me and the insane was that I had not only all the horrors and suffering of insanity but the duties of doctor, nurse, and strait-jacket imposed upon me, too. Conceive of never being without the sense that if you let yourself go for a moment your mechanism will fall into pie and that at some given moment you must abandon it all, let the dykes break and the flood sweep in, acknowledging yourself abjectly impotent before the immutable laws. When all one's moral and natural stock in trade is a temperament forbidding the abandonment of an inch or the relaxation of a muscle, 'tis a never-ending fight. When the fancy took me of a morning at school to *study* my lessons by way of variety instead of shirking or wiggling thro' the most impossible sensations of upheaval, violent revolt in my head overtook me so that I had to "abandon" my brain, as it were. So it has always been, anything that sticks of itself is free to do so, but conscious and continuous cerebration is an impossible exercise and from just behind the eyes my head feels like a dense jungle into which no ray of light has ever penetrated. So, with the rest, you abandon the pit of your stomach, the palms of your hands, the soles of your feet, and refuse to keep them sane when you find in turn one moral impression after another producing despair in the one, terror in the other, anxiety in the third and so on until life becomes one long flight from remote suggestion and complicated eluding of the multifold traps set for your undoing.

Alice presented her "never-ending fight" again and again in terms of diametric opposites: body and mind, power and weakness, dissolution and control, violence and stillness, murder and suicide, immutable laws and an impotent self. Against raging impulses she pitted a doomed effort at self-control. She knew that the forces of evil — the body aligned with violence, upheaval, dissolution — would be victorious. She located these forces outside herself: waves invaded her muscles, dikes broke and the flood swept in, revolt overtook her. Her body became something alien, powerful, terrifying, bad. She traced the conversion of her moral struggle into physical symptoms that affected the pit of her stomach, the palms of her hands, the soles of her feet. On the side of good she placed will power, self-control, muscular sanity — warring against the forces of murderous (and, less clearly, sexual) impulses and the body's impossible sensations. Her strong will seemed suddenly helpless; yet to give way, to satisfy these inchoate urges, spelled certain if obscure disaster.

Alice was nearly twenty when she first came up against the full force of these conflicts. Her experience echoed in certain respects her father's "vastation." He, too, placed evil outside himself in a hideous apparition squatting before his English hearth, and he, too, found the confrontation incapacitating. But his paralysis lasted only a few months: soon, with the help of Swedenborg, he conquered his dread by universalizing his private struggle and explaining evil as part of a process toward good. Alice found no similar balm. She was convinced from the first that she would lose her battle — that the unnamable force within her was stronger than her ability to contain it.

She placed the blame for her collapse on a "physical weakness, excess of nervous susceptibility . . ." How, she may have asked herself, did other people maintain a more favorable balance? Did they have these "inclinations," these flood tides of feeling? If not, why did she? If so, were other people simply stronger than she was, better at controlling their own base natures, more capable of "constabulary functions"?

William — or, rather, Janet — had an answer. "How far this splitting up of the mind into separate consciousnesses may obtain in each one of us is a problem. M. Janet holds that it is only possible where there is abnormal weakness, and consequently a defect of unifying or coordinating power. An hysteric woman abandons part of her consciousness because she is too weak nervously to hold it all together. The abandoned part . . . may solidify into a secondary or sub-conscious self. In a perfectly sound subject . . . what is dropped out of mind at one moment keeps coming back at the next." Alice appears to have accepted this explanation, which also fitted into the nineteenth-century conception of inherited tendencies toward nervous weakness. If something beyond her control was causing her illness — a physical weakness, an inherited tendency — then she bore

no responsibility for it and could place her true self on the side of a resisting moral power.*

Alice did see a personal history in her illness, but she was not inclined
to generalize about it. Because of her "physical weakness" and "excess of
nervous susceptibility," slight exaggerations of ideal nineteenth-century
femininity, she came face to face with insanity. Even if she could assume
the duties of doctor, nurse, and straitjacket, she could not ward off this
invasion of her body. But she could resist it. She could teach herself to
face the terrors and, in spite of them, lead a life of moral integrity.

•

Alice described wanting to "knock off the head of the benignant pater as
he sat with his silver locks, writing at his table." She disguised this murderous wish thinly, with compliments and jokes, and slipped it into her
narrative as a casual aside. She could not turn the towering rage that
comes through in her writing even twenty years after the experience itself
against the kind father who had so blithely stimulated and thwarted her.
Instead, she turned the full force of her fury on herself, making herself
literally ill.

Both the incidents she alluded to in this description of her early hysteric attacks occurred when she tried to do intellectual work — "conscious and continuous cerebration." First, she recalled sitting still in the
library, reading, when violent "inclinations" invaded her muscles and
made her want to throw herself out the window or knock her father's
head off. Next, she described trying to study at school — as a change
from shirking or wriggling with "impossible sensations of upheaval"; instead of being able to focus her mind on study, however, she watched it
go altogether out of her control.

Study was the primary occupation of the three Jameses to whom Alice

* She did not comment on William's question a little farther on in the essay —
"Who knows how many pathological states (not simply nervous and functional ones,
but organic ones too) may be due to the existence of some perverse buried fragment
of consciousness obstinately nourishing its narrow memory or delusion, and thereby
inhibiting the normal flow of life?" That, of course, was the question being asked just
then in Vienna by Sigmund Freud and Josef Breuer, who were studying illnesses remarkably similar to Alice's and who would begin to formulate answers in their 1895
Studies on Hysteria. William did not pursue it much further, though years later, when
Freud delivered his famous lectures at Clark University in Worcester, Massachusetts,
in 1909, James put his arm around Ernest Jones's shoulder and said, "The future of
psychology belongs to your work."

felt closest: in the late 1860s William was studying medicine for his career and philosophy for his private questions, Harry was reading literature and criticism in his formative years as a novelist, and their father, the perpetually eager devourer of books and ideas, had advised his children to describe his profession to their friends as "student." In her late adolescence Alice was trying to find out whether she could engage in studious activities and assert her intellectual potential, or whether she must accept that she was not equipped with whatever made men capable of "cerebration." To use her mind productively would have meant entering the lists in competition with Henry, William, and Henry Sr.; and though beneath her self-derogations Alice respected her own intelligence, she was convinced that her mind was not on a par with theirs. Besides, competing with men would have been an extraordinarily inappropriate form of "spiritual snatching" for a girl.

Not pursuing her studies, however, turning instead to the womanly sphere, would have meant competing with her mother and aunt. And since being a woman meant being mindless, selfless, and effortlessly good, turning in that direction would have required Alice to relinquish her sense of superior intelligence and her desire to be something more than her mother and aunt. It seemed impossible either to measure up to their domestic virtues or to step down to their intellectual level. The "feminine" alternative was as fraught with hazard as the masculine.

In trying to keep still and study, Alice tried to live up to a number of ideals. At Newport she had determined to be neutral, silent, self-effacing, sexless. At school she had tried to be "still" in a different way — to control her "inclinations" and apply her mind to taking things in. But her body revolted, writhing with "impossible" sensations. Physical upheaval and thoughts of suicide and murder prevented her from carrying out the mental activity she had set for herself. These forces would be "triumphant to the end," causing her to "abandon" her attempt to find an androgynous middle way between the polarities of gender.

What Alice described, in this retrospective account, was not neurasthenic languor but full-blown hysteria. Such hysterical attacks "sabotaged" the norm of civilized refinement by bursting through it with violent emotion and by rendering women truly incapacitated, caricaturing the idea of their helpless frailty. Alice's illness served several purposes of this kind. It provided her with an escape route — a way out of having to choose between a safe boring life of devotion to others and a dangerous assertion of intellectual competence. And it justified her failure to achieve while allowing her to preserve a sense of potent capacity. Henry noted this function of nervous illness in his description of Winterbourne's aunt in *Daisy Miller*: "Mrs. Costello was a widow of fortune, a person of much distinction, and who frequently intimated that if she hadn't been so dreadfully liable to sick-headaches she would probably have left a deeper impress on her time."

•

Alice's reflections on this first breakdown have all the advantages and drawbacks of twenty years of hindsight. They place the experience in the context of what came before and after, but they provide little sense of her daily life during the 1868 crisis. The chorus of her family's letters helps fill in the picture.

Mary James wrote once a week to the absent younger brothers, Bob in Wisconsin and Wilky in Florida. She tended to gear her information to her audience: to Bob, whom she saw as having a weak nature with a tendency to morbid self-absorption, she pointed a moral in Alice's valor: "The fortitude with which our daughter carries the load which has been given her to bear is truly beautiful." And in the spring of 1868 she described Alice to Bob as "the sweetest and most patient of invalids and I only wish we could all be as patient under her sickness as she is herself."

For Wilky, the stronger brother, Mary provided fuller description. At the beginning of March she wrote, "Alice says tell Wilky I would write to him if I were able. — The truth is she has been very much run down the last month. The little strength she has had of late is much diminished. We think we have got at the secret of all her nervous weakness, and have put her under a new medical treatment [a massage therapy Aunt Kate had tried earlier in the year], which we hope after a time will bring her up. In the meantime she must be kept carefully from any over exertion, and visiting is a thing that seems to try her very much."

A week later, she added, "We are as well as usual except Alice who is very miserable. Poor dear child she bears her confinement patiently. She is obliged to give up all out of door exercise, and lies upon the bed or sofa pretty much all day, with the windows open as much as possible."

In April, things took a turn for the worse. "All our time and thoughts are given now to dear Alice who is not better," reported her mother. "Her nervous turns are very frequent and brought on by the slightest exertion. It is a case of genuine hysteria for which no cause as yet can be discovered. It is a most distressing form of illness, and the most difficult to reach, because so little is known about it. In her case it has many ameliorations. It is not in the least degree morbid in its character — her mind does not seem at all involved in it* — she never dreads an attack, and seems perfectly happy when they are over. She is full of patience and affection instead of being inconsiderate and irritable as is so often the case."

In enduring her illness so virtuously, Alice made a strong claim to moral superiority: her body and mind might be weaker than those of the people around her, but no one could deny her goodness and strength of soul. In addition, she had her parents at her beck and call. Her "healthy-minded" mother praised her patient fortitude, and Henry Sr. hovered constantly at her bedside, vibrating with sympathetic suffering. He wrote to William in April that he had cancelled a visit to Emerson because "poor dear Alice has been so very much prostrated for a few hours past, that though I was ready to leave for Concord a while ago, I dare not do it for fear of her being worse."

William's letters from Dresden show both the commiseration that illness guaranteed and the self-centered seductiveness that still characterized his relations with Alice: "I am excessively sorry to hear all the time from home that you are still delicate. I would give anything if I could help you my dearest Alice, but you will probably soon grow out of it ... Meanwhile count upon the sword, purse & strong right arm of yr. bro. W.J. in the hour of trouble." He accompanied this chivalrous offer with a lengthy story about a handsome young American wandering through the streets of Dresden, returning the "glances of interest & curiosity with wh. the ladies greeted him ... Anon a cloud wd. cross his noble brow, anon some more genial thought wd. seem to visit him, for he wd. smile, displaying a row of teeth like orient pearls, and mutter some words of which '... Alice ... beloved child ...' were the only ones caught by the bystanders. Who was the noble stranger? Never I ween a maiden of all those faire ones (faire, aye, and rich, & titled too) whom he met, but tossed sleepless upon her couch that night, & asked herself that question! ... Well, to thee, O my Alice, I will whisper that the youth was

---

* Mary's description highlighted the *belle indifférence* that Freud noted in hysteria. He attributed the phrase to Charcot.

none other than *me,* & the Alice of whom he thought none other than the peerless child of Quincy Street, i.e., *Thou!*" Then he shifted the focus of concern from Alice's pain to his own. He had recently been ill at Teplitz, "crying all the time for to have you sitting by me stroking my brow, and asking me if there was nothing, *nothing* you could do to alleviate my sufferings. And me casting up my eyes to heaven & solemnly shaking my head, like Harry, to command sympathy, and saying in a feeble voice, 'no! dear, nothing' and then you saying how beautiful and patient I was. Whole dialogues did I frame of how I wd. work on your feelings if you were there, and longed to cleave the Ocean once more to press you in my arms."

William was absorbed during this period in his own struggles, not the least of which were sexual. He wrote constantly to his sister about women, comparing American and European girls, playfully cataloguing his infatuations, critically evaluating each member of the opposite sex who passed within his view. Like the nineteenth-century doctors who treated female hysterics, William moved with confident authority between expressions of concern about Alice's illness and prescriptions for true femininity: "Let Alice cultivate a manner clinging yet self sustained, reserved yet confidential, let her face beam with serious beauty, & glow with quiet delight at having you speak to her; let her exhibit short glimpses of a soul with *wings,* as it were (but very short ones) let her voice be musical and the tones of her voice full of caressing, and every movement of her full of grace, & you have no idea how lovely she will become."

William cast his ambivalent vote in 1868 not for strong, competent, healthy-minded women like his mother and the Europeans he was observing (though ten years later he would marry a woman of this type), but for delicate flowers of American femininity: "What pleases me most in the female of my dear country is her moral unstainedness — her proud, sensitive, & reserved nature — and a total absence of that worldly wisdom, or rather that muscular ability and joy to cope with all the commercial and material details of life which characterizes her european sister." Although strong women impressed William favorably, he was troubled by his own sense of weakness, and seemed to want to make sure that women were not better equipped than he to deal with "this tough world." Neither, however, should they give way to sickliness: in June of 1868 he advised his sister to "keep a stiff upper lip & snap your fingers at fate — read as much comic literature as you can, and your sickness will wear itself out as it almost always does. Time and the hour run through the roughest day."*

This sort of counsel from her mother and oldest brother encouraged Alice's stoicism. Looking back later on her adolescence, she saw that "a spark then kindled which every experience great and small has fed into a steady flame which has illuminated my little journey and which, altho' it may have burned low as the waters rose, has never flickered out — 'une pensée, unique, éternelle, toujours mêlée a l'heure présente.' How profoundly grateful I am for the temperament which saves from the wretched fate of those poor creatures who never find their bearings, but are tossed like dryed leaves hither, thither and yon at the mercy of every event which o'ertakes them. Who feel no shame at being vanquished, or at crying out at the common lot of pain and sorrow . . ."

By "those poor creatures" Alice may have meant the invalid women and hypochondriacal brother(s) she had determined to prove herself superior to. She looked at her own limited life without complaint and without the distortions of religious optimism or justification. Detachment enabled her to submit and resist at the same time. It was as if she ceded her body to the "feminine" principle of frailty and submission, while cultivating with her mind a "masculine" strength and indifference to pain.

•

William's and Robertson's crises of the late 1860s differed significantly from Alice's, but they shed background light on her troubles. Robertson, a restless, moody young man, was now settled in Wisconsin. He had fallen in love with his cousin Kitty Temple, and became secretly engaged to her in the fall of 1869. He confided in William, who fired off a lengthy piece of unsolicited advice drawing a direct connection between the body's ills and the world's evils. Both Kitty and Bob were afflicted with the family "dorsal infirmity," noted William, and "feeling as strongly as I do that the greater part of the whole evil of this wicked world is the result of infirm health, I account it as a true crime against humanity for any one to run the probable risk of generating unhealthy offspring. For

* Minny Temple wrote to a friend as she was dying of consumption the following year, "Willy James sometimes tells me to behave like a man and a gentleman if I wish to outwit fate."

myself I have long since fully determined never to marry with any one, were she as healthy as the Venus of Milo, for this dorsal trouble is evidently s'thing in the blood. I confess that the flesh is weak and passion will overthrow strong reasons, and I may fail in keeping such a resolve; but I *mean* not to fail. I want to feel on my death bed when I look back that whatever evil I was born with I kept to myself, and did so much toward extinguishing it from the world."

Two months later there was no more talk of Kitty Temple, but Bob wrote from Wisconsin complaining of exacerbated physical troubles that were only too familiar to the family at 20 Quincy Street. In addition to his bad back, he suffered from poor digestion, kidney trouble, depression, constipation, and nocturnal emissions: he worried about becoming impotent. William, now an M.D., prescribed iron, moderate exercise, painting the back with coats of iodine until the skin peeled off, and a stiff upper lip. Later, he made light of Bob's sexual fears: "Your case as you describe it belongs to the most trifling class, amenable to treatment in some form; and if continuing in spite of medical treatment, ready to cease when sexual intercourse begins regularly." But these remedies and reassurances had little effect on Bob's troubles. He continued to be plagued with violent alterations of mood and to worry about his impure nature. His father wrote to him in 1874, "You say in your letter to Willy: 'I burn one day with lust and vengeance and conceit; and then all strength seems to leave me, and I have nothing but content and peace and beauty springing up all round ... I have unutterable longings &c but no attainments apparently. But I cling to you [William] and father and the good everywhere. Don't think I forget you when I forget to write: at these times I am in the suburbs of hell but not in the town.' "

Bob tended even more than the other Jameses to divide the world into moral absolutes. And although both William and Henry Sr. tried to share with him their own struggles with temptation and despair, he persisted throughout his life in seeing his father and brother as purely virtuous and himself as all wrong. He tried to find solace in religion, alcohol, women — but never managed to obtain any lasting relief from his cycles of self-loathing and elation.

William, meanwhile, was trying in the late 1860s to find a philosophy that would reconcile his own tormented nature with the laws of the universe. In 1869 he gave up the idea of practicing medicine, and looked to biological or psychological research as more fitted to his temperament.

But he could not work. He felt "disgusted" with his life, and paralyzed. Everyone else seemed productive; he alone, a waste. He longed for some guide to action. In his diary in 1868 he wrote, "Tonight while listening [to music] my feelings came to a sort of crisis. The intuition of something here in a measure absolute gave me such an unspeakable disgust for the dead drifting of my own life for some time past. I can revive the feeling perhaps by thinking of men of genius. It ought to have a practical effect on my own will — a horror of waste life since life can be *such* —and oh God! an end to the idle, idiotic, sinking into *vorstellungen* disproportionate to the object."

He saw man as a mere "bundle of desires, more or less numerous." These were the base line of existence, the "lowest terms to which man can be reduced"; if desire were gratified, man could live, if not he would die. Should he accept this baseness in himself, the counterpart of evil in the universe? — or protest against it? The alternatives were struggle and resignation.

On February 1, 1870, he recorded in his diary, "Today I about touched bottom, and perceive plainly that I must face the choice with open eyes: shall I *frankly* throw the moral business overboard, as one unsuited to my innate aptitudes, or shall I follow it, and it alone, making everything else mere stuff for it? I will give the latter alternative a fair trial." In other words, he would opt for struggle, attempting to make some moral sense of the world and himself. If he could not be purely good, he could at least refuse to give way to evil. But militant refusal required "vigor of will enough to look the universal death in the face without blinking." And at the heart of William's trouble was his lack of moral vigor, his impotent will.

This state of affairs came to a crisis James described in *The Varieties of Religious Experience* (1902). There he presented the case of a Frenchman "in a bad nervous condition." He claimed to have translated freely from the man's own account of his case, but both the Frenchman and the translation were a fiction. According to William's biographers, he was describing himself:

"Whilst in this state of philosophic pessimism and general depression of spirits about my prospects, I went one evening into a dressing-room in the twilight to procure some article that was there; when suddenly there fell upon me without any warning, just as if it came out of the darkness, a horrible fear of my own existence. Simultaneously there arose in my mind the image of an epileptic patient whom I had seen in the asylum, a black-haired youth with greenish skin, entirely idiotic, who used to sit all day on one of the benches, or rather shelves against the wall, with his knees drawn up against his chin, and the coarse gray undershirt, which was his only garment, drawn over them in-closing his entire figure. He sat there like a sort of sculptured Egyptian cat or Peruvian mummy, moving nothing but his black eyes and looking absolutely non-human. This image and my fear entered into a species of combination with each other. *That shape am I,* I felt, potentially. Nothing that I possess can defend me against that fate, if the hour for it should strike for me as it struck for him. There was such a horror of him, and such a perception of my own merely momentary discrepancy from him, that it was as if something hitherto solid within my breast gave way entirely, and I became a mass of quivering fear. After this the universe was changed for me altogether. I awoke morning after morning with a horrible dread at the pit of my stomach, and with a sense of the insecurity of life that I never knew before, and that I have never felt since. It was like a revelation; and although the immediate feelings passed away, the experience has made me sympathetic with the morbid feelings of others ever since. It gradually faded, but for months I was unable to go out into the dark alone.

"In general I dreaded to be left alone. I remember wondering how other people could live, how I myself had ever lived, so unconscious of that pit of insecurity beneath the surface of life. My mother in particular, a very cheerful person, seemed to me a perfect paradox in her unconsciousness of danger, which you may well believe I was very careful not to disturb by revelations of my own state of mind. I have always thought that this experience of melan-cholia of mine had a religious bearing."

William recoiled from what he might become — a sick body with no capacity of mind. This specter reflected everything he refused to accept in himself, and it might at any moment overwhelm his higher self: *"That shape am I."*

Alice, too, had located defect and evil in her body, in overwhelming forces of dissolution and rage. But whereas William dreaded giving way, Alice experienced the disintegration itself. Like Alice, William knew that this "evil" could conquer all power to resist. "Nothing that I possess," he wrote, "can defend me against that fate, if the hour for it should strike . . ."

William's vision also resembles his father's "vastation" (experienced at approximately the same age). William saw a green-skinned, epileptic idiot; his father, a damnèd shape "raying out from his fetid personality influences fatal to life." These visions confronted both men with incontrovertible evidence of the terror that lay beneath the surface of life, and left both paralyzed with fear. But whereas Henry Sr. had turned to the optimistic monism suggested by Swedenborg, William could not bring himself "so to sympathize with the total process of the universe as heartily to assent to the evil that seems inherent in its details."

He had begun in the late 1860s to read Charles Renouvier, who addressed exactly the questions he struggled with: how to find a way to act and believe that did not seem blind to the nature of evil. If man were a mere bundle of desires, if the laws of the universe were fixed and evil an irrefutable presence, what hope could there be for moral action — especially when action required a strength of will he could not find in himself? Renouvier proposed that one could assert moral freedom regardless of the laws of the universe. In his diary on April 30, 1870, William James wrote: "I think that yesterday was a crisis in my life. I finished the first part of Renouvier's *Essais* and I see no reason why his definition of free will — 'the sustaining of a thought *because I choose to* when I might have other thoughts' — need be the definition of an illusion. At any rate, I will assume for the present — until next year — that it is no illusion. My first act of free will shall be to believe in free will."

This resolution did prove to be a turning point in William James's life. From here on — though not without setbacks and further struggles — his health and ability to work began to improve.

•

Life had to be met on special terms by each junior member of the James family. Alice and her brothers, having been exhorted to "take in" all the cultural riches the world had to offer, came up in adolescence against severe limitations on their capacities for full participation in life. There seemed to be a "family curse" of ill health, weak nerves, delicate constitutions. It was as if each had received a devastating wound — a "moral equivalent" to their father's amputation.

The theme of suffering ran through their lives in a major key. Stephen Spender has observed of Henry's novels, "The amount his characters have to suffer, whether love or gain be their aim, is prodigious. Intelligence is all, and intelligence is the costliest of all." The aim, within the family, was not, of course, gain but love; and love, as uniquely defined by Henry

James, Sr., in terms of innocent goodness, was often at odds with that other Jamesian aim, self-knowledge.

The refusal to accept or even acknowledge "sinful" desires has been so widely attributed to the nineteenth century that the name given the era — Victorian — stands for an atmosphere of repression and moral rectitude. Scholars recently have began to question the extent of nineteenth-century sexual repression, but the James family, for all its sensuous education and intellectual freedom, did exhibit the moral severity that is commonly associated with "Victorian." Henry Sr. believed passionately in his children's goodness: they would gravitate toward virtue "by love for it or a sympathetic delight in it." With doting fervor he shielded them from the harsh realities of the world and their own "baser" instincts, preaching his private gospel of spontaneous selflessness and Divine Natural Humanity.

Keeping his children ignorant of the world's ills was not altogether possible, but insofar as it was, it did not foster the freedom of choice he intended. Having been sheltered from certain kinds of knowledge, the young Jameses found themselves at adolescence ill equipped to deal with the world's complexities and their own troubled natures. On the edge of adulthood, facing large choices about what to do with their lives, each one paused, tormented by self-doubt and fear.

Confronted with the evil that was supposed not to exist, William, Robertson, and Alice found it impossible to give way and impossible to maintain control. Even if evil was outside the soul — in sweeping floods and devilish temptations and green-skinned, epileptic idiots — it did not go away. Henry Sr., whose own "redemption" (and entire philosophy) had come through his anguished confrontation with evil, had a cheerful confidence in the ultimate triumph of good that seemed to deny the validity of his children's suffering. William wrote to Bob, in 1870, about their father's apparent lack of sympathy, "His religious optimism has I think a tendency to make him think too lightly of anyone's temporal troubles, even to neglecting to look closely into them at all." If "father's ideas" did not explain away the pain, one was truly alone in hell.

In 1868, Alice faced what her father had called "the obscene bird of night."* Unlike him, she could not make it out to be good. Her life was

* "The natural inheritance of everyone who is capable of spiritual life is an unsubdued forest where the wolf howls and the obscene bird of night chatters," wrote Henry James, Sr.

a constant struggle, and she foresaw no ultimate victory. "What *is* living in this deadness called life," she wrote in 1889 (echoing her adolescent edict about "the resistance we bring to life"), "is the struggle of the creature in the grip of its inheritance and against the consequences of its acts."

Chapter Eight
"Trying to Idle"

A FTER HER NERVOUS CRISIS had passed in 1868, Alice began slowly to
resume a more active life — though always trying not to "overexert" herself or otherwise disturb her convalescence. It was clear that she
could not now direct her mind to serious study; her breakdown had effectively proved what her father had been saying all along — that she was
not cut out for the "conscious and continuous cerebration" of intellectual endeavor. She gave no thought to preparing for a career; there, too,
she tacitly endorsed her father's views. Instead of studying or learning a
marketable skill, she now filled her days with visits, light reading, and the
charitable work that provided middle-class women with a sense of usefulness.

The sewing bee she had joined became, after 1868, not only the font of
gossip she had promised to share with William but the social center of
her life. Among the other members were Susan Hunt Dixwell (whose
sister Fanny married Wendell Holmes in 1872), Caroline Parsons, daughter of Harvard law professor Theophilus Parsons, Charlotte and Elizabeth
Dana, whose father had written *Two Years Before the Mast,* Clara Crowninshield Thies, whose house at 20 Quincy Street the Jameses were renting, Margaret Woodbury Storer, Mabel Lowell (daughter of James Russell Lowell), Grace Hopkinson, and Florence Sparks.

The Bee, as Alice had written to William, had been started during the
Civil War. In October 1861, Mrs. Asa Gray, the wife of Harvard's famous botanist, had invited fifteen Cambridge girls to her house to meet
her niece, Julia Bragg, and sew for the soldiers and hospitals. The follow-

ing week the sixteen girls met again at the home of Susan Dixwell on Garden Street and decided to organize into a working unit. It was then that they took the name Banks Brigade, in honor of General Nathaniel Prentiss Banks, who was leading the Massachusetts troops at the front.* They wrote to the general for permission to use his name, and elected Sue Dixwell head, or "Colonel," of the brigade, because (explained the group's chronicler) "she had knitted for the soldiers more socks than any one else, and of course we must needs give her a military title to express our intimate connection with the army."

From then on, these fourteen- and fifteen-year-old girls met once a week, on Fridays at four o'clock, each time at the home of a different girl. Until half past six they worked and talked, making shirts, hospital drawers, nightclothes, quilts, and blue knitted socks with red and white borders. Then they were served a supper of waffles, graham toast, cold tongue, cold ham, and occasionally oysters, with rich chocolate to drink and desserts of sponge cake with tall pyramids of pink ice cream. Mothers presided over these Friday gatherings; fathers and brothers were not invited. Some of the girls' older sisters suggested inviting Harvard students to join the group for dancing after supper. The suggestion, recalled Mary Towle Palmer (whose memoir, *The Story of the Bee,* was published privately in 1924) "was submitted to the Colonel, who turned it down summarily with inimitable scorn. The question was never again raised, and often have I blessed Sue's quick decision, for she saved the life of the Bee that day." After supper, instead of dancing, came songs and piano-playing until nine o'clock.

When the war ended, the name Banks Brigade was dropped for the civilian "Bee," the colonel became the president, and meetings slowed to once a fortnight. Carrie Parsons' sister Emily had returned from a job as a nurse with the Union Army to establish a new Cambridge Hospital on Mount Auburn Street; the Bee helped furnish the hospital with bedding, towels, and nightshirts, and also sewed clothes for poor families "down on the marsh" — a shantytown on the mud flats in the area now occupied by the Massachusetts Institute of Technology.

Alice James joined the Bee in 1867 and served as president in the 1870s. Mary Palmer recalled that "our witty ones, Marnie Storer, Lizzie

* Banks was outmaneuvered by Thomas J. (Stonewall) Jackson in the Shenandoah Campaign in 1861-1862, and later (1863-1864) aided Ulysses S. Grant in the West.

Simmons, and Alice James, tossed the talk across the table until we were in gales of laughter." Though the group was proud of its solidarity, continued Palmer, "it was one of our glories that we were not afraid of 'cliques,' but cheerfully showed partiality to those we loved best. Alice James left a classical remark for us to remember when she said: 'It is astonishing how fond we are of the Bees, even of those we don't like.' "

In the late 1860s, the charitable work of sewing for the poor continued, but the young women harbored no pious illusions about their good works. They met primarily for fun, and staged theatrical productions, tableaux, coffee parties, and fairs. They took bicycle rides, had country picnics, went rowing on the Merrimac River. For these outings, the young women were elaborately dressed: "The members of the Bee, like the rest of womankind, wore hoop-skirts, nor could we imagine that a time would ever come when our dresses would be less than six yards around," wrote Mary Palmer. "Sitting down in a hoop-skirt was an art that needed to be well practised, otherwise the hoops would flare up in front revealing a 'limb,' which was something always invisible in those Victorian days. We learned to sit down very carefully, bestowing our skirts behind the calves of our legs, so that we looked as demure as the Puritan maidens we were."

Men were still not invited to participate in the Bee or the group's outings; but as the young women began to reach their late teens and early twenties, the opposite sex began to play a larger role in their lives. "Engagements and marriages were events to which we were becoming accustomed, while still there was wonder in our eyes as we saw our members stolen away into a region of romance of which as yet some of us were only dreaming. I remember my awakening thrill when I first saw Mabel Lowell dressed in a low-cut gown of heliotrope satin, an amethyst necklace resting on her white neck, while her eyes shone like stars. She was like a sumptuous moth emerging from its chrysalis." The members of the Bee gave a gold thimble engraved with the letters "B.B." to each girl who got married.

Several of the new young wives left the Boston area with their husbands. But those who married men connected with Harvard or Boston, and those who did not marry (they lived on in the "dignified old houses, Colonial or Victorian, of their parents and kept the beauty of the old days in their surroundings") remained "Bees." They continued to meet, sew, and keep in close touch with each other for over sixty years. As grandmothers and great-aunts, the surviving members of the Bee cele-brated their sixtieth anniversary in 1921.

•

The members of the Bee sewed by hand, to facilitate talk. But in 1867, Alice and her mother bought a sewing machine — a Florence, reported Alice to William, "which is considered the best and seems to be very simple and easy to learn to use. By the time you get back you will proba-bly find Harry and father dressed in suits made by mother and me. Apropos of making clothes," she continued, "father came in the other day with some story from the Lowells about the goodness of Mr. Paige the artist* who allowed his wife to make his clothes. We disputed for some time who was the most virtuous, Mrs. Paige for making them or Mr. Paige for wearing them, when Harry came in and settled the matter in his cool way, by saying that they were all very good but the clothes."

Alice now began to take an interest in the poor that went beyond the donations of the Bee. Years later, when she was living in England, the struggles of the working class occupied a great deal of her attention and sympathy, and some of the most interesting passages in her diary reflect on the contrasts between rich and poor. In the late 1860s she started to learn, in a limited way, about people outside her own class. In spite of the fun constantly poked by her father and brothers at the earnest reforming ladies of Boston, Alice began to call on Elizabeth Peabody, the quintes-sential reformer who had elicited such mirth in Newport when Henry Sr. described her as "one of the most d-d-dissolute old creatures that walks the earth!" Miss Peabody had been a transcendentalist and a friend of Emerson, Alcott, and George Bradford; her brothers-in-law were Horace Mann and Nathaniel Hawthorne. She had founded several schools in the Boston area, and at the time of Alice's first visit was leading a kindergar-ten movement in Boston. Henry advised his sister to cultivate this new friendship with the woman whose displaced spectacles, falling down the

---

* William Page (1811–1885) — Alice misspelled his name — was a portrait painter, originally from Albany, whose famous works include portraits of John Quincy Adams, Josiah Quincy, James Russell Lowell, Charles Sumner, Wendell Phillips, Charles W. Eliot, and Colonel Robert Gould Shaw. He was a Swedenborgian, and a friend of Emerson, Hawthorne, and the Brownings. He moved to Italy in 1849, and was the leading American painter in Rome for several years; he returned to the United States — New York City — in 1860, where he remained until his death, in 1885. The Mrs. Page Alice refers to was his third wife, Sophia Hitchcock.

bridge of her nose, reflected (in his portrait of Miss Birdseye in *The Bosto-nians*) "the whole moral history of Boston."*

Alice enjoyed listening to Miss Peabody talk about her work, and had begun to take on more of her own. In 1868 she and her mother had joined the Female Humane Society of Cambridge, a charitable organization founded in 1814 for the relief of women who were indigent or sick.† The majority of cases helped by the society in the year Mary and Alice James joined were widows and single women with no source of income beyond what they were able to earn with their own hands; many had large families to feed and clothe. In 1869 the society set up a "department of usefulness": twice a week, members came to a central work place with fabric to be made into clothes; indigent seamstresses were paid for their work and could buy what they made at cost. What they did not buy was given away to people who could not work at all. The society, in the best Boston tradition, was interested in providing profitable work for the poor to encourage a sense of useful productivity. It did not underrate the importance of cash: it simply placed greater value on the ability to earn it.

Sara Sedgwick now became Alice's closest friend. The daughter of Theodore and Sara Ashburner Sedgwick, she had grown up in Stock-bridge, Massachusetts, and New York. Her mother had died when Sara was seventeen, in 1856; her father, three years later. In 1860 the four Sedgwick children — Susan, Arthur, Sara, and Theodora — had moved to Cambridge so that Arthur‡ could attend Harvard; the girls were cared for by their two maiden English aunts, Anne and Grace Ashburner.

* "It was the perennial freshness of Miss Birdseye's faith that had had such a contagion for these modern maidens [Olive Chancellor and Verena Tarrant], the unquenched flame of her transcendentalism, the simplicity of her vision, the way in which, in spite of mistakes, deceptions, the changing fashions of reform, which made the remedies of a previous generation look as ridiculous as their bonnets, the only thing that was still actual for her was the elevation of the species by the reading of Emerson and the frequentation of the Tremont Temple."

† The roster of the Female Humane Society, like that of the Bee, reads like a Cambridge Social Register. The members in the 1860s included Mrs. Louis Agassiz, Mrs. Richard Henry Dana, Mrs. Asa Gray, Mrs. James Russell Lowell, Mrs. Charles Russell Lowell, Julia Ward Howe, Melusina Fay Peirce, Ellen Hooper Gurney, Mrs. John Singer Sargent, Jane and Grace Norton, Anne and Grace Ashburner, and Sara Sedgwick.

‡ Arthur George Sedgwick (1844–1915) graduated from Harvard College in 1864 and from the law school in 1866. He practiced law in Boston until 1872, then moved to New York, where he worked as a lawyer and as an editor on the *Evening Post* and *The Nation*. He delivered Harvard's Godkin Lectures in 1909, "Some Unsettled Questions Relating to Popular Government" (published by Scribner's in 1912 as *The Democratic Mistake*).

Sara's older sister, Susan, soon married Charles Eliot Norton, at the time a writer, editor of the *North American Review* (with James Russell Lowell), and translator; later, he became a professor of art history at Harvard. The Nortons lived at Shady Hill, in an enormous house surrounded by fifty acres, just off Kirkland Street to the east of Harvard Yard. In 1864 the Sedgwick-Ashburner clan moved to a house on the Shady Hill property, not far from Quincy Street. The Jameses had known the Nortons since their Newport years; now the Sedgwicks, too, became friends as well as neighbors.

Alice never particularly liked Norton or his sisters, Jane and Grace. She found them intellectually pretentious, and was probably envious of Grace's lifelong friendship with Henry Jr. When Norton (whom she nicknamed Charlemagne) was editing Carlyle's letters and reminiscences in 1887, Alice wrote to William, "I am amused to here [sic] that the ancient houri of Kirkland St. [Grace] is still sowing her belated crop of wild oats. I suppose her mouthing ineptitudes, her 3 century old anecdotes and her snobbish pretentiousness are as great as ever. Instead of Froude why does not Charles expurgate her? — Was there ever anything so exquisitely delicious as Charles pruning Carlyle?"*

But though Alice made fun of the Nortons, she grew quite as close to the Sedgwick girls as she had to Fanny Morse. In 1869 Sara, too, went traveling abroad — with the Nortons. Henry Jr. met them in London in March. While William had struggled in Europe with ill health, Henry had thrived at home. As soon as William returned in the fall of 1868, however, Henry stopped writing and developed back pains. The younger brother had been longing for the life abroad that William found so unsatisfactory, and in February of 1869 the second James son left for Europe. In London, his first stop, the Nortons introduced him to Ruskin, Darwin, Rossetti, William and Jane Morris, George Eliot, and G. H. Lewes. He saw a good deal of Leslie Stephen, whom he had met when Stephen visited America in 1863 and 1868. He breakfasted, lunched, and dined with Sara and the Nortons.

This trip, Henry's first prolonged separation from his family, marks the

---

* Carlyle's opinion of Norton may have coincided more with Alice's than with Norton's own. Mark de Wolfe Howe's daughter Helen, in *The Gentle Americans*, reports, "A Sedgwick cousin of the family has told me, though I am not sure that the anecdote has been substantiated, that on the same day that Professor Norton wrote in his diary: 'Dined with the dear Carlyles,' Carlyle wrote in *his* diary: 'Goose N. came to dinner.' "

real beginning of his copious correspondence with his sister. He wrote
Alice long, evocative letters full of his European experience. Eager to resume the sensuous education that had begun so many years before, he
"inhaled" the Old World — the art, history, cultural traditions, and
physical beauty that provided setting and subject matter for his novels.
As always, he took fullest possession of his experience in the process of
rendering it for someone else — converting the rich materials at hand
into communication. "I hope you are not already sick of my frequent
letters," he wrote to Alice in April. "In time the nuisance may abate, but
for the present I feel an irresistible need to let off steam periodically & to
confide to a sympathetic ear the impressions which the week has gen-
erated in my soul . . . I exhale all my pleasurable emotions by means of
inarticulate groans & grunts & sighs. Whenever I see anything very
stunning I long for the presence of my lovely sister, & in default of it
promise myself to make the object present to her eyes by means of the
most graphic and 'spirituelle' descriptions."

Henry's letters to Alice assume a shared world of reference and discrimination. After visiting Ruskin at Denmark Hill near Sydenham, he asked
William to tell Alice that the house was just like Miss Austen's novels.
Confident of her Wordsworth, he described Mary and Edmund Tweedy
abroad as " 'whirled round in earth's diurnal course' at very much the
same rate as ever." He knew she would want to hear all about his meeting Matthew Arnold ("He is not delicately beautiful, but he has a powerful face and an easy, mundane, somewhat gushing manner") and Mrs.
William Morris ("Ah, *ma chère,* such a wife! *Je n'en reviens pas* — she
haunts me still. A figure cut out of a missal — out of one of Rossetti's or
Hunt's pictures . . . It's hard to say [whether] she's a grand synthesis of
all the pre-Raphaelite pictures ever made — or they a 'keen analysis' of
her . . . in either case she's a wonder"). He called on George Eliot (whom
he called "Mrs. Lewes") on a Sunday afternoon in 1869 with Grace Norton and Sara Sedgwick, and reported her "magnificently ugly — deliciously hideous. She has a low forehead, a dull grey eye, a vast pendulous
nose, a huge mouth, full of uneven teeth and a chin and jaw-bone *qui
n'en finessent pas* . . . Now in this vast ugliness resides a most powerful
beauty which, in a very few minutes, steals forth and charms the mind, so
that you end as I ended, in falling in love with her. Yes behold me literally in love with this great horse-faced bluestocking."

His letters were shared with the entire family. Alice treasured them, and William told Henry that he ought to send his notes about his physical ailments ("I blush to say that detailed bulletins of your bowels, stomach, &c. as well as back are of the most enthralling interest to me") on separate slips of paper marked private "so that I may then give freely the rest of the letter to Alice to carry about and re-read and wear in her bosom as she is wont to do."

More than any other member of the James family, Henry treated Alice as an equal, and rejoiced as if he were a participant in her improving health. Every letter from home, he wrote, "brings me such reiterated assurance of your amendment that I feel an awful desire to get home & see it with my eyes. Were I there there were much we could do together — we could mingle the streams of our common improvement & walk about together hand in hand smiling so 'peacefully.' " This artful fraternal empathy differed markedly from the sexually charged idylls offered by William. William's scenarios highlighted the polarities of their two natures — he the masculine force and she his nurturing complement. Henry envisioned a sexually neutral scene in which brother and sister offer mutual consolation, hand in hand.

His health *was* improving — he had hiked over the Simplon Pass into Italy — and so was his sister's. He wrote that he was glad to hear of her "dropping her elegant invalidity." In March, Alice went to Newport, where Aunt Kate was staying with friends. She was escorted on this venture by John Bancroft, a painter and friend from the Newport years (and son of the American historian and diplomat George Bancroft). William reported to Henry that "Father was loath to let her go without him, but she said to me and mother that her main wish in going was to get rid of him and Mother, and I was very glad to find her understanding so clearly her position."

Alice knew, then, that she wanted to "get rid of" her parents for a vacation — and the perspicacious William endorsed that desire. She could voice this wish to her mother, apparently, but not to her father. Still, she rarely left home, and during her brief absences she and Henry Sr. proclaimed how they longed for each other. Once when Mary and Alice were off in the country and Henry Sr. was ailing at home, Mary wrote to her husband, "I saw how [Alice's] spirits sunk last evening, in hearing of the recital of all your troubles — and she sighed a deep sigh, and said Oh! how I wish father was here — She bids me however say that she does not want *at all* to see you."

Alice's rare vacations from her parents generally took her to cool summer retreats, for everyone agreed that hot weather was bad for her health. None of the Jameses liked the humid heat of Boston, and now that they were established in Quincy Street they began taking vacations in the country. The whole family did not always go for the whole three months, but whoever happened to be ailing (usually Alice, and often William) would spend the summer with one or two of the others, in the woods or mountains, or by the ocean.

In June of 1869, Alice, William, and their parents went to stay in a comfortable farmhouse surrounded by pine trees in Pomfret, Connecticut. Just before they left, William wrote to Henry that Alice was much better, "lively all day, visiting &c. She never thinks now of lying down, and the slow steadiness of her improvement is a great thing in favor of its durability. If it keeps on at the same rate this summer she'll be as good for social purposes next winter as any one."

Her improvement did continue at Pomfret. The Jameses' friends Francis and Elizabeth Boott, a widower and his daughter who had recently moved from Europe to Boston, had taken a house nearby. The quiet days passed, with William reclining in a hammock he had strung up between two trees, Lizzie Boott painting at her easel, Henry Sr. and Mr. Boott engaged in discussions of philosophy, music, and literature, while Alice and Mary James read and did their needlework. (Aunt Kate was traveling in Europe.) On August 7, the entire party at Pomfret celebrated Alice's twenty-first birthday, marked by a solar eclipse. Then the Bootts left, but the Jameses stayed on from week to week while the August heat lasted, returning to Cambridge in early September.

For the most part, Alice was succeeding at the full-time job of getting well.* In July, Mary James sent Henry a description from Pomfret that would have made Alice laugh, had she read it, at the unintended paradox. "Alice is busy trying to idle," wrote Mary James, "and it is always very hard depressing work, this to her; but I think it will tell in the end."

•

* Her father wrote to a Swedenborgian friend on July 26: "Alice has been a little under the weather for a day or two, and I consequently have been invaded by the infernal crew as usual, infusing doubts & anxieties of the most tormenting nature in my bosom. Now I see that the D.N. [Divine Nature] is the sole truth of my relationship to her, while I have been privily appropriating it always to myself, and that I cannot master the influence of evil but by that acknowledgment."

At home that winter, as William had predicted, Alice proved "as good for social purposes as any one." She traveled with Fanny Morse to Lenox for several days, and went to Milton with Theodora Sedgwick. She took daily walks and began a program of "lifting" — an exercise system using mechanical weights, pulleys, and levers. In December, William reported to Henry, "To prove to you how well Alice is, I may tell you that today (Saturday) she started before eleven for town, where she is to go to the lifting cure, thence to lunch at a restaurant, alone, then to be caught up by Mother & Annie Ashburner* and to go to the Boston theatre to hear Maggie Mitchell in the Pearl of Savoy and then home to dinner. Last night she was at her bee. They hoped to hear M.M. in her great new play, 'Lorlie, the tiny belle of Canton,' but the play has been changed." The next day he reported that Alice was "not tired a bit by her theatre," and Henry wrote back about the delicious letter "telling of Alice's dissolute life."

Alice's life was, of course, as far from dissolute as reformer Elizabeth Peabody's. Carefully regulated and supervised, Alice's social world revolved almost entirely around her family and female friends. One evening she gave a dinner party for William, Fanny Morse, Theodora Sedgwick, Mary Mead (the sister of Mrs. William Dean Howells), and a young friend of William's named Charles Atkinson. The next day Howells wrote to Henry that he had been to pick up his sister-in-law at the end of the evening: "I don't know whether your sister is really so much better than she used to be, but she looks so, and I've found a very great resemblance to you in her — a fact you've both reason to be proud of."

Her improving health allowed Alice to enjoy a greater range of intellectual life than before. She went to the theater — in March 1870 she saw Charles Albert Fechter play Hugo's *Ruy Blas* with her mother and William. And she was reading a great deal, particularly the novels of Charles Reade. She wrote to Fanny Morse that *Hard Cash,* a two-volume novel published in 1863, was "most certainly interesting although not one of Reade's best"; she preferred *The Cloister and the Hearth,* as has posterity.

She had also begun to watch the world of politics. In July 1870, war broke out between the French and the Prussians. Alice avidly followed

* She had met Sara Sedgwick's cousin, Annie Ashburner, during the summer at Pomfret.

the news and editorial analyses, convinced that the French stood no chance, schooled in her opinions by the editorials in *The Nation* written by her father's friend E. L. Godkin.

War, empire, tyranny, and liberty were the live issues in the pages of *The Nation*. The intellectual fare in Cambridge was somewhat tamer. At Harvard, Alice was attending a series of lectures for the nonstudent community. All the Cambridge young ladies were going in a rush (reported Henry Sr. to the traveling Theodora Sedgwick), "taking notes that embarrass the lecturer" and hearing Mr. Emerson tell of the remark that Plutarch made about Pythagoras — only since Emerson couldn't find the right page in his manuscript, they had to be satisfied with hearing *about* the remark.

The Jameses spent the summer of 1870 again at Pomfret, but in 1871 they took a place on the ocean near Scarborough, Maine. It was called the Atlantic House, at Oak Hill. The younger boys were home for the summer. Henry and Wilky stayed in Cambridge while their parents, Alice, William, Rob, and Aunt Kate retreated to the quiet charm and cool ocean air of Maine. The Bootts and Wendell Holmes were there, along with the Sedgwicks, the Ashburners, and two other families of friends, the Andrews and the Lombards.

A favorite pastime of the group at the Atlantic House was sitting on the piazza, cooled by sea breezes, listening to Mr. Boott read aloud. William Dean Howells' *Their Wedding Journey* was being serialized in the *Atlantic* beginning in July,* and the Maine contingent was so enthusiastic that a round-robin letter was composed to convey their delight to the author. Lizzie Boott painted a singing robin on a branch, and Henry James, Sr., was the chirographer for Grace Ashburner's verse:

> A little round-robin, from Scarboro' sands,
> Has promised full well to obey our commands,
> To flap at your window, & peck at your pane,
> and to whistle our thanks, again and again.
>
> Your humour sheds light on a desperate lot,
> Whether wearied with waiting, if fainting, if hot;
> Good wishes we send to both husband & wife
> and a properous jaunt o'er the rail-road of life!

---

* It appeared in six installments, from July to December. Henry Jr.'s first novel, *Watch and Ward,* was running simultaneously in the *Atlantic,* in five installments, from August to December.

Managing her vacationing flock was by now second nature to Mary James, who showed few signs of fatigue, though she had turned sixty in 1870. She sent bundles of laundry home from Maine to be washed and sent back by the servant girl, Lizzie, who was keeping house for Wilky and Henry. She supervised 20 Quincy Street in absentia: "Did Tom come and cut the grass as desired and trim the wisteria? If not let him be sent for." And she reported to the boys at home on her patients: "Your Father seems happy and is an immense favorite among the ladies — As this is nothing unusual, a common experience, I do not so much dread the effect upon him. Will took one sea bath, and is going in again today — He keeps up bravely, which is saying a good deal, when one considers the great change in his habits here. Wendell Holmes ... has read Browning aloud to us most charmingly — and I hear him now in the next room reading to Will, who will feel a great void when he is gone." And "Alice had yesterday some unusual experiences — She began the day with a sea-bath, and ended it with a ride on top of the hay cart in the barn — She was the leader in the frolic, which will give you an idea of her improving condition."

Alice's main task continued to be to improve her health. "Trying to idle" meant trying to strike the right balance between activity and relaxation, thinking and feeling, interest and ennui, society and solitude. And though she seemed to be keeping this balance quite successfully in the early 1870s, her life was still dominated by the threat of illness. Even when she felt fine, she was seen not as normal but as "better" or distinctly not sick. Implicit in each evaluation of her improvement was an apprehension of possible relapse.

Chapter Nine

A Grand Tour

E UROPE had always served as the ultimate James family panacea. In
the 1840s it had offered a refuge for Henry Sr., with his pressing social and religious questions, and in the fifties had provided an educational
antidote to the plainer American scene. In the 1860s both Henry Jr. and
William sought physical cure and fresh intellectual stimulation abroad,
with varying degrees of success. And Aunt Kate, too, traveled to Europe
in the winter of 1869 for pleasure and restoration. Several of Alice's
friends had taken the "grand tour" in the late 1860s, including Fanny
Morse and Sara Sedgwick, and Alice had followed their progress with
mixed enjoyment and envy. She had accepted with pleasure Henry's invitation in 1869 to participate vicariously in his higher sensuous education.
But no matter how evocative his regular letters from abroad were, the experience they offered his sister in Cambridge was secondhand. By 1872
she was ready for more. She made plans in the early spring to travel in
Europe for six months with Henry and Aunt Kate. Fanny Morse, who
visited Alice in April, expressed what everyone was thinking about the
prospective trip: "It will do her a great deal of good."

In early May, Alice, Henry, and Kate took the train from Boston to
New York and sailed for England on the Cunard Line's *Algeria* on May
11. The passage was relatively easy — the two occasionally seasick women
bore up well, reported Henry to his parents; he himself did not miss a
meal. After ten days at sea they arrived at Queenstown and steamed up
St. George's Channel toward Liverpool under clear skies. They were delighted to set foot on land at last, and to sleep in beds that did not pitch

and roll. In Liverpool, they spent a leisurely day resting, exploring, booking return passage for Alice and Kate in a stateroom on the *Algeria* for October 15; then they proceeded through the blooming gardens and velvet green of an English May to Chester.

Alice, now twenty-three, was twelve when she had last left Europe, in 1860. She had only vague memories of most of her traveling childhood: apartments, hotels, train rides, blurred into one another, and she had been too young to have more than a superficial response to the art, theater, music, and architecture that had fed her older brothers' imaginations. When she returned for her grand tour in 1872, it was as if she were seeing everything for the first time. Years later, in her diary, she confessed to having been terrified, in the months before this trip, that her responses would be inadequate. "I needn't have been in such a *funk* as I was before I left home that summer, lest being such an entirely inartistic organization I should not know what to *do* with the pictures, like poor Mrs. Ogle with a joke, looking, as some one said, so helpless, as if she wanted to hand it on as fast as possible . . . Imagine the bliss of finding that I too was a 'sensitive,' and that I was not only 'mute before a Botticelli,' but that a Botticelli said an infinity of things to me — and this in a flash of mutual recognition, after the years of toil in trying to establish some sort of relation, either of speech or silence, with the Botticelli of Boston." Once launched in Europe, she found she could participate, after all, in the Jamesian dialogue with culture, effecting her own sensuous education.

Alice's letters from her European tour were enthusiastically received and lavishly praised. Bob wrote that Alice was "turning out the genius of the house," and William observed that she "must be tired ere now of the epithet of Mme. de Sévigné." But not one of the letters she wrote two or three times a week to Quincy Street during her six months abroad has survived.

From the Queen's Hotel in Chester, Henry reported his pleasure at seeing Alice not only rested and revived but "ravished and transported by what she finds here." He drew his parents a sketch (see picture following page 80) of his sister as she sat in the window of their common sitting room: it was a cold, wet English May, and the travelers kept a fire going on the hearth; Alice was composing a letter and gazing out through the ivy-framed glass at the hotel's elegant, high-walled garden, absorbing with quiet pleasure what it meant to be at last "abroad."

As Lambert Strether does in the opening pages of Henry's 1903 novel, *The Ambassadors,* brother, sister, and aunt wandered all over the ancient town of Chester, exploring on foot the two-mile stone wall, first built by the Romans, that girdles the city in a winding, rambling, uneven circuit. The town itself was a "perfect feast of crookedness," of winding streets and architectural idiosyncrasy that charmed its American visitors. They visited churches, drove through country villages and lanes, and lingered in the Rows, Chester's Gothic arcades. "If the picturesque be measured by its hostility to our modern notions of convenience," wrote Henry in an unsigned article on Chester that appeared in *The Nation* that summer, "Chester is probably the most romantic city in the world."

After a week, the little group proceeded to Rawseley, Derbyshire, with an overnight stop at Lichfield. With its superb cathedral and literary interest as the birthplace of Dr. Johnson, Lichfield was a great success. Rawseley, however, where Henry had thought of settling for a while, proved less interesting. The travelers stayed at a lovely inn just at the confluence of the Derwent and the Wye, and spent pleasant hours at Haddon Hall and Chatsworth; but at the end of two days they had had enough — the landscape, wrote Henry in *The Nation,* was "too ovine, too bovine, it is almost asinine." On they went to Oxford, stopping en route to admire the Van Dycks at Warwick Castle and to see Royal Leamington Spa. The next day found them wandering through Oxford's colleges, rapturous over the June profusion in garden after garden; and the day after that they returned from a visit to Blenheim, "ready to die," Henry reported to Quincy Street — and "not with fatigue." He went on, "Alice enjoys everything to ravishment, and what is better, endures everything *à merveille* . . . She is really making a capital traveller and when we have done what she is able to do we have all pretty well done what we desire to do. In short, her undertaking has already proved a most distinct and brilliant success. She enjoys, admires, appreciates and observes to the utmost possible extent. Aunt Kate is of course, inestimable, invaluable, and invulnerable."

From Oxford, on June 9, they went to Devonshire, stopping one night at Exeter (where they found the cathedral fine but not on a par with Lichfield) and another at the exquisite little coastal town of Ilfracombe. Better even than Ilfracombe was Lynton, North Devon — an earthly paradise too perfect, Alice later told a friend, to be real. Lynton was "niched in mid-air," wrote Henry, "in a fold of hills, and looking down into their blooming bosoms as it overhangs . . . the ocean." Their little hotel was ideally situated for morning explorations on foot and afternoons in the garden with a book, surrounded by the lush blooms of rare plants, looking out over the blue harbor to great rocky cliffs and wooded headlands facing the sea. "Alice's exploits (there is hardly another word for them)," Henry told to his parents, "have become such a matter of course that A.K. and I have almost ceased to notice them. She simply does everything . . ."

Both Henry and Kate had begun the trip by handling Alice with kid gloves. They had not headed immediately for London because they feared it might exhaust her; instead, they had chosen to take things slowly, in the country, watching for a place to settle down and acclimate their excitable companion. Alice, however, proved quite equal to the rigors of travel and sightseeing, requiring no more rest or special care than the ordinary exigencies of touring demanded. Henry hovered dutifully in his role as escort. Kate reported to her sister that he was "always at our door about five or ten minutes before breakfast hour, and if you were to see him invariably folding in the most precise manner, the shawls and rugs, which are brought in from our drives, and smoothing them down in some quiet corner, with the parasols and umbrellas, tears would flow from your eyes, and you would say, he is my own son indeed. *He forgets nothing,* and his care and consideration for Alice is unceasing." And Kate, like her nephew, reported to Quincy Street with a certain astonishment on Alice's new vigor: "Alice is bright and not in the least over-fatigued . . . and I think . . . that she is gaining strength by her travels . . . She takes it all very calmly, and is never at any time unduly excited, which of course enables her to bear her pleasures in a more lastingly beneficial way."

After four perfect days at Lynton (Henry feared that nothing else could seem quite as good after this time in the "lap of Paradise"), they turned at last toward London. They spent a Sunday at Wells — "an immense hit" — and then proceeded to Salisbury, a cool pleasant dinner, and a twilight visit to the splendid Close. From the White Hart Inn they "did" Salisbury Cathedral, Stonehenge, and Wilton House. Salisbury struck them as slightly banal — too obviously beautiful to be aesthetically interesting. The mystery of Stonehenge caught them in its magic for a quiet afternoon. But the feature of these last rural days that most appealed to Alice's imagination was Wilton House, the home of the

Earls of Pembroke, granted to William, the first earl, by Henry VIII in 1539. Van Dyck had come to Wilton in the early seventeenth century to paint the Pembrokes, and one portrait of the whole family during the reign of James I remained vivid to Alice for the rest of her life. Almost twenty years later, when she and Henry were living in England, she noted in her diary, "H. writes that he has been spending Sunday at Wilton House, next best to having been there myself, for we saw the great Van Dyck together in '73 [it was actually 72], when Aunt Kate, he and I drove from the White Hart, humble pilgrims!" She recalls "living for 48 hours in the house with that glorious object . . . It is as if it were yesterday that I saw it — a breathless moment."

The following day saw them in London, at the Charing Cross Hotel. Alice found the hubbub of the city less than "hygienic," and after a quick conference the little group determined to stay in London only four or five days, then head for Paris and Switzerland. Alice wrote later to Annie Ashburner that she was not in London "long enough to be anything but oppressed and depressed by its size and by the great seething multitude which it contains, but that, as one grows familiar with it passes off, after awhile I suppose." In four days they went shopping (hats for the women, suits for Henry), made tours of the Royal Academy and the British Museum, rested in the shade of Kensington Gardens, visited their old friends the Wilkinsons, sauntered through Hyde Park and along Rotten Row, and dined at the St. James's Restaurant in Piccadilly. At the National Gallery, Alice noticed the Boston portrait painter Benjamin Curtis Porter. As he came in, she observed, "It was his first sight of an old master and he sauntered about glancing casually here and there with no more ripple of emotion than if he were at Doll and Richards' [Boston art dealers, on Tremont Street]. How the cheap quality of his personality stood out." She was gloating over her own new-found powers of appreciation: "I can never forgive these excellent folk for being such an inartistic race. Amidst such opportunities for the picturesque, born to a medium which transmutes all things thro' such infinite degrees of the beautiful and the grim, to think of their having had only one great Master!"* She could readily understand how the English landscape might not inspire great art — how, for all its beauty, it might "by its arranged, respectable expectedness exasperate to the last degree the irritable spontaneous genius, holding within it, as it does, the possibilities of the *bête;* but

* Probably she meant Turner.

think of Rembrandtesque London!! One must acknowledge, however, that the one Master took the atmosphere with sufficient solemnity and put it thro' all its paces."

To save money after an expensive week in London, the three travelers did not stop at Boulogne for a sentimental return visit, but made the journey to Paris in one day, on June 26. On arrival, they were completely enchanted; one evening at the Théâtre Français drove "grimy uproarious London" out of their heads. Alice delighted in each detail of the French capital, enjoying her ease with its language and visits to the dimly remembered scenes of her childhood. She wandered along the broad avenues, lingered over the treasures of the Louvre, and rested in the afternoon shade of a favorite café. She went with Henry and Kate to spend a day with the Nortons, who were living just outside Paris at St.-Germain-en-Laye. (In February, Norton's wife, Susan — Sara Sedgwick's sister — had died at Dresden a few days after the birth of a son. Norton, with his mother, his sisters, and his children, had determined to stay in Europe, and spent the spring and early summer at St.-Germain.) Bismarck, the 1871 Commune, and the savage suppression that had left tens of thousands dead, had not cast the shadow over Paris that Henry had prepared his sister to expect. Instead of battle scars, the Americans found Paris "still the perfection of brightness and neatness and form and taste." Alice, wrote Henry, had not been so well since they left home as she was during their three days in France. She seemed "like a new — like a rejuvenated creature, and displayed more gaiety, more elasticity, more genuine youthful animal spirits than I have ever seen in her." She wanted to stay a month.

"My daughter a child of France!" wrote Mary James in mock shock from Cambridge after receiving a packet of letters from Paris. Though teasing, she called attention to the extremes of self-restraint and "dissolute" indulgence that caused Alice so much trouble: "What has become of that high moral nature on which I have always based such hopes for her, for this world and the next? That you should so soon have succumbed to this assault upon your senses, so easily have been carried captive by the mere delights of eating and drinking and seeing and dressing, I should not have believed; and indeed I see it all now, to be merely the effect of a little cerebral derangement produced by the supernatural effort you made in crossing the Channel. It will be a lesson to you not to exercise such self restraint in the future.

"How marvellous my dear child your progress seems to be! what a benign medicine this journey is proving to you!"

Mary James believed fully in the travel cure. Her husband, however, counseled caution: Henry's accounts of Alice's "exploits" frightened him. He would be much happier, he wrote his daughter, to hear they were taking things in a leisurely way and "never fatiguing yourself beyond a good *honest* fatigue such as a little lie-down will easily recruit you from. You have always had such power to control imprudence, however, that I count upon you now, to say nothing of Aunt Kate, who is a sure fortress."

Both parents made these epistolary reaches across the Atlantic all summer long, sometimes joking, sometimes anxious, always depicting their twenty-three-year-old daughter as a fragile child. Mary sent a double-edged message at midsummer, describing to her traveling offspring how their father delighted in their correspondence, then adding that he was greatly enjoying his freedom from all responsibility, with "no little girl on hand to manage or inspect him."

Henry Sr.'s abundant, newsy letters expressed his eagerness to participate from home in his daughter's pleasure. He had moved into her room, in the afternoons, to read and write. "I am alone with my darling," he wrote to Alice shortly after she left. "I don't know what to say except that I rejoice in you, never so much as now that you are having your heart and mind and senses so filled with beauty."

•

The news from Quincy Street was largely matrimonial. Clover Hooper married Henry Adams on June 27 at Beverly Farms; a week later they sailed for Europe — where Henry and Alice met up with them toward the end of the summer. In July, Wendell Holmes married Fanny Dixwell, sister of the Bee "Colonel," Sue. Henry wrote, "Father's account of Wendell Holmes' marriage was interesting but we would fain have known how Miss Dixwell *looked*."

Robertson James, living now in Milwaukee, had gotten engaged to a young woman in Wisconsin named Mary Holton before Alice and Henry left for Europe; in late June, Wilky announced *his* engagement to a friend of Mary Holton's, Caroline Cary. Neither young woman, wrote their prospective mother-in-law to Alice, was "at all intellectual. Miss

Cary is probably a person of more sentiment and stronger affections than Mary Holton. She will ask more from Wilky in a sentimental way than Mary will from Bob — and this is just right — How she is on the practical side I have not found out."* From Milwaukee, Wilky wrote to Alice and Henry that he now felt closer to his sister than ever before: "She will have a role in life now which she has never played before. Her role has been so far a very loving & cherished one to her brothers, but it must now expand into one of far greater importance in their eyes than ever before. — It will be that of standing before Bob & myself in a sort of double sisterhood, a sisterhood which will give us a double solicitude — in the future."

William, spending the summer of 1872 at Mount Desert Island in Maine, was still ailing and trying to cure his "philosophical hypochondria" with sea baths and fresh air. The Sedgwicks and Ashburners were also in Maine, and William's letters to Henry and Alice throughout the

---

* She had tried to find out by writing to Wilky. His reply is at once a defense of privacy and a compliance with her request:

Milwaukee, Wis.
August 7, 1872

My dearest mother.

Your letter arrived yesterday, and I was glad to hear from you and shall be only too glad to answer all your questions about Miss Cary.

I should have done so voluntarily if you had given me a little while longer to do so, but the sensation of love to me, the true love which fills my bosom for this pure lovely girl is so deep and so strange that it becomes daily & daily a less familiar subject to my mind, & simply fills me with an inward contentedness & acquiescence so great as to make the relation subside into comparative obscurity & privacy so far as any approach at analysis is concerned. We are different in disposition and temperament, as different as we can be. She is exceedingly reserved & unimpassioned & never betrays an emotion of feeling on any subject scarcely; but the outward lack of it is only the sign of an inward fullness which cannot be computed.

— I know this instinctively & feel it all the time so deeply that I cannot help liking it & respecting it. She has had no mother since she was 8 years old & ever since she has been able she has been the head of her father's house, directing it & managing it for him ...

She is the centre of the family and although they are all rather undemonstrative in their feelings it is evident that she cements them altogether. There is in her a capacity for improvement greater than any woman I ever knew, & when one thinks of the deadening influences she has all her life been under, it is wonderful to think what she has made of herself in the way of simple womanly trueness & purity & gracefulness ...

summer catalogue the relative attractions of his female companions.
Mary James wrote to Europe that she had no fear of any harm being done
to William's heart, however, and by August William was complaining of
"petticoat sway." He had, as usual, some ex cathedra advice for his sister:* "Don't overdo your exercise . . ." he wrote her, "but let your mind
go to sleep and lead a mere life of the senses. Forget your conscience and
religion, which will return tenfold better for it when you are home again
by my side. Tell Aunt Kate & Harry to do the same. 'Tis the object of my
life at present." And, also as usual, he teased: he expected to find Alice on
her return "sprung into full possession and exercise of faculties of mind
and I trust heart, hitherto undreamt of by any of us, and only dreamt of
by herself. She will be the lioness of the next season."

•

By the end of June, Henry was eager to get Alice away from the heat of
cities up into Swiss mountain air. So, although Alice would have pre-

* William's constant advice to his younger brothers and sister was often aggressive
and not always welcome. He freely criticized Henry's writing, for instance. In the
summer of 1872, he told Henry that the letters to *The Nation* showed a tendency to
"over-refinement" and suggested that a broader treatment would hit a broader mark.
Two months later, he confessed that he was surprised at the numbers of people who
were enjoying the pieces in *The Nation,* "as I thought the style ran a little more to
curliness than suited the average mind . . . In my opinion what you should cultivate is
directness of style. Delicacy, subtlety and ingenuity will take care of themselves." He
protested against his brother's "constant use of french phrases. There is an order of
taste — and certainly a respectable one — to which they are simply maddening," and
he found in certain phrases "something cold, thin blooded & priggish suddenly pop-
ping in and freezing the genial current."
Throughout the brothers' lives, William offered this kind of pronouncement on
Henry's work — not as a question of *taste* (many have agreed with William's objec-
tions to Henry's ornate style), but as if the novelist did not quite know what he was
doing. Henry, for the most part, listened, offered polite thanks, and ignored the advice. He never made similar criticisms of William's work, though he did read it, and
usually responded with warm, if vague, praise. Finally, when William urged Henry to
write a book with no "twilight or mustiness" in the plot, with straightforward action
and "no fencing in the dialogue," the younger brother hit back — softly. He offered
to write such a book — "but let me say, dear William, that I shall greatly be humiliated if you *do* like it, and thereby lump it in your affection with things of the current
age, that I have heard you express admiration for and that I would sooner descend to a
dishonoured grave than have written . . ." And he concluded, "I'm always sorry to
hear of your reading anything of mine, and always hope you won't — you seem to me
so constitutionally unable to 'enjoy' it."

ferred to linger for several more weeks in Paris, and though Henry was half afraid to break the spell of pleasure by bringing her away, the little group proceeded by overnight express train to Geneva. They stopped only a day in the city they had lived in fifteen years before, staying at the familiar Hôtel de l'Ecu, refreshing their memories with visits to their old haunts. The following afternoon they made straight for the country — the Hôtel Byron at Villeneuve — "nothing but comfort and pleasantness and cool breezes and the perpetual vision of this blue lake and these purple mountains."

For two weeks they remained at the quiet hotel, resting from their travels and deliberating slowly which way next to bend their steps. They took little day trips, to Vevey, the Gorge du Trient, and Martigny. The days, wrote Henry to his parents, broke "one by one on the shores of eternity very much as the blue waves do on the white strand." Alice seemed very well: the more she did, the more she was able to do. But she did like "a little more society" than was available at Villeneuve.

Then Lizzie and Francis Boott arrived. At first, they fitted comfortably into the James party's hotel life. Lizzie, two years older than Alice, had, like the James children, been exposed to Europe at an early age: she had grown up alone with her father in Italy. But unlike the rather haphazard education the Jameses had had abroad, Lizzie's training had been closely planned and supervised. Her father, a composer, had nurtured his only child's talents for singing and painting. Henry later described her as "the admirable, the infinitely civilised and sympathetic, the markedly *produced* Lizzie" — she was "educated, cultivated, accomplished, toned." He confessed that Lizzie had served as the model for Pansy Osmond, the carefully cultivated if somewhat ordinary flower in his *Portrait of a Lady*; and Leon Edel suggests that Henry also drew on the Bootts' intense father-daughter attachment for his portrait of the Ververs in *The Golden Bowl.*

The company of the Bootts at Villeneuve seemed a decided advantage, Henry reported to his parents, although planned excursions had occasionally to be postponed because Lizzie, not Alice, was *"hors de combat."* Soon the enlarged little group set off for Bern, Interlaken, and Grindelwald, in search of higher altitudes and cooler air. Other American friends joined them in Grindelwald, at 3400 feet above sea level. The air was cool, the company abundant, the view of the Wetterhorn and the Eiger spectacular. Alice declared it, next to Paris, the loveliest place in the world; their tranquil existence was "heavenly."

But there is an undertone of concern in Henry's letters from Switzerland. He was learning (he told Quincy Street) something of the cares of paternity, "in spite of the fact that Alice is everywhere, invariably & obstinately taken for my *wife!* & addressed as Madame — A.K. passes of course for our *mamman.*" His observation that Alice liked "a little more society" than she had at Villeneuve hints at an undiagnosed problem. He would not alarm Quincy Street by telling them anything less than splendid news of Alice's health, but he did warn his parents from Grindelwald not to be alarmed if they heard of a sudden change in plans: *change,* he wrote, seemed to have been the great agent in Alice's improvement during the course of their travels. His attempts to link her health to environmental factors — cool weather, society, change — show him searching for a solution to a problem he did not dare mention.

At the end of July they did suddenly opt for change, leaving the Bootts and Grindelwald for the mountaintops of the Engadine. The weather everywhere was hot. They pressed on from Meiringen to Lucerne, Andermatt, and Thusis, keeping as high and cool as possible. Ten days of driving, Henry hoped, would be just the thing to solve their "Swiss difficulties," which he now attributed to the heat, the lack of stimulus, and the absence of suitable walks. Also, a week of Lizzie Boott's "*unshared* society" had proved "a little heavy." The Bootts would be perfect, Henry told Quincy Street, "if we could only have them à discrétion; but as attachés of our party they conduce a little to nervous exhaustion. This is especially the case in travelling when it makes some difference in Alice's buoyancy whether she is the centre of a body of three members or of six."

The James parents had expressed their concern that too much excitement would bring on a reaction. From Villeneuve, Henry had replied that Alice had not had one hour of excessive excitement and that the increase in her strength and activity had been, on the contrary, natural, solid, tranquil. She was like "a person coming at last into possession of the faculty and pleasure of movement, and it is the most *active* part of her life now which does her most good and leaves the most substantial effects behind it." At Thusis, however, in early August, the crisis everyone had been fearing came on. Henry alluded to it lightly at the time, hoping to spare Quincy Street a parallel crisis of anxiety. But later he referred to the "episodes" at Thusis and Meiringen and confessed to his parents once it was safely past that Alice's attack had been severe. They were traveling again, in spite of his first enthusiastic reports from Thusis, because after a couple of days "the air seemed over-exciting to Alice. It made her nervous — rather acutely so — for the 1st time since we have been abroad." They had accordingly taken a three-hour drive to Chur, capital of the Grisons. "Alice's sensations were not produced by over excitement of any other kind," Henry continued, anticipating criticism from Quincy Street, "for she had notice of them only after two or three days of perfect quietude. It was a case of climatic antipathy ... Alice has tested stiff mountain air to its condemnation ... [her] verdict is that there is such a thing as being over stimulated." She was longing for towns and people: "Alice's own impulse and curiosity is almost altogether towards cities, monuments, and the *human picturesque,* of which she has seen, during her lifetime, so little; I think our month of mountains has been a little over-solemn sort of entertainment for her."

Since there is no record of these weeks in Alice's own voice, it is difficult to guess at what besides the air might have precipitated her crisis in the Swiss mountains. But two factors in Henry's account of the preceding weeks stand out as possibly connected with the Thusis episode. The first is the decision to leave Paris. Alice appears to have agreed that it was best to head for Switzerland, coolness, and country tranquillity — certainly Henry and Kate did not force her to go. But in Paris she was at last taking possession of Europe in true Jamesian fashion — responding to history, art, and human diversity and converting them into experience of her own. Having to leave for the remedial countryside may have served as an unwelcome hint that she was not, after all, "up to" the belated sensuous education that had provided her elder brothers (and some of her friends) with such cultural wealth.

A second factor in Alice's attacks may have been, as Henry suggests, the proximity of the Bootts. At first she welcomed companionship through the long country days, but the society of the Bootts quickly became more of a burden than a pleasure. Alice had grown accustomed, by this time, to making triumvirate decisions and to having the undivided attention of Aunt Kate and Henry. Veiled in Henry's observation that "it makes some difference in Alice's buoyancy whether she is the centre of a body of three members or of six" may have been Alice's resentment that Lizzie now had a voice in their plans, and that the "body" catered as much to Lizzie's health as to her own. The James group had left Grindelwald abruptly, and the crises at Meiringen and Thusis follo

Nothing could have regained the center of the stage for Alice more effectively than a nervous attack.

Her health began to improve as soon as she left Thusis. From Chur the little party proceeded to Zürich, and thence to Bern, which was full of Bostonians. The Bootts were there ("not especially changed," reported Henry to Quincy Street, "Lizzie being still a little too passive, and Boott a little too active"), along with some of Fanny Morse's Lee cousins, various Jacksons, Parkmans, Lombards, and Whitwells, and soon Mr. and Mrs. Henry Adams. The "mild lionising" that was now possible in this company quickly dispelled all remaining traces of Alice's nervousness, but the Jameses did not linger in Bern. They were headed for Italy. ("I do hope you are not starting [for Italy] *too* early!" wrote their father from Cambridge. "That you are not risking those precious gains you have made by undue precipitancy! Of course it is too late now to be heard in reference to this step, but I pray you once more to be cautious in general, and do nothing upon impulse ... I have really nothing to say except the old story — that we love you consumedly as usual and rejoice in every letter that comes as a love letter ... believe me my darling little maid your devoted parent, HJ.")

Since Alice now wanted to avoid mountaintops, they decided to go through the Mont Cenis tunnel rather than over the Simplon Pass. That way they would see Turin and miss the lakes, but "Alice will give a lake for a city any day. If she could be put through a course of all the cities of Europe," wrote her new "doctor" to his parents, "I think she would have little left in the way of invalidism to get rid of ..." That she had compressed such an acute attack and full recovery into ten days, concluded Henry, clearly signaled a general convalescent tendency.

Leaving Bern, they stopped at Fribourg, Lausanne, Geneva, and Chambéry; on August 26 they passed through the Mont Cenis tunnel into Italy. This was Alice's first visit to Italy, and she was captivated by Turin's piazzas and arcades, by the frescoed ceilings, marble floors, and long balconied windows of their hotel. From Turin they went on to Cadennabia, on Lake Como, and then took a boat down the lake, slept at Milan, and arrived in Venice on September 2. The heat and mosquitoes of nighttime Venice in the late summer outweighed its aesthetic attractions. As a result, the travelers did as much as they could in four days (exploring churches, visiting Torcello, Murano, and the Lido, dining al fresco, lingering in St Mark's, eating figs all day and ice cream every night at Florian's) and departed on the 5th for Verona.

Years later, Henry James compared Venice to a nervous woman: favorable to both the city and the woman, the comparison indicates his covert appreciation of Alice's delicate health (just as, in a similar vein, he appreciated the "interesting" illnesses of his cousin Minny Temple and the fictional Milly Theale). Venice, he wrote in *Italian Hours* (1909), "varies like a nervous woman, whom you know only when you know all the aspects of her beauty. She has high spirits or low, she is pale or red, grey or pink, cold or warm, fresh or wan, according to the weather or the hour. She is always interesting and almost always sad; but she has a thousand occasional graces and is always liable to happy accidents."

●

At last the touring Americans were heading back toward Paris. Alice, thoroughly well, was panting (reported Henry) "for the Riviera and her beloved southern France." They went first to Austria and southern Germany, pausing only when necessary to rest. William had prescribed Germany as a cure-all, but Henry found Munich a "nightmare of pretentious vacuity" and concluded that it was all right with regard to Germany to listen to the voice of the spirit and "treat oneself to a good square antipathy."

September 17 found them delighted to be back in Paris, at the Hôtel Rastadt in the Rue Neuve St. Augustin. Alice was well, "indefatigable" even after a month of hard travel, and eager to enjoy every minute of three full weeks in Paris. The morning after their arrival she was up early, "shaking her invincible locks and walking over Paris with unabated elasticity," reported her brother. She and Kate indulged in orgies of shopping for the first week, and then, with all their orders placed and packages mailed, turned to revel in the cultural *richesse* of Paris. They had plenty of American company. Edmund and Mary Tweedy, who were also at the Rastadt, dined with them every day. The Nortons were at the Hotel Windsor en route to England,* and Mr. and Mrs. James Russell Lowell were staying nearby along with William's friend Chauncy Wright. The Jameses welcomed all this company to relieve the "mutual

---

* Henry found them "excellent," he told William, but he shared Alice's reservations: "I feel less and less at home with them, owing to a high moral je ne sais quoi which passes quite above my head. I went with Charles the other day to the Louvre, where he made some excellent criticisms, but he takes art altogether too hard for me to follow him ... I daily pray *not* to grow in discrimination and to be suffered to aim at superficial pleasure."

monotony of our by this time extremely familiar selves," confessed Henry.

For all the James children, travel inevitably meant worry about drawing on the "sacred" family funds. But illness proved a great exonerator: whenever Henry received an admonitory letter from his mother about his extravagance abroad, he replied with a full accounting of his ailments and the benefits derived from first-class train compartments and good food, proclaiming his gratitude and the guilt he felt at exhibiting any semblance of selfish indulgence. Mary would then capitulate, urging him to spend as much as he needed in order to get well.

From Europe in 1872 Henry sent home regular statements of his and Alice's expenses, justifying the amount (about $500 each in the first three months) by the improvement in Alice's health. It had been absolutely necessary, he wrote, to travel first class and engage sitting rooms at the English inns; little had been spent on extra luxuries, and the money represented an "immense gain" for Alice — he didn't think she could have got the same for less. From Paris at the end of September he gave a final accounting. By the time he had seen Alice off on the *Algeria,* he predicted, they would have spent about £480 — roughly $2400 — including all Paris purchases. The money had been well spent in every way, he assured his parents: the journey had been a "very fruitful one and I think that when Alice is fairly established at home again you will feel that for her its fruits have been considerable ... We have really I suppose, become considerably older and wiser by it and we shall measure our profits little by little as life goes on. In retrospect it all seems now to have been absurdly easy — and indeed our wheels have been liberally oiled by the paternal bounty."

On October 9, they crossed the English Channel to stay a few days more in London, at the Charing Cross Hotel, before the women embarked from Liverpool. They found London the same "terrible murky Babylon" as ever. Henry and Alice took a drive to see the new Bethnal Green Museum, which Henry wrote up for the *Atlantic.* The ineluctable Nortons were there, living now at Cleveland Square in Bayswater, and so was Annie Ashburner. One day Alice and Henry had lunch with Annie and then walked round to visit the Nortons: "I don't think," Alice wrote later to Annie, "that I was ever more impressed with the size of the place than by seeing this great quarter [Bayswater], the existence of which I had never heard before, with its interminable rows of houses all packed with human beings." From London they went directly to Liverpool. Alice and Kate boarded the *Algeria* on October 15, exchanged tearful good-byes with Henry, and turned toward home.

•

Quincy Street embraced its wanderers and questioned them eagerly about every detail of the trip. Henry warned his family not to conclude anything too quickly about the results of Alice's travels, as her "mind, like her trunk, was so heavily packed with treasures that it can empty itself only in successive *trays,* or layers of information. I wish I were there that I might officiate as showman or *déballeur.*" He needn't have have worried. The family was immensely impressed with Alice's physical and moral improvement. William told Henry that she had showed no languor since her return, and was in all respects more "elastic* and toned up. Her journey was a great thing for her in every way and her talk about things and people seen has been very abundant and good."

To Alice, the tour had been truly a great thing. Everything had been arranged for her pleasure. She had had Henry and Kate all to herself — two experienced travelers and sensitive companions who encouraged her independence. They had managed to take just the right amount of care, making clear their concern for her welfare, yet not worrying excessively about what she could bear. Though her success in Europe (with the brief failure at Thusis) leaned on the support of Henry and Aunt Kate, it was nonetheless real. She had been able to range as freely and pursue pleasure as avidly as a young unmarried American woman could. She had absorbed, participated, acted — proving able to live more fully than she ever had done at home. And the question she faced on return was whether she could find some way of sustaining this new strength in Cambridge.

For several weeks the answer seemed to be yes. She was carried along by the fresh memory and constant retelling of her six months abroad, and her new energy and elasticity astounded her family. But by December, Mary James was writing to Henry that Alice now found too stimulating the breakfast of chocolate and rolls that she had come to love abroad: "She continues to seem much stronger than she was before she went away, but the life here offers her so few distractions, and she has so

---

* The word *elastic,* applied frequently to Alice in her periods of improvement, points up the brittle character of her nervous frailty.

little spontaneous activity in a practical way, that I fear she may suffer from the temptation to fall back upon her books too much."

And in the spring: "A. is full of the most vivid memories of all your love and care last summer, and is so eloquent on the subject, that she brings wrath upon Will's countenance, while she brings tears into my eyes. I think she enjoys her journey more and more in thinking it over, and her greatest delight would be to go again and stay longer. This is not to be thought of now, but nor will it ever be possible during Father's life time — still, it is a great source of pleasure to her both in the past and in the future."

Returning home from Europe at the age of twenty-four meant for Alice returning to a tedious present and an uncertain future. Mary James was right, insofar as her diagnosis went, about the lack of interesting activity for Alice in Cambridge. Too little action and too many books did not, of course, explain "Alice's nerves," but her health did improve when she had something to do other than contemplate her own uselessness. She could not keep traveling, both for practical reasons and because her father would not sacrifice his pleasure in her company to her pleasure at independence. She came home, then, after a welcome respite from the Quincy Street life of internal conflicts and external boredom, to realize that she could not "have" Henry, Kate, and Europe as a steady diet. Cambridge daily life had to be met on its own terms.

And what would happen to her after Quincy Street was no longer home? Her parents were getting old. Some day her father would not be there to require her companionship. He had written to Henry in Europe that he hoped she would always "enjoy her husband's appreciation to the same extent her mother does mine." Would she find a husband and establish a family of her own? It was time, as her marrying friends and William's exhortations repeatedly reminded her.

As she began to face these troubling questions, the success and freedom of her European adventure came increasingly to seem the high point of her life. "I am frightened sometimes," she wrote to Annie Ashburner, five years after the trip, "when I suddenly become conscious of how constantly I dwell on the memory of that summer I spent abroad."

Chapter Ten

Love and Work

T HE ISSUE of central interest in Alice's Cambridge social circle during the 1870s was marriage. One by one her friends and brothers were pairing up. In letters on this subject to Sara Sedgwick in New York and Annie Ashburner in London, Alice shows herself by turns caustic, funny, defensive, hopeful, self-depreciating, superior, and resigned, as it became more and more apparent that her own turn (as she put it) was never going to come. After all, as she told Annie, matrimony was the only successful occupation a woman could undertake.

Robertson James had married Mary Holton just after Alice returned from Europe in 1872. Alice took to this sweet, docile sister-in-law from the first: William wrote to Henry in November that "even the fastidious Alice is loud in praise of [Mary's] native 'refinement'" and the two "spend a good part of the day rapt in each other's arms or with arms round waists and cheek to cheek &c &c." In the fall of 1873, Wilky married Caroline Cary, Thomas Sergeant Perry was engaged to Lilla Cabot, Alice's friend Sylvia Watson announced her engagement to William Emerson, and several members of the Bee got married or betrothed.

To Sara, Alice wrote early in 1874, "Sargy and Lilla are to be married in a month or two and to live on no one knows what, they themselves less than any one I fancy. Sargy's philosophy can hardly be of the fashionable positivist school exclusively or he would never run the risk of assuming the entire responsibility of Lilla's solid proportions in addition to his own six feet of muscle, on such slender expectations as a summer to be passed in the sylvan shades of Park Square in Dr. Cabot's house, which is the only tangible provision for the future with which they seem to be provided. Isn't it wild?"

When Sara postponed her return from New York to Cambridge, Alice threatened, "If you don't come soon I shall in desperation elope with the handsome butcher-boy, with whom I have an interview every morning for the purpose of telling him that Mrs. J. does *not* wish anything. He must think that we are a curious race, living on our own fat, unless he knows that madam only has him come for looks and galavants herself to market every morning. He is very good-looking and is filled with emotion whenever he sees me, so you had better fly to the rescue." Her old friend Bessy Ward, continued Alice, was engaged to a Saxon, Baron von Schönberg: "I think that if I condescended to a title I should draw the line at a duke. Aren't you sick of these flimsy Barons who are always on hand to be converted into husbands? How much more respectable a good solid shoemaker would sound, even better than a butcher boy!" And then, "What do you suppose I heard the other day? Nothing less than that those dreadful Loverings had had no end of offers! It was insulting, but satisfactory as explaining the mystery of why the article had been so scarce in Quincy Street, for if such ragged growth as the Miss L.'s are what's wanted its no wonder that a rare exotic like — modesty forbids my saying who — is left unplucked upon its stem, to reach a bloom bordering, to put it delicately, on the full-blown."

The sharpened points of Alice's wit held venom when she was jealous. She anatomized feminine flaws and scrutinized connubial financial arrangements as if she were narrating a Jane Austen novel. After Sargy Perry married Lilla Cabot, Alice told Sara she had been "struggling to like" the new Mrs. Perry "for a long period . . . but it is a struggle that I can no longer keep up. I was thoroughly routed . . . the last time. When she confined her wonder & admiration to her intellectual achievements I could stand her, but now that she rams her moral perfections down your throat it's a little more than my imperfect digestion can stand. Sargy always had the capacities of a cormorant, so he is able to swallow her whole, not having to think about her as she is going down must make it easier."

In early 1875, Ellen Tappan got engaged ("wonder of wonders") to a Mr. Dixey. "Between ourselves," whispered Alice across the Atlantic to Annie, "can you conceive what the youth wants her for? You may say money, but after all she hasn't got enough in her own right to make it worth while and her mother may live half a century. She has only between six and seven thousand, a sum not to be despised for a spinster but hardly enough to make an inducement to matrimony with such an extravagant unpractical creature as Ellen . . ."

Ridiculing other women as physically gross, dreadfully ragged, or morally conceited, Alice implicitly compared them with her own delicacy of body and sensibility. These coarse females had something she didn't have — men — but she could claim a superior refinement.

When discussing her close friends, she deployed gentler mockery and drew softer (though still critical) portraits of marriage. Ellen Hooper, Clover's sister, had married Ephraim Whitman Gurney, a professor of history and dean of the faculty at Harvard. "Ellen Gurney was so funny the other day," reported Alice to Annie; "she was repeating some one's having intimated that the matrimonial state was rather a complicated one and subject to more or less rubs of one sort or another, when she said suddenly, 'can you conceive what she meant? I can't I'm sure!' Whereupon I burst out laughing and told her that she must not take her blissful condition with her beloved Whitman as a sample of marriage generally. She is certainly the most *married* and the most happy woman I know. It has wonderfully improved her, she grows all the time more and more delightful. I seem to have laid myself out on the marriage question rather extensively, you mustn't be alarmed, for I have no plans for myself just yet, but it is a topic always interesting you know to the spinster mind."

The story of another close friend's courtship and wedding runs like a serial through Alice's correspondence in the mid-seventies. Margaret Storer, a member of the Bee, had begun seeing a young man named Joseph B. Warner, who would become the James family's lawyer in later years. "Marny has the most Boston arrangement with Mr. Warner," Alice told Annie. "What do you suppose they do? Why, they read Constitutional History and meet once a week to discuss it! Doesn't it savour of the soil? If it had been any thing but Constitutional one could conceive of it, but thus are the youths and maidens made in these latitudes!"

The Warner-Storer wedding took place more than two years later, in September 1876. Alice regaled Sara with the full story, concluding, "We staid till about ten o'clock, and then came away congratulating ourselves upon our single-blessedness."

Utterly absorbed in the "marriage question," Alice disguised her longing to participate with this sort of falsely hearty self-congratulation. Envy lay beneath her running commentary on marriage and the "insignificant" women who were successfully doing the usual thing. When she heard a rumor that Annie Ashburner had a suitor in London, Alice advised her friend to "nail him" and confessed, "I am becoming ardently matrimonial, and if I could get any sort of man to be impassioned about me I should not let him escape."

Alice was neither coy nor flirtatious, and did not find conversation with the opposite sex easy. Her brothers' friends — all "suitable" young men — came through the house in a steady stream; but if her parents made any attempt to encourage a romance or introduce her to a wider circle of acquaintance, it was not recorded. Alice found most men, aside from her brothers, "queer" and rather frightening. Her remarks about them to her female friends ranged from scathing to belittling.

In the winter of 1875, Lizzie Boott gave an engagement party for Ellen Tappan. Alice reported to Annie that the party was "not eminently successful owing to rather a scarcity of the male sex, to which on social occasions, whether we have the vote or not, we are and shall always be slaves." She found Ellen's fiancé disappointing: "Mr. Dixey . . . is about the lightest weight that I have ever had the pleasure of knowing. He seems like nothing but a little society creature, and rather a snobbish one too. I imagine he is very amiable and good, and he has a certain physical refinement, but I should say that was all . . . Oh! he is so flimsy, so flimsy . . ." William's friend Charles Atkinson was also at the party, and Alice told Annie that

he asked as usual with interest after you, what a pity it is that he always thinks it necessary to talk nothing but nonsense at parties, its dreadfully tiresome after awhile. The poor fellow looks thin & pale, I wonder whether it is still Miss Loring. Why is it that love affairs appeal so much less in real life to one's sympathy than they do in the silliest novel, even in a double-column Harper's reprint? Lizzy had fortunately refrained from inviting the odious Mr. Frank Loring* whose sentimental goody compliments are a little more than I can

---

* Frank Loring was the Boston publisher who, early in 1880, pirated an American edition of Henry James's tale *A Bundle of Letters.* The tale had been originally published in an Anglo-French journal, *The Parisian,* edited by Theodore Child. Loring printed his unauthorized edition in Boston and sold it for twenty-five cents a copy. Henry had not taken out a United States copyright on the story, and consequently had no legal redress, but was nonetheless annoyed at losing the income to Loring and not being consulted. Two years earlier, he had confided to Lizzie Boott that the character of Mr. Wentworth, in *The Europeans, "was* a reminiscence of Mr. Frank Loring, whose frosty personality I had always in my mind in dealing with this figure." Frank Loring was not related to Alice's friend Katharine.

stand. But she had there a funny little man a Mr. Bancroft, do you know him? He had been talking for a long time to Fanny Morse, during a respite I went & spoke to her, when suddenly Mr. Bancroft appeared behind a large cake-basket which he offered first to Fanny & I supposing he meant to do the same to me bowed my head & said, "no, thank you," whereupon he became much convulsed and said, "Oh, good-evening, Miss James," & then turned and fled with the cake-basket never again to reappear, whether he was so frightened at having called me Miss James without having been introduced or whether he thought that I was a bold-faced jig and needed snubbing I can't tell, but the effect was most peculiar ... It is a queer world and people behave in the strangest way. The absurd little Wm. Apthorp who has been introduced to me more than once comported himself as usual last night, looking everywhere but at me; as Mrs. Child says they seem to think that if you bow to them across the room that you are trying to hook them in to talking to you. They have got about as much manners and civilization as gorillas. I hope you don't think that I am in a very ill-tempered condition, but they all provoke me dreadfully, for it is so easy to be gracious and courteous, and it makes life run so much more smoothly, and there are so many, many corners to turn.

Very few members of the male fraternity escaped the scorch of Alice's pen. One who did was Fanny Morse's first cousin Charles Cabot Jackson. Jackson had graduated from Harvard College in 1863 and from the law school in 1864. Instead of practicing law, however, he spent a few years learning the iron-smelting and railway-supply businesses, traveled abroad, and worked with the wool-brokers, Richardson and Jackson, in Boston. Then, in 1870, he had joined the eminent banking firm of his uncles and cousins, Lee, Higginson & Company.

Alice was first impressed by Charles Jackson on a visit with Lizzie Boott to the Morses' at Beverly in 1873. She wrote to Annie Ashburner that Mr. Jackson would instantly have captivated her affections "had I not been told that his were already engaged with Miss Fanny Appleton,* not openly I believe as yet but in aspiration. Isn't he lovely and hasn't he got the nicest face and the sweetest smile you ever saw? I hope I shan't see him again or I am afraid the illusion will be dispelled." But she did see him again the next month, and the illusion was not dispelled. She was attending another party, and, though she "only had word" with "the beautiful Mr. Charles Jackson," she concluded it was "perhaps well ... for it would be melancholy to throw away one's affections hopelessly

* Frances Elizabeth Appleton, daughter of Robert and Rebecca Wentworth Appleton of Brookline, was exactly the same age as Alice. Her father was a distant cousin of the Frances Elizabeth Appleton who married Henry Wadsworth Longfellow.

from the start. His hair is what I find now my greatest snare, but I must say its beauty is somewhat counterbalanced by the tone of his voice which you may remember is not particularly musical in its quality."

Over a year later she told Annie that she was about to attend a dinner party at the Morses', "where I shall see the beautiful Mr. Charley Jackson, for whom I still cherish an unhappy and perfectly hopeless passion, he being still equally hopeless and passionate about Miss Fanny Appleton. Things are all wrong aren't they?" And several months after that she and William dined with E. L. Godkin and Charles Jackson, "the former as uproarious and the latter as beautiful and seductive as usual. My passion grows, its fortunate I see him rarely for I am told that it wd. be altogether wild in me to nourish the faintest hope, Miss Appleton still reigning supreme over his affections. I saw her the other day at the Morses. She does not attract me in the least, but I am forced to confess that she is not bad-looking, its painful, but true. I refrained from looking in the glass for some time after I got home. Its most inconvenient to be possessed of so tender and apparently undesired an organ as mine."

Alice then turned from the wistful to the comic, presenting her tender, undesired heart as "seriously threatened again the other night at Ellen Gurney's dinner-table, and it was only through immense self-control and the knowledge of his married condition to which I couldn't shut my eyes for a minute, but what they would open upon his stout washer-womany wife who sat like a great sun-flower opposite me, that I preserved any tolerable equanimity. Perhaps you will be surprised when you hear that my charmer was Mr. Moorfield Story.* I used to know him slightly long ago but never then understood my advantages, perhaps if I had I might have sat in the place of the sun-flower! Now what under the sun did he want to go off to Washington for that creature [for]! its a mystery of mysteries! But he is an adorable creature at any rate."

There is no further mention of Charles Jackson, who did marry Frances Elizabeth Appleton in 1876.† Alice's description of her non-romance

---

* Moorfield Story (1845–1929) was a lawyer, author, and publicist. He had graduated from Harvard College and then from the law school in the late 1860s. Immediately after finishing law school, he served as clerk for the Senate Foreign Relations Committee in Washington, and as secretary to its chairman, Charles Sumner. Then in 1869 he began a law practice in Boston. Although he was quite successful as a lawyer, Story failed to fulfill his own political ambitions. He was a frank advocate of unpopular causes, supporting the rights of black people and American Indians. In 1870 he married Gertrude Cutts, the "stout washer-womany wife" to whom Alice refers.

† They had five children. In 1879, Jackson and Lawrence Curtis went into partner-

with Jackson sounds more like an adolescent crush than a grand passion. Because she was diffident about her own feelings, it is impossible to tell how strong they were. The episode may have been more painful than Alice lets on. It may also have been largely invented to provide a lively story for her correspondence with Annie, and to include herself in the tide of romance that seemed to be sweeping up everyone around her.

Whatever Alice's feelings for Charles Jackson were, they brought her as close as she ever came to a conventional "affair of the heart." She appears never to have entered seriously into a relationship with a man, or even to have surmised what that might mean. The men she liked were involved with other women; the rest were rude gorillas or flimsy sentimentalists. Love affairs, as she told Annie, had much more appeal in novels than they did in real life.

Alice envied men and resented the disadvantages femininity entailed. When Rob's first child, Edward Holton James, was born in 1873, William wrote to his sister from Florence, "I congratulate you on the noble sex of the creature. The hollowness of your dogmas about women are shown by your joy (impossible to conceal from me even at this distance) that it is not one." And when Wilky's first child, Joseph Cary, arrived in 1874, Alice announced to Annie Ashburner, "I am so glad that it is a boy and not another miserable girl brought into existence." (Robertson's wife gave birth to a girl, Mary Walsh James, in August 1875; four months later, Wilky and his wife had a girl and named her Alice. The first Alice told Annie only that "we have had one good present in the shape of a little niece born on the 24th, making the fourth grandchild.")

In the summer of 1874, Alice had gone with Aunt Kate to the Breadloaf Inn at Ripton, Vermont. There she found horseback-riding the "greatest of all delights." With "excellent" horses, "your humble servant" (she told Annie) "has had two ecstatic experiences. More she would have had if it were not for her disgusting sex." An incident that autumn at Brattleboro, where she went with Kate and the Bootts in search of good saddle horses,* exacerbated her sense of the "disgusting" quality of her sex. An old gentleman came to see them there one eve-

---

ship to form the Boston banking and brokerage firm of Jackson and Curtis. It is still in business as Paine Webber Jackson and Curtis.

* There was a famous water-cure sanatorium at Brattleboro, to which a number of ailing Bostonians periodically retired for rest and convalescence. Alice may have gone to "take the waters," in 1874, as well as to find good horses.

ning, and the next day (reported Alice later to Annie) he asked one of the other ladies "whether she thought Miss James would have him. Imagine the flutteration within my bosom! At last I was to have the privilege of declining matrimony and of escaping the mortification of descending to the grave a spinster, not from choice of the sweet lot, but from dire necessity. But, alas! no such fate for me, the man was a wretch, it being his habit to destroy the peace of any maiden who might come along, by this airy little remark. My fate, which if he had only spoken I should look upon as rapturous, is as humdrum and hopeless as ever."

Alice's response to this cruel joke was surprisingly mild for someone so capable of scornful fury. It was as if she looked for nothing better from men, expecting them to prey on female weakness. Flimsy, discourteous, obtuse (for not seeing her superiority to the women they chose to marry), men lived up to her expectation that they would fail to live up to her expectations.

•

Alice's sense of her adult self derived much more from her relations with other women than from her relations with men. Her loving, playful, even flirtatious language in letters to her friends is characteristic of nineteenth-century correspondence between women and should not be misread as literally sexual.* Nonetheless, the warmth and intensity in these letters to female friends present striking contrasts to the awkwardness and stiff formality of Alice's relations with extrafamilial men.

When Sara Sedgwick did not return to Cambridge on time, Alice threatened to elope with the butcher boy. When Alice did not hear from Annie Ashburner, she feared "that you are growing to despise yr. humble American friend. If such be the case, pray Oh! pray never let me know, for it would afflict me deeply, my sentiments for thee being unalterable! How strange it will be after all these years to meet and have a regular talk once more, such as we were wont to indulge in on those Sunday afternoons when you used to come and sit with me whilst I lay on the bed. I do not pine for the lyings on the bed, but I must say that an occasional confabulation wd. be refreshing to the soul." And when she heard Annie was homesick in London, Alice asked if there were not in all London "some one young woman with whom you can commune? . . . or mayhap

---

* See Caroll Smith-Rosenberg, "The Female World of Love and Ritual: Relations between Women in Nineteenth-Century America," *Signs,* vol. I, no. 1 (Autumn 1975), p. 1.

is my Nancy difficult to suit? Would you like to know what would fulfill, at the present moment, my highest ideal of earthly happiness? Nothing more than to be driving thro' the streets of London town, with thee by my side, in a hansom-cab! Now, this consummation of bliss, with the exception of one trifling element, is constantly attainable by you — so why, oh! why, are you not happy? It can't be possible that the absence of the few molecules which go to make up the person of yr. humble servant, shd. poison all yr. joy. I am too modest to think that!"

When men failed to get "impassioned" about Alice, she reacted with derision and reproof. When she felt unloved by her female friends, she was undone. The familiar sense of her own *badness* came to the surface with women. To Sara she wrote, "My joy at receiving your letter this morning was somewhat tempered by my having so little deserved it. But I shall not bother you with excuses for the very good reason that I have none to give. Original sin is my only refuge, I was born bad and I never have recovered." Only the love of her virtuous friends could save her, at least temporarily, from herself. To Fanny Morse: ". . . I have been quite consoled for this bothersome world by a little sight of Sara the other day. When I got home & reflected that you and she were both in it & that you both condescended to look upon me in a friendly manner I came to the conclusion that I couldn't be so abjectly base as I seemed to be to myself. Pray don't abandon me in disgust for my only hope of salvation will be gone."

Though Alice was quick to find herself and her sex "disgusting," she was also a fierce public defender of female solidarity. One evening at E. L. Godkin's, Jane Norton was expounding on women and marriage in "the most idiotic conversation," Alice reported to Annie. "She said that she thought all these Boston women instead of devoting themselves to painting, clubs, societies, etc. ought to stay at home in a constant state of matrimonial expectation. They were all so happy together that men said to themselves, Oh! she's so happy we won't marry her! which was a new view that men were attracted by depressed & gloomy females, and also that they generally married them from compassion. She also abused their habit of wearing waterproofs — her own gown as she was speaking was of so hideous a description that I shd. have been only too thankful if I had only had a water proof to cover her up with. Whether it was all palaver to please Mr. G. I do not know but whatever it was it was *awfully* foolish. Don't you think its despicable for women to run each other

down before men? I always have thought it the shabbiest sort of syco-
phancy."

•

In the late 1870s, Alice found something to do besides "stay at home in a
constant state of matrimonial expectation." She began work with a
group of Boston women called the Society to Encourage Studies at
Home, a correspondence school for women started by Anna Eliot Ticknor in 1873. "The purpose of this society," announced a pamphlet published in 1876,

> is to induce young ladies to form the habit of devoting some part of every day
> to study of a systematic and thorough kind. Even if the time devoted daily to
> this use is short, much can be accomplished by perseverance; and the habit
> soon becomes a delightful one. To carry out this purpose, it is proposed to
> arrange courses of reading and plans of work, from which ladies may select
> one or more, according to their taste and leisure; to aid them from time to
> time with directions and advice; and, finally, to distribute to them annually,
> certificates of progress . . .
>
> This Society does not, however, wish to attain its end by any factitious ex-
> citement, and does not desire publicity . . .

Statement of Purpose, Society to
Encourage Studies at Home

Anna Eliot Ticknor lived in downtown Boston in her parents' man-
sion at 9 Park Street. Her father, George Ticknor, the first professor of
modern languages at Harvard, was the author of *History of Spanish Literature.* He was also a founder and the first president of the Boston Public
Library. In an attempt to reform the educational system at Harvard, he
introduced elective courses for undergraduates. Miss Ticknor's mother,
the former Anna Eliot, held a famous literary salon in her parlor and even
more select gatherings in the library upstairs. Miss Ticknor inherited her
father's concern for education and both her parents' interest in literature;
she also developed a special interest of her own, the education of women.

In the decades following the Civil War, small colleges and academies
for women had begun to spring up across the United States.* Anna

---

* In 1872, the Women's Education Association petitioned the Harvard Corporation
to consider granting degrees to women. The corporation, through Harvard president
Charles W. Eliot, turned down the request. Seven years later, in 1879, the Harvard
"Annex" (predecessor of Radcliffe College) was founded.

Ticknor, who had had all the educational advantages of Boston's schools for girls as well as proximity to the Harvard intellectual community, determined to share her education with women who lived far from the new academies and established centers of learning. She decided on a flexible organization that could reach out to women all over the country and meet their special educational needs by mail. Her aims were not radical. She did not challenge prevalent assumptions about woman's place in the home; instead, she intended to provide support and instruction for women in order to make possible "new sources of progress and pleasure to mothers and their children within their own homes, and without hindering in any way domestic duties and claims." She wanted to assist women "to form habits of study, without professing anything technical or learned," and she told a friend, "It is, after all, not absolute instruction that we offer so much as guidance, criticism and sympathy." ·But though she was no revolutionary, Anna Eliot Ticknor was original in trying to interest all classes of women in her program; she saw education as an enhancing of life rather than as training for a particular career, and she had more in mind than book-learning.

In her work with the society, Miss Ticknor constantly stressed the importance of health in women's lives. In the first months of the society's existence she wrote to a friend, "I am enjoying the feeling that I dare to be busy, for the first time in many years, during which I have been an invalid." Knowing from personal experience about the problems of ill health and the obstacles they posed to mental development, Miss Ticknor aimed to help "delicate" women cultivate their minds and to keep young girls from falling into lifelong habits of debility.

In 1874 the society issued a little paper called *Health,* giving the titles of some useful books for the readers' further consideration.* Soon, however, a more extensive primer on hygiene seemed in order, and Miss Ticknor drafted a manuscript with the head of the society's science department. Published in 1878, it was distributed to the students of the society free of charge. "Between the old ascetic idea that there is virtue in disregarding the body, and the opposite tendency, always common, to

---

* Four had been published by the London Society for the Promotion of Christian Knowledge: *Personal Care of Health,* by E. A. Parkes; *Food,* by A. J. Bernays; and *Guild of Good Life* and *Household Health,* both by B. W. Richardson. Also listed were *The Human Body,* by H. N. Martin (Henry Holt, New York), the *Primer of Physiology,* by M. Foster (Appleton, New York), *Home Sanitation, a Manual for Housekeepers* (Ticknor & Fields, Boston), and *American Health Primers* (Blakiston, Philadelphia).

indulge the body by luxurious living, lies the truth," begins the *Health* pamphlet, "that the human body is a wonderful instrument, on the wise management of which depends our power of accomplishing, through its use, certain objects, held in high esteem by thinking people." Science had revealed the true laws of physical health, and all educated people had a duty to study and obey them. The body, like a machine, ran on air, water, and food, and women as homemakers had in their hands the power to control humanity's fuel supplies — to keep their homes free of "dangerous air" and polluted water, and provide their families with nourishing food.

But the body was not moved only by mechanical forces. The second half of the *Health* tract discusses "the motor power seated in the brain and the nerves" and relations between mind and body. "If the mind needs a healthy body for its service, the body also needs an active, healthy mind to act upon it, and there must not be too great a difference between mental and muscular development." The nerves and brain, like the body, could be overtaxed, but they could also *lack* healthful exercise — and it was this understimulation that seemed to the society most conducive to insanity. "The best preventive of mental disease, even in those predisposed to it, is education, or wisely directed mental activity, leading to a knowledge of the proper ways of living."

The authors of the pamphlet saw education as a preventive, rather than a cause, of mental disease; but Miss Ticknor, like the nineteenth-century doctors who treated neurasthenics, advocated a "right balance of mental and physical growth." To avoid excitement and overstimulation of the nerves,* women should shun the extremes of absorption in the "carking cares" of housework with no intellectual activity on the one hand, and concentration on the intellect with no physical exercise on the other. Taken a little at a time, brain work should alternate with exercise and

* "The high-strung nerves respond to an eager craving, which, like the mediaeval saintly asceticism, puts conscience on the side of work, reasonable or unreasonable. Delighting in the use of their intellects, intensely alive to all kinds of responsibility, desirous to crowd every waking moment with interest and action, these women fancy that, because they enjoy all this, it is right and wholesome. It is no more right and wholesome than over-indulgence in eating and drinking. For them, when the inevitable results come, there must be rest and fresh air; rest *in* fresh air; frequent nourishment; variety of small amusements, acting on the mind as fresh air does on the body; not much direct expression of sympathy. When the normal state is restored, they will know better how to use mind and body as not abusing them."

housework. A woman's day should consist of eight hours of sleep, three or four hours of meals and rest, and an equal division of the remaining twelve between mental and physical activity. Each woman must learn to accept her personal limitations and live with them in mind. Susceptibility to climate was one; another was social — "our quicker pace of living, the effect of modern invention and enterprise," which made life more stimulating to eager, sensitive temperaments and increased the susceptibility of the nervous system. The pamphlet closed with an encomium to self-control:

> Lose not thyself nor give thy humors way,
> God gave them to thee under lock and key.

Every student of the society received a copy of *Health*, which was revised and reprinted four times. In addition, individuals and women's educational associations from all over the United States wrote in for copies. Health and hygiene were topics of absorbing interest to women throughout the country in the last decades of the nineteenth century; a tract that proposed guidelines for good housekeeping and a personal balance of mental and physical work had tremendous popular appeal.

•

From the first, Miss Ticknor was determined not to advertise the society, saying that "if it is really needed it will make itself known." She was right. In 1873, several Boston women from backgrounds similar to hers volunteered to teach the courses.* Some had teaching experience. Others simply wanted to share with others whatever knowledge they had. The teachers, called managers, made up a large lending library from their own bookshelves, and organized themselves into departments of history, art, English, French and German literature, and natural science. (Credit for the inclusion of science in the society's curriculum, at a time when science was just beginning to be recognized as important in the liberal education of men, goes to Elizabeth Cary Agassiz.) Students had to be at least seventeen years old. They paid $2.00 (eventually $3.00) a term, and

---

* They were Elizabeth Cary Agassiz, Elizabeth Cleveland, Lucretia Crocker, Ellen Hooper Gurney, Katharine Peabody Loring, Ellen Mason, Elizabeth Perkins, and Mrs. Ticknor. Miss Ticknor was the society's secretary and treasurer. Her cousin Samuel Eliot, who was a historian, an educator, and a philanthropist, was appointed chairman.

their numbers increased so rapidly that the society soon became self-supporting. In the first term, forty-five women from seven states studied twenty-nine subjects in six departments. Each student received an announcement of the subjects offered; she then chose her subject, paid her fee, and received a receipt, along with three questions: How old was she? Had she been educated at public or private schools? Was she a teacher? She also received a letter from the head of her department with further questions about the subject she wanted to study. When she had answered these, she was assigned a correspondent. Teacher and student planned their reading together. Then the teacher sent off the first book and the student began to read and make notes from memory. At the beginning of each month she wrote to her adviser, enclosing a specimen of her notes. The teacher's reply sometimes asked for an abstract of the reading, and sometimes posed questions as an exam to be taken on the honor system.

In the society's second year, still without advertising, the number of students doubled to 82. William Dean Howells published an account of the society's work in the *Atlantic* in September 1875; other papers and magazines picked up the story; and by the fall of 1875 the enrollment was up to 213 students from 24 states and Canada.* More teachers were needed, and the departments could now be more extensively subdivided. In December 1875, Fanny Morse recruited Alice James to teach history for the society.

Alice's interest in history had grown from curiosity about contemporary politics into an avocation. She studied history books, devoured historical novels, and read all the memoirs, biographies, and volumes of letters she could get her hands on. In the late 1870s she was reading, among other things, Macaulay's *Life and Letters* (by his nephew Sir George Otto Trevelyan), Madame de Staël's memoirs, Mackenzie Wallace's *Russia, Daniel Deronda,* and Mérimée. Her favorite historians were English: William E. H. Lecky and John Richard Green. From London in 1877 Henry reported on glimpsing these two favorites at his club, the Athenaeum: "Lecky the historian, and Green *ditto* (author of Alice's favorite work [*A Short History of the English People*] — the fat volume which she gave me) have just come and seated themselves in front of me: two such grotesque specimens of the rickety, intellectual Oxford cad that I can't forbear

---

* By the time the society ceased to function in 1897, it had taught a total of 7086 students, with a high-water mark of 1000 in 1882.

mentioning them. Only du Maurier, in *Punch,* could do them justice; and if Alice could see in the flesh her little wizened, crawling Green, with eyes like ill-made button-holes, she would take to her bed for a month and renounce her 'historic-reveries.' The delights of London are only equalled by its disillusionments."

This satirical vision did not send Alice to bed or precipitate a renunciation. Just after Christmas in 1875 she wrote to Annie Ashburner about her new "job": "I am with Miss Katharine Loring and have charge of the historical young women. I think I shall enjoy it and I know it will do me lots of good. Don't you want to become one of my students? I will write you the wisest of letters about any period of the world you choose."

Katharine Peabody Loring, of Beverly, was head of history, the largest of the society's departments. Working under her in 1876 were Alice and Fanny Appleton, Alice's rival for Charles Jackson's affections. That year the course covered the sixteenth century. The following year, the department expanded to offer courses in ancient, medieval, modern (beginning with the sixteenth century), and American history.

Alice's new career provided fresh fodder for teasing. When Annie made fun of it, Alice replied, "I was deeply hurt at your ridicule of my professional character. I assure you it is not a thing to be laughed at. Some day you may be only too happy to sit at my feet." The usual teaser, William, however, saw how important it was for Alice to have some work she cared about. He had been trying to find a job for her at Harvard's Museum of Comparative Anatomy, and when she began work with the society he reported to Henry that "Alice has got her historical professorship which will no doubt be an immense thing for her."

To be able to extend intellectual help to other women gave Alice more gratification than any work she had ever tried. Though she had failed to develop for herself the "systematic and thorough" habits of study free from "factitious excitement" advocated by the society, she welcomed the opportunity to help others achieve that end. "I had a letter this morning," she told Annie in the fall of 1876, "from a new student, who has as Wm. says the spirit of a Crusader. She has been most anxious to improve herself but owing to the discouragement she has received on all occasions she has feared that she would be nothing but 'a cipher in the world's history.' She is truly pathetic & lovely and I am sure I shall enjoy her greatly."

Six months later, in a letter to cheer up the homesick Annie in London, Alice indicated how much this new endeavor meant to her:

I wish that you had some work to do that amused you half as much as my society work does me ... You may laugh as much as you please, but I am nevertheless speaking the truth ... You see it can do very little harm to a poor uneducated maiden in the wilds of California, Kansas, Missouri, Michigan, Kentucky, Florida, Iowa, & Illinois (I have students in all those states) who have never seen but half-a-dozen books in their lives, to get a letter once a month from a semi-educated being in Boston who recommends and sends her good books to read and who has a very beneficial effect upon [*their* was crossed out and made into *her*] spelling (mind I don't say grammar, so you needn't laugh at my hers and theirs being somewhat mixed). We who have had all our lives more books than we know what to do with can't conceive of the feelings that people have for them who have been shut out from them always. They look upon them as something sacred apparently ... Now this is the sort of being that we want to help and that we do help, so I do not see that there can possibly be any harm in it ... I have to write between thirty and forty letters every month, but I have nought else of importance to do. Perhaps you may wonder at my sudden onslaught upon your indolent self, but I feared it must seem very silly to you, and as it is what I care most about just now, I did not want you to judge it without a hearing.

Chapter Eleven

Dark Waters

SINCE ALICE'S RETURN from Europe in 1872, her health had gone through its usual (by this time) range of improvements and reversals. When she could be active, she thrived — working with Miss Ticknor's society, riding and driving horses, traveling, keeping a greenhouse, organizing a women's luncheon club for intellectual discussion. In the fall of 1876 she reported herself to Sara Sedgwick "so well that to be any better would be quite superfluous."

Riding and driving, in particular, renewed the sense of autonomy that had meant so much to her in Europe. Her first letter from Vermont in the summer of 1874, all about riding, was pronounced a "squeal of delight" by her family, and Mary James answered, "Your career in life is at last opened to you, what a blessing!" Alice's father bought her a phaeton, and Aunt Kate reported to Rob in June of 1876 that the ailing Henry Sr. had "just come in from a two hours' drive in Alice's little wagon. Of course she always holds the reins, as in it she considers herself in her own kingdom — and he seems to have enjoyed it, in spite of rather a summerish temperature."

Characteristically, Alice made light of her low points in letters to her friends. In the winter of 1873 she told Annie Ashburner of "an increase of feebleness in my upper story which though lofty never was you know particularly distinguished for its solidity." During that winter, her mother emitted a cry of mystified anguish to Henry about Alice's relapse: "Poor child! *why* is it that she has gone back so? Can there be any thing in this climate to account for it? . . . She does not feel from her experience that any other climate would suit her better to *live* in, but says she thinks that change is the thing for her; and it was altogether that that did her good last summer."

Alice wanted simultaneously to "take the reins" in her own hands and to be taken care of. Events toward the end of the 1870s highlighted her dependence on her family and her failure to find a new domestic harbor of her own. Within one year, 1877–1878, three of her closest allies among the still-unmarried in effect deserted her.

In the spring of 1877 Sara Sedgwick had gone to live for a while with relatives in England. In September, Alice wrote, "So you have betaken yourself, madam to Yarmouth to find a spouse after the manner of your great grandmother. It seems a strange matrimonial fishing-ground, herring, having hitherto been my only association with those waters. Good luck to you, however! May he only not carry with him too strong a reminder of whence you have hooked him. If they bite in numbers, bear in mind the lone lorn spinster you have left behind." That fall, Sara fell in love not with a herring but with a banker named William Erasmus Darwin, eldest son of the great naturalist.* She was married in November, at the Darwins' home at Basset in Southampton. Henry James, who spent a day there shortly after the wedding, described William Darwin to Quincy Street as a "gentle, kindly, reasonable, liberal, bald-headed, dull-eyed British-featured, sandy-haired little *insulaire,* who will to a certainty never fail of goodness and carefulness towards his wife and who must have merit, and a great deal of it, to have appreciated merit so retiring, appealing, and delicate as Sara's ... Altogether, she struck me as very happy and comfortable, and I should have great confidence in Darwin and his prosaic virtues."

Alice pressed for details of the wedding, Sara's state of mind, and Mr. Darwin's character. Though worried by reports that Sara's sister Theodora was "not rapturous about brother William ... I consoled myself very soon, by remembering that rapture was not her way and that Sir Philip Sidney himself would doubtless have met with but mild approval at her hands. She would have been afraid of compromising herself by showing what she calls 'Boston enthusiasm.' "

* The Darwins and the Charles Eliot Nortons had become close friends when the Nortons were living in England in the late 1860s, and Sara, as Mrs. Norton's sister, was included in the family friendship, which led eventually to her own marriage.

When the newly married couple came to Boston the following fall, Alice found herself delighted with Mr. Darwin and disappointed in Sara, who seemed "wretchedly forlorn and unhappy." Alice could not forgive her, she told Fanny Morse, "for not being able to make some enthusiastic expression about her delightful husband, for how is existence possible unless we resolutely make the most of all our blessings?"

A year after Sara's wedding, in the fall of 1878, Annie Ashburner announced her engagement to Francis Gardiner Richards of Gardiner, Maine. Alice answered that she rejoiced in the announcement but news it was not, as she had followed the progress of the romance all winter: "I have always had a weakness for having my friends married but I confess that I began to feel rather hopeless about you buried among all those wretched John Bulls. I am therefore proportionally grateful to Mr. Richards for showing himself to be a man of so much discrimination & I congratulate you most warmly dear Nanny upon having secured the affection of a man so highly esteemed as Mr. Richards seems to be by all who know him." Annie and Richards were married in London in February of 1879.*

On August 7, 1878, Alice would turn thirty. She had no prospect of marriage, and "nought else of importance to do" (as she told Annie) besides her work with the Society to Encourage Studies at Home. In May, Sara Darwin was a bride of six months, Annie was being courted by Mr. Richards, and William James announced that he, too, would do "the usual thing": he was going to marry — a woman named Alice.

He had met Alice Howe Gibbens early in 1876 after his father came home from a meeting of the Radical Club in Boston to announce that he had just seen William's future wife. Intrigued, William went to the next meeting of the club to have a look at the attractive, frank, natural young woman he would, in fact, marry. She had just turned twenty-seven, and was living with her widowed mother and sisters at 18 Garden Street, in Cambridge. Her father, a physician and an alcoholic, had shot himself in 1865. The Gibbenses were not rich, and the highly practical Alice had

---

* Henry reported to Alice on the wedding: "Annie A. looked extremely pretty (in yellow satin, with a yellow veil) and appeared to great advantage. The breakfast was very sumptuous and agreeable and the whole affair pleasant, save that at the end, her angry father, coming with me to the door, broke out into a torrent of protestations and imprecations. I am afraid she has had no easy time — but S[amuel] Ashburner is a selfish old turk."

worked as a schoolteacher for several years in Europe and Boston to support their female household.

William courted Alice Gibbens for two long, difficult years. Still tormented by physical and mental troubles, he doubted whether he had the right to inflict himself on a healthy young woman (he was thirty-six) or on their eventual offspring. After some months of his agonizing indecision, Miss Gibbens decided that, though she loved him, she would burden his life, and went off to Canada for the summer of 1877 in order to allow their feelings to subside. At the end of the summer William wrote Bob that "the affair I confided to you at Newport is fallen through. I charge you to breathe no word of it *ever,* to any one. It is a painful business, but she is an angel incarnate." She was pure, straight, and true, said William; he was a sinner, a child, an errant soul. But by the spring of 1878 he had persuaded Alice Gibbens to be his wife. Still hypochondriacal and troubled by his back and eyes, he wrote to Bob the night before his wedding that he now thought the strain of the year plus the "probably unwholesome excitement of an engagement" was the cause, and that he would be cured by a combination of his wife and a honeymoon in the Adirondacks. "Every Dr. I have ever spoken to has said that matrimony ought to be the best possible mode of life, for me. Alice Gibbens is an angel if ever there was one — I take her for her moral more than her intellectual qualities."*

In later years, he would see her as having saved his life. William's successful marriage probably contributed even more toward the "cure" of his emotional troubles than his philosophical resolutions of the early 1870s did. His wife's calm practicality offset his fitful nervousness: she understood his moods, catered to his whims, protected him from the outside world and the cares of domesticity, and provided an order within which he was free to come and go as he pleased. She was not afraid to oppose him, and frequently won her point. Directly descended, in the line of selfless devotion and divine maternity, from William's mother and grandmothers, she seemed all goodness and capability, asking nothing for herself, nurturing her husband and children in equal measure. William later said he had been a diseased boy whom she lifted from the dust and transformed into a man. And his description of her when their infant son Herman was dying in 1885 bears a strong resemblance to what

---

* Almost twenty years earlier, Henry James, Sr., had written to his mother from Europe describing William as "much dearer to my heart for his moral worth than for his intellectual."

he called, in *The Principles of Psychology,* "the most simply beautiful moral spectacle that human life affords ... the passionate devotion of a mother — ill herself, perhaps — to a sick or dying child." At eighteen months, Herman came down with whooping cough; the other children were taken off to the country. Herman's mother, who caught the disease herself, nursed him round the clock, but he contracted pneumonia and died on July 9, 1885. William wrote to Henry: "The great part of it to me has been the spectacle of Alice through it all. The old word Motherhood, like so many other old words, suddenly gets and [sic] unsuspected meaning. For six weeks not a night of adequate sleep — for 9 days and nights never as much as three hours in the whole 24, and yet every day as fresh and passionate and eager to do and work as if it were the first. Of course there will now be a collapse. But she is so essentially mellow and free from morbidness, that with all her sensibility I fear nothing bad."

•

Henry Jr., writing from London in 1878, wanted to know what system the family had worked out to distinguish between the two Alices; he got no reply. Six months after the wedding he beseeched his sister, "What *do* you call each other, for distinction's sake? — *please answer this!*" There was no answer because there was no system. William's wife was referred to on occasion as "Mrs. William," "William's Alice," "Mrs. Alice," and by William as "my Alice"; her sister-in-law was sometimes designated "sister Alice" or "our Alice."

Another Alice James, a "peerless specimen of 'New England womanhood,' " possessed of all the health, strength, virtue, and competence that the first Alice James lacked, presented serious competition. The romance between William James and his sister had, if anything, intensified during the 1870s, with William addressing her always as "little beauty" and "sweetlington," and writing his familiar self-absorbed love letters. From Dresden in 1873: "Thou seemest to me so beautiful from here, so intelligent, so affectionate, so in all respects *the thing* that a brother should most desire that I don't see how when I get home I can do any thing else than sit with my arm round thy waist appealing to the [sic] for confirmation of every thing I say, for approbation of everything I do, and admiration for everything I am, and never, never for a moment being disappointed. What I shall do for you in return for this excellence 'tis for you rather than me to say, but I hope not to fall short of any of your exactions." He still teased about her role in his romantic life: "Beloved beautlet ... You will have to provide a substitute if you don't wish me to pop the question to Miss Whitwell." And Mary James had reported to Henry Jr. that Alice's health, spirits, wit, intelligence, and personal charm had greatly impressed William on his return from Europe: "He is very sweet upon her, in his own original way, and I think she enjoys very much his charming badinage."

Teasing about female rivals was one thing. Marrying one was another. Whatever agitation William's flirtatious attentions caused his sister, they also flattered and excited her — and they were the only consistent, overt, amorous attentions she ever received from a man. To this brother, whom she admired and loved, she seemed at times the most important woman on earth. She returned his mocking banter, and undoubtedly, in a suppressed way, his sexual curiosity. His engagement to a paragon of health and virtue was a profound betrayal.

William James and Alice Gibbens announced their engagement in May 1878,* but its imminence was clear earlier in the spring. In April,

---

* Wilky greeted the news with a strange, joking mix of congratulation and hostility. He was working at the North Chicago Rolling Mill Company in Milwaukee, and he wrote on May 16:

> My beloved brother William James
>
> Your letter announcing your engagement was received today: It fills my soul with joy unutterable at the thought of what must be your contentment and happiness. It is certainly the greatest piece of news you have ever inflicted upon the world, and I suppose the greatest event that has ever transpired in the family. I feel a good deal like going out to our works and blowing them up or setting fire to the town, or doing something equally momentous at the thought of such a proceeding and such a consummation for you. — I wish you would take Miss Gibbens by the hand for me and tell her that she must certainly be the best specimen of womankind that has ever adorned the earth; that you are a being (take you for all you are) who are worthy of such a woman and would be likely only to choose just such a one for your wife. On a le droit de parler franchement pour une fois de sa vie upon such events as these, and I most heartily and lovingly congratulate you both ...
>
> I can imagine seriously speaking no greater good to befall you than a love of this kind. — It will probably be the one thing that will do you the most good in the world: — My own experience is of course just what I anticipate for you, only in a far greater sense than can ever befall you. — I should have been by this time deep down in Hell if it had not been for my wife.
>
> — You have other qualities and other features of character which would save you *any way*, but you have an intellectual force to your being, which must be very much helped and softened by the influence of love and all that it brings with it. —
>
> Your loving brother,
> Garth W. James

"sister Alice" took spectacularly to her bed. Mary James described this new crisis to Robertson as "a nervous breakdown of a very serious character — an aggravated recurrence of her old troubles."

When William announced his engagement, Mary wrote to Alice Gibbens how disappointed she was not to be able to call on her prospective daughter-in-law, "and Alice much more so if that be possible, but she is too unwell to make such an effort herself, and also too unwell for me to be willing to leave her." The two Alices had become cordial but not intimate friends. In March of 1877, Alice James invited Alice Gibbens to a meeting of the lunch club she had organized (a group unconnected with the Bee), in order to introduce the object of William's affections to some of her own friends.* No further record of the two young women's reactions to each other at this period has survived.† From later evidence, it appears that William's fiancée took an early dislike to the querulous future sister-in-law whose illness so disrupted the pleasures of her engagement and wedding. And though sister Alice may not have written down her thoughts on this formidable foe, her breakdown constituted, among other things, a dramatic objection.

In the middle of May, the family summoned Aunt Kate from New York to help "share the cares and anxieties" of the Quincy Street household.

In June came a slight improvement. Alice's "periods of depression and feeling of inability to meet life are less frequent," reported Mrs. James to Bob, "and in the interval she is quite cheerful and like herself. She is able now when driving to take the reins herself, and has done so for an hour and a half at a time. She always enjoyed this very much, and the country is so exquisitely lovely just now, that I am in hopes she will get great gain by being out in this way."

From England, Henry wrote Alice of his sadness at the news of her troubles, observing that "it seems rather inconsiderate of William to have selected such a moment for making merry." He told Lizzie Boott that his parents' "satisfaction in William's engagement appears to have

* The club met fortnightly, for intellectual discussion. Several years after Alice left Boston for London, Marny Storer Warner revived the lunch party "you started so long ago," wrote William's wife to her sister-in-law, "save that it is confined to Cambridge ladies and only eight of them."

† All the correspondence between William and his wife has been donated to the Houghton Library at Harvard with the stipulation that it not be opened to the public until the year 2023.

been a good deal toned down by the fact that when it occurred poor Alice was alarmingly ill — they were much distressed about her." And he commiserated with William: "Yes, I know it must be a sad summer in Cambridge."

Alice was too ill to attend the wedding ceremony in July. "I hope her abnegation," wrote Henry to his mother, "will bear rich fruits in the way of enabling her to enjoy their conjugal and fraternal society afterwards. I think of her — tell her — all the while." Three months later, he instructed his father to tell Alice that the worse her health was, the more her brother cared for her — "only, if she takes that as an alleviation, she must not take it as an encouragement to sickliness." Henry's warning, issued in jest, came years too late. Alice had long since learned that "the worse" her health got, the more tender, solicitous care she would receive.

Throughout her life, but especially in these acute breakdowns, Alice saw herself as bad and weak, and everyone else as perfect and strong. At her worst moments, she turned on herself as if some awful other person lived in her body; then the "good" Alice would revile the sinner. At other times, she simply sank into silent depression, feeling (as her mother told Rob) incapable of meeting life, needing others to care for her as they would a young child. "In the old days," she wrote later in her diary, "when, month after month, and year after year, I used to get my 'attacks,' and Mother and Father would watch by me through the long nights, I used to cry out to them to know what would become of me when I lost them."

William's engagement and marriage precipitated Alice's 1878 breakdown not simply because it seemed a desertion, but also because it brought her face to face with familiar questions about love and what would happen to her without it. And beneath those torments lay an unacknowledged sense that she had never really *had* it. Later, long after her parents had died, she looked back at the "vast and responsive reservoirs of the past," and it seemed to her "incredible that I should have drunk, as a matter of course, at that ever springing fountain of responsive love and bathed all unconscious in that flood of human tenderness." Those memories housed the inverse truth of illusion. Alice longed for fountains of responsive love. Her father and William, in particular, kept talking about their floodlike, overwhelming tides of feeling for her; but the emotion directed her way usually had more to do with the giver than the receiver: in its extravagance and drama, it drew insistent attention to itself.

For Alice to have acknowledged the absence of love in her life, however, would have meant giving up hope of receiving it. Instead, she extolled the "responsive reservoirs" of family affection and turned on herself, through illness and depression,* for the sense of lack she did experience. This way, she kept alive the hope of getting what she wanted. And in punishing herself, in effect, with physical suffering, she exacted a measure of revenge — making her family suffer in sympathy, and forcing them to care for her (in both senses of the phrase).

Her father acted as principal caretaker — nurse, companion, and confidant — throughout the long siege of this illness. In a letter he wrote to Robertson in the fall of 1878, his own optimism colored his description of Alice's "fantastic" troubles. And this apology to Bob, who was also in emotional straits, indicates how completely Alice's illness had gained for her the center of the family attention. "The truth is," wrote Henry Sr. to his youngest son, "that we are so wholly immersed in Alice's malady, that we are apt to think there is no one else sick and suffering in the world, unless we are distinctly told of it." He wanted, he said, to invite Bob's family for a visit but felt unfit to entertain them "while Alice is half the time, indeed more than half, on the verge of insanity and suicide. Any other care upon our hands, while this absorbing state of things endures, would be intolerable, especially to me whose own nerves would bear no stouter tension than they now have."

He then presented a singular view of the nature of Alice's breakdowns: "I feel very untroubled in mind about the *issue* of Alice's troubles, whatever material aspect it may assume. Her own inward peace and *inmost*

---

* Writing "Mourning and Melancholia" in 1917, Freud might have been describing Alice James during this illness: the "melancholic" patient represents himself as "worthless, incapable of any achievement and morally despicable; he reproaches himself, vilifies himself and expects to be cast out and punished. He abases himself before everyone and commiserates with his own relatives for being connected with anyone so unworthy. He . . . extends his self-criticism back over the past; he declares that he was never any better. This picture of a delusion of (mainly moral) inferiority is completed by sleeplessness and refusal to take nourishment, and — what is psychologically very remarkable — by an overcoming of the instinct which compels every living thing to cling to life."

William James, too, wrote about the kind of depression his sister was struggling with when he described, in a chapter of *The Principles of Psychology* called "The Consciousness of Self," how the "good or bad fortunes" of one's "social self," in the eyes of a loved one, cause the "most intense elation and dejection": "To his own consciousness he *is* not, so long as this particular social self fails to get recognition, and when it is recognized his contentment passes all bounds."

sanity are so clearly promoted by them as we see whenever she emerges from them. She has perfectly understood for a long time past that her frightful nervousness was a part of our trouble as a race, struggling to get free: that there was nothing in it peculiar to herself, and she never regards it as having the least sinister bearing upon her immortal interests. About these latter indeed I know no one whose mind is more clear & serene than hers. It is only the burden of the mortal life that she groans under, or is even distressed at. Poverty, sickness, pain, suffering of all sorts abounds around her, and when she falls under an influx of 'nervousness,' she seems to believe that these evils are just as consciously *present* to other minds as to her own, and that the whole world."

Alice had contemplated suicide:

One day . . . [continued her father to Robertson] when I was telling her that this persuasion grows out of a diabolic influx into the human mind from the spiritual world, to which something in her temperament rendered her peculiarly susceptible, and that we should all feel grateful to her for so stoutly resisting the persuasion, and fighting against it, she laughed at the idea of her not succumbing to it, "though she must confess that she hated it with all [her] heart," and then asked me whether I thought that suicide, to which at times she felt very strongly tempted, was a sin. I told her that I thought it was not a sin except where it was wanton, as when a person from a mere love of pleasurable excitement indulged in drink or opium to the utter degradation of her faculties, and often to the ruin of the human form in him; but that it was absurd to think it sinful when one was driven to it in order to escape bitter suffering, from spiritual influx, as in her case, or from some loathsome form of disease, as in others. I told her so far as I was concerned she had my full permission to end her life whenever she pleased; only I hoped that if ever she felt like doing that sort of justice to her circumstances, she would do it in a perfectly gentle way in order not to distress her friends. She then remarked that she was very thankful to me, but she felt that now she could perceive it to be her *right* to dispose of her own body when life had become intolerable, she could never do it: that when she had felt tempted to it, it was with a view to break bonds, or assert her freedom, but that now I had given her freedom to do in the premises what she pleased, she was more than content to stay by my side, and battle in concert with me against the evil that is in the world. I don't fear suicide much since this conversation, though she often tells me that she is strongly tempted still. But you see darling boy that as no three days slip by without some break down on her part, and my thoughts and fears are all claimed by her acute distress, I cannot do justice to interest so near and dear to me as the entertainment of you & dear little Mary and the children.

It is doubtful that Alice found much comfort in the idea that these paroxysms of mental and physical anguish had nothing to do with *her* but were simply part of the troubles of the race. Once again, her father insisted on her primal innocence, although she expressed in this crisis what she had told Sara Sedgwick lightly: "Original sin is my only refuge, I was born bad and I never have recovered." By refusing to acknowledge the truth of what Alice felt — by seeing good where she saw bad — Henry Sr. seems likely to have robbed this painful breakdown of whatever personal value it might have had. Alice was fighting for self-control and for a strengthening sense of moral responsibility. In placing blame on an external "diabolic influx" at war with her pristine soul, her father's exonerating analysis took responsibility and control out of her hands.

She clung to him during this protracted crisis but left no evidence that she shared his view of the situation. She laughed at his notion that she could fight off evil for all mankind. She had learned too well, ten years before, that evil conquered good and that she would succumb in the end even while hating the diabolical "with all her heart."

Exhausted from her struggle, unable to believe in victory, she thought about suicide. As far as the record shows, she never tried to kill herself, but the subject always fascinated her, and in her diary she commented approvingly on those whose suicides struck her as acts of moral autonomy. She read *Hamlet* again and again, and in the copybook at the front of her diary inscribed from Act I, scene 5:

> Why, what should be the fear?
> I do not set my life at a pin's fee;
> And for my soul, what can it do to that,
> Being a thing immortal?

(The last line of that speech, in fact, reads, "Being a thing immortal as itself," for Hamlet is talking of his father's ghost. Alice wrote out the whole line as it appears in the play, then crossed out "as itself.")

Her discussion with her father about suicide and sin suggests that she was more interested in the threat than in the act. Why, otherwise, ask? The question nodded to his theological authority, reaffirmed her interest in being good (she wouldn't want to commit a sin), and let him know she felt bad enough to self-inflict the ultimate wound. In 1868, Alice had wanted to knock her father's head off but had turned her fury on herself instead. Now, she threatened him with suicide. In this complicated way, she kept herself connected to him by adopting his covert view of her as unlovable except when helpless, fragile, childlike. At the same time, she defied him, seeing her inmost nature as anything but innocent. And in announcing that she might be evil enough to commit suicide, she put herself in a position of considerable power.

Her father gave her permission to kill herself. Pleasure was a sin, he said — a wanton indulgence in the excitement of self-destruction. And hostility was a sin — if she did kill herself, it should be in a perfectly gentle way so as not to distress her friends. But no sin attached to suicide as an escape from bitter suffering: not a free choice but a necessity, neither a sensual pleasure nor an act of anger, suicide as a "way of doing justice to your circumstances" would not damn her soul. This shrewd piece of exposition divested the act of its most attractive features. In addition, it skillfully parried one of the primary motives for the question — Alice's desire to hurt others by hurting herself (although it is hard to imagine either father or daughter actually believing that her suicide, even if committed in a perfectly gentle way, would not distress her "friends").

If he was contriving to stop her from killing herself — and perhaps a parent may be justified in going to any lengths to achieve that end — he nonetheless committed an act of moral violence of the sort he practiced on all his children with loving impunity throughout his life. If, however, her question was pleading covertly for recognition of a reality of her own, he failed to see it or respond. Taking credit, in his letter to Robertson, for preventing her suicide by granting her the right to commit it, he concluded that she was "more than content to stay by my side, and battle in concert with me against the evil that is in the world."

Alice's own remarks on her '78 breakdown, though even more than usually sparse, indicate how far this cheerful account diverged from the truth. Years later she described giving way to the "dominion" of physical symptoms, in particular "that mighty organ," her stomach: "No fiat of the fateful three was ever more irresistible than the decrees sent forth by that pivot of my being! Mentally no fate appalls me, but morally no crawling worm was ever so abject as I am before the convolutions of that nest of snakes coiling and uncoiling themselves. What pain remotely approaches the horror of those hours, which may swamp one at any moment, passed, second by second, hanging as it were by a cobweb to Sanity!" Her legs, too, exercised their "dominion" during this illness, for

Alice told Fanny Morse a full year later that "I am growing stronger all the time although I cannot do much or walk much yet."

She found what she called "moral prostration" much harder to bear than physical pain. Recovering slowly, she thanked Fanny late in the fall of 1878 for writing letters steadily throughout the long months of illness; Alice had been unable to reply, and now proclaimed, as usual, how little she deserved her friend's generosity. She had just resumed her correspondence at the end of November, and reported that at last she was no longer "an object of compassion. I shall have to admit, however, that I was pretty wretched through the summer and gave my poor family an immense amount of trouble, but for the last couple of months I have been learning to behave myself better and better all the time.

"My physical sufferings would have given me no concern, but my patience, courage & self-control all seemed to leave me like a flash & I was left high and dry. For a young woman who not only likes to manage herself but the rest of the world too, such a moral prostration taxed my common sense a good deal. But, I suppose I needed the lesson greatly and I only hope that it will bear some of the fruits that it ought."

Alice was sorry to hear that Fanny's sister, Mary, had been "shut up through the summer" in Paris, "losing so many of the beautiful sights that you were all enjoying. But how much I envy her! — convalescence in Europe seems such an easy process, where there are so many helps on every hand. When one can only take a passive part in life, the base, crude, blankness of nature here with nothing to call one out of one's self plays upon the soul, and makes the process of getting well a task and not a pleasure."

Almost fifteen years later, Alice added one more note to this spare account of what had really happened to her in 1878, a cryptic sentence written in her diary a month before she died. She described there what amounted to the death of her spirit — as if she had concluded in 1878 that *feeling* itself had to be abandoned: rather than suffer such despair again, she would prefer to feel nothing. She took, then, one more step along the difficult path of renunciation or spiritual suicide that she had started on at Newport in her adolescence.

If she could be concerned about the fate of her soul, she wrote in 1892, it would undoubtedly give a "savor of uncertainty" to the last moments of life, "but I never felt so absolutely uninterested in the poor, shabby old thing. The fact is, I have been dead so long and it has been simply such a grim shoving of the hours behind me as I faced a ceaseless possible horror, since that hideous summer of '78 when I went down to the deep sea, its dark waters closed over me, and I knew neither hope nor peace; that now it's only the shrivelling of an empty pea pod that has to be completed."

Chapter Twelve

Gains and Losses

ALICE HAD DESCRIBED to Fanny the bleak prospect of a passive convalescence in Cambridge — "the base, crude blankness of nature here
with nothing to call one out of one's self." She did, however, have something — actually, someone — to call her out of herself in the late 1870s:
Katharine Peabody Loring, the head of the history department at the Society to Encourage Studies at Home. Alice and Katharine had first met in
1873, but did not become friends until they worked together teaching
history. "I wish you could know Katharine Loring," wrote Alice to Sara
Darwin in the summer of 1879; "she is a most wonderful being. She has
all the mere brute superiority which distinguishes man from woman
combined with all the distinctively feminine virtues. There is nothing
she cannot do from hewing wood and drawing water to driving run-away
horses and educating all the women in North America."

Katharine Loring had been born on May 21, 1849, nearly a year after
Alice James. Her family traced its way back through the history of New
England to 1634, when the first Loring came to Hingham, Massachusetts, from Devonshire, England. Her male ancestors were shipowners,
merchants, distillers, lawyers, judges, and state senators; most of them
went to Harvard. Her father, Caleb William Loring, practiced law and
was president of the Plymouth Cordage Company. Her mother, Elizabeth, the daughter of Louisa Putnam and Joseph Augustus Peabody, died
in 1869, when Katharine was twenty. Katharine had two younger brothers, William Caleb and Augustus Peabody, both trained in law, and a
younger sister, Louisa Putnam, a consumptive beauty with a nervous
temperament.

In 1844, Katharine's grandfather, lawyer Charles Greeley Loring, had bought a twenty-five-acre farm on the sea at Prides Crossing, a patrician little enclave in Beverly Farms on what is sometimes referred to as Boston's Gold Coast. Harvard botanist Asa Gray, whom Loring had asked for advice about planting and landscaping the property's grounds, met Loring's daughter Jane in 1847 and married her in 1848.* Jane's brother (Katharine's father) built a house called Burnside on the property at Prides Crossing in 1852. For years Katharine's family spent winters in Boston, at 33 Mount Vernon Street, and summers at Burnside. Then, in 1872, three years after Mrs. Loring's death, the family moved to live at Prides Crossing all year round.

By the time Alice James met Katharine, the two young Loring women were keeping house for their father and brothers at Prides. Louisa, the more domestic of the sisters, played the piano, kept pigeons, loved to cook, and gave lavish dinner parties. She was something of a social lion hunter, and included among her friends William Howard Taft, Oliver Wendell Holmes (both neighbors at Beverly), and John Singer Sargent, who made several sketches of her. His 1917 watercolor of Louisa and Katharine, *Study in Greens,* was destroyed by fire in 1969; a photograph of it is reprinted here, following page 272. When Louisa was well enough, she did her proper Bostonian's share of good works in the field she knew most about — health. Having gone to South Carolina for a tuberculosis cure, she founded a sanatorium in Aiken. Later, she became a director of the Beverly Hospital, secretary of the Essex County chapter of the Red Cross, and a founder of the Anti-Tuberculosis Society in Beverly. Her surviving relatives recall her as rather tart and strong-willed, a domineering presence who all her life (she died in 1924) kept her elder sister in the background.

Katharine, however, the more intellectual of the sisters, appears to have been a powerful enough figure long before Louisa's death. When Henry James, Jr., first heard about her, he replied from London that her "strength of wind and limb, to say nothing of her nobler qualities, must make her a valuable addition to the Quincy circle." Katharine was a good deal less pretty than Louisa — her photographs show a stern, prim, rather forbidding visage — and much stronger. A Loring family story describes the terrible hurricane that hit Boston's North Shore in 1938 as

---

* Jane Loring Gray suffered from chronic ill health, reports her husband's biographer, A. Hunter Dupree, with bouts of "dyspepsia, headaches, dizziness, &c."

the first cataclysm that "Aunt K." couldn't top. Her brothers, both energetic and dynamic men, deferred to her opinions throughout their lives
(William Caleb became a supreme court justice of the Commonwealth
of Massachusetts in 1899; Augustus Peabody was active in Republican
politics and a member of the Constitutional Convention of 1917).

Although Katharine, like Alice, had no formal education, she took an
avid interest in politics and foreign affairs, traveled widely, and read vo-
luminously. She had had weak eyes since childhood, and taught herself
Braille early on. She once said that there was no more delicious sensation
than lying in bed reading under a cosy quilt and never having to get up
to turn out the light. By the end of her life she was blind, and dictated
her correspondence to secretaries. Her active interest in women's education kept her teaching with the Society to Encourage Studies at Home
(which she had helped Anna Ticknor start) for twenty years. In addition,
she founded the Saturday Morning Club of Boston in 1871 with Julia
Ward Howe; it was a literary and social discussion group for girls from
Miss Hubbard's School on Bowdoin Street.* She was also instrumental in
setting up the Beverly Public Library, and worked with the Mayflower
Club in Boston, the Red Cross during World War I, the Women's Education Association, the Harvard Annex, and the Massachusetts Library
Club.

Her surviving descendants recall her as "the most loving and understanding person in the world" and "extraordinarily fond of children."
She knew crow-calls and kept Lincoln Logs for the entertainment of her
nieces and nephews, but had no natural ease with the very young, who
found her, as a consequence, rather frightening. As her nieces and great-
nieces grew older, they often spent vacations at Burnside, where meals
featured thick cream fresh from the cow and lettuce home grown in a
cold frame. Katharine once explained to her adolescent guests that the
reason there were so many maiden ladies in her generation was that the
Civil War had killed off such masses of young men — and the girls, of
course, assumed that she had lost a beau. Rules at Burnside were firm:
Katharine did not like anyone to be late, and "always let you know if she
didn't approve." One day her sharp-eyed personal maid and companion,

* In 1871 the club met at Katharine's house on Mount Vernon Street; in 1872 she
served as president. The speakers on Saturday mornings included Henry James ("A
Tour in Provence," 1883), Robertson James ("Colored Troops in the Civil War,"
1887), and Katharine Loring ("The Great Trees of California," 1874, and "A Memorial Tribute to Julia Ward Howe," 1911).

Rosa, spied the fourteen- and fifteen-year-old girls skinny-dipping on the beach. Aunt K. was horrified at this violation of maidenly propriety — and was no less so years later, when bloomers and bare legs made their appearance. A great-niece described her as "Victorian but avant-garde" — always interested in the world and up on the vast changes that took place during her long life (she lived to be ninety-four).

In 1879, Katharine began to take over much of the care of her friend Alice James.

After a year of collapse, Alice first ventured out of Cambridge on an excursion with Katharine to the Adirondacks. The two women set off on July 1, 1879, to stay at William's "panacea for all earthly ills, the Putnam shanty" — a log cabin near Lake Placid that had been converted into a vacation camp by the combined efforts of William, the physician brothers Charles and James Jackson Putnam, and Harvard physiologist Henry P. Bowditch. (William spent his honeymoon there in 1878.) Surrounded by Adirondack peaks, the camp was set in a forest wilderness. The uneven ground around the roughly made cabin, covered with mossy stones and logs, ran in the near distance into hills dense with trees. Alice described the trip to Sara Darwin, announcing that "the bosom of nature" had proved to be "just about as much of a humbug as I always knew it was." She relished her irreverence for life in the wild:

You will never find me being taken in again by any of her [nature's] snobbish votaries who are half of them only too craven to say how squalid it all is. We made a very thorough trial for between ourselves the shanty lacks nothing in the way of discomfort and is no doubt after camping the next worst thing. We stumbled gracefully over the stones in the brook and K. bathed therein, but I assure you that for purposes of cutaneous refreshment one tub in the hand is worth fifty brooks in the bush. We perched ourselves on the sharpest stones we could find and religiously spent endless hours in listening to the babbling water, the gentle hum of the mosquito, giving joy untold to the sportive midge who found me quite the loveliest production civilization had as yet sent to him. The beauty of the sylvan scenes was sadly marred by the excellent but prosaic K. who would insist upon inserting a hideous rubber blanket between my fair form and all the mossy logs upon which I wished to extend it, thereby putting a cruel barrier between me and all the dear little crawlers I had come so far to feel and who would no doubt have found me as delectable and succulent a feast as did their winged brethren. We had the shanty fortunately all to ourselves and the only romance in the situation was at night when we sat by our bonfire the woods all round us and no one else within a mile, save some lively cows who in the middle of the night with that unreasonableness characteristic of their sex would charge the shanty with their horns driving K. to her revolver and me under the bed. But this joy was soon denied us for a male protector presented himself in the person of the virtuous Dr. Charles Putnam who stayed a few days. He ate and consorted with us through the day but when the deeper shades of night fell he with great and unexpected propriety betook himself to the other house. It just occurs to me that perhaps those new friends of yours in Basset, for whom you have so easily abandoned the old, might be shocked to hear of two virgins of thirty summers living alone in the woods with a bachelor, but I think if they were to see the piety of his mould, his virtuous spectacles, and the general maiden-aunt like turn of his figure the veriest prig of them all would fall back abashed. Our food was sent to us from the other house under the auspices of "Si Ware, the gentleman-cook, and a hired girl," which shows you that the same inequality between the sexes exists in the wilderness as that which disgraces the effete civilizations to which you so passionately cling."*

This detached, ironic tone — sometimes bitter, sometimes bemused — characterizes her writing from this point on. She mocked her frailty while creating an impression of energetic vehemence and mildly erotic wit. The "dear little crawlers," sportive midges, and humming mosquitoes found her body not weak and vulnerable but a "lovely production," a "delectable and succulent feast." Charging cows inspired Katharine's chivalrous protection while demure Alice dove under the bed.

The "excellent but prosaic K." was the only subject of Alice's report to Sara that escaped with only an ounce of irony. And it was at the end of this letter that Alice extolled Katharine's androgynous merits, echoing a number of popular nineteenth-century female novelists who created heroines with the strengths and aptitudes of men as well as the domestic skills and sensitivities of women.† There were probably as many private reasons

* A later visitor to the Putnam camp shared Alice's sense of its discomforts. Sigmund Freud visited James Jackson Putnam there in September 1909, with Carl Jung and Sandor Ferenczi. He wrote to his family that his visit to the "very rough and primitive" camp was the most amazing of his American experiences. He had been invited upon arriving to walk up the nearest mountain to see the "utter wildness" of the landscape: "We took trails and came down slopes to which even my horns and hoofs were not equal. Fortunately it is raining today . . ." He was surprised to find "mixing bowls serve as wash bowls, china mugs for glasses, etc." And "this morning I sorely missed a barber for all I can do is comb my hair."

† For example, in *The Minister's Wooing* (1887), Harriet Beecher Stowe wrote, "Katy could harness a chaise, or row a boat; she could saddle and ride any horse in the neighborhood; she could cut any garment that ever was seen or thought of, make cake, jelly, and wine . . . all without seeming to derange a sort of trim, well-kept air of ladyhood that sat jauntily on her."

for this fictional cross-dressing as there were writers; viewed socially, these heroines probably represented the longings of nineteenth-century women for a world in which roles divided less absolutely along sexual lines — one in which they could become whole, active, fully functioning individuals.

Alice, cataloguing Katharine's virtues, made her friend sound amazonian — superior in competence even to Mary James, Aunt Kate, and Alice Gibbens James. She had always looked to her friends to "save" her. Now Katharine, who had all the strength of wind and limb that Alice lacked, seemed able and willing to do just that. Recounting the Adirondacks trip to Fanny Morse, Alice reported herself "consoled for all its disappointments by the revelation of Katharine Loring's virtues whose depths I had thought I had sounded long ago but I found that I had only stirred the surface thereof. She is a phenomenal being and no one knows what she has been and done for me these trying months I have been through . . ."* Others echoed this secular canonization. Henry referred to Katharine from abroad as a "celestial being." William told Fanny at Christmas, 1879, that "my sister Alice is a good deal tougher than she was last year, but still pretty frail. One hardly knows whether most to pity her sufferings or to admire the toughness of her character. Miss Loring has been a real savior to her. I really don't know how Alice cd. have got through this year without her."

Now that his marriage-cure had begun to work, William established his distance from the "neurotic" unhappiness of his sister (and of his brother Bob). He alone, among Alice's relatives and friends, never understood that she hated to be pitied. Henry learned, with Alice's cues, to feel with rather than for her. And Katharine knew it from the start. She took better care of her invalid friend than anyone else had ever done; she entered into Alice's pain with unconditional love and sympathy, and proved her allegiance by adopting Alice's own stoical attitude toward her troubles.

---

* In the same letter, Alice told Fanny, "I had a dream the other night at once amusing and distressing, in which your Mother came into the room & said, with wrath and indignation in her face and voice, that you must not write to me again until I had answered your letters that my conduct was past forgiveness, which shows you that I am haunted with remorse by night as well as by day for the evil of my ways." Alice continued to see and write to Fanny, but with Katharine's advent this first close friend dropped into the background; in fact, at this point she virtually disappears from Alice's story, to show up again only at the end.

Alice had at last exactly what she wanted: a devoted companion who could be everything to her — man and woman, father and mother, nurse and protector, intellectual partner and friend. Where Alice's father had wanted to be everything to his children in a way that satisfied primarily his own desires, Katharine appears to have played all these parts for Alice out of a more generous kind of love. In the security of this new friendship, Alice found mobility and the freedom to strike out on her own. With Katharine, she was finally leaving home.

The two women took a number of trips around New England in 1879 and 1880. To the amazement of the James family, they traveled without mishap to the White Mountains, Lake Winnepesaukee, Maine, Newport, and Cape Cod. But the most dramatic departure came in the summer of 1881, when Alice ventured with Katharine to England.

They sailed from Boston on May 21. Although Alice and Henry had been on opposite sides of the Atlantic for six years, the bond between them had held strong. She reported to him on her travels, her friends, her reading — and read everything he wrote.* He, in turn, continued to amuse her with reflections on his literary and social life ("I confess," he reported after an exhausting round of dinner parties in London, "it is most sweet, after a series of such performances, to mumble one's bone, as Thackeray says, in solitude, without the need of swallowing inscrutable *entrées* and tugging at the relaxed bell-rope of one's brain for a feeble tinkle of conversation").

In 1881, Henry had not yet met the "celestial" Miss Loring, nor did he know how his sister would bear up as a traveler after the ravages of 1878. When the two women landed in England in June, he was away in Venice

---

* When *The Portrait of a Lady* appeared, serialized in the *Atlantic* early in 1881, Alice objected to her brother that it seemed unnatural for the bright, imaginative Isabel Archer to be intimate with the rather vacuous American journalist, Henrietta Stackpole. Henry answered that it did appear unnatural, "but it wouldn't if I explained it. I have been afraid to do this, because there are so many explanations in the story, which, I think, is rather overburdened with them." However, when he wrote a preface to *The Portrait* for the complete New York Edition of his work in 1907–1909, he took up several pages explaining his use of "so broken a reed (from her slightness of cohesion) as Henrietta Stackpole." She serves, he wrote, like Maria Gostrey in *The Ambassadors,* as merely the "wheels to the coach" of the novel — not the true agent but "the light *ficelle* . . . She exemplifies, I fear, in her superabundance, not an element of my plan, but only an excess of my zeal." He had felt in this novel a special obligation to be amusing; the danger of a "thinness" of plot was "to be averted, tooth and nail, by cultivation of the lively. That is at least how I see it today. Henrietta must have been at that time a part of my wonderful notion of the lively."

and somewhat annoyed at not having been informed of their plans. He was trying uneasily to decipher just what might be expected of him as host, chaperon, guide, and friend. "From what you intimate," he wrote to his father, "I am all ready to believe that any practical aid I can render her will be quite thrown into the shade by Miss Loring's mighty arts."

Alice and Katharine toured slowly through the North Country on their own, and did not meet up with Henry until the middle of July, when he returned from the Continent. By this time the two women were staying at Richmond. Alice found him physically changed — at thirty-eight, Henry James had become a large, stout, vigorous-looking man with a full beard and a receding hairline — but she described him as "the same delightful kind creature as of old." He found her, he told Quincy Street, "rather weaker in body than I expected, but stronger in spirits, cheerfulness, &c," and he delighted in her brilliant talk, her "animation, vivacity, gladness to see me, wit, grace, gayety &c." He added, "The blessing that Miss Loring is to her it would be of course impossible to exaggerate. She is the most perfect companion she could have found, if she had picked over the whole human family." Alice and Katharine were headed for Scotland; Henry would put them on the train but would not "pursue them" there, he told his mother, "both because I have a good deal to do besides, and because they seem to prefer the liberty and irresponsibility of being by themselves."

A few days later, a breakdown curtailed the trip to Scotland and this happy liberty. "In an evil hour," reported Henry, the travelers had moved from Richmond to Kew so that Katharine could have a three-day visit with her aunt and uncle, the Asa Grays. Alice took to her bed on their arrival at the Grays' and stayed there, with Katharine nursing her, for over two weeks, until she got well enough to depart for Sevenoaks and a peaceful country inn. Henry blamed the accommodations at Kew — her quarters were so small, "so unsuitable and uncomfortable (the Grays are very primitive) as to prevent her getting better as quickly as she otherwise would." The collapse was an accident, Henry assured Quincy Street, and Alice was not discouraged by it: "She appears to think her attack . . . is a positive indication of her nervous tendencies working themselves off. She has much less general nervousness than at home, and believes that her troubles are, to a considerable extent, the expiring kicks of the malady. I sincerely hope so. Meanwhile, her spirits seem very good — and Miss Loring's devotion has been what you may imagine. She is certainly worth her weight in gold to Alice."

This minor collapse was no accident. It repeated itself under similar circumstances again and again over the next ten years — whenever Alice had to share Katharine's affections. Katharine did seem worth her weight in gold, and Alice was not about to share her new-found wealth with the Grays or Katharine's invalid sister or even Henry. Illness, as usual, guaranteed a loved one's undivided attention.

As soon as Alice's health improved, she and Katharine moved up to London, taking rooms in Clarges Street, just around the corner from Henry's flat at 3 Bolton Street in Piccadilly. In 1872, Alice had found London depressing, but now it seemed endlessly entertaining. With Katharine, she took long walks, shopped, went to the theater, discussed English politics, and compared the British and Yankee characters. Henry, returning to town from Somersetshire at the end of August, reported her bright and well. In his notebooks he registered his delight in the long August afternoons making "a cool grey light in the empty West End. Delightful to me, too, it was to see how *she* enjoyed it — how interesting was the impression of the huge, mild city." He planned an early September visit to Scotland, and Alice received an "urgent invitation" from his hosts, Sir John and Lady Clark, to accompany him. She preferred to remain in London, however. When the Clarges Street arrangement proved difficult, she and Katharine moved into Henry's empty Bolton Street rooms.

Henry had expected to see his sister off at Liverpool on September 20, but Alice and Katharine assured him it would not be necessary. They insisted they were attended to "in perfection" by a hired guide, and that (Henry told Quincy Street) "I shall be a fifth wheel to their coach." While glad to be relieved of responsibility for his invalid sister and free to travel as he pleased in the summer of 1881, Henry found himself mystified and slightly hurt by this exclusive new devotion. The theme of his irrelevance repeats throughout the summer in his letters home: "Alice and Miss L. are very independent of me — & A. indeed seems so extraordinarily fond of Miss L. that a third person is rather a superfluous appendage."

Henry had been accustomed in the past to his sister's full attention and affection. If her invalidism and dependence could be a burden, her company and wit were a pleasure, her adoration a reward. In 1881, however, Katharine's presence altered the connection between brother and sister. With Katharine on hand to share Alice's travels, dissect politics and literature, make the social rounds, and do the necessary nursing, Henry did seem like a fifth wheel.

The kind of intense, exclusive relationship Alice and Katharine had developed became so common between upper-class single women in late nineteenth-century America that people called it a "Boston marriage." The poet Sarah Orne Jewett and the widowed Annie Fields had a similar arrangement at Mrs. Fields's house in Charles Street, and when Alice and Katharine were living in London several years later, Miss Jewett wrote from Maine, "Dear Katharine and Alice . . . I can think of you together in the closest way, and how you think together and know each other's thoughts as only those friends can who are very near and very dear." She had spent Christmas with her sisters and taken the night train to Boston: "Mrs. Fields had gone to *her* sister's and I waited an hour or two before she came back — and I stretched myself in comfort on the green couch in the library and contemplated the heap of nice white paper bundles on the piano — Then I was a surprise-party to A.F. and we sat up late and talked of many things. It is ten years since Mr. Fields died and I spent my first Christmas there!"

Of Miss Jewett and Mrs. Fields, Henry James wrote that "their reach together was of the firmest and easiest and I verily remember being struck with the stretch of wings that the spirit of Charles Street could bring off." About the "marriage" between Alice and Katharine, however, Henry was not quite so sanguine. Something in its intensity troubled him, and he would express this unease in *The Bostonians.*

•

When Alice returned home from England in the fall of 1881, she impressed her family, again, as vastly improved. The focus of parental concern shifted now to the younger two brothers. Robertson, separated from his wife, had moved home temporarily, where he struggled unsuccessfully against philandering and alcoholism. Wilky, suffering from rheumatism and heart disease, had gone bankrupt with a debt of $80,000; Henry James, Sr., had lost a good deal of money in the crash of 1879 and could not avert Wilky's ruin. Both younger sons appeared more than ever, to themselves and the rest of the world, to have failed.

William, however, despite continuing trouble with his eyes, was thriving. He held the title of assistant professor of philosophy at Harvard, was writing (slowly — it would take him twelve years) a book about the workings of the mind and nervous system, and was living with his pregnant wife and young son, Henry, in rooms on Louisburg Square near the Massachusetts State House. (He had considered moving in with his parents after his honeymoon, but his sister's illness had prevented it.) William made daily trips across the Charles River to Cambridge on the horse cars, often accompanied by his wife and son, who visited the grandparental enclaves on Garden and Quincy streets. William's sister described her nephew to Fanny Morse as "a dear little soul ... we have a delightful visit from him every day, the day seems quite lost if we don't see him."

Relations between the two Alices had by this time improved. However, Henry's hope that his sister's "abnegation" in missing the wedding would "bear rich fruits in the way of enabling her to enjoy their conjugal and fraternal society afterwards" did not come true. William's wife suspected Alice and Katharine of being lovers — though she confessed that thought only to William. And William's sister resented having to share with a rival not only her brother but her parents, as well. Only years later, after the first Alice James moved to England, did the animosity between the two women relax; then their letters grew quite warm and friendly.

Through the filter of that late rapprochement, Alice Gibbens James looked back in 1892, just after her sister-in-law's death, to draw a picture for Henry Jr. of the "dear old Quincy Street circle as I knew it. I can see it now — your father, mother and Alice gathered in the library evenings, the time I oftenest visited them. Your mother beside the little table on the left of the fire, reading, Alice on the sofa, your father in his deep chair talking to us all or making Alice talk. One Monday night while Wm. was at the Faculty meeting he [Henry Sr.] told us of his boyhood and of the wild pranks in which he was leader, then of the Class in Sunday school he taught at the age of seven at which point in the story Alice declared her entire disbelief in so preposterous a tale — and he swore it was a true one and your mother dropped her book on her lap to watch them both with her sweet smile of amusement at their audacious retorts ... For years I have looked forward to seeing Alice again, to being something to her from out the larger knowledge that life brings to us all, but it was not to be and the loss is mine."

•

In November of 1881, Henry Jr. came back to Cambridge from London for an extended visit to his aging parents. He had postponed the trip several times, promising in his inimitable way in August that "it is absolutely certain (as certainties go) that I shall sail not later than October 14th." With Alice, Rob, and Henry at home, and with constant visits from William's family, 20 Quincy Street was nearly full again for the first time in years. Three-year-old Harry went around telling everyone proudly that he was "Uncle Harry's fascinating little nephew."

Four months after Alice's return from England, at the end of January 1882, Mary James contracted bronchial asthma. Alice took over the management of the household, saw to her father's needs, and seemed to "thrive," reported Bob, "under the ordeal of nursing." On January 29, Bob wrote to Henry Jr. (who was visiting friends in Washington) that their mother was making a thorough, cheerful recovery and she wanted Henry to know he had no cause for anxiety. The next evening, however, with Alice and Henry Sr. sitting by her bed in the twilight, Mary James quietly died.

Henry arrived home twenty-four hours later. Wilky came from Wisconsin, and the four brothers carried their mother's body to the Cambridge Cemetery on "one of those splendid days of winter that are frequent here — when the snow is high and deep, but the sky as blue as the south, and the air brilliant and still." Henry went on: "She was the perfection of a mother — the sweetest, gentlest, most beneficent human being I have ever known . . . I thank heaven . . . that it is given to us to feel this particular pang but once. My father is infirm, but very tranquil; he has a way of his own of taking the sorrows of life — a way so perfect that one almost envies him his troubles. Alice, I am happy to say, after many years of ill health has been better for the last few months than for a long time; she is able to look after my father and take care of his house — and as she is a person of great ability it is an extreme good fortune that she is now able to exert herself."

Everyone watched Alice for signs of collapse.* But contrary to all expectations, she seemed to flourish. Aunt Kate reported her cheerful, happy, equal to all her new responsibilities — "taking up of household duties what her mother laid down." Kate even went so far as to observe that "her Mother's death seems to have brought new life to Alice," and to repeat a month later that if Mary James were looking down from

---

* Henry's friend Constance Fenimore Woolson wrote from Italy, "A daughter feels it [the death of a parent] more than a son of course, because her life is so limited, bounded by home life."

heaven, "how must she rejoice that to the dear child to whom she gave material existence, she has by her death given spiritual life."

Alice did not envision her mother looking down from heaven. Once her parents died (she wrote later in her diary), she could think of them only "as a sublimation of their qualities." Her mother, in particular, now seemed simply "a beautiful illumined memory, the essence of divine maternity."

There had been a sharp contrast between the celebrated family vision of perfect maternity and Alice's unsatisfied yearnings for love; she had "resolved" the contradiction by denying her sense of deprivation and idealizing her mother. It was an uneasy resolution at best. But in death, Mary James could become an ideal — the abstract essence of divine maternity — and Alice could believe in her image. She wrote to Kitty Prince in March, "Instead of having lost her it seems sometimes as if I had never known or loved her before."

Alice had defaulted in competition with her mother for managerial skills and physical strength. Now Mary was gone and Alice, having longed to be useful and to "manage," rose to meet her new responsibilities with pleasure. Katharine Loring stayed close at hand, with love and moral support; Aunt Kate got gracefully out of the way by going back to New York. Henry Jr. left for England. Henry Sr. had grown old and sad — and he needed his daughter to care for him. She did — nursing, feeding, keeping house. Father and daughter settled into a new domestic regime. "My father and Alice are almost happy!" exclaimed Henry Jr. in February to his old friend, Harvard's Chaucerian, Francis Child.

•

Alice and her father agreed that the house on Quincy Street would not do for the two of them: it was too haunted with the past, and too large. Early in the spring of 1882, they moved to a little brick house at 131 Mount Vernon Street on Beacon Hill in Boston. Mount Vernon Street runs down the hill from the state house to the embankment of the Charles River. Number 131 sits at the bottom of the hill, just west of Charles Street, next to a fire station. Alice described it as a "very pleasant little house in a most convenient situation for housekeeping and for father. We feel more and more content all the time with the change, Father was growing too old and feeble to go back and forth in the horse-cars every day and . . . he is not happy if he is kept for long away from his dear book stores." The Bootts lived up the hill, at number 47. Half the furniture from the Quincy Street house easily filled the smaller one on Mount Vernon Street. The other half went into a house at Manchester-by-the-Sea that Alice was having built on some land she had bought there in 1881.

Manchester, a tiny coastal town on the North Shore, is about two miles up the coast past Prides Crossing. Alice had bought 1.3 acres on a small peninsula called Proctor's Point, or Point of Rocks, just across from the Manchester Harbor and a mile and a half from town. She paid $4000 for the land as well as the rights to use a pier that extended out into the bay from Proctor's Point and a common beach just to the south and west. Her property looked out past several little islands toward the open sea.

She began building a "cottage" there as soon as she signed the deed and the weather permitted. In May 1882, she made plans to move into the still-unfinished house with her father for the summer. Alice had sided with Robertson's wife, Mary, in all the couple's marital difficulties, and she now invited this sister-in-law to visit Manchester with her children in July. At the beginning of July, even though the house was not quite ready for occupancy, Alice wrote to Mary Holton James, "We moved on Saturday, in the pouring rain with ten workmen still in the house, but we are alive to tell the tale and are delighted with our situation and the little house which will be quite perfect when we get the painters and paperers out of it." The "little" house had three stories. Alice had it built on the model of an old English country cottage, multigabled and shingled, with a red-brick chimney running up the outside. It had casement windows, hardwood floors, and a verandah running along two sides. Since the house faced on the water, breezes graced it even on the hottest days of the New England summer. Henry Jr. came out for a visit just before sailing back to England and recorded in his notebooks that the Manchester house seemed "very pretty — bating the American scragginess; with the sea close to the piazzas, and the smell of bayberries in the air. Rest, coolness, peace, society enough, charming drives; they will have all that." For the charming drives, Alice and her father kept a horse and carriage. They docked a rowboat at the pier. And they hired a young Irish sailor to do maintenance work.

By the middle of July, housekeeping conditions were still primitive: the plumbing couldn't supply enough water to do laundry, and work-

men still traipsed in and out. But Alice and her father were enjoying
their solitude and the fresh sea air. Henry Sr. got up between five and six
every morning and wrote until one. Alice managed the house, the meals,
the workmen, and the visitors — just as her mother had done. "Our life
is very quiet," she wrote to Robertson's wife, "Father and I being neither
of us strong enough to go about much or see much company, but it is
lovely and cool and the views are as pretty as they can be."

The visit of young Mary James and her children had been postponed
by the continuing presence of the workmen, but finally on August 1 the
contingent from the Midwest arrived. Mary and Bob had been separated
for about a year. His Cambridge family had been entirely sympathetic
with her, admiring her strength and dignity in the face of what Bob's
mother had called his "selfish and tyrannical turbulent spirit." In May
1881, Bob had committed himself to "the Asylum" (probably the
McLean Hospital, then in Somerville), "where he might rest and be
taken care of." After his mother's death, in 1882, he took a long trip
alone to Egypt and England. Alice did not have much residual fondness
for Bob, whom she described to Henry in the fall of 1882 by exclaiming,
"Poor boy! his vices and his virtues his joys and his agonies are all equally
superficial, he seems to be without any interiors at all." Bob *was* pathetic,
and Alice was quick to put a critical distance between his difficulties and
her own. Shortly after the elder Mary James died, Alice wrote to the
younger, "I can never hope to be half the help to you that she was, but
you must remember that I have a perfect understanding of all your troubles and a complete sympathy throughout with you. Your sweetness and
patience in all these last years fills me with wonder and admiration."

Mary and the children stayed two weeks.* As soon as they left, Aunt
Kate arrived. Then, at the beginning of September, Bob turned up unex-
pectedly from England, hoping to find work in Boston. Instead, he left
suddenly after a week to join his wife in Wisconsin. Alice reported to
Henry, "How long it will last of course no one can tell, but we must be

---

* Wilkie sent Mary a piece of unsolicited advice about living with his father and
sister: "I know that father and Alice think that they lead rather hum-drum existences.
The truth is that they do not: they do not value by half as much the richness of their
lives as they might do, and you must stir them up and boss them and not allow them
to boss you. The more noise the children make, the better it will be for them, and
don't restrain the children a particle from any sense you may have that they are going
to be a charge upon father's tranquility of mind or body. This is all I have to say, and
it is entirely true."

thank full for the present respite ... I am looking for a letter from Mary every day, she poor little thing will be very much set up by the change."

Alice and her father stayed on through September, with Katharine Loring a constant visitor from nearby Prides Crossing. At the end of the month they moved back to Mount Vernon Street, because Henry Sr. was longing (Alice told Henry) "for the bricks and mortar which he finds a much more succulent pasturage than the rocks and sands. The house here seems quite home-like on getting back to it ... Kath. was as usual the guardian angel of our move and has done everything for us since we arrived and has provided among other things an ultra-refined parlor-maid who has mastered the mysteries of the nominative case after the verb *to be*, but whose desire for 'Sabbath privileges,' 'attendance at Sabbath-school and the communion table,' will interfere too much, I am afraid, with our noonday alimentation. She will doubtless soon feel her unfitness to this ungodly house and depart."

Fanny Morse wrote, hinting that she had been worried about Alice all summer. Alice begged her not to be: "Now that the moves are all over and this little box is pretty much in order the paddling of the domestic canoe through the placid waters of Mt. Vernon St. will be child's play.

"The last seven months have brought such changes in so many ways and to me so many new responsibilities that I feel at times that I may not be equal to them, but I find I am from day to day and I try to keep in mind as much as possible the invaluable thought that one has only to live one day at a time and that all the vague terrors of the future vanish as the future at every moment becomes the present."

•

Alice dreaded the day — among the "vague terrors of the future" — when her father would no longer be there to give her life a center. She was finding herself more than equal to her new responsibilities, but she could not paddle the domestic canoe toward a safe mooring. Her father, growing increasingly frail, was longing to join his wife, whom he now worshiped even more devoutly than he had done while she was alive. He had already bid Henry a "distinctly widowed farewell" by letter in the spring of 1882: "How loving a farewell it is, I can't say, but only that it is most loving. All my children have been very good and sweet from their infancy, and I have been very proud of you and Willy. But I can't help feeling that you are the one that has cost us the least trouble, and given us always the most delight. Especially do I mind mother's perfect joy in you the last few months of her life, and your perfect sweetness to her . . . I feel that I have fallen heir to all dear mother's fondness for you, as well as my proper own . . . That blessed mother, what a link her memory is to us all henceforth! I think none of us who remember her natural unaffected ways of goodness, and especially her sleepless sense of justice, will ever again feel tempted to do a dishonest or unhandsome thing . . . The sum of it all is, that I would sooner rejoin her in her modesty, and find my eternal lot in association with her, than have the gift of a noisy delirious world!"

In November of 1882 he began to decline rapidly. He stopped eating, since food would only keep his body alive, and talked incessantly of joining his wife. Alice collapsed. She did not emerge from her room for ten days, and Aunt Kate came up from New York to take care of her brother-in-law.

On William's recommendation, Alice consulted a new physician named Henry Harris Aubrey Beach. The doctor suspected "something lying back of her nervousness, and the cause of it, and he was bound to find it out," reported Aunt Kate to Henry. "A three weeks investigation has persuaded him that it is gout, rheumatic gout! and he promises her exemption from her nervous attacks."

While Beach diagnosed Alice's latest ills, Henry Sr. consulted with a Boston homeopath named Ahlborn. Dr. Ahlborn insisted that there was nothing in the old man's condition that rest of body, stomach, and brain could not cure. But James knew better. "It is weary work this dying," he pronounced, and continued to starve himself. In late December he summoned Marny Storer's lawyer husband, Joseph Warner, to make out his will.

The James sons (with the exception of Wilky) more or less supported themselves by this time, but Alice had no wage-earning capacity and no prospect of a husband. Henry Sr. worried about what would happen to her after he died (Mary James had left all *her* property to Alice, but most of it was railroad stock that had greatly diminished in value in the panic of 1879) and intended to leave her more money than he left the boys. Alice protested vehemently against being set apart in this way, however, and finally convinced her father not to discriminate in her favor by explaining exactly how she would "get on" without him.

Her health had improved after Dr. Beach's optimistic diagnosis, but in early December she collapsed again — "and no wonder," wrote Aunt Kate to Henry, "that she did break down as 'father's' two successive swoons, when she and I were alone with him, were very alarming. She thought he was dying, and I did too ... Alice kept up all day, but at night she gave way, but the faithful Katharine was at her side, and has not left her since." Through Kate, Alice told Henry not to worry about them — she would telegraph him in London to start for home as soon as the end seemed near.

William, too, was in London, on a year's leave of absence from Harvard. His wife, who had just had her second son, Billy, had moved with both boys to her mother's house on Garden Street.* Henry Sr. insisted that William not interrupt his year abroad. He would consent to let Henry come as the end approached because, he said, Henry had no family to support and could better afford to leave his work. There was a certain illogic to this paternal decree, since William was on leave from work: Henry Sr. now simply favored Henry Jr., having fallen heir (as he put it) to Mary's special fondness for her "angel."

On December 9, Alice telegraphed Henry to start at once. He answered that he and William would leave on the 12th. Alice replied that William must not come, and added "brain softening" to explain their father's condition. Henry Sr. now talked constantly about the spiritual life, objecting to food and railing against "this disgusting world." "He gets over the delay in dying by asserting that he has already died," reported Katharine to Rob on December 11. "He has to be kept very quiet — seeing Alice yesterday left him very excited, and of course excitement is bad. He is very happy and perfectly comfortable." Refusing to have his room darkened, he lay facing the windows and "yearned unspeakably" to die. On the night of December 17, Alice saw him for the last time. She then retired to her room, where Katharine and William's Alice watched over her while Aunt Kate and a nurse stayed with the dying Henry James. The next morning the old man's speech grew thick and incomprehensible; a draft of opium cleared his throat and eased him into unconsciousness. Aunt Kate, watching through the last hours, heard him say, "Oh, I have such good boys — *such* good boys!" Henry was still two days from home on the Atlantic; Alice had a note waiting for him when his boat docked.

---

* William tended to leave the country whenever his wife had a child.

Wednesday 20th

My darling Harry

Darling father's weary longings were all happily ended on Monday at 3 P.M. The last words on his lips were "There is my Mary!" For the last 2 hrs. he had said perpetually "My Mary." He had no suffering but we were devoutly thankful when the rest came to him and he went and I am sure you will feel as thankfull as I do that the weary burden of life is over for him. I have no terrors for the future for I know I shall have strength to meet all that is in store for me, with a heartfull of love and counting the minutes till you get here

Always yr devoted

A——

The funeral is to be tomorrow Thursday 20th [actually Thursday was the 21st] at 11 A.M. There seemed no use in waiting for you the uncertainty was so great.

Henry James — no longer Jr. — arrived in Boston on the night of the 21st. The funeral was over, and the elder Henry now lay beside his wife in the Cambridge Cemetery. The next morning Alice took to her bed; Katharine Loring bundled her off to Beverly for a complete rest and change of scene. Rob had stayed for two days and gone back to Wisconsin. Henry came down with a headache that kept him in bed for several days. Christmas came and went. Alice stayed on with Katharine at Beverly, and Henry alone with Aunt Kate on Beacon Hill.

During this period Kate took it upon herself to destroy a great many of the family letters. Almost forty years later, Katharine Loring wrote to William's eldest son, Harry, in response to a request for James letters, "Most unfortunately, when your Grandfather died in Mt. Vernon St. your Aunt Alice was very ill, and while she was still in bed, Mrs. Walsh burned up great numbers of letters that your Grandfather had in a chest of drawers. I happened to see her doing it (just as she finished) & remonstrated, but she said they were family papers & she thought it better that 'the children' should not see them.

"Of course your Aunt Alice felt terribly grieved, but there was no remedy."

As soon as Henry could get up, he went out to the Cambridge Cemetery to read aloud over the fresh grave a letter William had written from London in farewell to the dying old man. The message had arrived too late, but Henry told William he was sure their father heard it "some-

where out of the depths of the still, bright winter air." The letter expresses poignantly all the love, faith, guilt, tenderness, and confusion this
complex man had inspired in his children.

Darling old father ... We have been so long accustomed to the hypothesis of
your being taken away from us, especially during the past 10 months, that the
thought that this may be your last illness conveys no very sudden shock. You
are old enough, you've given your message to the world in many ways and
will not be forgotten, you are here left alone, and on the other side, let us
hope and pray, dear, dear old Mother is waiting for you to join her. If you go,
it will not be an inharmonious thing. Only if you are still in possession of
your normal consciousness, I should like to see you once again before we part.
I stayed here only in obedience to the last telegram, and am waiting now for
Harry, who knows the exact state of my mind, and who will know yours, to
telegraph again what I shall do. Meanwhile, my blessed old father, I scribble
this line (which may reach you though I should come too late) just to tell
you how full of the tenderest memories and feelings about you my heart has
for the last few days been filled. In that mysterious gulf of the past into which
the present soon will fall and go back and back, yours is still for me the central
figure. All my intellectual life I derive from you; and though we have often
seemed at odds in the expression thereof I'm sure there's a harmony somewhere, and that our strivings will combine. What my debt to you is goes beyond all my power of estimating — so early, so penetrating and so constant
has been the influence ... [William then promised to take care of his father's
literary remains by bringing them out in a collection of extracts.] As for us,
we shall live on each in his way, feeling somewhat unprotected, old as we are,
for the absence of the parental bosoms as a refuge, but holding fast together in
that common sacred memory. We will stand by each other and by Alice, try to
transmit the torch in our offspring as you did in us, and when the time comes
for being gathered in I pray we may, if not all, some at least be as ripe as you.
As for myself, I know what trouble I've given you at various times through
my peculiarities; and as my own boys grow up, I shall learn more and more of
the kind of trial you had to overcome in superintending the development of a
creature different from yourself for whom you felt responsible. I say this
merely to show how my *sympathy* with you is likely to grow much livelier,
rather than to fade — & not for the sake of regrets. — As for the other side, &
Mother, and our all possible meeting, I *can't* say anything. More than ever at
this moment do I feel that if that *were* true, all would be solved and justified.
And it comes strangely over me in bidding you good bye, how a life is but a
day and expresses mainly but a single note — it is so much like the act of bid-

ding an ordinary good night. Good night my sacred old Father. If I don't see you again — Farewell, a blessed farewell! Your William.

•

As executor of his will, Henry Sr. named Henry Jr., the aesthete who had embarked on the kind of artistic career the elder James had seen as dangerous to his children's spiritual welfare. William, the eldest and ostensibly more practical son, was made an ordinary beneficiary — and he was still 3000 miles away. Henry now moved effortlessly into the position of paterfamilias, apprising himself of the financial situation, mediating disputes, and insisting that William remain abroad.

Henry James, Sr., had left an estate valued at approximately $95,000 (translated into 1979 standards, about $700,000). His will, like his own father's, discriminated among his children. Alice received property and stocks worth about $20,000, including the house on Mount Vernon Street and railway bonds and shares bought with the proceeds from the sale of the Quincy Street house. The remaining $75,000 of the estate, invested in land and houses in Syracuse (and yielding about $5000 a year), was to be divided equally among William, Henry, and Robertson. Henry Sr. omitted the spendthrift Wilky, to whom he had been advancing funds without reimbursement ever since the failed plantation venture in Florida in the late 1860s. The most recent "loan" had been $5000 to help ward off bankruptcy, but "poor old Wilk" had failed nonetheless. Enraged by this "unjust and damnable" discrimination, Wilky wrote to Bob that it was "a base cowardly act of father's, a death stab" at a son "who dared to fight through the war for the defense of the family."

At the time of his father's death, Wilky James was seriously ill with heart trouble and Bright's disease. He had been to Boston for medical consultations in the fall of 1882, and doctors had pronounced his prognosis poor. By the end of the year he could no longer work at all. Henry, visiting him early in January, found him "sadly broken and changed . . . for his spirits have gone a good deal, as well as his health." In view of Wilky's misery, Alice and Henry felt the financial discrimination to be more than he could bear, and they worked out with William and Rob a redivision of their father's property so that Wilky would get almost a full share. He would repay a $1000 debt he had to Bob, and give each of his brothers $1000 as partial repayment to the estate of the recent $5000 loan. This arrangement left Wilky with property worth about $15,000, and William, Henry, Alice, and Rob with $20,000 each. Alice would have about $2500 a year in income from her investments; in addition, she planned to build a stable on her Manchester property and rent the house for $1000 a year. With a total income, then, of about $3500 a year (roughly, $26,000 in 1979 terms), she would be "perfectly well off," Henry assured William in February. Nonetheless, he made over to her his share of the income from the Syracuse property several months later. "She assures me," he told William, "that she will have no occasion to use it — will save and invest it for my benefit &c. But I wish her to have it, to cover all the contingencies of her new existence."

•

Just what shape that new existence would take remained to be seen at the end of 1882. William, writing from London, made a general prediction: "For you, my dear sister, this is the most important change in all your life. In some ways it will be a great nakedness, in others a great freedom."

Alice's father had figured as the most important person in her life. For the past year she had devoted herself entirely to his care and comfort. Now he had virtually killed himself, by starvation, in just the manner he had recommended to her in 1878 — gently, so as not to distress one's friends. And in dying, he forgot her. "I have such good boys," he had said, and "There is my Mary!"

Alice left no record of her sense of loss beyond the fact of her collapse. Even in death, however, her father exerted a powerful influence on her life. He died eagerly, declaring himself so delighted to be released from this "disgusting world" that to mourn would have seemed selfish. For Alice to reproach his memory — for having included (and deserted) her along with the things of this disgusting world — would have been unthinkable. She did not cry when her father died.

A year and a half later she told Sara Darwin that "we were so glad to have him go and that he was not kept in weariness and desolation any longer after Mother's death that we could give no thought to our own loss. It has fallen most heavily upon me, but I am gradually getting used to my loneliness and I find as every one else does that no burden is given that one cannot fit one's self to, after the necessary hewing and hacking. I have every consolation in having so many kind friends and brothers, Boston surpasses itself, you know, when trouble comes."

Several years later, when her English friend Constance Maud described praying to God to spare her own mother's life, Alice wrote, "The sincerity and strength of the feeling which she showed increased the shocked sense which filled me as I listened. One cries out, bowed down in supplication, for strength, but how can any creature measure her judgment with that of the Doer of all Good, how can she propose to make her paltry necessities an element for the modification of another's destiny, how can she thrust her miserable plaints into the presence of Majestic Death? I remember how horrified I was to the core of my being when some said to me in that month when Father lay dying that he must eat *for my sake*!! Imagine my wanting to stay the will of God and add a second to the old man's hours!"

Alice did not mourn her father's death until eight years had passed. Then, reading some old letters from both her parents, she had

one of the most intense, exquisite, and profoundly interesting experiences I ever had ... As I read it seemed as if I had opened up a postscript of the past and that I had had, in order to find them *truly*, really to lose them. It seems now incredible to me that I should have drunk, as a matter of course, at that ever springing fountain of responsive love and bathed all unconscious in that flood of human tenderness. The letters are made of the daily events of their pure simple lives, with souls unruffled by the ways of men, like special creatures, spiritualized and remote from coarser clay. Father ringing the changes upon Mother's perfections, he not being of the order of "charming man who hangs up his fiddle outside his own front door," for his fireside inspired his sweetest music. And Mother's words breathing her extraordinary selfless devotion as if she simply embodied the unconscious essence of wife and motherhood. What a beautiful picture do they make for the thoughts of their children to dwell upon! How the emotions of those two dreadful years, when I was wrenching myself away from them, surge thro' me! — The first haunted by the terror that I should fail him as I watched the poor old man fade day by day — "his fine fibre," William said, "wearing and burning itself out at things too heavy for it" — until the longing cry of his soul was answered and the dear old shrunken body was "lying beside Mary on the hilltop in Cambridge." — Mother died Sunday evening, January 29th, 1882, Father on Monday midday, December 19th, 1882, and now I am shedding the tears I didn't shed then!

Chapter Thirteen

Alone

T HE SECOND "dreadful" year of Alice's "wrenching" herself free from
her parents still lay ahead of her at the beginning of 1883. She returned in January from Beverly to Henry and the silent house on Mount
Vernon Street, profoundly depressed. "She would be utterly lonely, a sort
of waif in the great human family, but for Harry," wrote Sara Darwin's
aunt, Grace Ashburner, reporting to another family friend that Alice's
"old hysteria is just now as bad as ever." Alice was thinking of moving to
England eventually, to live near Henry, but first she wanted to regain her
health. In order to live alone she would have to be well. From now on, it
was clear, she would be living alone.

For the time being, however, as she recovered from this last hysterical
attack, she and Henry kept house together on Mount Vernon Street. At
the end of January, he wrote to his London publisher, "I feel strangely
settled here for the present, and shall probably remain for the summer . . .
My sister and I make an harmonious little *ménage,* and I feel a good deal
as if I were married." They did make a neat little nearly conjugal unit,
much like the one Alice had the previous year with her father. When she
was well enough, she managed the house, the meals, and some of their
social life. Henry slept in his father's bed, tended to the family finances,
urged William to stay in Europe, traveled to Milwaukee to check up on
the ailing Wilkie (who now looked on Henry and Alice as substitute
parents*), and spent long quiet hours in companionable conversation

---

* They invited Wilky to Boston for a rest. The invitation, he wrote, "fills my heart
to the bottom with gratitude and love for you and Alice," and Henry's visit with its

with his sister. He proposed to her that they "set up a common *ménage*" in London, but Alice "shrewdly declined the proposal," he told Fanny Kemble, "for we are really both much too fond of our individual independence, and she has a dread of exchanging the comfortable *known* of Boston for the vast unknown of London." Henry looked forward to returning to his beloved vast London, but felt he had to stay with Alice until she was fairly on her feet. ("If it were not wicked to plume one's self on one's virtues," he confided to Mrs. Kemble, "I should risk the remark that I do this at a certain sacrifice, for I care not for this place and ne m'y amuse pas du tout — mais pas du tout!")

Brother and sister stayed on alone together at Mount Vernon Street through the winter. Henry found a great deal more to interest him in the social landscape of the Puritan capital than he had expected. He observed it carefully, and was impressed above all by the extent to which Boston seemed a city of women. He felt himself in a "deluge of petticoats" among the "sisterhood of 'shoppers,'" writers, hostesses, visitors, and suffragists then waging a campaign for the female vote.

In the early 1880s, Boston witnessed a great deal of activity around the issue of women's right to vote. In June of 1881, the National Women's Suffrage Association held its convention in Boston. The National, as it was called, had come into existence early in 1869 as a result of a split in the Equal Rights Association along radical versus conservative lines. The radicals, led by Elizabeth Cady Stanton and Susan B. Anthony, believed that the E.R.A. had been betrayed by male leadership, and they formed a separate organization for women only. Its primary goal remained the passage of an amendment to the federal Constitution, granting women the right to vote, and any woman who was for suffrage could join. But the National spoke out vociferously on women's issues in other areas as well, such as the organization of women workers and the complicated question of divorce. The more conservative faction of the suffrage movement had formed a second organization in 1869, the American Women's

---

"loving, tender, moderate and wise counsels to me, had peremptorily disarmed me of all the fancied abuses and isolations under which my existence labored." The visit, he continued, had left him almost a redeemed man, as it helped him shake off "all the evil omens and surroundings which my mind had invited to me," and the kindness of his brother's and sister's invitation furthered this sense of redemption. But he would not come — he was determined to work off some of his debt, to free himself of "constant disquietude and mortification." Only then could he leave the Midwest to work at improving his health.

Suffrage Association, under the leadership of Lucy Stone and Julia Ward Howe. The members of the American believed the goal of suffrage could be achieved only by women focusing entirely on that one issue, and by working within the individual states rather than on the federal level. Frankly elitist, organized on a delegate basis, the American made use of alliances with powerful political groups outside the women's movement.

Throughout the tumultuous 1870s, the schism between the two factions had widened. National economic and social change had been rapid and unpredictable: burgeoning cities, increasing poverty, industrialization, capital expansion, and massive immigration had caused social problems America had never had to face before. At the bottom of the social scale were female workers, poor housewives, immigrant mothers who could not speak English — and the women's movement polarized into radicals, who believed in the efficacy of organizing women in labor unions, settlement houses, temperance unions, and working girls' clubs, and conservatives, who were single-mindedly interested in suffrage.

In the upper classes, college-educated and professional women had, in the years following the Civil War, become increasingly visible and active in favor of women's right to vote. By the 1880s the suffrage movement no longer looked like a collection of harebrained fanatics threatening to destroy the structure of family and society. It had achieved a certain legitimacy — partly in contrast to the widespread social turmoil associated with poverty and organized labor, and partly as a result of the movement's years of hard work educating the public, organizing state suffrage associations, keeping the question of the vote alive through state referenda, and urging Congress to amend the Constitution.*

It was against this background that the National Women's Suffrage Association met in Boston in the spring of 1881. The New England "city of reform" proved fertile ground for the seeds of female suffrage, and out of the convention came a Massachusetts chapter of the National. A movement to enfranchise the women of Massachusetts in municipal elections began in 1882, and by early 1883 female suffrage had become Boston's leading social question: newspapers and lecture halls publicized the debate that continued in every educated household in the state. Alice, Henry, and Katharine watched the flurry of feminist activity with inter-

---

* In 1882 both houses of Congress appointed select committees to study woman suffrage, and both committees came out in favor of it.

est. Katharine, in fact, did more than watch: she supported the suffragists' cause at least to the extent of inviting some of her Boston friends to meet one of the leaders who came to Boston in May 1881 — May Eliza Wright Sewall.* And although Alice did not participate actively, the "situation of women" occupied a central place in her conversations with Katharine: it came up again and again in their discussions of history, literature, contemporary politics, and private life.

Everywhere they found evidence of woman's oppression. Alice noted that her friend Constance Maud wanted to devote herself seriously to music as a profession,† "but as she is a daughter and not a son her tastes are set aside and she has to do parish work!" Alice joked with Katharine about the restrictions imposed on women, observing that when she felt "one of those longings to commit sin that come over us every now and then," she remembered that "all but gastronomic vice" was "denied by my miserable sex" and sent out for éclairs. She quoted Fanny Morse on the " 'busy ineffectiveness' of our kind." But it was the theme of women's superiority to men that came up again and again in her discussions with Katharine and her private diary entries.

Her views had changed in the ten years since she wrote of Wilky's first-born, "I am so glad that it is a boy and not another miserable girl brought into existence." When William's third son, Herman,‡ was born in January 1884, Alice wrote her sister-in-law a "congratulatory" note: "I am sorry that he has chosen the inferior sex though I suppose it is less on

* The poet Lucy Larcom sent Katharine a note saying that she would be glad to come meet Mrs. Sewall and her husband, "but I don't want to be advertised as present at the 'Suffrage Convention.' I never have raised that banner, and prefer not to appear under false colors. Not that I object, — what difference would it make if I did? And it may be the noblest banner in the world, only I am not yet convinced, any further than to be *sure* that women ought to control their *own* affairs. Whether they ought to help rule the men, legally and visibly, is another point."

† Constance Maud did become a musician, however, and a writer, as well. In addition to novels and memoirs, she published *Wagner's Heroes* (1896), *Wagner's Heroines* (1896), and *Heroines of Poetry* (1902).

‡ It was Herman who died of whooping cough and pneumonia in the summer of 1885, prompting William's remarks to Henry about his wife's nobility as a mother and nurse. The baby, born on January 31, 1884, looked (announced William) like a "little Israelite." The search for a name took some time, because William and Alice already had sons named Henry and William. Finally, the parents named him after their friend Hermann Hagen, a professor at Harvard's Scientific School. When the baby died, he was buried in a tiny grave at the Cambridge Cemetery, beside the grandparents he never knew.

one's conscience to have brought forth an oppressor ... than one of the oppressed." And when William and his Alice had a daughter in 1887, Alice was overjoyed with "the happy news of 'la belle fillette!' ... That 'he is a girl' delights me, it will be so good for the boys, elevate the tone of the house and be some one for *me* to associate with in the future! You and she," she wrote her sister-in-law, "will be two against three, Mother and I, however, maintained the fight more unequally still, two against five and I think I may add not altogether unsuccessfully." Two weeks later she added to William, "I am more and more delighted with the *sex* of the babe, your 'affectional-side,' as Aunt Kate wd. say will have a chance to develop in your relations with her. I feel as if I must hurry ... and protect the innocent darling before she is analyzed, labeled & pigeon-holed out of existence."

Alice's fears about sex and childbearing were inadvertently the subject of a letter she wrote a few years later, after she accidentally overheard an accouchement. A young couple had taken the apartment above hers at a rooming house in England for a fortnight, and on Christmas Day the woman went into labor. Alice, terrified, wanted to be moved to the hotel across the street, but her nurse "towed my heart back to its moorings by digitalis and poured a sufficient amount of Bromide upon my gunpowdery nerves [and] I returned to my ordinary passivity, although not serenity. It seems to have been more silliness than villainy in the people. It was very curious to lie here, and to hear the Xmas rejoicings through the gossamer walls on one side, and the groans of the woman in labour in the room above, where the mystery of Life and Death was acting itself out. How my heart burned within me at the cruelty of men! I have been haunted by the thought of Alice and all the child-bearing women ever since."

The idea of physical contact between the sexes seemed attractive only when abstract and innocent — and Alice cloaked it, characteristically, in Latinate mockery: "K. says this is a shocking hotel; she is always coming, at the turn of the stairs, upon a waiter and chambermaid, rebounding at sound of her, from osculatory relaxations. How different their life from ours! We toil not to be sure, but do we ever attain the Ideal as they must in the surreptitious kiss?"

Had she been less in the grip of this powerful subject, Alice might have laughed at her own euphemisms and the illogic of blaming men for the pain of childbirth. As it was, she saw sex and childbearing not as facts of nature or positive female functions, but as evidence of male cruelty. Men had power; they preyed on the weaker, suffering sex. Woman's only power lay in her moral superiority.

Again and again Alice praised women who had mastered men in one way or another. She congratulated Sara Darwin on the "subjection" of her husband. In the 1880s and nineties she repeatedly touted William's Alice as the better half of that couple, having converted some of her envy into a sense of solidarity. She wrote in 1888 to William that "ladies who come into the world featured, eyed & complected like Alice have little difficulty in managing shirking man." And she exhorted her sister-in-law to join her in superiority to William and the "ancient houri," Grace Norton: "Why try and like her because William does? — if he is a less highly organized being than you, why deny the most sacred instincts of yr. nature to fit a lower form? Every woman, wife or maid, knows that her fellow, Man, is to FLATTERY as blotting-paper to ink, he soaks in it, in no matter how crude a form, or how wreathed about in mouthing ineptitudes, with endless ecstasy!"

Some years earlier, she had threatened, reported her father to William's wife, to "expose some swindling concern in the papers, which from their Philadelphia offices advertise a silk-worm treatise and take in the public to the tune of a dollar a piece." Henry Sr. said he hoped she wouldn't use her own name in writing to the press. Alice retorted, "Yes, I will do so under my own name and add that I am the daughter of one Henry James, the sister of another, the aunt of a third, better than either."

In a less embattled frame of mind, she discussed in her diary the importance of a sense of self: "When will women begin to have the first glimmer that above all other loyalties is the loyalty to Truth, i.e., to yourself, that husband, children, friends and country are as nothing to that."

That "loyalty to Truth," Alice's paraphrase on women's behalf of Polonius' pompous "to thine own self be true," diverged radically from the idea of female selflessness embodied in her mother and Aunt Kate. Alice made the comparison extreme (devotion to others was *as nothing* next to loyalty to self) in the attempt to justify her own path and define an alternative.

In Katharine Loring she admired a woman free of enslavements to husband, children, and country. Katharine's devotion to Alice, which eventually did amount to "enslavement," looked all the more valuable because it bore no resemblance to the automatic selflessness of ordinary females. Paradoxically, Alice appreciated Katharine's ministrations precisely because they seemed to involve giving up the demands of a developed self. Once, as Katharine shuttled back and forth between her invalid sister and her invalid friend, Alice remarked to Aunt Kate that if Katharine had "not a crown of glory somewhere I don't know who will have! Her whole life & occupations broken up having to give up all she most wants to do and all taken as a matter of course. I wonder how much of courseness there would be about it if she happened to where [sic] trousers! Oh, the goodness of women!!" she exclaimed. "But you," she went on to her aunt, "certainly don't need any instruction . . ."

And again to Aunt Kate she mused, on observing that Katharine looked old and worn from the long strain of self-sacrifice, "Her existence must be a mild purgatory. Some day the rights of women will be respected, I suppose."

Alice James did not call herself a feminist. Her sympathy with the movement to establish women's rights was emotional rather than practical, personal rather than public. She believed in women's suffrage, education, physical and intellectual competence — but not in her own. Her lack of participation in feminist activities had partly to do with her sense of fatalism: she felt powerless to alter the position of women or her own sense of inferiority to Henry and William. But she saw her friends involved in activities that would in the long run make real differences in the fate of women — particularly, in the late seventies and early eighties, the founding of the Harvard Annex. In 1879, Katharine, Anna Ticknor, Annie Fields, Ellen Hooper Gurney, Lilian Horsford, Joseph Warner, Arthur Gilman, and Elizabeth Cary Agassiz (among others) were working to raise money, set up classes, and arrange for Harvard professors to teach the Annex students.

Alice was still recovering from her 1878 breakdown. The issues raised by the stirrings of feminism in women's education and suffrage touched intimately on her own conflicts — about the values attached to biological determinism, about equality, competition, the superiority of one sex over another. It was perhaps because she did care deeply about these issues that she did not attempt to participate. Emotional involvement in any kind of work or intellectual process seemed more than anything else to threaten her health. To work on behalf of her "miserable" and "disgusting" sex would have been, on the one hand, to diminish her sense of superiority to other women, and on the other, to make a dangerous self-assertion.

•

Even though Alice avoided the excitement of involvement in the "woman question" in the spring of 1883, her health did not improve. In mid-April, when Henry went off to visit friends in New York and Washington, Alice moved out to Beverly to spend two weeks with Katharine by the sea. Then, in early May, she placed herself in an institution that had recently been established in Jamaica Plain called the Adams Nervine Asylum.

The Adams Nervine, as it was called, treated "nervous people who are not insane." It had been founded in 1877 by the will of Seth Adams of Newton* for indigent, debilitated, "nervous" inhabitants of the Commonwealth of Massachusetts who needed "the benefit of a curative institution." It also took in paying cases, for fees determined by the managers of the institution according to the patients' means. The asylum had room for thirty patients, all of them women. Each applicant had to submit a statement, signed by her physician, certifying that she was suffering from a disease of the nervous system, that she was not insane, and that she could, in the doctor's opinion, be cured or materially benefited by treatment at the asylum.

Jamaica Plain was one of the most attractive of Boston's suburbs in the late nineteenth century. The estate of the asylum, on Centre Street, took up over sixteen acres of woods and lawns overlooking the grounds of the Arnold Arboretum. The buildings, constructed in the 1880s and still standing, are pure wood-frame Victorian Gothic, mixing architectural styles (Queen Anne Revival, Second Empire, Colonial) and extravagantly ornamented with scrollwork, wraparound porches, archways, dormer windows, and odd excrescences of cupola and gable. Enclosed corridors connect the buildings, and it is easy to imagine nurses and attendants scurrying through them, arms full of steaming basins and clean linens. The high-ceilinged patients' rooms, originally painted white, were

---

* Not related to the Henry Adams family, Seth Adams (1807–1872) made his money by inventing, with his brother Isaac, a printing press; later, he sold the press-manufacturing business and went into sugar refining. He had nervous troubles of his own, which took him out of business activities in the early 1860s and led to his ideas about a hospital that would treat nervous (but not psychotic) patients.

redone with wallpaper, ceiling tints, and ash picture molding when the "glaring whiteness" proved "trying to the vision of nervous invalids."

The corporation and the medical staff of the Adams Nervine consisted of Boston Brahmins. In 1883, the president of the corporation was Henry P. Kidder, the treasurer was Katharine Loring's father, the consulting physicians included James Jackson Putnam, Richard Edes, and Morrill Wyman. Katharine's sister, Louisa, headed one of the Visiting Committees of Ladies.

With its large endowment of real estate, stocks and bonds worth approximately $575,000, and its first-rate medical minds, the asylum presented an ideal situation for experiments in the treatment of nervous diseases in the last decades of the nineteenth century. The resident physician, Dr. Frank Page, noted in his 1883 report to the managers that the high rate of application (371 for the year 1882–1883) probably did not indicate a rise in the incidence of nervous disorders among women, but rather showed the urgent need for special facilities for the treatment of "nervous derangements."

In his 1882 report, Dr. Page offered a sociological analysis of his patient population and some observations on the causes of female breakdown. Although nervous diseases were generally assumed to be found among the upper and middle social classes (who are "free from the cares and responsibilities of life, delicate, sensitive, and easily excited to mental emotion"), Page reported from experience that these diseases were "confined to no one class." He cautioned that the numbers at the asylum were too small to yield reliable conclusions, but found his patients refuting the accepted notion that "the present system of education is largely operative in the production of the nervous invalids of today." Of the total number of women admitted to the asylum since it opened in 1880 — 136 — 34 percent had been housewives, 32 percent had listed no occupation, 4 percent were nurses, 16 percent were evenly distributed among a number of different occupations, and 14 percent were teachers. "Among housewives," continued Page, "overwork, care, anxiety, and sleeplessness, incident to domestic afflictions, were the assigned causes" of nervous distress — "worry being more largely operative than overwork . . .

"Among teachers, the causes assigned were, care of dependent and invalid relatives, overwork outside the school-room, and anxiety attendant upon an indifference to and lack of attachment for their work." Overwork in the schoolroom was only rarely attributed as the cause of breakdown: "on the contrary, it would seem that honest teaching, like any other honest mental work, is actually productive of sound health, and that it is rarely the cause of nervous exhaustion."

Page and his colleagues at the Adams Nervine held relatively enlightened views about the etiology of nervous disorders: they did not see nervous women as overeducated malingerers shirking their proper feminine functions or as histrionic victims of imaginary ills. Instead, they saw causes of nervous distress in the strain and fatigue of quintessential feminine functions — domestic overwork and excessive caring for others. That was a useful view as far as it went, but it did not account for women like Alice James, who were responding to subtler forms of pressure than domestic responsibility; and in assigning blame to the anxiety attendant on social functions, it failed to account for individual conflict. In addition, its implications for treatment were not clear. What the institution could offer its patients was primarily a respite from the cares and anxieties of their daily lives, a period of complete rest and freedom from responsibility.

Weir Mitchell's rest cure was by this time quite well known to doctors and nervous invalids throughout the East. "Weir Mitchell has been here curing all the dilapidated Bostonians," wrote Phillips Brooks in 1878. "His coming makes a great sensation for he is a very famous man." And a few years later William James wrote to his sister: "I dined at Phillips Brooks' 3 or 4 nights since in Co. with your friend Weir Mitchell, whose talked [sic] was very interesting but who struck me as if his intellectual and artistic nature might be developed at the expense of his moral stability . . . Mitchell said of the English 'they live in a climate which is a sort of poultice — no wonder their skins are good.'" And on the subject of female nervousness, William added, "I also sat next to Howells at dinner. He was very fat and good, asked about you, said his wife and [daughter] Winnie were both nervously prostrated."*

---

* Both Howells' wife, Elinor, and his daughter Winifred were nervous invalids. Van Wyck Brooks attributed the "squeamishness" of the "tender-minded" Howells to his experience with his wife — "a nervous invalid who required, if she did not exact, his continual devotion. He wrote much more for her than for anyone else, and his mind was unconsciously governed by her distaste for all that was disagreeable and unpleasant."

Winifred (1863-1889), Howells' eldest child, had been a nervous invalid since the age of fifteen. The mysterious disintegration of her health puzzled her family and doctors — including Mitchell and James Jackson Putnam. At sixteen, she had a severe breakdown: Putnam prescribed a regime of feeding and bed rest, à la Mitchell — and

William's reference to "your friend Weir Mitchell" probably meant only that Alice was interested in Mitchell's work, for she never ventured to Philadelphia to try his treatment. But the Adams Nervine experimented with a version of the rest cure, and Dr. Page discussed its selective efficacy in his annual report for 1883. Among his patients, he made distinctions between hysterics, melancholics, and neurasthenics — and even noted varieties of neurasthenia:

The value of "rest and seclusion" as remedial agents is an exceedingly interesting question [he reported to the asylum's trustees], in view of the rather indiscriminate application which has been made of this treatment to all forms of nervous disturbance ... In hysteria it assists by its discipline in regaining self-control, but *not* in melancholia, either of a mild or severe type. On the contrary, its uses in cases of *depression* invariably aggravates rather than soothes or mitigates the symptoms, and I do not resort to it in the treatment of this class

---

her eight meals a day prompted her father to nickname her "the lunch fiend." Later, in the 1880s, Mitchell himself advised force-feeding to restore her strength before her doctors could proceed to the psychological origins of her anorexia. But after Winny's death, in 1889, the autopsy showed evidence of an organic disease.

Alice wrote to Howells from England when Winny died, and, though her letter has not survived, his reply indicates that she had offered consolation by evoking their shared past. Howells wrote:

330 East 17th St., N.Y.
April 26, 1889

Dear Miss Alice:

I have not yet had the strength to reply to your brother Harry's beautiful letter about Winny; but I must try to send you some word of thanks for yours. It is strange, and not strange, either, that the greatest help and kindness in this bewildering grief of ours, should have come from your father's children; for your brother William said something that more than anything else enabled our hearts to lay hold on faith again, and supplemented with a hint of hope those perfect terms in which Harry expressed our loss. And now your message, with its memory of another world, completely past, is an intimation that we may somewhere else survive that of today, too, and of all earthly morrows. I cannot tell you with what tenderness I recurred to those Sundays, when you mentioned them, and with what vividness your dear father and mother's presence was with me again. I was greatly privileged to know such a man as he, and things that he said have enriched my life with a meaning that did not all appear in the moment. It consoles and encourages me that such a mind as his held fast to such a belief as his ...

The family join me in love, and in the warmest wishes for your welfare.

Yours sincerely,
W. D. Howells

of patients. In nervous exhaustion, so-called, whether of cerebral, spinal, or mixed types, it is more certain of satisfactory results than any other plan yet tried. It retards waste, checks morbid activities, and prevents the drains and lesser strains so fruitful in perpetuating this condition.

Page did not know, any more than Mitchell and other doctors of the late nineteenth century did, what caused the symptoms of neurasthenia, but the rest cure did seem to alleviate some of them. Warning again that his sample was too small for general conclusions, he hazarded the opinion that "heredity and temperament exert an important influence" in nervous disorders. Just as heredity could determine certain anatomical peculiarities, "so neurotic traits, whether psychological or not, to a much greater degree manifest themselves in parents and children for successive generations. Even disturbed nerve functions, like migraine and neuralgia, perpetuate themselves in different members of a family through a long line of descent."

Alice James had been diagnosed as hysterical *and* neurasthenic by various doctors at various times. She was also "melancholic," especially in 1883, feeling utterly alone and grieving, in a conflicted way, over the deaths of her parents. The Adams Nervine doctors advised her to rest, supervised her nutritional intake, gave her treatments of hot air, vapor baths, and massage. In 1883 the asylum acquired a popular new appliance called the Holtz Electrical Machine: hospital attendants applied its faradic and galvanic currents to Alice's nerves and muscles to relieve pain and stimulate normal functioning.

She remained at the asylum in Jamaica Plain for just over three months, from the beginning of May through early August. Then she returned to Katharine Loring at Beverly. Henry found her better, he told Francis Boott, "but there has been no miraculous cure."

Henry had enjoyed his own summer. "My sister is in the country. I have a house all to myself, wear no clothes, take 10 big baths a day, & dine on lemonade and ice-cream," he wrote to his London publisher. "Moreover, even under a torrid sun Boston is essentially breezy: so I do very well." But by August he was longing to be back in England, and since Alice appeared to be on the mend, he made plans to leave on the 22nd. She came down from Beverly to spend a last few days with him before his departure (she seemed "markedly and encouragingly better," he told William), and returned to Katharine immediately after he sailed. She stayed on at Beverly until the end of November.

In October, William traveled to Milwaukee for a last visit with Wilky, who had written to say that his heart trouble and Bright's disease had worsened and "it looks as if it would not be long before I shall peg out." On his way back, William reported to Alice that "my presence was evidently too exciting for him, — everything that interests him brings on attacks of hard breathing ... I had best not come again as long as poor Wilky lives, since all he wants is complete quiet and mental repose." Late in November, Caroline Cary James cabled William in Cambridge and Henry in London that Wilky had died. Alice wrote to Bob's wife, "I should like very much to hear from you how poor Carrie is, her letters are very touching. But what a blessing to think of that poor boy at rest." And from London, Henry asked William for news of Wilky's last hours: "May they have been easy. I suppose they were unconscious. I like to think that somewhere in the mysterious infinite of the universe, Father and Mother may exist together as pure, individual spirits, and that poor Wilkie, lightened of all his woes, may come to them and tell them of us, their poor *empêtrés* children on earth — This post brings me also a letter from Katharine Loring from which I gather, though she tries to dissimulate it, that on the whole since I have been away, Alice has been pretty poorly. I try to hope, however, that now she is in her own house, independent & surrounded with her own arrangements, she may pull herself together, if she doesn't languish from loneliness."

Throughout the fall, the ailing Louisa Loring had pre-empted Katharine's caretaking attentions, and in late November Alice moved back to Mount Vernon Street, to face the new nakedness and freedom William had forecast for her. With Henry off in London, Aunt Kate in New York, William and Alice preoccupied with their children, and Katharine with Louisa, Alice now faced exactly the alternatives Henry described: to pull herself together or languish from loneliness. She quickly established a daily routine of rest, galvinism, and massage treatments. Servants saw to the details of housekeeping; Alice had only to supervise. Friends came to call in the mornings, and she gave occasional dinner parties. Aunt Kate offered to come live with her, but Alice insisted on solitude. "She has always liked to be alone, and sought to be so a good deal," Kate told Rob's wife; besides, "any one in the house with her disturbs her life."

That was not quite true. Alice loved having Henry or Katharine Loring in the house. She specifically did not want Aunt Kate hovering anxiously in the foreground of her new life. Since Mary's death, Alice had proved able for the most part to manage alone, for her father and now for herself. She invited Kate as an occasional guest, but had no desire to depend on her too-solicitous aunt or share a household with her the way her mother had done. Besides, Alice now had a Katharine of her own.

Katharine Loring came to Mount Vernon Street whenever she could leave Louisa. During the winter of 1884, however, Louisa's health took a turn for the worse. Her weak lungs could no longer stand the bitter Boston winters, and her doctors suggested Katharine take her to Europe for the traditional cures of Swiss mountain air and the English seaside. Accordingly, the sisters departed in February. With both Henry and Katharine on the other side of the Atlantic, Alice now knew she was in danger of collapse. She made plans, as soon as Katharine left, to go to New York to try a new doctor and a new cure.

The doctor this time was William B. Neftel, a Russian émigré who specialized in nervous diseases. He had an office at 16 East 48 Street, and had treated a number of Bostonian friends of the Jameses, including Henry Adams' mother, Abigail Brooks Adams. His fees were high: Mrs. Adams reported to her husband that he saw one lady ten times and charged her $1000 (roughly $7400 in 1979 terms). But his skill was renowned, and wealthy nervous women were willing to pay a great deal for a cure.

Neftel treated his patients with galvanic electrical currents, on the theory that the nervous and muscular systems operated on the basis of transmitted electrical "messages." He believed that many spinal irritations and "neuralgias" symptomatic of hysteria could be treated by redirecting electrical currents that had gone wrong and stimulating those that were dormant. He disagreed with Weir Mitchell about the efficacy of rest in treating chronic female nervousness. In Neftel's view, exercise was the key to good health: nervous disorders affected body tissues and the "accumulated products of tissue-metamorphosis act in a deleterious manner upon all the vital processes, especially producing a depressing effect upon the muscular and nervous system, and a feeling of exhaustion." Exhausting substances deactivated the sensitive electromotor system of the muscles, resulting in nervous exhaustion throughout the body. Exercise, bringing fresh blood and lymph to the affected muscles, helped remove these "effete substances" so that the organs could resume normal function.

Having tried rest at the Adams Nervine, Alice now tried exercise with Neftel. At first she felt a "wonderfull change quite as if I had been transformed," she wrote to Fanny Morse. "The doctor is as kind and easy to get on with as he can be and the only thing I have to complain of is that 'Rome was not built in a day'; as I have known this fact for a month or two I was foolish to allow my hopes to rise through the specious representations of a non-Puritan temperament, to put it mildly." Neftel *was* expensive; she expected to come home a pauper, she told Fanny.

In the past she had liked New York; compared with Cambridge, its pace was faster, its women more fashionable, its intellectual climate more stimulating. Now, however, she hated the "alien, odious spot. How any one can live here and lead a virtuous and reputable life amidst the Jews, the tawdry, flimsy houses and the ash-barrels seems hard to understand, but I suppose there is some domestic existence somewhere." Before, she had liked the escape from parental constraints that New York offered; now, trying to establish a new kind of domestic life on her own, New York seemed hard and cold, and Boston, "that blessed humble city," began to seem like "a shrine of all the virtues." She told Fanny that she was "beginning to sympathize with the lady who died and found Heaven delightfull 'only it was *not* Boston.' "

When she returned after two months to blessed humble Boston, she reported to Sara Darwin that her stay in New York had been moderately successful: "I went to test the skill of a Russian electrician . . . of whom I had heard great things and who certainly either in spite or because of his quackish quality has done me a great deal of good in many ways. I was charmed at first with the Slavic flavour of our intercourse but I soon found myself sighing for unadulterated Jackson. To associate with and to have to take seriously a creature with the moral substance of a monkey becomes degrading after awhile, no matter how one may have been seduced by his 'shines' at the first going off. His electricity however has the starching properties of the longest Puritan descent, and I wish very much that you might try it some of these days." This pattern of initial enthusiasm for and ultimate disillusion with doctors, described sardonically in terms of seduction, intercourse, sighs, and charms, repeated itself again and again over the next several years. Neither the perpetual quest for cure nor the search for a medical man who could fully comprehend the intricate nature of Alice's trouble was ever to meet with success.

Back in Boston, Alice continued to try to manage on her own. She told Sara in the spring of 1884 that "I have been anxious to solve the problem . . . as to whether I could not make a home for myself here and to my great satisfaction I find that I can." Henry and William, guardedly optimistic about her, agreed that she had "spirit enough to survive anything." As always, Alice's stalwart comments on her life at the time contrast sharply with her reflections later in her diary, where she described the terrible loneliness of this year: "Those ghastly days, when I was by myself in the little house in Mt. Vernon Street, how I longed to flee in to the firemen next door and escape from the 'Alone, Alone!' that echoed thro' the house, rustled down the stairs, whispered from the walls, and confronted me, like a material presence, as I sat waiting, counting the moments as they turned themselves from today into tomorrow; for 'Time does not work until we have ceased to watch him.' "

She went in the summer of 1884 to Pomfret, Connecticut, where Katharine had engaged rooms for her earlier in the year. The country was lovely, but even lonelier than Boston. Alice had written to Sara in May that she might soon have questions about "ways and means in England, and the feeling that you are there, dear Sara, will strengthen my hands very much to undertake what would otherwise seem a very forlorn venture." Going to England, to be near Henry, Katharine, Sara, and Annie Richards, seemed like an admission of defeat. But by the fall of 1884, it had come to seem preferable to staying on alone in Boston.

Katharine came back from Europe on September 20, leaving her father and sister together at Bournemouth on the south coast of England, to "fetch" Alice. They booked passage on the *Pavonia* for November 1. Alice packed her trunks and rented her Manchester and Mount Vernon Street houses. She planned to go straight from the boat to London. Katharine would stay with Louisa at Bournemouth for the winter, within easy visiting distance.

On the clear cold November morning, Alice and Katharine sailed out of Boston Harbor on the *Pavonia*. From the deck of the ship Alice turned around for a parting glimpse of the Puritan capital that had been her home for over twenty years. She did not know it then, but she would never see America again. From England several years later, nostalgic under a "tide of homesickness," she wrote of her "longing to see a shaft of sunshine shimmering thro' the pines, breathe in the resinous air and throw my withered body down upon my mother earth, bury my face in the coarse grass, worshipping all that the ugly, raw emptiness of the blessed land stands for — the embodiment of a Huge Chance for hemmed in Humanity! Its flexible conditions stretching and lending themselves to all sizes of man; pallid and naked of necessity; undraped by the illusions and mystery of a moss-grown, cobwebby past, but overflowing with a divine good-humour and benignancy — a helping hand for the faltering, an indulgent thought for the discredited, a heart of hope for every outcast of tradition!"

Part III

The Wider Sphere of Reference

... Laura had not aspired to be coaxed or coddled into forgetfulness: she wanted rather to be taught a certain fortitude — how to live and hold up one's head even while knowing that things were very bad. A brazen indifference — it was not exactly that that she wished to acquire; but were there not some sorts of indifference that were philosophic and noble?

— Henry James, "A London Life"

It is the most supremely interesting moment in life, the only one in fact when living seems life ... It is as simple in one's own person as any fact of nature, the fall of a leaf or the blooming of a rose, and I have a delicious consciousness, ever present, of wide spaces close at hand, and whisperings of release in the air.

— Alice James to William James, July 30, 1891

Chapter Fourteen

"Peculiar Intense and Interesting Affections"

ALICE JAMES left behind more than her American past when she crossed the Atlantic with Katharine Loring in late 1884. The intermittent periods of health she had known between her long bouts of illness now also receded into the distance. Her body took over, as she had predicted it would in her first dramatic breakdown in 1868, when she had seen "so distinctly that it was a fight simply between my body and my will, a battle in which the former was to be triumphant to the end." The remaining years of her life were almost totally dominated by sickness and the struggle for a sense of moral triumph.

Although she later came to idealize America as the embodiment of a "Huge Chance for hemmed in Humanity," Alice found England a more congenial setting than Boston for a career of invalidism. America reproached the "chance" not taken. Like Rowland Mallett at the opening of Henry's *Roderick Hudson,** Alice found her sense of uselessness less troubling in Europe than in America. "It's rather strange that here," she wrote in her diary after living in England for several years, "among this robust and sanguine people, I feel not the least shame or degradation at being ill, as I used at home among the anaemic and the fagged. It comes of course in one way from the conditions being so easy, from the sense of leisure, work reduced to a minimum and the god *Holiday* worshipped so

---

* Explaining to Mary Garland why he is going, Mallett remarks, ". . . I have the misfortune to be rather an idle man, and in Europe both the burden and the obloquy of idleness are less heavy than here."

perpetually and effectually by all classes. Then what need to justify one's existence when one is simply one more amid a million of the superfluous?"

•

While Alice and Katharine were crossing the Atlantic, Henry James wrote from London to Grace Norton, who had expressed alarm at what Alice's advent in England might mean for him. He gently admonished his "dear anxious — too-anxious friend" for her "rare facility for taking the world tragically" and assured her that he was not in the least worried by Alice's impending visit: "She is not coming in any special sense, at all, 'to me,' — she is simply coming to Europe, and apparently will not even alight at my door when she arrives ... She is unspeakably un-dependent and independent, she *clings* no more than a bowsprit, has her own plans, purposes, preferences, practices, pursuits, more than any one I know, has also amply sufficient means, &c &c, in short, even putting her possible failure to improve at the worst, will be very unlikely to tinge or modify my existence in any uncomfortable way."

Alice, Katharine, and an American friend of Louisa Loring's named Mattie Whitney arrived at Liverpool on the morning of November 11. Henry was waiting to meet them with a maid he had brought from London. He boarded the ship out in the stream at seven-thirty, and found Alice (he reported to Aunt Kate) "in a *very* knocked up condition." The voyage had been brief and not particularly rough, but Alice had been ill before she left Boston and got worse at sea. Katharine and Miss Whitney had taken turns tending to her. She was carried off the *Pavonia* by two stewards to the rooms Henry had booked at the Adelphi Hotel. For several days she was too ill to travel. Katharine and Miss Whitney soon departed for Bournemouth, where Louisa was waiting for them. Henry stayed with his sister until she grew strong enough to be moved, then brought her up to London and established her with her maid in rooms at 40 Clarges Street, just off Green Park and around the corner from his Bolton Street flat.

As soon as word of her arrival in London got around, Alice began receiving invitations. Mrs. James Russell Lowell, whose husband was then the American minister to the Court of St. James's, wanted her for Thanksgiving dinner. Sara Darwin asked her to Basset for two weeks at Christmas. William's American friend Charlotte King invited her to

Versailles. But Alice accepted none of these engagements. She did not leave her room once in nine weeks, though she did receive occasional callers. Henry visited twice a day. Katharine and Miss Whitney came up from Bournemouth for two weeks at the end of November. The novelist Mrs. Humphry Ward, Matthew Arnold's niece, came to call, as did the widow of J. R. Green, and J. J. Garth Wilkinson's daughter, Mary. But most days Alice felt too ill even to see visitors.

Her symptoms, this time, were entirely somatic. She was "never nervous," reported Henry to Aunt Kate. She consulted a Dr. Garrod, recommended by Dr. Beach as "the only man in the world who knew anything about suppressed gout." At first she liked the English physician, "with whom I spent the most affable hour of my life," she told her sister-in-law Alice. Garrod had "listened with apparent interest and attention to my oft-repeated tale, which by the way to save breath and general exhaustion I am going to have printed in a small pamphlet." He thoroughly satisfied her with the "percussing and stethoscoping" of his careful examination, but not with his negligible remedial suggestions. He ordered her spine sponged with salt water and prescribed pills containing Indian hemp. He diagnosed no organic trouble: the disturbances in her legs and stomach were entirely functional, he said, and the weakness of her legs would not lead to paralysis, "a grim spectre which has been staring me in the face for a long time."

Dr. Garrod so pleased Alice that she consented to remain in London under his care even though Katharine stayed away at Bournemouth with Louisa. At the end of December, however, came a violent attack with "great distress of the heart." Alice thought she was dying. Katharine was summoned from Bournemouth. Henry hovered anxiously by his sister's bed. Dr. Garrod claimed she had struck the pneumogastric nerve in applying galvinism to the back of her neck to relieve a headache and had induced something like a paralytic stroke. Alice recovered quickly from this crisis, but she disagreed with Garrod. At first she saw the attack as simply a variation of her old hysteria, not as a condition brought on by galvinism; but then she decided it was a reaction to the hemp (*Cannabis sativa*) Garrod had prescribed, which she felt had affected her heart. This incident caused a "great reaction" against the doctor. Now her legs would not move at all. She no longer wanted to stay in London, and toward the end of January she moved to Bournemouth to be with Katharine.

With Henry doing the reporting to the interested William and Aunt

Kate, the nature of Alice's physical symptoms becomes much clearer than it had before. Since his parents were gone, Henry did not need to disguise his sister's pain and did not obscure her troubles with philosophical optimism. In addition, Alice wrote more during this period, and described her symptoms more concretely, than she ever had before. She could no longer deny that her "career" consisted of these ills.

Typically, in late 1884 and early '85, she experienced weeks of steady pain in her legs, head, or stomach — and then suddenly "went off" or "under" in an intense attack. Typically, too, she had a highly emotional reaction to her doctor. First, she adored him — time after time she or Henry reported on "the best," "the finest," "the first doctor she has ever liked"; then, inevitably, something went wrong. Each doctor failed to live up to her hope of perfect understanding and care. And, of course, each failed to cure her.

In her responses to her doctors, Alice was in part protesting against the limitations of nineteenth-century psychological science. She was also registering a complaint against men in general and "great" men of science in particular. And her reactions were charged with suppressed sexuality. Doctors were probably the only men who touched her adult body. In addition to whatever excitement or shame she may have felt on being physically examined, she brought extraordinarily high expectations to these encounters. In her family, the concern elicited by illness passed for love — and doctors were the scientifically sanctioned personification of solicitude and care. The understanding of Alice's physical troubles meant, by this time, the assessment of her whole complex being. But no doctor could understand or sympathize enough.

At the beginning of 1885, Alice reported to Aunt Kate, "I asked the doctor [Garrod] whether it was not unusual for a person to be so ill & have no organic trouble & he said 'Yes, very unusual indeed.' — I should have thought he would therefore have liked to do something for me, but it was only my folly in going to a great man — their only interest being in diagnosis & having absolutely no conscience in their way of dealing with one." The following year she told William, "It may seem supine to you that I don't descend into the medical arena, but I must confess my spirit quails before any more gladiatorial encounters. It requires the strength of a horse to survive the fatigue of waiting hour after hour for the great man and then the fierce struggle to recover one's self-respect." She then drew a direct parallel between being a patient and being a woman: "I think the difficulty is my inability to assume the receptive attitude, that cardinal virtue in woman, the absence of which has always made me so uncharming to and uncharmed by the male sex."

Alice did not know, any more than her doctors did, just what ailed her, but she sensed its relation to her sexuality and the ideals of nineteenth-century womanhood. Her illness was a form of self-assertion, among other things, and she took pleasure in baffling the medical experts. In the fall of 1886 another English doctor, Townsend, told her that she had a gouty diathesis complicated by an abnormally sensitive nervous organization, and that the neurosis in her legs was brought about by anxiety and strain. He predicted that her health would improve when she reached menopause* (which she called "middle life"), and she reported to William that "this seems highly probable as I have had sixteen periods the last year. Dr. Townsend," she went on, "is personally the flower of that type which makes the Briton valuable. I never came in contact with a more beautiful soul, manly, impersonal, intelligent, kind as a nursing mother, but with too pale-eyed a purity and unhumorousness of being to thread the mazes of trans-Atlantic neurasthenia. But it is a gain to know such creatures exist in the world."

It is impossible to see into the exact workings of Alice's psychological conflicts after a century has passed, but their general nature leaks from her writing in a number of ways. Few in the psychologically minded twentieth century could write the kind of autobiographical prose she did without an awareness of what they inadvertently gave away. In the 1880s, she said of Garrod, for instance, "My doctor turned out as usual a *fiasco,* an unprincipled one too. I could get nothing out of him & he slipped thro' my cramped & clinging grasp as skilfully as if his physical conformation had been that of an eel instead of a Dutch cheese — The gout he looks upon as a small part of my trouble, 'it being complicated with an excessive nervous sensibility,' but I could get no suggestions of any sort as to climate, baths or diet from him. The truth was he was entirely puzzled about me and had not the manliness to say so. I got from him however a very thorough examination . . ."

She described herself repeatedly as a weak vessel containing a powerful

---

* This view of menopause was not uncommon. If menstruation seemed a curse and called attention to a woman's sexual function, its cessation often seemed a blessing and a release. Many nineteenth-century doctors blamed female nervousness on female anatomy, and many saw the periodic loss of blood as contributing to nervous weakness and exhaustion. Menopause, then, was often welcomed as the beginning of a new freedom from the pain and sufferings of womanhood.

substance that threatened to overflow, explode, spurt out of her. When she began to keep a diary, it was as "an outlet to that geyser of emotions, sensations, speculations and reflections which ferments perpetually within my poor old carcass for its sins." She saw herself as "an emotional volcano within, with the outward reverberation of a mouse and the physical significance of a chip of lead pencil." After a visit from Katharine, she remarked, "What an indigestion of remarks *rentrés* I've had since Kath. left! I shall learn to cork myself up again before long and return to my state of 'bottled lightning' as Wm. calls it."

The nature of the stuff inside her changed with her changing moods and circumstances: it was her blood, "a pale fluid that stagnates in my veins," and a "congenital faith" that "flows through me like a limpid stream." Another time it represented life force:

Yesterday Nurse and I had a good laugh but I must allow that decidedly she "had" me. I was thinking of something that interested me very much and my mind was suddenly flooded by one of those luminous waves that sweep out of consciousness all but the living sense and overpower one with joy in the rich, throbbing complexity of life, when suddenly I looked up at Nurse, who was dressing me, and saw her primitive, rudimentary expression . . . as of no inherited quarrel with her destiny of putting petticoats over my head; the poverty and deadness of it contrasted to the tide of speculation that was coursing thro' my brain made me exclaim, "Oh! Nurse, don't you wish you were inside of *me!*" — her look of dismay and vehement disclaimer — "Inside of you, Miss, when you have just had a sick head-ache for five days!" — gave a greater blow to my vanity, than that much battered article has ever received. The headache had gone off in the night and I had clean forgotten it — when the little wretch confronted me with it, at this sublime moment when I was feeling within me the potency of a Bismarck, and left me powerless before the immutable law that however great we may seem to our own consciousness no human being would exchange his for ours, and before the fact that *my* glorious role was to stand for *Sick headache* to mankind! What a grotesque I am to be sure! Lying in this room, with the resistance of a thistle-down, having illusory moments of throbbing with the pulse of the Race, the Mystery to be solved at the next breath and the fountain of all Happiness within me — . . .

This passage, in which Alice cast herself both as a frail receptacle and an explosive force, reflected her continuing conflicts about sexual identity. She wanted to be chaste, pure, innocent, and delicate, as well as strong, angry, imperial, vital. This scheme differed from the simpler good-bad, mind-body distinctions she had made in her early breakdowns. In these later descriptions, the body was not simply bad: she admired the force in these coursing liquids. If doomed to be a frail vessel, she could still feel within herself the potency of a Bismarck — though perhaps it was *because* of that sense of power that she had to be a frail vessel. Recognizing the nature of this ratio, she noted "the sense of vitality, in short, simply proportionate to the excess of weakness!"

•

Behind the scenes of the illness that dominated Alice's life in the 1880s, two other complex dramas were being enacted, both interpersonal, both triadic. One involved Alice, Katharine, and Louisa Loring; the other, Alice, Katharine, and Henry James.

Alice wanted Katharine all to herself. But Louisa, with her weak lungs and nervous prostrations, stood (or, rather, lay) in the way. From London, in January 1885, Alice wrote to Aunt Kate, "Kath. comes in of course every day and does all my marketing for me. They [the Lorings] seem to be quiescent for the present but I tremble every time I see her lest their plans change. Louisa seems to be doing well & of course from my point of view seems like an Amazon but she may take a fancy to move at any moment." Henry, reporting on Louisa's "peculiar, nervous . . . somewhat obstreperous condition," felt sorry for Katharine, caught "between 'nervousness' *in* her family and out of it!" And Katharine herself observed that there appeared to be a "regular boom in invalids."

Alice's worst attacks came when Katharine was off with her sister. Summoned by telegram, Katharine would race back to Alice's side and stay there until the crisis had passed. Inevitably, it did pass, but Alice did not usually improve in Katharine's presence. On the contrary, she appeared to grow weaker and more dependent with Katharine there to be depended on.

For instance, when Alice left London to join the Lorings at Bournemouth in 1885, her legs would not move, and the journey caused such a "bad upset" that she did not get out of bed for months. At Bournemouth, Katharine ministered alternately to her sister and her friend. When the Lorings went up to London in April, planning a summer of European travel, Alice's spine condition became so "delicate and critical" that she could not move at all. Henry came down to Bournemouth, with a nurse-companion for his sister, to stay with her indefinitely. Fortunately for Henry, Robert Louis Stevenson was living at Bournemouth. James described the "deadly consumptive" novelist to Grace Norton as "an old acquaintance . . . ripening now into a friend," and the two writers spent long, pleasurable evenings together over literature and claret in Stevenson's rooms by the sea. Katharine hovered in London within convenient reach. In May, Alice had a "cataclysmic" attack of palpitations. The nurse Henry had brought, whose previous experience had been at Dr. Daniel Hack Tuke's London insane asylum, treated Alice as merely morbid and hysterical — a disastrous tack. Furious that Alice would not obey her orders, the nurse quit. Alice implored Henry to send for Katharine, who hurried down from London. Henry described the scene to Aunt Kate: Louisa "having nervous fits in one house, produced by her impatience to get away," while Alice "in a state of great prostration, was having nervous fits in another (aggravated by a knowledge of Louisa's)." Katharine flew between them and finally "calmed the waters." Henry went up to London to find a new nurse.

The Lorings decided in May to go to Switzerland for a month, after which Katharine would come back to Alice, since Louisa's health was improving and their father and brother were coming out to join her. "The plan," wrote Henry to Aunt Kate, "is doubtless subject to variations of detail, from possible fluctuations in Louisa's health, but what it means is that, *virtually,* Katharine comes back to Alice for a permanency. Her being with her may be interrupted by absences, but evidently it is the beginning of a living-together, for the rest of such time as Alice's life may last. I think that a conviction on K.'s part at *bottom,* beneath her superficial optimism, that it *may* not last long, has something to do with the arrangement — for evidently it is a kind of definite understanding between them . . ."

And then Henry confided to Aunt Kate something of his own reactions to this "arrangement" of Alice's and Katharine's — a topic he had discussed with his aunt before:

We must accept it with gratitude. One may think that her being with A. is not in the long run the best thing for A.; but the latter is *too ill* to make the long run the main thing to think about. There *may* be no "long run" at all; and if there is, a *long* period with K. will work better than a *short* one, especially if it is free from the baleful element of Louisa's conflicting claims and K.'s divided duty — which had much to do with Alice's downward course after going to B[ournemouth]. Lastly a devotion so perfect and generous as K.L.'s is a gift of providence. Moreover, there is about as much possibility of Alice's giving Katharine up on the ground I speak of as of her giving her legs to be sawed off. She said to me a few days ago that she believed if she could have Katharine *quietly & uninterruptedly,* for a year, "to relieve her of all responsibility!" she would get well. Amen! She will get well, or she won't but, either way, it lies between themselves. I shall devote my best energies to taking the whole situation less hard in the future than I have done hitherto.

Henry's repeated protestations as to how grateful the James family ought to be for Katharine and Alice's "definite understanding" indicates how little he really cared for it. He told Aunt Kate not to come out to help care for Alice because "while *she* is with her any one else is simply a complication, for the simple reason that she is the one person or thing in the world that Alice really cares about!" He believed Katharine's caretaking did Alice "more harm than good," but "even if it were a much worse prospect than it is, there would be no possibility of averting it, for it is a matter between themselves." The "harm" he saw in the relations between the two women appears to have had to do with Alice's absolute and tenacious dependence on Katharine. When Louisa Loring was competing for Katharine's attention, Alice's health got dramatically worse; Henry reported the situation "improved distinctly" by the elimination of Louisa. But even without competition, Henry concluded, Alice did not get better. When Alice, "in an acute nervous fit, *implores* that K. be sent for," wrote Henry to Aunt Kate, "one must do it: & it would be an impossible situation that we should say to Katharine that she is bad for Alice and must stay away, and yet should expect her to hold herself ready to rush to the rescue when Alice cried out for her. I think her foolish optimism is now rapidly passing away and that she judges Alice's state very much as I do." He vowed again, for the future, to "assent" to Katharine's return "with a good grace, for the simple reason that it is the only thing I can do unless I take Alice completely on my own shoulders — which is obviously impossible from every point of view."

For the first and virtually only time, Henry appears to have seen less than the whole truth about his sister's emotional life. His assessment of the rivalry between Louisa and Alice was correct, as was his observation that Alice did not get well even when she had Katharine all to herself. But his belief that Katharine did Alice more harm than good showed a curious lapse of perspicacity. He may not have been especially fond of his sister's friend: she was energetic, high-minded, sometimes astringent, and thoroughly Yankee, whereas he generally preferred women with more roundness and curves in their characters. But Alice genuinely loved Katharine and felt loved in return. In seeing the relationship as harmful, Henry was mistaking an effect for a cause: Alice used illness as a way to ensure Katharine's continuing care; once she had that, she reported herself fulfilled, content, at peace — though not cured.

Henry had assured Grace Norton that Alice in England would not modify his existence "in any uncomfortable way." Whether he had believed in this cheery assertion (and he may have been defending his sister by laughing at Grace's anxiety), it was now apparent that Alice's tyrannical helplessness might drastically modify his existence. He knew how she relished independence, yet her illness made her rely on others for every detail of daily life. He was neither willing nor able to assume total responsibility for her welfare, and Katharine was. Besides, as he had told Aunt Kate, there was about as much possibility of Alice's giving up Katharine as of her giving her legs to be sawed off. His grisly figure of speech was singularly appropriate: Alice, suffering from "nervous paralysis," *had* virtually given up the power of independent mobility.* The more helpless she grew, the more Katharine took over. And Katharine had told Henry it was her desire "quite as strongly as Alice's" to be with her to the end. Henry knew he had no alternative to assent.

The two women rented a cottage together at the top of Hampstead Heath for the summer of 1885. It consisted of only four small rooms, but they squeezed in happily. In a Bath chair bought and wheeled by the "munificent" Katharine, Alice went out on sunny days for long excursions around the Heath. Her letters and diary entries generally stopped when Katharine came to stay, and she left no record of this summer at Hampstead; but from later remarks, a picture of her feelings about her "beloved K." comes into focus.

When Katharine departed for America after a two-month visit in 1889, Alice wrote in her diary, "She seems as large a joke as ever, an embodiment of the stretchable, a purely transatlantic and modern possibility

---

* Each of the James children had at one time or another felt wounded or crippled, just as their father had been, and Alice's illness curtailed her life even more severely than her father's amputation had done his; the similarity grew particularly striking when she lost the use of her legs.

... I feel like a creature who, after a long draught of fresh air, has crept back under an exhausted receiver closing down over her again with a hopeless and all too familiar click."

Her own version of what Henry had called (though Alice did not know it) Katharine's "foolish optimism" shows her able to laugh at herself without the usual biting sarcasm: "Katharine is a most sustaining optimist; she proposed writing for me this morning. I said, 'Why, you won't have time.' 'Oh, yes, I'm not going until twelve, and by that time you are always back again in bed, fainted.'"

Living with Katharine and a nurse at a hotel in London's South Kensington in 1890, Alice described her pleasure at being taken care of: "It is so amusing watching Katharine and even little Nurse managing me, and the feeling of acquiescence and sense of their wisdom and desire to play into their hands and meet them half way, is very curious and diverting." Then, with no transition, she quoted Christina Rossetti's lines:

> When I am dead, my dearest,
>   Sing no sad songs for me.
> Plant thou no roses at my head
>   Nor shady cypress tree.
> Be the green grass above me
>   With showers and dewdrops wet;
> And if thou wilt, remember,
>   And if thou wilt, forget.

Alice repeatedly drew attention to Katharine's energy and activity, her competent, "elastic," "stretchable," "flexible" character — just the qualities Alice herself lacked. One day in 1890, surveying her own bleak, crippled existence, she elucidated the feeling of potential power she got through her attachment to Katharine: "A life lifted out of all material care or temptation to which all the rudimentary impulses were unknown, a collection simply of fantastic *un*productive emotions enclosed within tissue paper. Walls, rent equally by pleasure as by pain — animated by a never-ceasing belief in and longing for *action,* relentlessly denied, all safety-valves shut down in the way of 'the busy ineffectiveness of women.' As I look up and find my better half Katharine effectually removing certain streaks of grime from the wall paper with a bit of india rubber my spirits rise in the hope that the unremitting and various na-

ture of her muscular contractions may shed a glamour over her humiliated appendage."*

•

Henry's continuing unease about Alice's relations with Katharine
showed up in the novel he was working on in the 1880s. He had first
sketched out the idea for *The Bostonians* when he was living on Mount
Vernon Street with Alice in 1883, after their parents' deaths. Henry
James had come of age as a novelist in Europe in the 1870s. His themes
had been transatlantic; his scenes, European. In the early eighties he was
looking to construct a particularly American tale, and had asked himself
"what was the most salient and particular point in our social life." The
answer, as he observed it in Boston's parlors, streets, and periodicals during his sojourn there, presented itself as "the situation of women, the decline of the sentiment of sex, the agitation on their behalf." He would
set his story in Boston, he told his American publisher in 1883, and focus
it on "an episode connected with the so-called 'woman's movement.'"
Its characters would be for the most part of "the radical reforming type,
who are especially interested in the emancipation of women, giving them
the suffrage, releasing them from bondage, co-educating them with men,
etc. They regard this as the great question of the day — the most urgent
and sacred reform."

On the issues and facts of American feminism in the 1880s Henry was
rather vague. Feminism provided the setting rather than the subject for
the novel he began to write in 1884-1885, with his sister living near him
in London. The woman's movement, which he put in quotes, offered a
vehicle for his portrait of the reforming New England spirit in its decline; but more important still, it seemed to him the appropriate back-
drop for the sexual drama he planned to portray. The real subject, as he
sketched it in his notebooks in 1883, was "one of those friendships between women which are so common in New England" — and for which
he had a model close at hand. The novel, published in 1885, presents
such a friendship and the struggle over one of the women between the
other woman and a man. In this struggle, James dramatized a confrontation between conservative masculine values and the new "feminine" age,
and raised disturbing questions about what it meant to be a man or a

---

* Henry had described himself when he first encountered Alice and Katharine together in 1881 as a "superfluous appendage."

woman in late nineteenth-century America. He depicted a decaying social order in which the passionate intensities of the old and new values were equally unattractive.

In the novel, patrician Bostonian Olive Chancellor and her conservative southern cousin, Basil Ransom, struggle over Verena Tarrant. Verena's lineage traces back to Boston transcendentalists, but the fine old flame of high-minded social thinking that characterized Emerson and Thoreau has burned down to nothing in her father, a "moralist without a moral sense," a false preacher and nostrum-monger who lives off his daughter's gifts. Out of her father's shabby world of mesmerism, faith healing, spiritualism, and public display, the innocent Verena has emerged with a talent for inspirational speaking on practically any topic. Her subject at the opening of *The Bostonians* is feminism.

Verena's pliable femininity contrasts sharply with Olive's brittle, hysterical feminism. Olive, as rich as Verena is poor, as cold as the girl is warm, has a heritage as Puritan as Verena's is heterodox. The Brahmin Olive lives in a small elegant house on Charles Street (as did Mrs. James T. Fields, in her "Boston marriage" with Sarah Orne Jewett), and her sister describes her as "full of rectitude ... She would reform the solar system if she could get hold of it." Pale, nervous, high-strung, given to sudden outbursts of gesture and speech, Olive trembles with fury at men and vibrates with ardent devotion to Verena and the feminist cause. She radiates suffering and makes an ideology of pain. After meeting Verena at a feminist gathering (described by another character as a "rendezvous of witches on the Brocken"), Olive determines that she and Verena will work together to redress the collective feminine grievance, Olive providing the money and ideas, Verena inspiring others to join them with her remarkable oratorical powers.

Olive's feminism, far more emotional than political, is in essence a sharp cry of protest against the "exquisite" weakness of women and the "odious" strength of men. James described her as

very eloquent when she reminded Verena how the exquisite weakness of women had never been their defense, but had only exposed them to sufferings more acute than masculine grossness can conceive. Their odious partner had trampled upon them from the beginning of time, and their tenderness, their abnegation, had been his opportunity. All the bullied wives, the stricken mothers, the dishonored, deserted maidens who have lived on the earth and longed to leave it, passed and repassed before her eyes, and the interminable

dim procession seemed to stretch out a myriad hands to her . . . She had analyzed to an extraordinary fineness their susceptibility, their softness; she knew
(or thought she knew) all the possible tortures of anxiety, of suspense and
dread; and she had made up her mind that it was women, in the end, who had
paid for everything. In the last resort the whole burden of the human lot came
upon them; it pressed upon them far more than on the others, the intolerable
load of fate. It was they who sat cramped and chained to receive it; it was they
who had done all the waiting and taken all the wounds. The sacrifices, the
blood, the tears, the terrors were theirs. Their organism was in itself a challenge to suffering, and men had practiced upon it with an impudence that
knew no bounds. As they were the weakest most had been wrung from them,
and as they were the most generous they had been most deceived. Olive
Chancellor would have rested her case, had it been necessary, on these general
facts; and her simple and comprehensive contention was that the peculiar
wretchedness which had been the very essence of the feminine lot was a monstrous artificial imposition, crying aloud for redress. She was willing to admit
that women, too, could be bad; that there were many about the world who
were false, immoral, vile. But their errors were as nothing to their sufferings;
they had expiated, in advance, an eternity, if need be, of misconduct.

Verena's softness arouses a passionate possessiveness in Olive, and
James's language describing their relation is rich in sexual nuance. When
Olive, in a "tremulous, tentative tone," accuses Verena of wanting to see
Mr. Ransom, Verena, "panting" with eloquence, insists that she has renounced men and is "more wedded to our old dreams than ever." Olive
"stilled herself, while the girl uttered one soft, pleading sentence after
another . . . She looked at Verena fixedly, felt that she was stirred to her
depths, that she was exquisitely passionate and sincere, that she was a
quivering, spotless, consecrated maiden, that she really had renounced,
that they were both safe, and that her own injustice and indelicacy had
been great. She came to her slowly, took her in her arms and held her
long — giving her a silent kiss."

Basil Ransom is as determined to win Verena for himself as Olive is to
keep her. His views on women are those of a southern traditionalist —
and they are remarkably close to the views of Alice and Henry's father.
Ransom held that women were delicate, agreeable creatures, whom Providence had

placed under the protection of the bearded sex; and it was not merely a humorous idea with him that whatever might be the defects of Southern gentle-

men, they were at any rate remarkable for their chivalry. He was a man who still, in a slangy age, could pronounce that word with a perfectly serious face.

This boldness did not prevent him from thinking that women were essentially inferior to men, and infinitely tiresome when they declined to accept the lot which men had made for them. He had the most definite notions about their place in nature, in society, and was perfectly easy in his mind as to whether it excluded them from any proper homage. The chivalrous man paid that tax with alacrity. He admitted their rights; these consisted in a standing claim to the generosity and tenderness of the stronger race. The exercise of such feelings was full of advantage for both sexes, and they flowed most freely, of course, when women were gracious and grateful.

That *The Bostonians* was one of James's least popular novels (Mark Twain said he would rather be condemned to John Bunyan's heaven than read it)* may be attributed to the fact that none of its major characters elicits much sympathy. Pretty Verena has no substance. Olive and Ransom struggle over her precisely because she is a blank: she will submit to, and thereby, each hopes, validate, their respective positions. It was the struggle between these two opposing forces that interested Henry James — a grasping, tyrannical, "modern" feminism versus a more relaxed but equally despotic and self-seeking male tradition. Ransom expresses, in hyperbole, the threat to American masculinity posed by the postwar era. "The whole generation is womanized," he declares; "the masculine tone is passing out of the world; it's a feminine, a nervous, hysterical, chattering, canting age, an age of hollow sensibilities, which, if we don't soon look out, will usher in the reign of mediocrity, of the feeblest and flattest and the most pretentious that has ever been."

Neither the new feminism embodied in Olive nor the old tradition espoused by Ransom invites affection, and no third choice emerges. The climactic final scene of the novel, in which Verena chooses Basil, provides no happy ending. As the pair goes off together, Basil discovers Verena in tears, and the novel concludes: "It is to be feared that with the

---

* However, F. R. Leavis, in *The Great Tradition,* calls *The Bostonians* "a wonderfully rich, intelligent and brilliant book. I said that it is an acknowledged masterpiece, but I don't in fact think that it has anything like the reputation it deserves. It could have been written only by James, and it has an overt richness of life such as is not commonly associated with him. It is incomparably witty and completely serious, and it makes the imputed classical status of all but a few of the admired works of Victorian fiction look silly. It is one of James's achieved major classics, and among the works that he devoted to American life it is supreme."

union, so far from brilliant, into which she was about to enter, these were not the last she was destined to shed."

Verena has been forced to choose between two forms of tyranny, and, though neither looks attractive, Ransom throughout seems less unattractive than Olive. He is reactionary and not particularly astute (an editor tells him that the ideas in an essay he has submitted for publication are about 300 years behind the times), but he is genial, for the most part, and rather strong in his blind assertion of masculine rights under threat. But Olive exists outside the range of James's sympathy. (F. W. Dupee has observed that "we pity her all the more because James pities her so little.") In her desperate arid passion and thinly cloaked perversity, Olive presents the more terrible of two awful alternatives. James's fictional women fall generally into two groups: in one they are pure, fresh, innocent, ripe to learn about the world (Daisy Miller, Isabel Archer, Milly Theale, Maggie Verver, Maisie Farange, Nanda Brookenham); in the other they tend to be already knowledgeable, compromised, duplicitous, or malevolent (Madame Merle, Kate Croy, Charlotte Stant, Mrs. Farange, Mrs. Brookenham). Verena falls into the former group, but she learns nothing. Olive has about her not only the soiled quality associated with sexuality in James's novels, but the disfiguring attributes of an inverted passion, as well. The sexual implications, more direct in this novel than in anything else James wrote during this period, may have prompted him to apologize in a letter to William for putting so much "descriptive psychology" into the book. When Verena does finally choose Basil, she knows that "Olive would never get over the disappointment. It would touch her in the point where she felt everything most keenly; she would be incurably lonely and eternally humiliated. It was a very peculiar thing, their friendship; it had elements which made it probably as complete as any (between women) that had ever existed."

The friendship between Alice James and Katharine Loring seemed to Henry a very peculiar thing, perhaps as complete as any between women that he had ever known. If William's Alice had confided to Henry her suspicion of something more than friendship in the relations between Alice and Katharine, or if he shared that suspicion, he left no record of it beyond the suggestive language of *The Bostonians*. More than any other Henry James novel, this one was criticized for drawing too closely from life. Bostonians gave a lukewarm reception to their city's critical portrait, and a number of people (including Aunt Kate, William, and James

Russell Lowell) scolded Henry for basing his reformer-lady, Miss Birds-eye, on Hawthorne's sister-in-law Elizabeth Peabody.*

If connections did exist between real people and the characters in *The Bostonians,* they did not amount to equations. Nonetheless, James did incorporate elements of the relations in his life into this story. Olive Chancellor's views on the "exquisite weakness" of women expressed in exaggerated form ideas Henry had heard his sister and her friend discussing on Mount Vernon Street in 1883. He may have modeled Olive on a number of women he knew, including Alice, Katharine and Louisa Loring, Kitty Prince, William Dean Howells' wife and daughter. To get from the brilliant, "inspired," untutored conversation of his sister to Verena's oratorical gifts required only a small imaginative leap; and Verena's choice between enslavement to masculine domination or feminist ideology paralleled Alice's unarticulated choice between her father's ideas about women and more "modern" views. When Henry described Olive's disappointment, loneliness, and deep humiliation "in the point where she felt everything most keenly," he drew on what he saw as Katharine's full possession of Alice, knowing how desolate either would feel at the defection of the other.

In the novel and in the novelist's life, a man and a woman waged a covert struggle over another woman. "Peculiar" was the word James used to characterize the relations between Olive and Verena in *The Bostonians.* He used the same word to describe the relations between a brother and sister in some notes he made for a story he never wrote.

One night in 1894, two years after Alice's death, Henry had an idea for a story based on "a peculiar intense and interesting affection between a brother and a sister." He noted the odd coincidence of this idea suggesting itself while he was driving to a house where he would see the correspondence between Lord Byron and his half sister, Augusta Leigh, who had conducted an incestuous affair for years. James claims not to have known he would see those particular letters, and denies that the "little relation" in his idea would have any of the "nefarious — abnormal —

---

* Henry replied to William that the character of Miss Birdseye, "like every person I have ever drawn," was not drawn from life. If he had made her *live,* he insisted, it was from an internal vision: "I had no sight or thought of her [Miss Peabody], but only of an imaginary figure, which was much nearer to me . . . in short . . . I have the vanity to claim that Miss Birdseye is a creation."

character" of the Byron-Leigh connection.* He imagined for his story "some unspeakable intensity of feeling, of tenderness, of sacred compunction ... a deep participating devotion of one to the other ..." His brother and sister "see with the same sensibilities and the same imagination, vibrate with the same nerves, suffer with the same suffering: have, in a word, exactly, identically, the same experience of life. Two lives, two beings, and *one* experience ..."

Henry and Alice James did not live out the "unspeakable" union of two lives, two beings, and one experience. But a deep intensity characterized their feelings for one another, and Henry's story idea had grown out of his relations with his own sister. The brother in his sketch goes out into the world and has "the experience and the effect of the experience ... and the sister understands, perceives, shares with every pulse of her being. He has to tell her nothing — she *knows:* it's identity of sensation, of vibration. It's, for *her,* the Pain of Sympathy: *that* would be the subject, the formula."

Pulsing with mutual feeling, this intense connection has a definite sexual tenor — though to read it as literally incestuous would be as great a mistake as to read lesbianism into *The Bostonians.* James in both cases used the sexual chemistry in human relations to convey their emotional values, not to imply physical facts. Henry describes the "little relation" repeatedly as not vile and physical, but cerebral and good — "such a union (of blood and sympathy and tenderness) that, on the part of each, it can only operate for intelligence and perception of the other's conditions and feelings and impulses — as is the case with *most* affectionate wisdoms, guiding devotions, which enter into the nature of the loved object for its good and to protect it sometimes against itself, its native dangers, etc."

What is more unusual than a suggestion of incest in Henry's story idea

* James never wrote his story, but the notes are preserved in his *Notebooks,* published in 1947 as edited by F. O. Matthiessen and Kenneth B. Murdock. As a footnote to this story idea, the editors of the notebooks quote John Buchan, who says, in *Memory Holds the Door,* that he and Henry James were invited by a descendant of Byron's to examine some family letters in order to judge the merits of the poet's matrimonial quarrel and to destroy some of the letters after depositing a statement of their contents in the British Museum. "So," writes Buchan, "during a summer week-end, Henry James and I waded through masses of ancient indecency, and duly wrote an opinion ... My colleague never turned a hair. His only words for some special vileness were 'singular' — 'most curious' — 'nauseating, perhaps, but how quite inexpressibly significant.'"

is the notion of a shared identity across the boundaries of gender. ".I fancy the pair understanding each other too well — fatally well. Neither can protect the character of the other against itself — for the other in each case is, also, equally the very self against whom the protection is called for." And the consummation of this throbbingly virtuous union is death: "The manner in which the thing (the climax) hovered before me was the incident of their dying together as the only thing they *can* do that does not a little fall short of absolutely ideally perfect agreement." They perform a "kind of resigned, inevitable, disenchanted, double suicide."

In dying together, the brother and sister, like Maggie and Tom Tulliver at the end of *The Mill on the Floss,* surrender themselves to a force that denies all distinctions. No matter how close and profound the sharing in James's story notes, neither brother nor sister can know what it is to inhabit the other's body. A perfect union beckons — impossible in life, absolute in death.

In the contrast between the "peculiar" affections in *The Bostonians* and those in Henry's notes for this story lie two kinds of sexuality: guilty and innocent, adult and childlike. Olive Chancellor looms darkly over *The Bostonians*: her passion is felt as malevolent, devouring, hysterically intense, and Verena escapes to the lesser evil of a conventionally unhappy marriage. By contrast, the affection between the brother and sister in Henry's unwritten tale radiates goodness, protective wisdom, guiding, disinterested love. These paradigms reflected James's vague sense that Katharine was "bad" for Alice, and his preference for a different kind of unusual affection.

Although Katharine, like Olive, was pure Boston Brahmin, she bore little real resemblance to the fictional doyenne of Charles Street. If anything, it was Alice whose brittle nervousness and defensive championing of women can be traced in Olive's lineaments. Katharine urged no ideology on her strong-willed friend, and if there was anything grasping or self-serving in her ministrations, it lay far beneath the surface. In *The Bostonians,* Henry expressed his reservations about the relationship between Alice and Katharine — his obscure sense of its unnatural intensity, its dangers, and his own jealousy. The novel pits an evil woman against a strong man — and it is the man in the end who gets, for better or worse, the innocent girl.

Alice, however, did not have to choose between Henry and Katharine the way Verena chose between Olive and Basil. She could have both. In January 1885, she described them to William as her "anchorages." Of Henry's devotion she had always been sure. Once she felt she had Katharine's undivided attention as well, she declared herself happy. And she managed to carry on these two odd love affairs simultaneously for the remaining seven years of her life.

Chapter Fifteen

A London Life

IN THE FALL of 1885, Alice and Katharine moved from Hampstead to 7 Bolton Row, at the end of Curzon Street in Mayfair. The little flank of ten houses no longer exists in modern London. What was Bolton Row is now the end of Curzon Street as it curves up toward Berkeley Square. Alice's rooms at number 7 faced Bolton Street in front, and in the back looked out on a "vast sea of mews," she wrote to Aunt Kate in November. "I have all the light vouchsafed by Heaven at this season of the London year. The rooms are very good and as our landlady is a Swiss she is possessed of a larger repertory for the manipulation of the potatoe than were her origin British." Though by no means well, Alice had more energy and strength now than she had had since arriving in London the previous year, and in the winter of 1886 she led a relatively active social and intellectual life. Henry lived five minutes off, at the other end of Bolton Street. Katharine stayed for months at a stretch. In her own flat, with a carefully maintained regimen of rest, Alice now began to hold a London salon.

Early in 1886, she told William that "a few virtuous matrons have come to nibble at me," and wrote to Sara Darwin, "How can you expect that a lady holding a salon in London can write to plain country folk?" By midwinter she was receiving four calls a day. She presented her new social success to Aunt Kate with characteristic self-mockery: "There are two views taken of me that rather neutralize each other, unfortunately, one 'so subtle, just like your brother,' the other '& above all *so* original,' this by a lady who every now and then finds a little refreshment in Plato and Emerson, don't you think I must have put on a good many frills since we parted? — It may sound fatuous but I divine from a certain greenish tinge which is coming over Henry's features, that after the manner of canines a little modest day is dawning for me, rather late, to be sure."

That divination probably had more to do with Alice's sense of competition, her objection to being compared with Henry, and the old Jamesian notion that one person's success must be balanced by another's failure, than with envy on Henry's part. He praised her London success extravagantly. "A great many people come to see her," he told William. "She is highly appreciated, and might easily, if she were to stay here, getting sufficiently better to exert herself more &c, become a great success and queen of society. Her vigour of mind, decision of character, &c wax daily, and her conversation is brilliant and trenchant. She could easily . . . beat the British female all round." For himself, he found that "she is the best company in the place."

Alice's callers included men and women, Americans and Britons, her brothers' friends and her own. Sara Darwin and Annie Richards came regularly. So did Fanny Kemble and Mrs. John Richard Green, widow of the historian. James Russell Lowell stopped in on occasion. E. L. Godkin visited from America. Henry's friend Constance Fenimore Woolson called when she visited London. George Eliot's sisters-in-law, Mary and Florence Cross, were welcome guests, as was Mrs. William Sidgwick, sister-in-law of the Cambridge philosopher Henry Sidgwick.

Alice found in all this new society a rich source of raw material for the Jamesian practice of conversion — into the conversation that Henry praised, and into the writing of her letters and diary. Her letters during this period show her honing her wit and literary skills. She described one of the "amiable ladies who inflict themselves on me," for instance, an American named Mrs. Mason, as "incredibly crude . . . like a raw turnip to one's mental palate." A Sunday evening was "made memorable by the advent of Mr. [Sir Frederick] Pollock led in by his wife's rippling laughter . . . He was quiet for the most part, but every now and then he suddenly jerked his profile round and shot forth a volley of deafening sound at the side-board." William's friend Charles Atkinson "came a few days ago to see me and exhaled a perfume of resinous purity and prosing virtue which filled my heart with joy."

Like a character in one of Henry's novels, Alice "abroad" was taking in new worlds in her own London sitting room. But she was no American ingénue come to absorb the traditions and values of an older civilization. Never adopting her brother's Anglophile tastes, she grew more staunchly American and critical of England the longer she stayed. "Patriotism," she observed to her sister-in-law Alice, "is a centrifugal emotion intensifying at the outskirts."

•

William, too, had a tendency to intense patriotism abroad — and to nostalgia for Europe when at home. Alice laughed over his perpetual eagerness for the side of the Atlantic opposite to the one he happened to be on. Once, after visiting her in England, he headed off to Paris for a meeting of physiological psychologists and planned to end up with a vacation in the Swiss mountains. Instead, wrote Alice in her diary, he "came suddenly back from Paris and went home, having as usual exhausted Europe in a few weeks and finding it stale, flat and unprofitable. The only necessity being to get home, the first letter after his arrival was, of course, full of plans for his return plus wife and infants! he is just like a blob of mercury, you can't put a mental finger on him."

The relative merits of America and England repeat as a favorite theme throughout the transatlantic correspondence between Alice and William, now that she was a virtual expatriate. She entertained him with elaborate tirades on British ineptitude: "A moribund Yankee is worth twenty of the deadly, stupid, lazy, doughy lumps when there is anything to be done . . . It is perpetually like running your hand into a feather-bed. The minds of the most intelligent even are simply cul-de-sacs, more or less long, of course, but the dead wall you will always come to in time." William delighted in these perorations, agreeing that "all round :.. one misses strangely the American edge and lucidity in England." But because he was at home he readily declared Americans inferior to the English — "inferior in culture, I mean. And as long as mankind has once for all *gone in* on the line of culture (as he has) that means everything." Alice replied that his remarks on "our inferiority as a race were very crude. I will put you right some day when I have energy, it is a subject which I have mastered."

Alice and her eldest brother continued their affectionate verbal jousting even across 3000 miles of ocean. Each seemed to make a point of going after whatever the other held dear. In his relentless curiosity about human consciousness, William had in the 1880s taken an interest in psychic phenomena — spiritual healing, mediums, and the Mind Cure

movement. Alice ridiculed spiritualism in general and William's flirtations with it in particular. At the end of 1885, he was attending the
séances of a Boston medium, Mrs. William J. Piper. He asked Alice to
send a lock of her hair from England for Mrs. Piper to hold, as she went
into trance, so as to "conduct" information about his sister into her
mind from the spirit world. Alice complied, but confessed later that
she had "played you a base trick about the hair. It was a lock, not of
my hair, but that of a friend of Miss Ward's [her nurse] who died four
years ago. I thought it a much better test of whether the medium were
simply a mind reader or not, if she is something more I should greatly
dislike to have the secrets of my organisation laid bare to a wondering
public. I hope you will forgive my frivolous treatment of so serious a
science."

Her contrition was short-lived. Thinking about death a few years later,
Alice hoped "to Heaven that the dreadful Mrs. Piper won't be let loose
upon my defenceless soul. I suppose the thing 'medium' has done more
to degrade spiritual conception than the grossest forms of materialism or
idolatry: was there ever anything transmitted but the pettiest, meanest,
coarsest facts and details: anything rising above the squalid intestines of
human affairs? And oh, the curious spongy minds that sop it all up and
lose all sense of taste and humour!"

Though she did not mean William specifically — his curiosity about
spiritualism did not involve the loss of taste and humor — she skated on
thin ice here, nearly ridiculing the "superior" intellect of the brother to
whom she had once written that her own "having so little mind may account for your having so much." Her responses to William were always
admiring, respectful, often loving — and also challenging, wary, defensive. She never relaxed, with him, into the comfortable assurance of mutual understanding that she found with Henry. Both she and William
seemed to stay, in relation to each other, permanently on guard.

He never ceased to offer her unsolicited advice and diagnoses, nor to
treat her with condescending pity — perhaps in order to keep the greatest
possible distance between himself and the "neurotic" suffering that had
so plagued his own earlier life. She once turned his own phraseology
against him, accusing him of "an artless healthy-mindedness suggestive
of primitive man and not attainable by, but very refreshing to, the more
perverted." He suggested that she try mesmerism in 1890 for her nervous
troubles, since his interest in psychopathology had led him to Paris in
1882 to witness Charcot's work with hypnosis in the treatment of hyster-

ics. Alice, however, ignored the suggestion, along with most of William's advice about climate, medication, exercise, and rest.

Except for an occasional contretemps between William and Alice (and these were always mediated by Henry), most of the tension remained between the lines of their correspondence — they did maintain their old fondness and a wary mutual respect. She loved his original use of language, quoting in her diary a line he had written after a New England snowstorm: "The light is shrieking away outside." And after *The Principles of Psychology* was published in 1890, she noted in her diary a discussion she had with Henry about the reviews, "which reprobate his [William's] mental pirouettes and squirm at his daring to go lightly amid the solemnities, H. said, 'Yes; they can't understand intellectual larking.' "

In 1884, William published a collection of his father's work in a volume called *The Literary Remains of the Late Henry James,* with a long introduction of his own. Henry and Alice received copies in London early in 1885. Alice's came at a bad time, Henry told William, for she had just had another crisis; but though she had only been able to hold the book in her hand for a moment, "it evidently gives her great pleasure. She burst into tears when I gave it to her, exclaiming, 'How beautiful it is that William should have done it! Isn't it, isn't it beautiful? And how good William is, how good, how good!' "

On a later occasion, Alice and Henry laughed over William's antics, recalling (she wrote) "Father and William's resemblance in these ways to him. Tho' the results were the same, it seems to come from such a different nature in the two, in Wm., an entire inability or indifference 'to stick to a thing for the sake of sticking,' as some [one] said of him once, whilst Father, the delicious infant! couldn't submit even to the thraldom of his own whim." But she summed up William's mercurial temperament best in a comment that also displayed her own bemused admiration: in 1886 she asked him to describe the country house he had just bought in Chocorua, New Hampshire. He "expressed himself and his environment to perfection," she noted in her diary, when he replied, "Oh, it's the most delightful house you ever saw; has 14 doors all opening outside." Commented Alice, "His brain isn't limited to 14, perhaps unfortunately."

•

While Alice was building a new life in London in the mid-1880s, she received sad news from Boston. Her old friend Clover Hooper Adams had always been troubled with long periods of melancholy and "over-sensi-tive" nerves. Clover's adored father had died in the spring of 1885, and the young Mrs. Adams had lapsed into a profound depression. She could not work at her photography, and would not go out or receive visitors. The incisive wit that had inspired Henry James to call her a "Voltaire in petticoats" now fell silent. Adams took his wife to the Virginia moun-tains and to her old home in Beverly, but her spirits did not lift. The couple returned to Washington, where Henry Hobson Richardson was just finishing their new house, and on December 6, when her husband went out for a walk, Clover killed herself by swallowing some of the chemicals she used to develop photographs.

Henry attributed her suicide to hereditary melancholy. Alice, full of sorrow, now renewed her friendship with Clover's sister, Ellen Gurney. From Cambridge, in the spring, William's Alice wrote that Ellen was still showing the great strain of her sister's death, and that for a time "she so dreaded to write her own name that she simply could not write let-ters." That fall, Ellen's husband, Ephraim, died. She confessed to William in her mourning that she longed to join her sister and husband. William re-ported this to Alice, who replied, "My heart is wrung for poor dear, dear Ellen Gurney, how can you be so cruel as to wish her to live, nothing would rejoice me more than to hear that she was gone." In November, al-most two years after Clover's death, Ellen threw herself in front of a train.

Alice told William's wife that she was glad Ellen's "bruised wings are folded, no more desperate flapping to prolong that weary flight. In view of what *might* have been, one cannot murmur at the manner of her end, but with our imbecile, physical clinging to what we know to be dust and ashes the thought of that poor wandering body violated by that hideous iron monster has given a ghastly wrench to my feeble frame ... How noble she seems ... Beside our silent and dignified dead, how trivial we living folk seem do we not? We are being *lopped* on every side, may the tender shoots that have sprung up about you and William over grow all your scars and make your days fragrant with their innocence."

But Alice could not accept the manner of Ellen's death, and her reflec-tions on the subject continued the debate with her father about suicide. Alice found herself haunted by the thought of Ellen's "hideous . . . ghastly" act, particularly as it brought home to her (she told William) "cruelly what paralytics we all are, so remote from our nearest and dearest that we are helpless to save them from such a desecration of their personal sanctity." At the end of the year her nerves were "still quivering from the shock": "That *her* hyper-aesthetic personality should have had such violence done to it is a hideous incongruity and the longer one contemplates it the harder it is to be reconciled to. Her going makes a great void, although of late years I saw so little of her, but she goes far back in our lives . . . It is a struggle this fitting oneself to the middle volume of life from the pages of which all the ripe and mellow are vanishing so fast leaving our own crude generation to fill their place. Can Time ever round our angles & deepen our tone so that some day we shall impose upon the innocents behind us and seem to them low-toned & harmonious?"

•

One of Alice's preferred new friends was the American novelist Constance Fenimore Woolson. "Fenimore," as Henry called her, descended from James Fenimore Cooper, was living most of the year in Italy by the 1880s, and wrote to Katharine from Florence in 1887, "I am grieved to hear that Miss James has been suffering. Tell her that an exclamation burst from me irresistibly, night before last — namely — 'I wish she were here this minute!' [Lizzie Boott] was paying me a visit, & we were speaking of Miss James. The broad doors stood wide open; the moonlight outside lighted up my old garden, & the dark, rugged outline of Hawthorne's tower; perfume from a thousand flowers filled the room; & I was so happy to be here that it was almost wickedness! It seemed to me, then, that if Miss James' couch could be drawn across that door, she would enjoy it so much. And *she* would not be wicked. (I hear her exclaiming, 'Yes, I should!')"

When she was not in Italy or traveling, Miss Woolson often took rooms at Cheltenham, near Oxford, to work and be near Henry James. (The story of the complicated friendship she and Henry established over fifteen years — from their meeting in 1880 until her death in 1894 — is told in full detail in volumes 2 and 3 of Leon Edel's *Henry James*.) She appears to have fallen in love with her American colleague from the first. Alice wrote home in a light tone about this romance. "Henry is somewhere on the continent flirting with Constance," she told William, and the next month she wrote to Aunt Kate, "Henry has been galavanting on the continent with a *she*-novelist, when I remonstrated he told me he thought it a 'mild excess.'" Alice admired Fenimore as a writer, and if she felt jealous of the "galavanting" she concealed it well. Constance, with her plainness, deafness, and superior age (she was three years older than Henry), probably did not strike Alice as a serious rival for her brother's love. From Cheltenham, in 1890, Miss Woolson wrote to Katharine, "I hope Mr. James has given a good account of me? If he mentions me as 'worthy,' let me know in private, that I may think of a revenge. Curiously enough, he considers it a complimentary adjective, I believe!"

Alice was willing to share not only Henry but also Katharine with Constance Woolson. Katharine went up from London occasionally to visit Constance at Cheltenham, and the two corresponded about everything from recipes for baked beans to Ruskin ("I am now going to enrage myself over Ruskin," wrote Constance; "I hate him, and hate's very enlivening when one is shut up in a British Promenade") and the medical education of women. "It opens a new field for women," replied Constance to an inquiry from Katharine, "& one that belongs to them fairly; one for which they are fitted. But do insist that they shall be educated with the students of the other sex, and not kept by themselves; it is the only way, in my opinion, to widen the feminine mind. Do not suppose from that that I think the feminine mind inferior to the masculine. For I do not. But it has been kept back, & enfeebled, & limited, by ages of ignorance, & almost servitude.

"Give my love to Miss James . . ."

Miss James, holding her salon in Bolton Row, took a special interest in the female relatives of great men and women, usually comparing them unfavorably with their distinguished kin. She liked Mary and Florence Cross, "but as a link between one and the immortal George [Eliot, they are] rather calculated to lessen the mystic heights upon which she has always dwelt in one's imagination." When the tables were turned, however, and other people viewed her in relation to the famous members of the James family, Alice hooted. She reported to Sara Darwin on a "most delicious Philistine who calls upon me and makes 'literary' remarks owing to my unfortunate family connections. The other day talking about Geo. Eliot something was said about her excursions from the conventional whereupon [the caller] said — 'That terrible rationalism leads so to Mormonism & that kind of thing.' It was physically impossible not to laugh. 'Why, isn't Mormonism a plurality of wives?' Imagine the immortal George and the complacent rationalist likened to the vile and degraded Mormon!"

As always, Alice's derogations of others served as a form of self-defense to establish her own intellectual superiority — if not to her "literary" family connections, then at least to these other sisters, daughters, and granddaughters. She had always taken satisfaction in being subtler and smarter than other women, and showed little sympathy or generosity in these mocking sketches. She admired Fanny Kemble's ability to deal with female foolishness, for Alice herself was too schooled in indirection and concealment to do anything more than gossip about it. When the widow of J. R. Green had prattled her way through two "absolutely night-marish" calls, Alice wrote to Sara that "I have mentally clasped Mrs. Kemble to my bosom finding that she [Mrs. Green] has the same effect upon her — only Mrs. K. can say to her, 'Why, what very *wise* things you do say!' — Mrs. G. asked H. whether Mrs. K. was laughing at her. H. will not tell me what he replied."

In London, in the late 1880s, Alice was recognizing the cost of her own squeamishness. "One day," she entered in her diary, "when my shawls were falling off to the left my cushions falling out to the right and the duvet off my knees, one of those crises of misery in short which are all in the day's work for an invalid Kath. exclaimed, 'What an awful pity it is that you can't say *damn*.' I agreed with her from my heart. It is an immense loss to have all robust and sustaining expletives refined away from one! at such moments of trial refinement is a feeble reed to lean upon."

"Refinement" came in for a massive dose of ridicule. Alice described a fifty-year-old English spinster as a "refined mortal" who embodies "the Wordsworthian maiden, having that wearying quality which always oozes from attenuated purity." When she heard that Grace Norton, her old antagonist from Shady Hill, was preparing a series of lectures on eighteenth-century Frenchwomen, and had presented a friend with a wedding present of Montaigne with the "naughty" pages gummed together, she exclaimed in her diary, "Could anything be more deliciously droll!" To William's wife she continued: "You must have heard me shouting over your account of Grace Norton's dissolute pruderies. A being writing about the nieces of Mazarin whose chaste lips cannot emit the word 'Mistress,' the sticky Montaigne and the condition of poor Mabel Quincy's fingers as she turns the glued leaves, wh. I do her the justice of thinking she immediately applied to the spout of the tea-kettle — is the ludicrous carried to the sublime and a rare treat to hear of! Oh Lord, how thankful

I am I didn't take to refined spinsterhood, to be able, if only once in one's life, to call a spade a spade is more productive of labial and mental health than all the prunes and prisms and prudish evasions of a life time."

The difference, in Alice's view, between herself and refined spinsters was that she did not pretend to virtue. She could not say "damn" or "hell." But she admired people who could, and her antipathy to mincing pruderies gave her a comic perspective on the whole question: "What a devil of a bore it must be, to be the superior person! those mental anaemics, who never read about murders, divorces, or whatever their especial squeamishness may be . . . as grotesque as going to the play and boasting that you shut your eyes tight whenever the villain walks across."

Through books, Alice had access to a world morally freer and larger than her own. Unlike Grace Norton, she read straight through Montaigne without flinching. She saved Zola for Sundays, "to cheer up the Lord's day." Her reading throughout the rest of the week in the late 1880s included the letters of Charles Lamb and John Lothrop Motley; the Old Testament; Froude and Carlyle; the *Revue des Deux Mondes, La Nouvelle Revue,* and the *Fortnightly Review;* everything Henry wrote; Pierre Loti ("pagan, miasmatic, exquisite"); the novels and stories of Miss Woolson; *Don Quixote; David Copperfield;* Emile Montégut, Anatole France, Marie Bashkirtseff, Mrs. Humphry Ward, François Coppée; Fanny Kemble's poems; *War and Peace* in French; Flaubert, Renan, de Maupassant. Acerbic about the standards of English literary criticism, Alice observed to William that "poor Harry has been pining" for a serious response to his recent work: "After toiling with endless conscientiousness over a book for months it is hard line [sic] to have no recognition of it but a few lines of superficial criticism which you know to be written by a child, but which sets the tune for the general public. The English papers are in one way worse than ours owing to the absolutely authentic fact that there is no independent literary criticism known. It is all *unblushing* cliques and sets worse even than Trollope made out."

She had read virtually all the fiction of George Sand and George Eliot. Now, in the late eighties, she was reading their published journals and letters. Sand's letters prompted further reflections on the contrast between full participation in life and the "attenuated purity" of excessive female refinement. Alice wrote to William in November 1887: "I have been reading lately with great enjoyment Geo. Sand's letters . . . The picture of her latter days among her grand-children is lovely. She is such a

great, healthy, rich, generous, human creature with such bursts of eloquence. She says somewhere that she has always been happy because she
never did anything wrong, never had any *mauvaises passions*! this might be
called carrying the anti-morbid to its extreme limit & perhaps stretching
it a little. Think of poor, dear Fanny Morse whose excellent mind has
been stunted from the cradle by the burden of uncommitted sin which
she clings to as her dearest possession, perhaps if she fell once it would
fascinate her less."

Alice knew all about the burdens of uncommitted sin and the stunting
of intellectual growth that came from excessive preoccupation with virtue. She had always in the past contrasted Fanny Morse's goodness with
her own sense of wickedness. But now, in her late thirties, her definitions
had begun to change: it was bad to be too good, to deny *mauvaises passions,* to choose the deadening virtue of refinement over passionate life. It
was too late for Alice to change the course of her life, but it was not too
late to change her views.

Now, she mocked Fanny's virtue, comparing it with some of the most
interesting female transgressions of the century. Poor, dear, stunted, un-
fallen Fanny was no match for the large-spirited, intellectual, *living* Sand.
Alice registered no trace of shock at Sand's sexual adventures; instead, she
endorsed the novelist's full-blooded embrace of life. More interested in
attitude than behavior, she delighted in Sand's moral and intellectual
freedom. And though she had doubts about the French writer's claim
never to have had *mauvaises passions,* she judged that slight self-deception
minor as compared with Puritanical virtue.

Alice returned to George Sand's letters the following year, comparing
the "admirable" grandmother period to the earlier letters in which Sand
seemed "to have been morally simply a boy — up to middle life. At the
core of all her fine phrases on love, friendship and humanity there is simply the boyish ideal of escaping all control, but it is very fine and most
interesting to see her sloughing it gradually off." Whether she meant
Sand sloughed off the control or the ideal is not clear — an interesting
ambiguity in light of Alice's own struggles with freedom and control. In
either case, she assumed that only boys dreamed of escaping control: girls
did not question the strictures of their lives, for they had no hope of
sloughing them off unless they were able, like Sand, to live "morally" as
men.

Again and again Alice established her distance from the mindless social chatter, absurd refinement, and intellectual poverty she saw in some members of her sex, aligning herself instead with men and with strong, capable women such as George Sand and Katharine Loring. If Sand represented one path not taken, George Eliot represented another. Alice adored *Middlemarch* and *The Mill on the Floss,* for they depicted fine, imaginative, intelligent women in conflict with social reality. What could these excellent creatures do? the novels asked. What destiny could adequately meet them, in a society that defines women entirely in terms of marriage and raises them in such radical innocence that they are unequipped for the complexities of adult life? Like Alice, Eliot and Maggie Tulliver in *The Mill on the Floss* were the younger sisters of boys. (The original title of the novel was to have been *Sister Maggie.*) Eliot constantly draws attention to the differences between a boy's world and a girl's. Maggie tells her friend Philip, "I begin to think there can never come much happiness to me from loving: I have always had so much pain mingled with it. I wish I could make a world outside it, as men do." In *Daniel Deronda,* which Alice read when it was published in 1876, "Anna Gascoigne felt herself much at home with the Meyrick girls, who knew what it was to have a brother, and to be generally regarded as of minor importance in the world." And a melodramatic chapter opening in *The Mill on the Floss* presents Maggie's life struggles as having "lain almost entirely within her own soul, one shadowy army fighting another, and the slain shadows forever rising again," while her brother, Tom, "was engaged in a dustier, noisier warfare, grappling with more substantial obstacles, and gaining more definite conquests. So it has been since the days of Hecuba, and of Hector, tamer of horses: inside the gates, the women with streaming hair and uplifted hands offering prayers, watching the world's combat from afar, filling their long, empty days with memories and fears; outside, the men, in fierce struggle with things divine and human, quenching memory in the stronger light of purpose, losing the sense of dread and even of wounds in the hurrying ardor of action."

Alice would have liked George Eliot to live out the answers to the questions her books raised — to be large, heroic, uncompromising. She defended her ideal George against the prosaic Misses Cross and against her philistine caller who linked rationalism to Mormonism. But though Eliot was in many ways brave and unconventional, and though her characters did grow out of personal experience, her life did not imitate her art. When Alice read the three-volume *Life,* edited by the novelist's husband, John Cross, she was bitterly disappointed.* Whereas in Sand's life she had found a fresh, lusty, animating spirit, in Eliot's she saw a nervous, solemn, hypochondriacal temperament giving way to the cardinal feminine sins of hypocrisy and self-pity:

Read the third volume of George Eliot's Letters and Journals at last. I'm glad I made myself do so for there is a faint spark of life and an occasional, remotely humorous touch in the last half. But what a monument of ponderous dreariness is the book! What a lifeless, diseased, self-conscious being she must have been! . . . Then to think of those books compact of wisdom, humour, and the richest humanity, and of her as the creator of the immortal *Maggie,* in short, what a horrible disillusion! Johnnie seems to have done his level best to wash out whatever little colour the letters may have had by the unfortunate form in which he has seen fit to print them. One hasn't at the end the faintest idea of how she signed her name even, or which of the three she used, whether her letters were long or short, all those details which are so characteristic . . . What an abject coward she seems to have been about physical pain, as if it weren't degrading eno' to have head-aches, without jotting them down in a row to stare at one for all time, thereby defeating the beneficent law which provides that physical pain is forgotten. If she related her diseases and her "depressions" and told for the good of others what armour she had forged against them, it would be conceivable, but they seem simply cherished as the vehicle for a moan. Where was the creature's vanity! And when you think of what she had in life to lift her out of futile whining! But the possession of what genius and what knowledge could reconcile one to the supreme boredom of having to take oneself with that superlative solemnity! What a contrast to George Sand who whatever her failings never committed that unpardonable sin; it even makes her greasy men of the moment less repulsive.

If there was one writer whose books Alice James would have liked to write, it was George Eliot. Eliot, as Henry wrote in the *Atlantic Monthly* in May 1885, had lived a larger, freer intellectual life than any woman he could think of — and Alice's admiration of her was tinged with envy. On the subject of private life, however, and particularly on private suffering, Alice considered herself an expert; her remarks on Eliot's physical cowardice and superlative solemnity served to place Alice in a

* William Ewart Gladstone, for one, agreed. He remarked that "it is not a Life at all. It is a Reticence in three volumes."

position of moral superiority to the greatest female novelist she knew.

She had resolved never to commit the "sins" of self-pity and whining. Though physical pain degraded the sufferer, it taught a moral lesson: one could give way to complaint and vanity, the way Eliot seemed to, or one could rise above them, recognizing "the beneficent law which provides that physical pain is forgotten," converting one's own pain into something useful — telling "for the good of others what armour she had forged against them."

Ever since her adolescence, Alice had struggled with her desire for intellectual competence, achievement, a sense of usefulness* — something more tangible than that elusive Jamesian ideal of being extraordinary. Though she fought to renounce ambition, to efface herself, to expect nothing of life, she did not entirely succeed. By the time she was thirty, she no longer had a choice about whether to make something of herself or accept divine female altruism. Her incapacitating illness dictated that she could do neither; it rendered her exempt, in-valid. But she did not stop there. Countless others, from Christian martyrs and eastern mystics to French philosophers and literary heroines, had found life a vale of tears and had forged private, internal means of transcendence. Alice had read the Bible, *King Lear,* Auguste Comte, Thomas Hardy, Henry James, and George Eliot. She had models for various kinds of resignation, for the heroic meeting of one's own fate. And she knew that the way in which she met her singular destiny would make a difference to herself, if not to the world.

In her attitude toward her own suffering, Alice was in the process of finding a plot of moral ground on which to stand. She did have a choice about how to bear what she could not change. She had learned detachment early. She had schooled herself, from the first, in a willed indifference to physical and spiritual pain. Now, like the high-minded, innocent American, Laura, in Henry's 1888 tale, "A London Life," she wanted to learn not "forgetfulness" but rather "a certain fortitude — how to live and hold up one's head even while knowing that things were very bad. A brazen indifference . . ."

•

* George Eliot had written to her former governess when she was twenty that she wished she "might be more useful in her own obscure and lowly station."

Alice's reading and letters of the late 1880s show her working over ideas about moral courage, forbearance, and a sense of personal value. She had always rejected pity as a proclamation of failure. When she explained something of this attitude to Fanny Morse in 1886, she took a sideswipe at William, who had still not learned the difference between empathic understanding and condescending pity. Lizzie Boott (whose pursuit of an artistic career had long before prompted Alice's reflection that feminine art was an excellent resource but "rather a broken reed" as an end in itself; that matrimony seemed the only successful occupation a woman could undertake) had just married her painting teacher, Frank Duveneck, and Alice was feeling sorry for Lizzie's father. Boott's "loyalty to Lizzie is absolute & he has swallowed this large human pill without allowing the world to see the twitching of a muscle ... But I have no doubt I am going thro' the most superfluous vicarious anguish, after the manner of my generation. This tendency is so often brought home to me in my own case! Pray dearest Fanny don't think of me as a forlorn failure but as a happy individual who has infinitely more in her life than she deserves. You know that ill or well one is never deprived of the power of standing for what one was meant to stand for and what more can life give us? — I hope this won't affect you as a somewhat similar remonstrance to William, who replied as if I were a hyena, 'I see you are still quite untamed and I shall condole no more but stand tremulously watching yr. course from this distant shore.' "

In "the power of standing for what one was meant to stand for," Alice found a measure of self-respect — but William kept trying, unwittingly, to take it away. In July 1886, he wrote: "You poor child! You are visited in a way that few are ever called to bear, and I have no words of consolation that would not seem barren. Stifling slowly in a quagmire of disgust and pain and impotence! 'Silence,' as Carlyle would say, 'must cover the pity I feel.' " She wrote back, thanking him for his recent "very fraternal, sympathetic and amusing letters ... The fraternity and amusingness are very gratefull to my heart and soul, but the sympathy makes me feel like a horrible humbug. Amidst the horrors of which I hear and read my woes seem of a very pale tint. Kath. and I roared over the 'stifling in a quagmire of disgust, pain, and impotence,' for I consider myself one of the most *potent* creations of my time, & though I may not have a group of Harvard students sitting at my feet drinking in psychic truth, I shall not tremble, I assure you, at the last trump."

When she was not fighting William, she could be more explicit about her philosophical aims. After Robertson broke down in 1888 and went to the Hartford Asylum, leaving his wife and children in Concord, Alice wrote to Mary, "The weary journey does not last forever and we do not take our successes with us only the manner in which we have met our failures, that never crumbles in the dust." And in a letter about an unhappy cousin, she wrote to William and his wife on assuming moral responsibility for one's own life: "To think of having no other armour than 'grimness' with which to meet 'the stings [sic] and arrows etc.' with all its cracks and crevasses for letting in despair. Surely there is nothing so true as that we are simply at the mercy of what we bring to life & not at what life brings to us."

Alice wanted desperately to find satisfaction in her manner of meeting failure. But she also still longed for some kind of success. In a letter to Aunt Kate filled with gossip and anecdotes about her admiring callers, she joked, "Forgive all this egotism but I have to be my own Boswell and it would be a pity for you to lose a little local colour by artificial bashfulness in me."

As a step toward becoming her own Boswell, Alice began in December of 1886 to copy quotations from her wide reading into the blank pages of a little leather-bound volume. The entries over the following two years show her absorption in the idea of triumph over worldly adversity, of private peace in the face of pain and death. The opening entry consists of lines from Edward FitzGerald's translation of the *Rubáiyát*:

> Whether at Naishpee or Babylon
> Whether the cup with sweet or bitter run,
> The wine of life keeps oozing drop by drop,
> The leaves of life keep falling one by one.

From Carlyle she quoted: "What is this — that thou hast been fretting and fuming and lamenting and self-tormenting on account of? Say it in a word: is it because thou art not *happy*? Foolish soul! What act of Legislature was there that *thou* shouldst be happy? There is in Man a higher than Happiness; he can do without Happiness & instead thereof find Blessedness. This is the Everlasting Yea, wherein all contradiction is solved."

From the French translation of *War and Peace* she entered the passages in which Prince Andrei, wounded in battle at Austerlitz, contemplates in the midst of war the immense calm of the sky (I use the English translation, though Alice wrote in French): "How was it I did not see that lofty sky before? And how happy I am to have found it at last. Yes! all is vanity, all is a cheat, except that infinite sky. There is nothing, nothing but that. But even that is not, there is nothing but peace and stillness. And thank God! . . ."

She copied out a line from Cotton Mather: "So the character of his daily conversation was a trembling walk with God." And from Howells: "Love is not strong eno' to save people from unhappiness thro' each other's faults."

On the theme of love and friendship she noted (ungrammatically), "Emerson says that we never love a friend really till we are willing for their sakes to do without them." Immediately following, she quoted from Thackeray's letters: "There go wit, fame, friendship, ambition, high repute! *Ah! aimons nous bien.* It seems to me that is the only thing we can carry away." And from "H.J.": "The nearness counts so as distance."

Well over half the entries were in French — long passages from George Sand, briefer lines from La Bruyère. Dumas *fils,* Edgar Quinet, Madame Roland, more Tolstoy, the Prince de Ligne, Droz, Châteaubriand, Legouvé, Joubert, Comte, Montaigne, Anatole France, and Flaubert (*"A force de s'élargir pour la souffrance l'âme en arrive à des capacités prodigieuses, ce qui la comblait naguère à la faire crever, en couvre à peine le fond maintenant"*).

With no attribution and no quotation marks, she entered miscellaneous single lines:

The frightful separateness of human experiences.

Conviction is the Conscience of the Mind.

Renunciation remains sorrow tho' a sorrow willingly born.

Nothing can make life worth the purchase money of pain.

From Comte she transcribed the phrase "An Unknowable reality behind Phenomena." From "a Jesuit," "God had graciously given to the frog the same delight in his croaking as the nightingale took in her song."

To George Eliot she paid homage with two brief quotations: a description of Maggie Tulliver as "a creature with a blind instinctive yearning for something that wd. link together the wonderfull impressions of this mysterious life and give her soul a sense of home in it"; and from

Eliot's letters, "There is something more piteous almost than soapless poverty in this application of feminine incapacity to literature."

And the subject of death came up again and again. Without attribution she wrote, "He didn't fear death but he feared dying." And from "Wm.": "All these deaths make the rest of life seem so insignificant & ephemeral as if the *weight* of things as well as the numbers were all on the other side."

•

Death had always interested Alice more than it had frightened her, and in the 1880s that interest intensified. Early in 1888, Lizzie Boott died suddenly. She had been spending the winter in Paris with Duveneck and their infant son. Three months after her death, Alice wrote to Fanny Morse, "The fact that Lizzy has gone still eludes one & will ever remain one of the most inscrutable freaks of providence. It has surely been the only violent action of her life ... What a new sense to the word *superfluous* a motherless babe gives ... A great bit of the past has gone with her & out of the present how much of faithfull friendship!"

According to all reports, Lizzie died of pneumonia. In using the word *violent* to describe a death caused by disease (and pneumonia *was* a ruthless killer in the late nineteenth century), Alice may have been thinking more of what that death did to the "motherless babe" and her own sense of the past than to Lizzie herself. However, Alice may have known more than the official story, for she returned to this idea even more explicitly several months later, in the fall of 1888, writing to William about how much she still missed Lizzie: "She didn't furrow the surface deeply when here but her continuity told more than one suspected. Her having so violently discontinued herself was a great shock."

Alice had long been fascinated by the idea of self-"discontinuance" and generally applauded those who found the courage to commit suicide. In June 1888, the English psychologist Edmund Gurney (a friend of William's and not related to Ellen Hooper's husband) killed himself with chloroform. Alice's reflections later that summer, as she observed the attempts of newspapers and family to obscure the cause of death, constitute a belated reply to her father's 1878 remarks on suicide. "What a pity to hide it," wrote Alice; "every educated person who kills himself does something towards lessening the superstition. It's bad that it is so untidy, there is no denying that, for one bespatters one's friends morally as well as physically, taking them so much more into one's secret than they want to be taken. But how heroic to be able to suppress one's vanity to the extent of confessing that the game is too hard. The most comic and apparently the chief argument used against it is that because you were born without being consulted, you would be very sinfull should you cut short your blissfull career! This has been said to me a dozen times, and they never can see how they have turned things topsy-turvy."

Like Henry, Alice tended to make emblems out of people after they had died, enshrining them in description, seeming to welcome the fixing of impression and meaning that death provided. She described this process in a letter to William about Edmund Gurney: "What an interest death lends to the most commonplace, making them so complete and clearcut, all the vague and wobbly lines lost in the revelation of what they were meant to stand for."

And throughout the late 1880s, Alice played with the idea of her own death. Telling Fanny Morse about her breakdown at Bournemouth, she wrote, "I passed through some rather dark hours last spring which I fondly hoped might lead me into celestial light, but I evidently did not deserve the best, so only got the second best, London fog in all its glory!" One day in 1890, unusually frustrated with her condition, Alice entered in her diary, "I'll not use that word recommended by Kath. [damn] but which is denied with her other rights to *Woman,* but I shall proclaim that any one who spends her life as an appendage to five cushions and three shawls is justified in committing the sloppiest kind of suicide at a moment's notice." A "sloppy" suicide could be counted on to distress one's friends.

A few months later, she touched more intimately on the sense of hopelessness that lay behind her own suicidal thoughts — and also reiterated her scorn for religious humbug. Reading in the papers, in January 1891, that the Duke of Bedford had died of "a congestion of the lungs," Alice either knew more than the papers printed or simply altered the facts to suit her own purposes, for she wrote, "How picturesque and instructive of the Duke ... to commit suicide at this moment of frozen misery, showing his destitution, before the affluence of the slums, of that apparently inextinguishable animal appetite for simple respiration, without which all power and splendour are inoperative against the canker of weariness. It makes it a more perfect whole, that, as his possessions were spoils of the Church, he should outrage the Canon against self slaughter, for the Church may say 'Here is our revenge.' "

•

Although eager to express her thoughts on death, life, and human experience, Alice was acutely conscious of having neither a Boswell nor the genius to speak directly to the world through creative work. For a time, the commonplace book served her purposes. She used other people's voices to express her own thoughts. In this way she remained safe, risking no ideas or phrases of her own, yet engaging in the world of ideas to express something about her own mind. Her preoccupations with love, intimacy, death, happiness, pain, women, endurance, and transcendence come through clearly, if indirectly. The effort itself expressed just what she responded to in Maggie Tulliver — "a blind instinctive yearning for something that would link together the wonderfull impressions of this mysterious life and give her soul a sense of home in it."

The commonplace book was a start, and Alice kept making entries in it all through 1887 and 1888. Then, in the spring of 1889, she relinquished this form of ventriloquism. At the end of May, she turned to a fresh page in the leather-bound volume and began to keep a diary.

ALICE JAMES, about 1873

HENRY JAMES, SR., about 1880

ROBERTSON JAMES, about 1880

GARTH WILKINSON JAMES
in Milwaukee, late 1870s

ALICE HOWE GIBBENS JAMES,
William's wife, with their son Henry,
1879 or 1880

THE BEE OR BANKS BRIGADE, taken in the garden of Theophilus Parsons on Garden Street, 1863. *Standing at left*: Lucy Nichols, Helen Allyn. *Seated left to right*: Mabel Lowell, Charlotte Dana, Mary Towle, Emily Atkinson, Katie Toffey, Marny Storer, Carrie Parsons, Mary Deane, Annie Abbott, Sue Dixwell, Molly Buttrick, Lily Dana, Mary Hastings, Mary Nichols, Lizzie Harris

ADAMS HOUSE, the central building of the Adams Nervine Asylum, built about 1880

KATHARINE PEABODY LORING
(*left*) and unidentified friend

KATHARINE (reading) and Louise Loring in *Study in Greens,* by John Singer Sargent,
inscribed "To my friend Miss Louisa Loring, Prides Crossing, October, 1917." The
original was destroyed by a fire in 1969.

KATHARINE PEABODY LORING
at the time of her friendship with
Alice James

THE HOUSE AT MANCHESTER (*right*) with its pier and stables, 1884

HENRY JAMES (*standing, rear*) at Aston Clinton, the country house of Sir Anthony de Rothschild in Buckinghamshire, probably March 1888. *On Henry James's left*: Lady de Rothschild and her daughter Mrs. Cyril Flower. *Middle row, left to right*: Lady Herschell, Mrs. Reginald Brett, George Russell, Mrs. W. E. Gladstone, Lord Herschell. *Front row, left to right*: James Bryce, Mr. Peale, Cyril Flower, the de Rothschilds' daughter Mrs. Eliot Constantine Yorke.

WILLIAM JAMES AND HIS DAUGHTER, Margaret Mary, in March 1892, the month of Alice's death

HENRY AND WILLIAM JAMES, about 1902

ALICE JAMES AND KATHARINE LORING at Royal Leamington Spa, 1889–1890

ARGYLL ROAD, KENSINGTON. Alice's house, number 41, is on the left, just opposite the street entering at right.

ALICE JAMES in London, September 1891

Chapter Sixteen

A Voice of One's Own

WHEN ALICE started the diary, she was living at Royal Leamington Spa in Warwickshire, about three hours by train to the north and west of London. Leamington, a fashionable nineteenth-century watering place, had been granted the right to call itself "Royal" after a visit by Queen Victoria and the Duchess of Kent in 1830. Its mineral springs had been discovered during the reign of Queen Elizabeth and had first become popular for medicinal purposes in the eighteenth century. By the middle of the nineteenth, invalids traveled from Europe and the United States to "take the waters" at Leamington. They drank and bathed in the naturally saline mineral springs that had high percentages of calcium chloride and were thought to cure gout, rheumatism, lumbago, sciatica, liver and digestive problems, anemia, chlorosis, and skin trouble. Alice's Dr. Garrod prescribed Leamington's therapeutic waters for gouty diathesis.

The town of Leamington had been designed for invalids, and in order to make "pleasure the handmaid of health," declared an official guide to the spa, "no social amenity that may be demanded by civilised tastes" was lacking. There were concerts, theatrical performances, libraries, art exhibits, and charming walks and drives. Among the eminent literary figures who had tasted the waters and pleasures of the little resort town earlier in the century were Hawthorne, Ruskin, Thackeray, and Dickens.

Alice had retreated from London to Leamington less for the waters than for solitude, however. She had tried it first in the summer of 1886, and returned the following July for an indefinite stay. Her many London friends had proven "altogether too stimulating for jangled nerves," she told Sara Darwin in the fall of 1887, and, as a result, "entire rest and a reducing of myself, if possible, to a lower level of imbecility than that already fixed by nature, has been decreed for me . . . I shall be densely dull and lonely of course, but the sands of my little hour-glass will run out as swiftly here as anywhere."

Katharine Loring's absence contributed to Alice's sense of desolation. Katharine had been called back to America in August 1887 to tend her ailing father and sister. "Since Kath. has been wrenched away from me and has now definitely passed from within my horizon for years," Alice wrote to William in November, "I am stranded here until my bones fall asunder, unless some magic transformation takes place in my state."

At Leamington she had taken rooms in a pleasant boarding house at 11 Hamilton Terrace, just off the town's main thoroughfare (called the Parade). Her bedroom faced south and her sitting room north. She spent mornings in bed, with the sun streaming in at her window. At half past noon she got up, and sometimes went out in a Bath chair wheeled by a Leamington man named Bowles. Her favorite excursion was to a little spot called Lillington, "where the trees meet overhead and where stands a manor house, an over grown farm house, a delicious little church in its grave-yard — a microcosm of England in short." These outings, however, depended on the unpredictable weather and Alice's even less predictable health. Most afternoons she established herself on a sofa in the drawing room to read, write, and receive occasional callers. It was here that she began to keep the diary.

"I think that if I can get into the habit of writing a little about what happens," she entered on May 31, 1889, "or rather doesn't happen, I may lose a little of the sense of loneliness and desolation which abides with me. My circumstances allowing of nothing but the ejaculation of one-syllabled reflections, a written monologue by that most interesting being, *myself*, may have its yet to be discovered consolations. I shall at least have it all my own way and it may bring relief as an outlet to that geyser of emotions, sensations, speculations and reflections which ferments perpetually within my poor old carcass for its sins; so here goes, my first Journal!"

All her life Alice had needed an outlet for her energy and ideas. Now, at the age of forty, she found a form that suited her purposes. A diary is private, making no claim as a work of art or an intellectual argument. She could have it all her own way because "it" was simply experience — *her* experience — and no objective standard could measure or condemn it. In the privacy of her own journal, she could feel safe from the kind of withering judgment George Eliot had made about the "feminine incapacity for literature," as well as from the criticism she might anticipate from her writer brothers. The anomalous literary realm occupied by the diary lay safely within the feminine province of the personal; Alice took no overt risk of appearing to compete either with men or with successful women like Eliot.

Yet diaries do, indirectly, lay claim to a certain kind of immortality, projecting a voice beyond the grave. Alice James's diary was her dialogue with the future. It gave form to her sense of ironic detachment. And it created a communion in her lonely life, providing an imaginary audience for the observations neither Henry nor Katharine was present to share. She addressed this audience at times as the formal "you," equivalent to the polite *vous* in French. At other times, she talked more intimately with an imaginary "other" — and then stepped back to note with irony her assumption that the gender of posterity was masculine: "I am as much amused, dear Inconnu (please note the sex! pale shadow of Romance still surviving even in the most rejected and despised of Man) as you can be by these microscopic observations recorded of this mighty race."

To a woman whose father had placed negative value on female intelligence and whose family suspected that one person's success was purchased by another's failure, addressing posterity even in this covert way seemed a dangerous undertaking, however. When Alice began to keep the journal, her parents had been dead for seven years, William was living 3000 miles away, and Henry didn't know about it.* The only people

---

* Indirectly, however, in essays that Alice no doubt read, Henry had endorsed the idea of keeping a journal — specifically in the context of an extraordinary relationship between a brother and sister. In *The Nation* he reviewed *The Journal of Eugénie de Guérin,* just translated into English, in 1865, and the *Lettres d'Eugénie de Guérin* in 1866. He told, in these two articles, the story of Mlle. de Guérin and her brother, Maurice: she had begun the journal in 1834, as a series of letters to Maurice, and continued to keep it for a year and a half after his death, in 1838, although she survived him by nine years. The journal, wrote Henry, left a "consummately pleasing impression" of "a delicate mind, an affectionate heart, a pious soul — the gift of feeling and of expression in equal measure — and this not from the poverty of the former faculty, but from the absolute richness of the latter . . . Her life — or perhaps we should rather say her faith — is like a small, still taper before a shrine, flickering in no fitful air-current, and steadily burning to its socket." He characterized the journal as "nothing more than a tissue of feelings, woven as simply, as easily, as closely, as rapidly, with the same interrupted continuity, as a piece of fireside knitting-work." It expressed a particular genius, and, continued Henry, "genius is not a private fact: sooner or later, in the nature of things, it becomes common property. Mlle. de Guérin pays from her present eminence the penalty of her admirable faculties."

who were aware of the diary while Alice was alive were Katharine Loring and Alice's nurse.

The diary shows Alice groping to find a voice in which to talk about her private experience and the world around her. The journal is not straight autobiography: as always, Alice's language about herself conceals as much as it reveals, and her passions and interests come through only indirectly. She depersonalizes her private observations and personalizes her general commentary. Self-deprecatory remarks run throughout: she repeatedly calls attention to her "restricted career," referring to her body as a "little rubbish heap," herself as a "coral insect building up . . . various reefs of theory by microscopic additions," a "friendless wisp of femininity tossed upon the breeze of hazard in the land of the stranger," a "mildewed toadstool," a "collection simply of fantastic *un*productive emotions enclosed within tissue paper."

Behind this barrage of self-mockery hid a strong, frustrated will. Again and again, Alice connected her incapacity to her ambition — just as she noted on feeling within herself the "potency of a Bismarck" that her "sense of vitality" was "simply proportionate to the excess of weakness." In 1888, she wrote to William and Alice about her physical reactions to the political situations she cared so much about (her insides "cramp themselves convulsively over every little public event here"), describing herself as "perfectly grotesque . . . a wretched shriveled alien . . . But just you see if I don't have a career somewhere! when perhaps Bismarck and some people who think a good deal of themselves now may have to take a back seat — a certain wife and mother and scientifico-philosopher whom I cd. mention, e.g." After that counterfeit swagger she returned to her fascination with Bismarck: "Isn't Bismarck a hideous spectacle? — like some huge moral cancer eating into the life of 42 millions of the human race!"

Twice she compared herself to the most potent force she could find on the European political scene. She wanted Bismarck's destructive power in her own hands. When George Sand's friend Juliette Adam was attacking Bismarck in the pages of *La Nouvelle Revue* and working against him for a Franco-Russian alliance,* Alice told William, "I would give all I possess to be inside of Mme. Juliette Adam for three months — imagine

---

* Bismarck is said to have cried, "Is there no one who can silence *cette diablesse de femme?*"

yourself & Bismarck as the only known quantities, you having got him by the throat writhing in yr. grasp — what state could be more glorious?"

Fervently radical, opposed to all forms of social oppression and restriction, Alice devoted page after page to the foibles of the British aristocracy, the evils of imperialism, the stifling weight of tradition in politics, education, and religion. " 'Noblesse oblige,' " she quipped, "doesn't seem to be the performance of noble deeds, but the doing of ignoble ones with social impunity and with an increase personally of your snobbish pretensions." On February 17, 1890, she fired a resounding salvo at British sanctimoniousness:

I find myself as the months pass more and more stifled by the all pervasive sense of pharisaism in the British constitution of things. You don't feel it at first and you can't put your finger upon it in your friends, but as the days go by you unfold it with your *Standard,* in the morn. It rises dense from the *P.M.G.* [*Pall Mall Gazette*] in the evening, it creeps thro' the cracks in the window frames like the fog and envelopes [sic] you thro' the day. I asked H. once how it struck him from his wider and varied field not wanting my view to become cramped upon conclusions drawn from my centimetre of observation, he said that he didn't think it could be exaggerated. It's woven of a multiplicity of minute details and incidents which elude you in the telling but which seem to exist in the texture of things and leave a dent in the mind as they file past. A monarchy to which they bow down in its tinsel capacity only, denying to it a manly movement of any sort; a boneless Church broadening itself out, up to date; the hysterical legislation over a dog with a broken leg whilst Society is engaged making bags of 4,000 pheasants, etc. etc., or gloating over foxes torn to pieces by a pack of hounds; the docility with which the classes enslave themselves to respectability or non-respectability as the "good-form" of the moment may be; the "sense of their betters" in the masses; the passivity with which the working man allows himself to be patted and legislated out of all independence; thus the profound ineradicables in the bone and sinew conviction that outlying regions are their preserves, that they alone of human races massacre savages out of pure virtue. It would ill-become an American to reflect upon the treatment of aboriginal races; but I never heard it suggested that our hideous dealings with the Indians was brotherly love masquerading under the disguise of pure cussedness.

Alice found her own province in politics. None of her male relatives had laid claim to it, and she ranged over the political events of the late

1880s and early nineties, offering a partisan commentary relatively free of apology and self-derogation. She favored the Irish nationalist Charles Stewart Parnell until he betrayed the cause of home rule late in 1890 by destroying the alliance between the Liberals and the Irish that he and Gladstone had built. Named as a corespondent in a divorce suit, Parnell refused to resign as head of the Irish Party even though it was clear that the Irish-Liberal alliance could not survive the scandal. When Gladstone urged a temporary resignation on political grounds, Parnell issued a manifesto to the Irish people in a tone of intransigent nationalism, accusing Gladstone of using and betraying the home rule cause. It was a "heart sickening day," wrote Alice in her journal. "Parnell after his years of desperate struggle, within a few months, more or less, of a superb victory . . . smirched and of necessity to be eclipsed only for a short time by the loathsome divorce-suit, pushed on by relentless fate not only to ruin himself in the present but by a few strokes of his pen to brand himself as infamous for all history . . . How I wept over [the] Manifesto with its portent of the possible death and burial of Home Rule, for if tomorrow the Irish pronounce for him one's ear must turn itself, one's heart close itself against the woes of that tragic land." The Irish did not pronounce for their adored hero, but the home rule cause lost ground nonetheless: the party split in two, and Parnell, deposed, married his mistress and died within the year.

Alice's admiration for Gladstone amounted to hero worship, and she regaled her diary and friends with stories about him. When he was temporarily out of power in 1887, she wrote to William, "Gladstone will come in with a rush before long. A Conservative lady asked Lord Hartington if he did not wish Gladstone were dead. God forbid! was the answer. 'What wd. become of us, he has got to get us out of this mess.' " When Katharine Loring returned in the fall of 1890 from visiting her family in the United States, she brought with her a Confederate $50 bill. She and Alice decided that the Grand Old Man would be the ideal recipient of this symbolic bit of history, and together they composed the following note:

South Kensington Hotel
Queen's Gate Terrace
London

Sept. 20, 1890

Hon. W.E. Gladstone,

It is absurd and presumptuous of me to start out of the unknown: but I cannot help writing to you and asking you to accept the enclosed genuine relic of a lost cause.

I offer it simply because I have such sincere admiration for you — for your noble championship of the oppressed in all parts of the world.

I am
very respectfully yours
Katharine P. Loring

Alice's fondness for Gladstone extended to his Liberal Party only when Ireland's interests might be advanced. She felt sorry that she would not live to be "in at the fun of seeing the poor, dear, 'respectable' Liberals dashed against their scruples and floating helpless spars upon the tidal wave of labour which will flood in as soon as the Irish question takes a back seat." The Conservatives presented no attractive alternative: she found the political reactionary "a curious nature . . . Being to the mind as some diseased vegetable growth which nips efflorescence, and burrowing all his days in a *cul-de-sac* instead of floating with the current of expansion and getting all the fun he can grasp at in passing."

She had a novelist's eye for the details marking social class distinctions, and delighted in contrasting the Briton's "sense of place" with the freer American sensibility. On February 8, 1891, she wrote:

To an American born to "rattle round" in space, who can have no representative value for his own consciousness or that of any one else, the sense of their place possessed by all sorts and conditions here is very instructive, and the skills they attain in keeping the balance of the exact measure of their worth, as between butler and baron, is most remarkable. There was a pathetic remnant in Leamington, a decayed gentlewoman, who gave one such an impression of an indestructible essence in proportion to her being a mere human shadow. Fortune had led her down the rungs of her ladder, to an income of ten shillings a week; Mrs. Nickleby was a stern logician as compared to her, and she had the mental range of an ant, — not a dear little burnished definite ant, who could tell you, if he only would, with such precision, all the architectural tragedies of his career, but a blurred vague ant, if such a thing is possible. On this little heap of social ruin, however, the *Gentlewoman* was impregnably intrenched, and how often have I gazed sadly through her atmosphere of *inherited* good breeding, and seen unfold itself the endless row of desperate ciphers, by which she is multiplied on this teeming island.

The class distinctions in English society, the "sense of place" that gave everyone the exact measure of his worth, provided endless interest to an American as concerned as Alice was with autonomy and determinism. In the privacy of her diary she scolded the English working poor for accepting their lot, and cheered when they organized strikes and demonstrations. When hundreds of workers gathered in Hyde Park in May 1890 to demonstrate their support for an eight-hour working day, Alice applauded: "How I wish I could have seen a few of the faces of these Masters of the world in whose hands our material future lies, who can say how immediately. Should the governments of Europe show the cowering abject attitude which they took on the first of May, what an impetus it will give, it will almost seem as if one might live to see the remodelling. I shall always be a bloated capitalist, I suppose, an ignominy which, considering all things, I may as well submit to, gracefully, for I shouldn't bring much body to the proletariat, but I can't help having an illogical feminine satisfaction that all my seven per cents and six per cents with which I left home have melted into fours. I don't feel as if four per cent were quite so base!"

Though eager for the revolutionary remodeling, she was aware that the genteel order of things, such as deference and courtesy, would be lost in consequence. One Christmas night in London Katharine was invited to a servants' ball at the hotel she and Alice were staying in. The housemaids and waiters greeted their American guest, sat beside her during the festivities, and conversed with her (Alice reports) "as if they were friends and hosts, till one's heart was melted to hear about it. These aesthetic decencies so wrap about the iniquities, and so explain and justify their long continuance, that one has flaccid moments of shivering at the raw edges that will be laid bare as democracy sweeps its pope's-head through the festooning cobwebs, and crumbles the richly hued mould into dust. Jennie [the housemaid] said to Nurse, with delight, the next morning: 'fancy Miss Loring shaking hands with me before the whole room.' Let us pray that our unconscious benefactions outweigh our unconscious cruelties!' "

•

Alice saw some sort of redistributive change as inevitable, and she was for it, just as she endorsed America as a symbol of freedom, openness, possibility — the "embodiment of a Huge Chance for hemmed in Humanity" — against stodgy, oppressive, tradition-bound England. While she was formulating these ideas in private, Henry was making his one fictional foray into the world of working-class revolutionary politics, *The Princess Casamassima,* a novel he published in 1886. Its hero is Hyacinth Robinson, the illegitimate son of a French seamstress and an English peer. Set in the murky subterrain of London prisons, gaslit shops, and shabby tenements, the novel depicts a world far removed from the drawing rooms and country houses that were usually the settings for James's plots. Hyacinth is a sensitive young craftsman, a bookbinder, who, like James, lives the life of an observer. His nature is as divided as his parentage: sympathetic with the plight of the working people among whom he lives, he is at the same time drawn to the aesthetic values of an aristocracy represented by his unknown father and the mysterious Princess Casamassima. He joins a group of anarchists and then, having committed himself to carry out for them an act of terrorism, comes into a small inheritance, which he decides to spend on travel. In Paris and Venice, he submerges himself in the culture of the society his anarchist friends are bent on destroying. When he gets his assignment — to kill a duke — he cannot bring himself to annihilate this symbol of his own paternity and newly discovered aesthetic heritage. He concludes, "I don't want every one to have a little piece of anything and I have a great horror of that kind of invidious jealousy which is at the bottom of the idea of a redistribution." Instead of killing the duke, he turns the pistol on himself.

Alice read *The Princess* twice in 1886 and pronounced it "magnificent." She told William's wife that there had rarely been "so tragic and perfect a picture as little Hyacinth and his heroic end," and the "seething" London background was "wonderfull." William, as usual, criticized Henry's book, and Alice leaped to the author's defense. She told William that she found "unaccountable" his "want of having in any way *felt* or *perceived*" the book. She had been "vehemently indignant for 24 hrs. but now I shrug my shoulders, the *Princesse* being one of those things apart that one rejoices in keeping and having to one's self. It is sad however to have to class one's eldest brother, the first fruits of one's Mother's womb among those whom Flaubert calls the bourgeois, but I have been there before! having had a holiday I was unnecessarily shocked at finding myself there again."*

Alice was no anarchist and did not, apparently, take issue with Hyacinth's final decision to destroy himself rather than the culture he has come to value. She might have argued with Henry that there were more shades of gray in the political spectrum than Hyacinth's choice between the destruction and preservation of culture suggests. But Henry came out as strongly against the exploitation and oppression of individuals, in political and in private life, as his sister did against the specific evils of capitalism, and she would not have found him the snobbish elitist others assumed him to be by virtue of his associations with the aristocracy.

The most interesting aspect of Alice's response to *The Princess Casamassima* is her silence on the character of Rosy Muniment, the invalid sister of the novel's anarchist leader, Paul. Hyacinth describes Paul and Rosy Muniment as a "most extraordinary pair." Rosy is a reactionary and a social snob; Alice James was a radical, an egalitarian. But in his portrait of this bright, passionate, tyrannical invalid, Henry James drew on some of his sister's attributes. He has the Princess describe Rosy in the language he used about Alice — as a "perfect little *femme du monde* — she talks so much better than most of society." Confined to her sofa in a pink dressing gown, Rosy is presented as brilliant and bizarre, a "strange, bedizened little invalid," a "small, odd, sharp, crippled, chattering sister" who makes "intensely individual little protests." Her brother, Paul, notes her "freakish inconsistency," and Hyacinth marvels at "the stoicism of the hard, bright creature, polished, as it were, by pain, whose imagination appeared never to concern itself with her own privations." Paul brings home everything he can to enrich the restricted life of his bedridden sister, and creates the impression that his radicalism exists only to get a "rise" out of her "and let their visitors see with what wit and spirit she could repudiate" his views. She strikes Paul the way Alice struck her brothers — as able to glean information from thin air: " 'Do I need to be told things to know them? I'm not a fine, strong, superior male; there-

---

* "There is some East wind for you!" she added at the end of her letter; "a striking contrast to the mild Southern zephyr in which your own Alice bathes you."

fore I can discover them for myself,' Rosy answered with a dauntless little laugh and a light in her eyes which might indeed have made it appear she was capable of wizardry."* When the Princess inquires about Rosy's health, Paul replies:

" 'Oh, her health will do. I mean that she'll continue to be, like all the most amiable women, just a kind of ornament to life' ...

" 'To *your* life of course. She can hardly be said to be an ornament to her own.'

" 'Her life and mine are all one.'

" 'She's a prodigious person.' "

That this prodigious invalid is rather awful becomes explicit toward the end of the novel, when the Princess suggests that Hyacinth pay Rosy a visit. " 'I don't like the sister,' Hyacinth frankly averred.

" 'Ah, neither do I!' the Princess said ...."

Rosy is not likeable — and neither was Alice, much of the time. But Henry admired the "prodigious" strength of mind and character in his own sister and in Paul Muniment's. Lionel Trilling observed that James gives his readers permission to dislike Rosy through this conversation between Hyacinth and the Princess, but does not "avail himself of the same privilege."†

---

* William echoed these descriptions in a letter characterizing his own sister just after she died in 1892: "Strange to say, altho' practically bedridden for years, her mental atmosphere barring a little overvehemence was altogether that of the *grande monde*, and the information about both people and public affairs which she had the art of absorbing from the air was astonishing in amount."

† Trilling draws attention to the "intensely autobiographical" nature of this novel. He sees Paul Muniment and the Princess, whom Henry describes as "the most remarkable woman in Europe," as standing for William and Alice. "When I say that Paul and the Princess 'stand for' William and Alice, I do not mean that they are portraits of William and Alice. It is true that, in the conditioning context of the novel, Paul suggests certain equivalences with William James: in his brisk masculinity, his intelligence, his downright common sense and practicality, most of all in his relation to Hyacinth. What we may most legitimately guess to be a representation is the *ratio* of the characters — Paul:Hyacinth :: William:Henry. The Princess had Alice's radical ideas; she is called 'the most remarkable woman in Europe,' which in effect is what Henry James said Alice would have been if the full exercise of her will and intellect had not been checked by her illness. But such equivalence is not portraiture and the novel is not a family *roman à clef*." Trilling then enumerates the points of similarity between Rosy and Alice, and concludes, "There is no reason why anyone interested in Henry James should not be aware of this, provided that it not be taken as the negation of Henry's expressed love for Alice and William — provided, too, that it be taken as an aspect of his particular moral imagination ...."

The double-edged nature of Henry's feelings about Alice emerged more clearly in this discreet likeness than in the letters he wrote about and to her. His exalted sense of his sister as potentially the most remarkable woman in Europe fitted her own grand conception of her latent capacities; but his sense of the deforming character of her illness differed qualitatively from her own self-evaluations. Rosy strikes people as freakish, bedizened, capable of wizardry. There is something other-worldly and threatening about her; the cruelty of her judgments and the brittle tenacity of her character were qualities that Henry could never allow himself to name in his own sister, but he did perceive them.

Just as Alice's diary represents her struggles to express and silence herself simultaneously, Henry reveals in this oblique way his own resolutions of the Jamesian conflict between speaking and concealing the truth. Which is not to say that he sketched his sister into *The Princess,* any more than he drew literal portraits in *The Bostonians.* He knew that Alice read every word he wrote, and he was much too kind and much too aware of her worshipful dependence on him to have engineered any such subtle slight. Alice appears to have recognized no hidden messages in these novels.

•

Two years after Alice died, when he first read her diary, Henry expressed to William his perception of the intimate connection between Alice's character and her invalidism — a connection she had implicitly made on several occasions but had never looked at straight on as Henry did now. The diary, he wrote, had impressed him immensely, "but it also puts before me what I was tremendously conscious of in her lifetime — that the extraordinary intensity of her will and personality really would have made the equal, the reciprocal life of a 'well' person — in the usual world — almost impossible to her — so that her disastrous, her tragic health was in a manner the only solution for her of the practical problem of life — as it suppressed the element of equality, reciprocity, etc."

•

On the 18th of July 1889, Henry came up from London to spend the day with Alice at Leamington. They had just finished lunch and were talking of something inconsequential, when Henry suddenly said, "with a queer look on his face" (Alice wrote in the diary a few days later), " 'I must tell you something!' 'You're not going to be married!' shrieked I. 'No, but William is here, he has been lunching upon Warwick Castle and is waiting now in the Holly Walk for the news to be broken to you and if you survive, I'm to tie my handkerchief to the balcony.' Enter Wm. *not* à la Romeo via the balcony; the prose of our century to say nothing of that of our consanguinity making it super[er]ogatory ... Poor Harry, over whom the moment had impended for two months, looked as white as a ghost before they went and well he may in his anxiety as to which 'going off' in my large repertory would 'come on' but with the assistance of 200 grains of Bromides I think I behaved with extreme propriety." William, whom she hadn't seen for five years, did not look much older: "All that there is to be said of him, of course, is that he is simply himself, a creature who speaks in another language as H. says from the rest of mankind and who would lend life and charm to a treadmill. What a strange experience it was, to have what had seemed so dead and gone all these years suddenly bloom before one, a flowing oasis in this alien desert, redolent with the exquisite *family* perfume of the days gone by, made of the allusions, the memories and the point of view in common, so that my floating-particle sense was lost for an hour or so in the illusion that what is forever shattered had sprung up anew, and existed outside of our memories — where it is forever green!"

The exquisite family past grew greener in memory — there it flourished, the perfect image of shared allusions, memories, and points of view — just as people grew clearer, easier to see and define, once they were dead. Contributing to Alice's sense of the receding past was the fact that, five months before William's visit to Leamington, Aunt Kate had died. She had been living for several years in a house left her by a cousin, at 121 West 44 Street in New York. In September of 1888, Alice and Henry had begun to notice a change in Kate's letters, an increasing mental feebleness and loss of memory. She had told Alice for years that she dreaded surviving her faculties more than any other fate, and when William diagnosed aphasia ("it is quite impossible for poor dear old A.K. to hold any conversation at all. She talks fluently, but with every word wrong"), Alice hoped that the end would come swiftly. It did not lessen her own grief and regret, she told William, to know that Kate was "as usual lying with folded hands fostering her own aches and pains." Her wish for a swift dénouement was granted. Kate died peacefully on March 5 at the age of seventy-eight, and Alice wrote to William, after hearing the details, "Poor Aunt Kate's life on looking back to it with the new distinctness which the completion always gives, must seem to our point of view such a failure, a person so apparently meant for independence and a 'position' to have been so unable to have worked her way to them & instead to have voluntarily relegated herself to the contrary. But the truth was, as her long life showed, that she had but one *motif,* the intense longing to absorb herself in a few individuals, how she missed this & how much the individuals resisted her, was, thank Heaven, but faintly suspected by her. My failing her, after Mother's and Father's death, must have seemed to her a great and ungrateful betrayal; my inability to explain myself and hers to understand, in any way, the situation made it all the sadder and more ugly."

Alice's sense of guilt and regret turned to annoyance when she learned that Kate had left the bulk of her estate to some cousins in Connecticut. The will barely mentioned Henry; William got $10,000; Alice received a life interest in some of Kate's possessions, including her silver and a shawl. ("A life interest in a shawl!" she expostulated to William, "with reversion to a *male* heir, is so extraordinary and ludicrous a bequest that I can hardly think it could have been seriously meant.") Possibly Kate did suspect how much some of the Jameses had "resisted" her; possibly, however, she had simply (and correctly) assumed that William, with his large family, and the Connecticut cousins needed money more than Alice or Henry did.

In any case, William financed his trip to Europe in the summer of 1889 with part of the legacy left him by Aunt Kate. He had feared his visit would upset Alice; but thanks to Henry and bromides, it went off smoothly. William reported to his wife that Henry had "covered himself, like some marine crustacean, with all sorts of material growth, rich sea-weeds and rigid barnacles and things, and lives hidden in the midst of his strange heavy alien manners and customs." To his sister he remarked, ". . . Beneath all the accretions of years and the world, he is still the same dear innocent old Harry of our youth. His anglicisms are but 'protective resemblances' — and he's really, I won't say a yankee, but a native of the James family, and has no other country . . ."

•

Alice's letters during this period describe Henry as a "treasure beyond price," an angel, the "excellent H." whose "virtues transcend the natural," and "*bon comme le pain* (not, however, as they knead it in Britain) and the staff, of course, of my life." By 1890, she no longer had any illusion of being on a mere visit abroad. She told William's Alice that Europe "is the place for me . . . during Henry's life, at any rate." She had "crossed the water and suspended myself like an old woman of the sea round his neck where to all appearances I shall remain for all time."

Henry had long since learned to make the distinction between empathy and commiseration that William failed to see. Alice rewarded him with a vivid appreciation of "Henry the patient": "I have given him endless care and anxiety but notwithstanding this and the fantastic nature of my troubles I have never seen an impatient look upon his face or heard an unsympathetic or misunderstanding sound cross his lips. He comes at my slightest sign and hangs on to whatever organ may be in eruption and gives me calm and solace by assuring me that my nerves are his nerves and my stomach his stomach — this last a pitch of brotherly devotion never before approached by the race. He has never remotely hinted that he expected me to be well at any given moment, that burden which fond friend and relative so inevitably impose upon the cherished invalid. But he has always been the same since I can remember and has almost as strongly as Father that personal susceptibility — what can one call it, it seems as if it were a matter of the scarfskin, as if they perceived thro' that your mood and were saved thereby from rubbing you raw with their theory of it, or blindness to it."

As if testifying to the "deep participating devotion" between a brother and sister that Henry sketched out several years later in his notebooks, Alice saw herself entering into his writing career as fully and sympathetically as he shared her physical ills. He had turned in the late 1880s to writing plays, for he had always been fascinated by the possibilities of stage drama, and though he was shy and wary of publicity, he hoped that theatrical success might earn him more money than his novels did and leave him free to write what he pleased. Early in 1890, he received a commission from the English actor-director Edward Compton to dramatize his 1877 novel, *The American*. Alice read the play in June and wrote her brother a few lines of ecstatic praise. They made him feel, he answered, "as if there had been a triumphant première and I had received overtures from every managerial quarter and had only to count my gold." The play opened in the English provinces early in 1891. "The great family event over which I have been palpitating for the last 18 months or more has come off," recorded Alice in her diary. "*The American* was acted for the first time at Southport, which they call the Brighton of Liverpool, on January 3rd, and seems to have been, as far as audience, Compton, and author were concerned, a brilliant success."

In spite of its provincial success, however, *The American* flopped in London. Alice's remarks on the closing show her experiencing this failure as if it were her own, and shifting awkwardly between "I," "we," "us," and "one" to express her gratitude and love for "H."

The American died an honourable death, on the 76th night . . . I have to thank the beautiful play for all the interest and expectancy with which it has filled the last two years. The excitement and brilliant success of the first night, then, the subsequent anxiety for a week or two about the "run," when failure brushed us as she flitted past, seemed too heavy a load of emotion and impressions for my weakness to profit from, but as I have lived on, have had time to assimilate the apparently indigestible mass and see all in its right proportions, it has explained so many hidden mysterious impulses, putting one in touch for the first time (and quadrupling one's indulgence) with the huge mass of strugglers after the concrete, that one seems to have added a new story to one's worldly store-house. Then the whole episode was so shot thro' with the golden thread of Comedy, that we grew fat with laughter. The best moment was one afternoon when H. came in, with the strangest, amused, amazed, disgusted-with-himself expression and said that he had just got a telegram from Compton, telling him that the Prince of Wales was coming to the theatre that night and wanting him to "dress" a couple of boxes with "smart people"; and in the most pathetic voice H. exclaimed: "here I am, having put away my self-respecting papers, come out to do it!" "I'd do anything for the good Comptons, but it will make me charitable to the end of my days." We stared at ourselves in our nakedness, and wonderingly found satisfaction within the germ at our core of the basest Tranby Crofter, moved to a common impulse of prostration before his tawdry Idol! 'Twas truly an instructively blushful moment . . . H. . . . . has toiled like a galley slave. He has been so manly, generous and unirritated by all the little petty incidents and exhibitions, so entirely occupied with the instructive side, that one has had infinite satisfaction in him.

Alice's gratitude to Henry, and her "infinite satisfaction" in him, did not, however, blind her to some of the problems in his work. In her diary in 1891 she wrote out a criticism of his latest play, *Mrs. Vibert,* that could be applied to his dramatic work in general. "I was surprised to find that H. didn't seem to see how much more dependent this play will be, for success, upon the actors than *The American* or The Comedy* that he has just written; it depending altogether upon the subtlety and art with which the delicate psychologic situations are introduced, and will only appeal to that limited public which suspects that art and subtlety exist." She was right — not just *Mrs. Vibert* but all the plays were too subtle, their dramas too internal, to work on the stage, and Henry never had the success in the theater that he longed for.

Alice incorporated many of Henry's anecdotes and bon mots into her diary, and he (she claimed) "has embedded in his pages many pearls fallen from my lips, which he steals in the most unblushing way, saying, simply, that he knew they had been said by the family, so it did not matter." But it did matter, just as it mattered when she sensed that people came to call on her because of her "Great Brother," or had the effrontery to assume she was literary because of her "unfortunate family connections." Finding a way to think and speak for herself was, for Alice, her life's highest aim. In beginning to keep a private journal, she had begun finally to distinguish herself, in both senses of the word — from her famous brothers, and as a person on her own.

William had often praised his sister's letters as "inestimable," "splendid, noble, etc." (the "etc." undercutting what preceded it), and suggested she keep a record of her impressions of England more permanent than letters. He inevitably took back with his left hand the encouragement he gave with his right. "I am entirely certain that you've got a book inside of you about England," he wrote her in August 1890, "which will come out yet. Perhaps it's the source of all your recent trouble." And a year later he took up the topic again: "I do hope that you will leave some notes on life and english life which Harry can work in hereafter, so as to make the best book he ever wrote.

When E. L. Godkin published a brief anonymous note by Alice in *The Nation* in 1890,† Henry called it her "swan song," the *London Daily News* reprinted it, and Alice exclaimed in her diary, "Imagine my entertain-

---

* Probably *Disengaged* (later called *Mrs. Jasper's Way*), which he wrote in Paris in the winter of 1891, based on his story "The Solution." The New York stage manager Augustin Daly took an option on the play, but it was never produced. Daly thought it lacked "story."

† To the Editor of the Nation:
    Sir: For several years past I have lived in provincial England. Although so far from home, every now and then a transatlantic blast, pure and undefiled, fans to a white heat the fervor of my patriotism.
    This morning, most appropriately to the day, a lady from one of our Eastern cities

ment in getting from Mary Cross the *Daily News* extract, a *European repu-tation* at the first go off! How fortunate for the male babes that I am physically so debile!" She pasted the clippings into her diary, and in fur-ther ironic reflections on her "work of genius" compared herself not only with Henry but with Shakespeare: "In comparing notes with H. I find that had I brought forth *The Tragic Muse,* I could not have gone through with more *author-processes.* As so often happens in works of ge-nius I had to leave out the chief points, fearing length and the editorial veto." She had wanted to point up the contrast between "the absence of reaction in the British masses against the accidents of life," and the "ag-gressive infant from beyond the sea" with its hapless "American mother,"* but consoled herself with the reflection that "Shakespeare may have felt Othello commonplace!"

One more passage in Alice's diary sheds light on her attitudes toward writing and competing with her famous brothers. In January 1892, she was reading the posthumously published poems of Emily Dickinson. She reflected: "It is reassuring to hear the English pronouncement that Emily Dickinson is fifth-rate, they have such a capacity for missing quality; the robust evades them equally with the subtle. Her being sicklied o'er with T. W. Higginson makes one quake lest there be a latent flaw which es-capes one's vision — but what tomes of philosophy *résumes* the cheap farce or expresses the highest point of view of the aspiring soul more completely than the following —

> How dreary to be somebody
> How public, like a frog
> To tell your name the livelong day
> To an admiring bog!"

Dickinson's lines accurately reflected Alice's sense of negative superior-ity. Immediately after quoting them, Alice wrote that her doctor had

---

applied to my landlady for apartments. In the process of telling her that she had no rooms to let, the landlady said that there was an invalid in the house, whereupon the lady exclaimed: "In that case perhaps it is just as well that you cannot take us in, for my little girl, who is thirteen, likes to have plenty of liberty and to *scream* through the house."

Yours very truly,
Invalid

ENGLAND, July 4, 1890

* Daisy Miller's brother, Randolph, and his mother, from Schenectady, are just such a pair.

asked "whether I had ever written for the press. I vehemently disclaimed the imputation. How sad it is that the purely innocuous should always be supposed to have the trail of the family serpent upon them." Abjuring all desire to write, compete, achieve the status of "somebody," she went on without even a paragraph break to compare her health to Henry's novels and William's psychology. "The domestic muse isn't considered very original; Mr. Cross* the Georgian widower asking K. whether William got his psychology from Mr. Frederick Myers, and Mrs. Lichfield† (née Darwin) speaking of having just read Miss Burney's letters,‡ asked whether 'Mr. Henry James had read them, and was it out of those books that he got the characters for his novels.' When I held my 'salon' in Bolton Row, she came to see me and asked what was the matter with me, I said: 'they call it latent gout': 'Oh! that's what we have, does it come from drink in your parents?' "

"I answered," continued Alice in a letter to William's wife, "that they were not to my knowledge victims of what Wm. euphuistically calls 'progressive nervous degeneration.' She says her Father's trouble was a gouty diathesis and they are all victims to it. Three of the sons have invalid wives besides!" In the diary she concluded, "It occurred to me that the Darwinian mind must be greater in science than in society."

A discussion with a Darwin about family tendencies to drink, gout, and invalid wives was implicitly about family tendencies to genius and intellectual superiority as well. All her life Alice had been in conflict over just who she could be in a family that appeared to include illness and intelligence in its genetic heritage. Though she had chosen, in effect, to be "nobody" and say nothing, she was (like the speaker in Dickinson's poem) a nobody with a difference, expressing her individuality even in the effort she made to control it. The intelligence and energy Alice might have used in some productive way went into the intricate work of being sick. Her comments about the Darwins recognized indirectly that her miserable health *was* her career. It grew out of her particular, troubled existence, just as Henry's novels and William's psychology grew out of their moral concerns and personal conflicts. All three careers expressed private experience, but two addressed themselves to the world and were crowned with public success, whereas Alice's "work" affected only her-

* John Cross, widower of George Eliot.
† Charles Darwin's daughter Henrietta had married R. B. Litchfield in 1871. Katharine, to whom Alice was dictating, misspelled Litchfield.
‡ Fanny Burney (1752–1840).

self — and by anybody's standards, a life of incapacitating illness denoted failure and waste.

Alice James was too intelligent, too competitive, and too much a James simply to give up and *be* nobody, however. If illness and failure marked her life distinctively, then they were its raw material, its "soluble stuff." Failure was a bedrock human experience she could claim as her own. An expert at suffering, she could *convert* the waste of her life into something more lasting than private unhappiness.

The diary made a start. In deciding to speak up at last, to articulate her life, Alice announced that private experience had inherent value, and that she had something to say about it. She was finding in the process of keeping a diary a nascent sense of self, much as William had done in determining that his first act of free will would be to believe in free will. Less assertively than William, less deliberately than Henry, Alice was taking hold of the reins at last.

The diary does not triumph resoundingly over adversity; it does not burst with hidden genius. Its subject is human suffering, and its achievement is the working-out of an attitude that accepts and moves beyond personal pain. "If I can get on my sofa," Alice wrote in May 1890, "and occupy myself for four hours, at intervals, thro' the day, scribbling my notes and able to read the books that belong to me, in that they clarify the density and shape the formless mass within, Life seems inconceivably rich — full of l'allégresse de la certitude acquise. La raison a aussi ses émotions et c'est par frissons que se propage la lumière."

At times, an arid, preaching tone dominates her attempts to define the inner life, and her sense of triumph seems false, as if she were talking herself into something she doesn't quite feel: a willed transcendence of pain, a mimicking of literary heroism, a moral superiority used as self-justification. On October 10, 1890, she wrote, in this vein, "How it fills one with wonder to see people old eno' to have stored experience never apparently suspecting that of all the arts the art of living is the most exquisite and rewarding and that it is not brought to perfection by wallowing in disabilities, ceaseless plaints of the machinery of life and the especial tasks fallen to their lot. The paralytic on his couch can have if he wants them wider experiences than Stanley slaughtering savages, the two roomed cottage may enclose an infinitely richer, sweeter domestic harmony than the palace; and the peaceful cotton-spinner win victories beside which those of the reverberating general are dust and ashes — let us not waste then the sacred fire and wear away the tissues in the vulgar pursuit of what others have and we have not; admitting defeat isn't the way to conquer and from every failure imperishable experience survives."

Elsewhere, however, her voice sounds quieter, less hortatory, more personal. Early in 1890, reflecting on a woman's ambition for her husband's political success, Alice asked, "But what of the success made up of all delicate shades and subtle tones — that makes no sign, but is known alone to the bosom that attains it? — that floods the mind with infinite delight when least expected — that has never mistaken pleasure for the shy bird happiness whose song is only to be heard of the ears of the soul?"

In no particular order, she works over the familiar themes of success and failure, power and impotence, public achievement and private growth —advancing ideas and retreating from them, despairing and exulting, recording the flux and process of her own mind. One day when she had a toothache, an attack of gout, and a crick in her neck, she took a small dose of morphine to steady her nerves and was consequently able to "*experience* the pain without distraction, for there is something very exhilarating in shivering whacks of crude pain which seem to lift you out of the present and its sophistications . . . and ally you to long gone generations . . ." She was practicing her own version of the interested detachment that Henry had called "pleasure under difficulties" almost thirty years before at Boulogne, when she had shared with him the "first dawning" of her intellect.

Alice was in the process of defining an attitude more than a faith — a wider realm, a broader perspective, a frame of reference beyond the accidents and dailiness of human life. At times, this attitude resembles Christian patience. Christ's example of accepting suffering served as a ready metaphor for the creed of inner peace toward which Alice was making her way, but she clung too fiercely to the unique quality of her experience, and had too much contempt for organized religion, to find solace in conventional faith.* Her voice rises to energetic heights of exco-

* Alice spent many delightful hours at Leamington arguing with the local clerics. Fenimore wrote to Katharine from Italy in 1887, "While I am grieved to hear that she [Alice] has been suffering, I feel a sort of jealous indignation that she sits up until after midnight discussing points of theology with the curates of Leamington. *I* belong to their fold, and *I* was in Leamington six months; but they never came to discuss theology, or anything else — with me!"

riation on the subject. "I used to wonder," she reflected after living in England for six years, "at Father's fulminations against what seemed so extinct, little dreaming until I came here what vitality the ugly things had. The parson they tell you is a link to soap in the slums; but what flavour of godliness can a cleanliness have which involves mental degradation, and what moral elevation can be brought about by a worship propped up by tortuous verbosity and emasculate evasions. Imagine a religion imposed from without, a virtue taught, not as a measure of self respect, but as a means of propitiating a repulsive, vainglorious, grasping deity, and purchasing from him, at a varying scale of prices, a certain moderation of temperature through the dark mystery of the future."

She appreciated the aesthetics of orthodoxy. When Robertson's son, Ned, was being urged by his mother toward a destiny as a "ministrant at the altar," Alice remarked, "Given the strain of Father that is inevitable in his blood, this is irresistibly funny: the altar, too, is to be after the episcopal order, that jerry-builder architecture of the soul, with none of the historic splendour of the Catholic Church to lend it romance and authority, nor the grim heroic nudity of austere and masculine Calvinism to brace the mental and moral sinews."

She delighted in the comic aspects of religion. William often read the Bible to his young sons, Harry and Billy, explaining passages as he went along. "The other day," recorded Alice after hearing from her brother in Cambridge, "little Billy exclaimed — 'But Father, who is Jehovah *anyhow?*' This must have been a blow, after three years of complacently supposed lucidity. Some years ago when Harry was five or thereabouts, Wm. undertook to explain to him the nature of God and hearing that he was everywhere asked whether he was the chair or the table.

" 'Oh no, God isn't a thing He is a spirit, He is everywhere about us, He pervades.'

"— 'Oh, then he is a skunk!'

"How," wondered Alice, "could the word 'pervades' suggest anything else to an American child!"

She had never subscribed wholeheartedly to her father's theological views. She had struggled alone with his ideas about her "immortal interests," about achievement and inner peace, about fighting off evil, in her nervous breakdowns, on behalf of the entire human race. In earlier years, she had believed in a sort of Christian afterlife, but in the 1880s she moved toward a self-taught existentialism that regarded only the present and made experience its religion. The clarity and calm she now expressed reflects a final covert rejection of her father's notion that there was "nothing peculiar to herself" in her sufferings, that they were only "part of our trouble as a race, struggling to get free." Alice found, on the contrary, that spiritual strength came precisely from the aspects of her experience that were peculiar to herself. She accepted her life on its own terms, with all its limitations, not as a path to something else; and she took far greater interest in moral responsibility and the freedom it gained than in the absolution offered by her father's deterministic, generalizing views. In August 1890, she observed in the diary: "There has come such a change in me. A congenital faith flows thro' me like a limpid stream, making the arid places green, a spontaneous irrigator of which the snags of doubt have never interrupted or made turbid the easily flowing current. A faith which is my mental and moral respiration which needs no revelation but experience and whose only ritual is daily conduct. Thro' my childhood and youth and until within the last few years, the thought of the end as an entrance into spiritual existence, where aspirations are a fulfilment, was a perpetual and necessary inspiration, but now, although intellectually non-existence is more ungraspable and inconceivable than ever, all longing for fulfilment, all passion to achieve has died down within me and whether the great Mystery resolves itself into eternal Death or glorious Life, I contemplate either with equal serenity."

Chapter Seventeen
Divine Cessation

As she calmly contemplated the prospect of her own "non-existence," in August 1890, Alice was in the midst of the worst breakdown of her English sojourn. Katharine had visited for three months in the fall of 1889 but had then gone back to Beverly Farms. Henry had left in May 1890 for four months on the Continent. Alone at Leamington with her nurse, Alice watched her health steadily decline. She had grown quite thin through the years of illness, and her face, framed in gray and hollowed by time and pain, now took on a beauty it had not had when she was young. Her clear gaze seemed to illuminate her sculpted features.

In August she "went under" with an attack of what she later called "squalid indigestions." Katharine called it stomachic gout. Henry rushed over from Italy, and Katharine from America. "I never have seen any one so thin as she was," reported Katharine to Fanny Morse, "so full of pain, and altogether wretched." The first order of business, it seemed to Henry and Katharine, was to get her away from Leamington. Alice's extreme weakness made travel difficult, but Katharine managed early in September to move her to London via an invalid carriage on the Great Western Railroad. They found rooms at the South Kensington Hotel in Queen's Gate Terrace, not far from Henry's new flat, at 34 De Vere Gardens.

Reflecting on these events several months later in her diary, Alice noted that "I had to get a little worse in order to lose all conscience about absorbing K. as a right." With Katharine back, Alice's lonely three years at Leamington came to seem "unspeakable," having "honeycombed all my moral being with their weary strain of the long desolate 'keeping up.'" But now the period of desolation had ended. Henry once again lived conveniently nearby, just as he had during Alice's sociable winter in London in 1886. He reported to William that Katharine would not leave Alice in her "present condition. She told me the other day that she shld. consider it 'inhuman' — . . . Alice *is*, really, too ill to be left."

No one any longer harbored the illusion that Alice's health was improving. She saw no point any more in "keeping up." Even reading, which had always been a bulwark against loneliness and boredom, now became impossible: "For a long time past I have only read what reads with the eyelashes, anything that stirs interest or reflection letting loose the fountain of tears." She was longing to die, and watched herself approach this consummation: "When death has come close, how the emptiness seems palpable and to permeate the very atmosphere, making the sounds of life reverberate therein so loud."

Henry and Katharine thought she would be better off outside London, where the climate was more bracing, and they accordingly rented lodgings for her at Tunbridge Wells. But just before the move, another collapse ("I have gone into pie") led them to conclude she should stay where she was. "Remaining here at loose ends," noted Alice, "seemed the only exit from chaos." For several weeks she and Katharine stayed on at the South Kensington Hotel, with Henry a daily visitor.

Then, in February 1891, Katharine found a house at 41 Argyll Road on Kensington's Campden Hill. The Italianate house had been built in the 1860s in the Renaissance revival style, with subdued, classical lines, four floors, arched bay windows, balustrades, and a garden in back.* Covered in front and behind with Virginia creeper, it had enough room for Alice, Katharine, Alice's nurse, a housemaid from Leamington, and a cook included in the lease of the house. Katharine had had "only to wave her magic wand," wrote Alice in her diary, "and in three weeks from our decision we found ourselves delightfully settled, she, after her usual manner, having levelled all the rough places and let sunlight into the dark corners of suggestion." From her sitting room, on spring afternoons, Alice could hear the rooks in Lord Holland's park and look out on the "good scraplet of garden which, with those of our neighbours, gives us a delightful glimpse of sky and many a feathery bit of green." Katharine was planting a flower garden with seeds sent by Fanny Morse. Watching Katharine dig and hoe, Alice sat at the window imagining being "carried

* The house still stands in London, three quarters of the way up the hill from Kensington High Street, near the Kensington Palace Gardens and Holland Park.

by my slaves through the tangled bloom" at midsummer, when sweet peas, mignonette, cornflowers, pyrethrum, poppies, pansies, carnations, daisies, musk, and nasturtiums would be in full flower. The setting seemed perfect, and she described herself in the diary on April 26 as "absurdly happy."

She had Katharine all to herself for as long as her life might last. Her "better half," the "beloved K.," now acted not only as Alice's legs, doing all the marketing, sightseeing, and socializing, but as her voice as well: beginning December 31, 1890, the diary is written entirely in Katharine's hand. Both friends took pleasure in their hours of dictating and transcribing. It made an odd little scenario: Alice addressing her thoughts about a life that featured this "excellent friend" to the friend herself, who took it all down just as if she were not the subject of Alice's anecdotes and the object of her love. After Katharine brought a photographer to take pictures of Alice in the fall of 1891 (Annie Richards had remarked that "Alice has fine features," and Katharine had "seized the 'psychologic moment' of titillated vanity and brought the one eyed monster to bear upon me; such can be woman's inhumanity to woman"), Alice dictated, "*Mes beaux restes* have returned from the photographer in refulgent beauty! so very much flattered that my heart now overflows with mansuetude for the admirable Katharine, so wise of counsel, so firm of purpose, so gentle in action!"

Elsewhere she joked through her amanuensis about the unequal nature of a relation that cast her once again as the passive recipient of emotional charity, with no right to protest or anger: "If K. knows the blessedness of giving, I certainly know the curse of receiving! No matter how great the iniquity she may commit, if I start up to confront her with it, there suddenly stares me in the face 3000 miles of solid sea-sickness, and my righteous indignation turns to pulp, and I flop back into a tangle of shawls swindled into savourless amiability."

In characteristically indirect fashion, Alice dressed up her greatest praise in mock criticism. "It must be allowed," she dictated to Katharine, that Katharine had "one most serious defect; she is most unbecoming to the race of man, and when he takes the shape of the British Doctor, the spectacle of impotent paralysis that he presents is truly pitiful. [William Wilberforce] Baldwin did keep his shape and colour, but even the great Sir Andrew Clark faded visibly to the eyes. When will men pass from the illusion of the intellectual, limited to sapless reason, and bow to the intelligent, juicy with the succulent science of life."

Alice had by no means resolved her conflicts over the relative merits of masculinity and femininity. At one moment she scolded the "emasculate evasions" of contemporary organized religion and praised "austere and masculine Calvinism." At the next, she associated men with pallid intellect, sapless reason, impotent paralysis, "dry husks" of science and philosophy, and women (in the person of Katharine) with intelligence, living emotion, and succulence.

The word *succulent* turns up again and again in her prose. It describes the juices exuding from the human comedy at the slightest pressure. Her body on her camping trip with Katharine in the Adirondacks was a "delectable and succulent feast" for insects and worms. She found the "recital of humanity's shortcomings more succulent than that of its perfections," and reading her parents' letters drew her "back into the succulent past out of this anomalous death in life." Most of the time Alice saw herself as dried up, shriveled, barren, desolate. She never mentioned feeling attractive to men (she appears delectable only to the lower forms of life) or capable of having children. In a rare moment of self-revelation, just after Katharine had left her in 1889, she admitted, "My soul will never stretch itself to allowing that it is anything else than a cruel and unnatural fate for a woman to live alone, to have no one to care and 'do for' daily is not only a sorrow, but a sterilizing process." She hastened to amend this reflection, however, with "This is a scientific statement, not a lament, for I am replete with the fertilization of the last three months."

Without Katharine's fertilization, Alice felt useless and sterile. Yet she did find, alone, a degree of fecundity in her mental life. She endowed her mind — just as she endowed her friend — with all the energetic life force that seemed denied to her feminine body. In the "succulent science" of life she found a latitude impossible to her in life itself.

With considerable amusement, for example, she related a story about "the great" Sir Andrew Clark, F.R.C.S., whom she had consulted in the spring of 1891. Sir Andrew, an eminent London physician and surgeon, doctor to Gladstone and later to King Edward VII, probably served as one of the models for Sir Luke Strett in *The Wings of the Dove*.* Alice recalled in her diary that when she was at Bournemouth in 1884, a

---

* Another, according to Leon Edel, was Dr. William Wilberforce Baldwin. The encounters between Sir Luke and Milly Theale as physician and patient focus more on her emotional life than on her physical ills. At their second meeting
she told him ... straightway, everything ... It was exactly as if, in the forty-

young American she knew had gone up to London to consult the great man: "Sir Andrew was a couple of hours after his appointed time; as he entered the room and was announced, he immediately added 'the *late* Sir Andrew Clark!' During *our* wait, I said to K., 'You bet' (as Mary Cross says in every one of her notes, to make us feel at home, and encouraged) 'he will make the same exclamation when he comes into this room.' When hark! the door opens, and a florid gentleman enters, and 'the *late* Sir Andrew' falls upon our ears, followed by the self same burst of hilarity, rippling down to us, thro' all these years. Imagine the martyrdom of a pun which has become an integral portion of one's organism to be lugged through life like the convict's ball and chain. Do you suppose he vainly tries to escape it, or is he passive in its clutches or can it

---

eight hours that had passed, her acquaintance with him had somehow increased, and his own knowledge in particular received mysterious additions. They had been together, before, scarce ten minutes; but the relation, the one the ten minutes had so beautifully created, was there to take straight up; and this not, on his own part, for mere professional heartiness, mere bedside manner, which she would have disliked — much rather from a quiet, pleasant air in him of having positively asked about her ... Of course he couldn't in the least have asked ... he had found out simply by his genius — and found out, she meant, literally everything. Now she knew not only that she didn't dislike this — the state of being found out about; but that, on the contrary, it was truly what she had come for, and that, for the time at least, it would give her something firm to stand on.

As she leaves this second encounter, Milly asks, " 'So you don't think I'm out of my mind?'

" 'Perhaps that is,' he smiled, 'all that's the matter.'

"She looked at him longer. 'No, that's too good. Shall I, at any rate, suffer?'

" 'Not a bit.'

" 'And then live?'

" 'My dear young lady,' said her distinguished friend, 'isn't to "live" exactly what I'm trying to persuade you to take the trouble to do?' "

Edmund Wilson said of James's story *The Turn of the Screw* that it was not a ghost story but a characterization of a hysterical governess — a poor country parson's daughter with "her English middle-class consciousness, her inability to admit to herself her sexual impulses and the relentless English 'authority' which enables her to put over on inferiors even purposes which are totally mistaken and not at all to the other people's best interests ... We see now that [the story] is simply a variation on one of James's familiar themes: the frustrated Anglo-Saxon spinster." And apropos of *The Wings of the Dove,* Wilson wrote to James Thurber in 1959: "It seems, by the way, that Henry James had seen quite a good deal of psychiatrists in connection with his sister Alice. I suppose that Alice and her ailments are also behind the Milly Theale situation."

be possible that some memory of the joy still survives which irradiated his being, the first time he heard it fall from his lips in the springtime of his practice?"

Sir Andrew had been called in by Henry and Katharine at the end of May 1891, for in spite of Alice's happiness and comfort in Argyll Road, her health had continued to decline. Shortly after the doctor's visit, she crowed in her diary, "To him who waits, all things come!" Her "eccentric" aspirations had at last been "brilliantly fulfilled": "Ever since I have been ill, I have longed and longed for some palpable disease, no matter how conventionally dreadful a label it might have, but I was always driven back to stagger alone under the monstrous mass of subjective sensations, which that sympathetic being 'the medical man' has had no higher inspiration than to assure me I was personally responsible for." Sir Andrew, she continued, had "endowed" her with cardiac complications, a spinal neurosis affecting her legs, a "delicate embroidery of 'the most distressing case of nervous hyperesthesia,'" and rheumatic gout in her stomach. (This panoply ought "to satisfy the most inflated pathologic vanity," she noted, and, though it seemed "decidedly indecent to catalogue oneself in this way," she "put it down in a scientific spirit, to show that though I have no productive worth, I have a certain value as an indestructible quantity.")

All these disorders, however, came under the heading of subjective sensations that Alice had been living with for years. What caused her to exult was Sir Andrew's pronouncement that a lump she had had for three months in one of her breasts was a tumor, and that she would soon die. She explained her bizarre jubilation the next day in her diary: "To any one who has not been there, it will be hard to understand the enormous relief of Sir A.C.'s uncompromising verdict, lifting us out of the formless vague and setting us within the very heart of the sustaining concrete. One would naturally not choose such an ugly and gruesome method of progression down the dark Valley of the Shadow of Death, and of course many of the moral sinews will snap by the way, but we shall gird up our loins and the blessed peace of the end will have no shadow cast upon it."

As always, she stepped back to watch. "I cannot make out," she wrote on June 5, "whether it is an entire absence or an excess of humor in Destiny to construct such an elaborate exit for my thistledown personality." She was savoring the new perspective afforded by Sir Andrew's verdict: "Having it to look forward to for a while seems to double the value of the event, for one becomes suddenly picturesque to oneself, and one's wavering little individuality stands out with a cameo effect . . . The grief is all for K. and H., who will *see* it all, whilst I shall only *feel* it,* but they are taking it, of course, like archangels, and care for me with infinite tenderness and patience. Poor dear William with his exaggerated sympathy for suffering isn't to know anything about it until it is all over."

All her adult life Alice had been preoccupied with death, not just as an escape from the "monstrous mass of subjective sensations" that had tortured her existence, but as something comfortingly absolute and complete. She had often *felt* dead, as a way of not having to feel despair, ever since the 1878 breakdown and her discussion with her father about suicide; "now it's only the shrivelling of an empty pea pod that has to be completed," she wrote in 1892. And she had been "killing herself," stifling her active, competitive nature, ever since her adolescence in Newport. However, she had also in the 1880s and nineties been finding not desiccation and emptiness inside, but the limpid flowing stream of a personal faith that enabled her to contemplate death and life with equal serenity. She had slowly, incrementally, lost her struggle to please her father, validate his ideas, see her own life through his eyes. That was a kind of death, a loss of hope. It was also a way of coming into her own life and views. Death now seemed to Alice to promise not eternal life but simply peace. It would annihilate all the questions of control, distinction, and selfhood that had plagued her life; it would obliterate the ceaseless conflicts between body and will, male and female, love and hate, good and evil, struggle and acceptance, success and failure. In the face of death, her life took on a new clarity. Death was the consummation of struggle and pain, the apotheosis and the cessation of suffering. Alice went out to meet it like a lover keeping a long-awaited assignation, yearning to surrender to its large, dark, overwhelming force.

•

At first Alice told "poor dear William" only that she had heart disease. As the weeks went by, however, it became impossible to keep the whole story a secret, and at the end of June she had Katharine write to him

---

* Here again, Alice points to one of the salient features of her lifelong illness — her sense that the people caring for her suffer more than she does, that watching pain is worse than experiencing it. That notion credited her caretakers with an ideal (and impossible) sympathy, the essence of selfless love — and also reflected her desire to hurt others by hurting herself.

about her tumor. The ensuing epistolary conversation between brother and sister about her impending demise reveals a moment of profound communion and the extraordinary forthrightness both Alice and William summoned in the face of death. From his summer home at Chocorua, William wrote, on July 6, 1891:

... So far from being shocked I am, although made more compassionate, yet (strange to say) rather relieved than shaken by this more tangible and immediately menacing source of woe. Katharine describes you as being so too; and I don't wonder. Vague nervousness has a character of ill about it that is all its own, and in comparison with which any organic disease has a good side. Of course, if the tumour should turn out to be cancerous, that means, as all men know, a finite length of days; and then, good-bye to neurasthenia and neuralgia and headache, and weariness and palpitation and disgust all at one stroke — I should think you would be reconciled to the prospect with all its pluses and minuses! I know you've never cared for life, and to me, now at the age of nearly fifty, life and death seem singularly close together in all of us — and life a mere farce of frustration in all, so far as the realization of the innermost ideals go to which we are made respectively capable of feeling an affinity and responding. Your frustrations are only rather more flagrant than the rule; and you've been saved many forms of self-dissatisfaction and misery which appertain to such a multiplication of responsible relations to different people as I, for instance, have got into. Your fortitude, good spirits and unsentimentality have been simply unexampled in the midst of your physical woes; and when you're relieved from your post, just *that* bright note will remain behind, together with the inscrutable and mysterious character of the doom of nervous weakness which has chained you down for all these years. As for that, there's more in it than has ever been told to so-called science. These inhibitions, these split-up selves, all these new facts that are gradually coming to light about our organization, these enlargements of the self in trance, etc., are bringing me to turn for light in the direction of all sorts of despised spiritualistic and unscientific ideas. Father would find in me today a much more receptive listener — all *that* philosophy has got to be brought in. And what a queer contradiction comes to the ordinary scientific argument against immortality (based on body being mind's condition and mind going *out* when body is gone), when one must believe (as now, in these neurotic cases) that some infernality in the body *prevents* really existing parts of the mind from coming to their effective rights at all, suppresses them, and blots them out from participation in this world's experiences, although they are *there* all the time. When that which is *you* passes out of the body, I am sure that there will be an explosion of liberated force and life till then eclipsed and kept down. I can hardly imagine *your* transition without a great oscillation of both "worlds" as they regain their new equilibrium aftrer the change! Everyone will feel the shock, but you yourself will be more surprised than anybody else.

It may seem odd for me to talk to you in this cool way about your end; but, my dear little sister, if one has things present to one's mind, and I know they are present enough to *your* mind, why not speak them out? I am sure you appreciate that best. How many times I have thought, in the past year, when my days were so full of strong and varied impressions and activities, of the long unchanging hours in bed which those days stood for with you, and wondered how you bore the slow-paced monotony at all, as you did! You can't tell how I've pitied you. But you *shall* come to your rights erelong. Meanwhile take things gently. Look for the little good in each day as if life were to last a hundred years. Above all things, save yourself from bodily pain, if it can be done. You've had too much of that. Take all the morphia (or other forms of opium if that disagrees) you want, and don't be afraid of becoming an opium-drunkard. What was opium created for except for such times as this? Beg the good Katharine (to whom *our* debt can never be extinguished) to write me a line every week, just to keep the currents flowing, and so farewell until I write again. Your ever loving,

W.J.

Alice replied from Argyll Road on July 30, dictating to Katharine:

My dearest William,

A thousand thanks for your beautiful and fraternal letter, which came, I know not when, owing to Katharine's iron despotism. Of course I could have wanted nothing else and should have felt, notwithstanding my "unsentimentality" very much wounded & *incomprise* had you walked round and not up to my demise.

It is the most supremely interesting moment in life, the only one in fact, when living seems life, and I count it as the greatest good fortune to have these few months so full of interest and instruction in the knowledge of my approaching death. It is as simple in one's own person as any fact of nature, the fall of a leaf or the blooming of a rose, and I have a delicious consciousness, ever present, of wide spaces close at hand, and whisperings of release in the air.

Your philosophy of the transition is entirely mine and at this remoteness I will venture upon the impertinence of congratulating you upon having arrived "at nearly fifty" at the point at which I started at fifteen! 'Twas always thus of old, but in time you usually, as now, caught up.

But you must believe that you greatly exaggerate the tragic element in my commonplace little journey; and so far from ever having thought that "my frustrations were more flagrant than the rule," I have always simmered complacently in my complete immunity therefrom. As from early days the elusive nature of concrete hopes shone forth, I always rejoiced that my temperament had set for my task the attainment of the simplest rudimentary ideal, which I could carry about in my pocket and work away upon equally in shower as in sunshine, in complete security from the grotesque obstructions supposed to be *life,* which have indeed only strengthened the sinews to whatever imperfect accomplishment I may have attained.

You must also remember that a woman, by nature, needs much less to feed upon than a man, a few emotions and she is satisfied; so when I am gone, pray don't think of me simply as a creature who might have been something else, had neurotic science been born. Notwithstanding the poverty of my outside experience, I have always had a significance for myself — every chance to stumble along my straight and narrow little path, and to worship at the feet of my Deity, and what more can a human soul ask for?

This year has been one of the happiest I have ever known, surrounded by such affection and devotion, but I won't enter into details, as I see the blush mantle the elderly cheek of my scribe ...

Give much love to Alice and to all the household, great and small ...

> Your always loving and grateful sister,
> Alice James

By the time Alice wrote this letter to William, she knew she had cancer. Sir Andrew had not positively diagnosed the painful lump in her breast as malignant, but at the end of July an American doctor passing through London declared it cancerous. This doctor, William Wilberforce Baldwin, was a friend of Henry's who resided in Florence. When Baldwin came to London in July 1891, Henry was off visiting friends in Ireland, and it was Constance Woolson, staying in Oxford, who recommended the American physician to Alice in the hope that he could provide (as Henry later put it) "some suggestion ... of more than British ingenuity, as to the alleviation of pain." Baldwin saw Alice four times, and concluded from a pain under the point of her right shoulder blade and an "earthy" hue in her complexion that the breast cancer had metastasized from an original malignancy in her liver.* He predicted that the

---

* Modern oncologists would conclude the opposite — that the cancer had probably metastasized to the liver from an original site in the breast. Radical mastectomy as a treatment for breast cancer had been perfected in 1889 by Dr. William Stewart Halsted, of the Johns Hopkins University, but surgery was never considered an option for Alice James. She wanted to die. Besides, surgical removal of her breast would have seemed unnecessary if the original site was thought to be in her liver.

progression of the liver cancer would be painless, and prescribed morphine to mitigate the breast pain.

Alice was delighted with Baldwin. "He appears to have been almost the only doctor that she has ever *liked* to see," Henry told William. To Baldwin he wrote that she "*yearns* to see you again." Alice sent the doctor as thanks a volume of Henry's stories, signing herself "Your limp & shadowy but sincerely grateful friend and patient, Alice James." Grateful, too, for the painkilling effects of morphine, she had begun taking it constantly by September. She struck Henry as extraordinarily serene, and with his usual astuteness he described her as in a "condition of greater comfort than she has known for years, or probably ever. The 'nervousness' engendered by (or engendering) her intense horror of life and contempt for it, is practically falling away from her in view of her future becoming thus a definite and not long — a rapidly shrinking, term."

For all William's knowledge of physiological psychology and his study of "nervous" pathology, Henry managed in his observations and unofficial diagnoses to characterize his sister's health more accurately than his older brother did. The familiar observation that William wrote psychology like a novelist and Henry wrote novels like a psychologist holds true with regard to Alice. William directed his efforts toward describing her troubles and establishing a narrative (and emotional) distance from them; Henry looked more closely and captured the subtler workings of her particular illness and character. William, generalizing, saw the "inscrutable and mysterious ... doom of nervous weakness which has chained you down all these years," and claimed that "some infernality in the body *prevents* really existing parts of the mind from coming to their effective rights at all." Henry caught the specific ambiguity in "the 'nervousness' engendered by (or engendering) her intense horror of life and contempt for it" and offered his trenchant summary analysis after she died — "her disastrous, her tragic health was in a manner the only solution for her of the practical problem of life — as it suppressed the element of equality, reciprocity, etc."

•

In the middle of September, William came to London for a brief farewell visit and found Henry and Alice in a fever of excitement over the London production of *The American,* which was to open on the 26th. William reported later to a Boston friend that Alice "altogether refused to waste a minute in talking about her disease, and conversed only of the english people and Harry's play. So her soul was not subdued! I wish that mine might ever be as little so!" Alice's preoccupation with *The American* and its reviews did prevent her from paying full attention to William, and he told her in a note from the *City of Paris* as he was returning to Boston that it seemed "absurd" for him to have "come and whisked about so soon after such short interviews and such contracted opportunities for conversation." He then reflected that in twelve years of marriage he had had no opportunity to talk with his wife about the "innumerable things that are of most importance," adding, "How *Harry* will miss *your* conversation when the opportunity for it is gone. Between us we promise you to try to work some of it into Philosophy and the Drama so that it shall become part of the world's inheritance!"

William still did not know that his sister was working on a legacy of her own. The diary has large gaps during the fall of 1891: it registered neither William's visit nor the London opening of *The American*. Alice offered a self-exonerating note to posterity: "These long pauses don't point to any mental aridity, my 'roomy forehead' is as full as ever of germinating thoughts, but alas the machinery is more and more out of kilter. I am sorry for you all, for I feel as if I hadn't even yet given my message. I would there were more bursts of enthusiasm, less of the carping tone, through this, but I fear it comes by nature . . ."

A number of Alice's friends and relatives now began to sum up her life. The admiration she had always so longed for was at last forthcoming at the end of her "weary journey." She observed, "It is very gratifying at this mortuary moment to learn how many people have been 'struck and impressed'!" Constance Woolson wrote to Dr. Baldwin, "Alice lives, and even enjoys, for every now and then I get a witty message from her. If she had had any health, what a brilliant woman she would have been . . ."

The most succinct and welcome praise came from William's Alice, in language she might have taken from one of Henry's novels. One night in November 1891, William was writing to his sister from Cambridge, when his wife came into the room and asked him to convey her warmest love to her sister-in-law. Then (added William), "She breaks out with: What a big void there'll be for us when Alice is gone! She stands for the wider sphere of reference!"

William took a more ambiguous retrospective look at his sister's life, striking in the midst of his praise the familiar note that she called "true fraternal condescension." In a letter to Henry that he knew Alice would read, William called her "the most remarkable member of the family . . . How one feels that the definiteness and comparative stability of her outlook rests and steadies her. It gives one an idea of how the state of suspense, agitation, trepidation, and uncertainty w. which she has lived for so many years is the hardest thing of all to bear. Poor dear girl! poor dear girl! But the back has been fitted to the burden as few 'backs' have; and . . . I am as sure as I am of anything that her life has been bearing its fruit, fruit not only for her, I mean, but for life at large."

Henry admired more generously, but even he put his acclaim in virtual quotation marks with his ineluctable "as it weres." He told Bob that Alice's suffering "only brings out her extraordinary fortitude and her wonderfully unconventional view of life, death, pain and her whole situation. Her state is very touching, but I can't call it tragic in the presence of her extraordinary mastery, as it were, of it, and superiority, as it were, to it."

These mixtures of praise and pity, jollying up and talking down, genuine admiration and undercutting irony, played as large a role in Alice's dying as they did in her living. Her indirect response can be read in two brief diary entries. Bitterly imagining her own "11th hour," Alice regretted that she would not be a member of the audience, for "it would complete it all so to watch the rags and tatters of one's Vanity in its insolent struggle with the Absolute, as the curtain rolls down on this jocose humbuggery called Life!" And looking back on the year 1890–1891, she noted that Henry had "published *The Tragic Muse*, brought out *The American*, and written a play, *Mrs. Vibert* . . . and his admirable comedy; combined with William's *Psychology*, not a bad show for one family! especially if I get myself dead, the hardest job of all."

•

The morphine that Henry had called an "ineffable blessing" in September had by November "disclosed its iniquities" to Alice and Katharine. It effectively killed the pain in Alice's breast, but it was also a "treacherous fiend" that kept her from sleeping and opened the door to "hideous nervous distresses . . . K. and I touched bottom more nearly than ever before." William had suggested that Alice try hypnosis for her nervous troubles late in 1890, months before the cancer diagnosis, and had sent her the name of Dr. Charles Lloyd Tuckey, an English physician who had written a "very creditable book" on its therapeutic effects. In the December 1891 issue of the *Fortnightly Review*, Tuckey published an article on hypnosis, which Alice, Henry, and Katharine read, and Katharine immediately looked up the author in Park Lane. She brought him to Alice, who reported that "K." had "turned on the hypnotic Tuckey, the mild radiance of whose moonbeam personality has penetrated with a little hope the black mists that enveloped us." She went into more detail to William on December 2, "supposing that your being is vibrating with more or less curiosity about the great hypnotic experiment on Camden Hill. [She was dictating to her nurse, who misspelled Campden.] As far as pain goes the result is nil . . . What I *do* experience is a calming of my nerves & a quiescent passive state, during which I fall asleep, without the sensations of terror which have accompanied that process for so many years, and I sleep five or six hours, uninterruptedly." Tuckey had taught Katharine how to hypnotize Alice, who concluded, "My pains are too much a part of my substance to have any modifications before the spirit and the flesh fall asunder. But I feel as if I had gained something in the way of a nerve pacifier and one of the most intense intellectual experiences of my life."

In hypnosis, she glimpsed a solution to the physical and psychological problems that had plagued her existence: "If it were possible, with Death so close at hand, to take anything which concerns one's ephemeral personality, with seriousness, I might pose to myself before the footlights of my last obscure little scene, as a delectably pathetic figure, for I have come to the knowledge within the last week or so that I was simply born a few years too soon." Hypnosis had opened up a "vast field of therapeutic possibilities . . . just at the moment when I have passed far beyond the workings of their beneficent laws, save most superficially." And it struck her as ironic that the "agent" — the hypnotic mechanism — took "the form and direction which, from experience, I learned, twenty-four years ago [during her first breakdown] was the some-day-to-be-revealed secret, of suspending for the time from his duties, the individual watch dog, worn out with his ceaseless vigil to maintain the sanity of the modern complicated mechanism. That the golden solution of the complex riddle should be a mechanical process of inconceivable simplicity, is only another of the myriad beautiful illustrations that the highest Divine order is brought about by the humblest means."

•

Through the end of 1891 and the beginning of '92, Alice continued, when she could, to dictate diary entries on her favorite subjects: politics, friends, America and England, the education of girls, language, religion, Ireland. She was also recording the progress of her decline. "It is curious to see 'subjects' and 'questions' slipping from out of the mental grasp, as the physical degeneracy advances; one lays them aside and turns from them as naturally as from any muscular exertion, so that the General Election, the 'Race,' those slight topics to which I felt myself so adequate, and tossed about so lightly, lie dormant under their present colossal expansion."

And she began to conclude the message of gratitude and love that she was dictating to Katharine Loring for all time: "As the ugliest things go to the making of the fairest, it is not wonderful that this unholy granite substance in my breast should be the soil propitious for the perfect flowering of Katharine's unexampled genius for friendship and devotion. The story of her watchfulness, patience and untiring resource cannot be told by my feeble pen, but all the pain and discomfort seem a slender price to pay for all the happiness and peace with which she fills my days."*

Her weakness increased daily, and she could only occasionally sit up and be read to, or work on the diary. At the beginning of February she rallied enough to dictate several long passages. On February 1, she declared, simply, "It isn't in the sorrows and the pains but in the inexorable inadequacy for happiness that the tragedy lies." The next day she related an "amusing episode" in which the "kind and usually understanding Tuckey" made the mistake of assuring her that she still had a good while to live: "I was terribly shocked and when he saw the havoc that he wrought, he reassuringly said: 'but you'll be comfortable, too,' at which I exclaimed: 'Oh I don't care about that, but boo-hoo, it's so *inconvenient!*' and the poor man burst into a roar of laughter. I was glad afterwards that it happened, as I was taken quite by surprise, and was able to test the sincerity of my mortuary inclinations. I have always *thought* that I wanted to die, but I felt quite uncertain as to what my muscular demonstrations might be at the moment of transition ... But my substance seemed equally outraged with my mind at Tuckey's dictum, so mayhap I shall be able to maintain a calm befitting so sublimated a spirit!"

The diary contains no entry from February 2 to 28. On the 15th, Henry described Alice to William as intensely ill: "There *is* nothing to

---

* Alice went over this passage after Katharine took it down, for the word "unexampled" toward the end of the first sentence is carated in above the line in her own handwriting.

tell, nowadays, of a condition so monotonous & intensely simplified . . . except that she lives and lives and lives through all her infinite Protean dying."

On the 19th she asked her nurse, her housemaid, and Annie Richards to come to her bedroom and witness her will. She had made out at least two previous wills, changing them as she changed her mind about whom she wanted to favor and exclude. The most recent version had been drawn up at Leamington, when Lizzie Putnam was visiting, "as it was so good to get a Boston witness." Annie Richards had been witness to an even earlier version, and as she entered Alice's room on Argyll Road in 1892, Alice remarked, "My wills give you a great deal of bother." Alice sat up in bed to sign the two-page document she had dictated to Katharine ("K. told me that as long as I indulged in no amateur legal terminology but confined myself strictly to my vernacular it would be all right, so she wouldn't allow me even one decorative bequeath"). Then Annie Richards, Emily Bradfield, and Louisa Griffin subscribed their names beneath hers.

The only real estate Alice now owned was the house and property in Manchester, and the will begins (in Katharine's hand): "I, Alice James, Spinster of the Town of Manchester in the County of Essex and Commonwealth of Massachusetts, in the United States of America, now living at 41 Argyll Road, Kensington, England, make this my will and testament as follows . . ." Her property and stocks amounted to an estate worth about $80,000. She left the bulk of it to William, Henry, and Katharine, to be divided into three equal shares amounting to approximately $20,000 each. To Robertson and his family she left about $10,000, justifying her discrimination by the fact that he had a rich father-in-law. The remaining $10,000 she gave in smaller portions to various female friends and relatives. To her namesake, Wilky's daughter, she left a gold watch and $2500. Robertson's daughter, Mary, and William's daughter, Peggy, were to receive $2500 apiece. And $1000 each went to her cousin Elizabeth Robertson Walsh, Francis J. Child's daughter Henrietta, and Katharine's cousin Alice Gray, who had earned Alice James's admiration by struggling for years without money to pursue a career in art and at last securing a job at the Boston Museum of Fine Arts. Finally, Alice left $100 to her Cambridge dressmaker and $50 to her gardener and handyman, Simon Hassett of Cambridge.

In addition, she willed her Boston furniture and Frank Duveneck's portrait of Henry James, Sr., to William, and her pictures, china, and English furniture to Henry. To Katharine she gave all her remaining personal effects, furniture, photographs, silver, jewelry, and £25 sterling "to be disposed of by her according to my written instructions." The earlier wills appointed Henry and William as executors. In this final version, Alice appointed Katharine Loring and Joseph B. Warner, Marny Storer's husband.

At the end of February, she rallied. But on March 2, she caught a cold from her nurse. It quickly turned to pleurisy, and Tuckey prescribed belladonna, predicting that she would not live more than three or four days. Henry told William that she was "really a tragic vessel, or receptacle, of recurrent, renewable, inexhaustible *forms* of disease," but that "her lucidity and moral command of the situation are unimpaired."

The acceptance and detachment that Alice had been trying out, simulating, working toward for years, became at the last entirely authentic and natural. On March 4, she dictated to Katharine: "I am being ground slowly on the grim grindstone of physical pain, and on two nights I had almost asked for K's lethal dose, but one steps hesitantly along such unaccustomed ways and endures from second to second; and I feel sure that it can't be possible but what the bewildered little hammer that keeps me going will very shortly see the decency of ending his distracted career; however this may be, physical pain however great ends in itself and falls away like dry husks from the mind, whilst moral discords and nervous horrors sear the soul. These last, Katharine has completely under the control of her rhythmic hand, so I go no longer in dread. Oh the wonderful moment when I felt myself floated for the first time into the deep sea of divine *cessation,* and saw all the dear old mysteries and miracles vanish into vapour! That first experience doesn't repeat itself, fortunately, for it might become a seduction."

The final words of the diary are in praise of Katharine, who was keeping a constant bedside vigil, reading aloud Constance Woolson's story "Dorothy"* and administering hypnotism with her "rhythmic hand"

* The story, which takes place in Florence, had just come out in the March issue of *Harper's New Monthly Magazine.* Alice sent a last message to Miss Woolson, then living at Cheltenham near Oxford, but its contents remain a mystery. A year after Alice's death, Constance wrote to her own nephew that leaving England for Italy meant "I am giving up being near my kind friend Mr. James." And then she added: "I don't know what made me tell you and Will that last message of his sister to me, that touched me so much. But I suppose it was simply the relief of having some of my own

every twenty minutes. "Katharine can't help it," declared Alice out of the blue in her last message to posterity; "she's made that way, a simple embodiment of Health, as Baldwin called her, 'the New England professor of doing things.'"

That night, Alice had a strange dream that both impressed and agitated her. It was a vision of Lizzie Boott and another good friend, Annie Dixwell, who had also died in the late 1880s. In the dream, they were standing up in a boat, just putting out into a tumbled sea. They seemed to pass from under the shadow of a cloud into sunlight, and they were looking back at Alice on the shore, as if beckoning her, in their mute departure, to join them.

The next morning Henry described to William the "supreme deathlike emaciation" that had come over Alice suddenly. The breast tumor had been growing steadily larger and harder. "Her lungs, her heart, her breast are all a great distress, and she has constant fever, which rises and falls. She has a most distressing, choking, retching cough, which tries her strength terribly." She could not sleep, but she was now too weak to be nervous. "She is perfectly clear and humorous and would talk if doing so didn't bring on spasms of coughing." But she could speak in a whisper, and into Henry's ear she dictated a final message to be cabled to William: TENDEREST LOVE TO ALL FAREWELL AM GOING SOON ALICE.

All through the day and night of Saturday, March 5, Alice was "making sentences," wrote Katharine in a note of her own at the end of her friend's diary. "One of the last things she said to me was to make a correction in the sentence of March 4th 'moral discords and nervous horrors.'

"This dictation of March 4th was rushing about in her brain all day, and although she was very weak & it tired her much to dictate, she could not get her head quiet until she had had it written; then she was relieved, I finished Miss Woolson's story of 'Dorothy' to her."

During the day on Saturday, all of Alice's painful symptoms disappeared. Her cough, her fever, the pain in her lungs simply fell away. Dr.

---

family to talk to, after being so long gone. I felt that I could say anything to you, without having to think whether it was safe or not, wise or not, prudent or not. — But Mr. James will come to Italy every year." One might surmise, from Miss Woolson's concern about safety, prudence, and wisdom — and her self-consolation that "Mr. James will come to Italy every year" — that Alice's message had something to do with Henry and his "*she*-novelist" friend; but it would be guessing.

Tuckey came twice. Henry left only to eat and sleep. Katharine remained at her post by Alice's bed through the night. Alice still did not sleep, but she was quiet and in no pain. She whispered to Katharine that she couldn't live another day, and begged that it might not be expected of her. Toward 6:00 A.M. she finally fell into a peaceful sleep. When Henry arrived at nine, she was still asleep, breathing in a loud, deep, "almost stertorous" way. Katharine, Henry, and the nurse sat by her all day. "For about seven hours this deep difficult, and almost automatic breathing continued," Henry wrote to William, "with *no* look of pain in the face — only more and more utterly the look of death. They were infinitely pathetic and, to me, most unspeakable hours. They would have been intolerable if it had not been so evident that all the hideous burden of suffering consciousness was utterly gone. As it is, they were the most appealing and pitiful thing I ever saw." Toward the middle of the afternoon her breathing slowed; her pulse flickered, stopped, revived. At three, a "blessed change" took place, and she seemed to sleep and breathe peacefully, like a child. After another hour the breathing slowed even more, until she was taking only about a breath a minute. "Her face," recorded Henry, "then seemed in a strange, dim, touching way, to become clearer. I went to the window to let in a little more of the afternoon light upon it (it was a bright, kind, soundless Sunday) and when I came back to the bed she had drawn the breath that was not succeeded by another."

Half an hour later he went out and cabled to William: ALICE JUST PASSED AWAY PAINLESS WIRE BOB HENRY.

•

Alice had thought a great deal about what she wanted to happen to her remains, imagining in mock horror the disgrace of having an Anglican priest supervise the "obsequies" of someone as opposed as she to clergy in general and Anglicans in particular. Since she had been neither baptized nor married, her funeral would be her "first and last ceremony; perhaps the impish part of me will hover about," she imagined months before her death, "and enjoy the fine and highly decorative rhetoric, to say nothing of the joke against the 'Not as other men' part of me." In order to minimize the ceremonial fuss, she had decided on cremation, at the Woking Crematorium outside London. Her ashes were to be carried across the Atlantic and placed beside her parents in the Cambridge Cemetery. And she wanted only Henry, Katharine, her devoted nurse, and Annie Richards to attend the ceremony.

Accordingly, on March 9, a sleeting, blustering, snowy English day, her body was taken in a hearse to the Waterloo Station and from there by train to Woking. Henry, Katharine, Annie, and Emily Bradfield followed in another train. An "inoffensive, sweet-voiced young clergyman," Henry told William, read a short, simple service, and then the body was cremated. "It was all somehow less dreadfull than I had feared," Henry continued that night to Francis Boott. He even felt "a positive joy" that Alice was not to be left alone and far off "in this damp, black alien English earth."

Henry's letters describing Alice's final days and her death would not arrive in Cambridge for another week. Meanwhile, William wrote on the 7th, after receiving both cables, "Poor little Alice! What a life! I can't believe that that imperious will and piercing judgment are snuffed out with the breath. Now that her outwardly so frustrated life is over, one sees that in the deepest sense it was a triumph. In her relations to her disease, her mind did not succumb. She never whined or complained or did anything but spurn it. She thus kept it from invading the tone of her soul. It made her doubtless despotic to others, but it didn't make her weak. And if one regards the working out of that particular problem as the particular burden that was laid on her, one can only say that it was well done, and that her life was anything but a failure. So much of her mysterious debt to this universe safely finished and paid off! That is the way her little life, shrunken and rounded in retrospect, has seemed to me to day."

Fanny Morse had been in constant touch through the last months from America, and Katharine wrote to her on March 12, "I cannot give you any idea of the beauty of that last night, those last hours when Alice knew that she was free at last: though she was too weak to say much . . . How fortunate and happy this year has been! Nothing has gone wrong . . ." Katharine was busy packing her own and Alice's things, and seeing the house cleaned up and put in order. "There is not a great deal to be done," she told Fanny, "but what there is has to be carefully done, and I do not want to hurry." She planned to sail for America some time in the early part of April.

From Concord, Robertson wrote to Fanny about death and "a sort of lifting of a curtain which has intervened between us and our childhood . . . In the past week, I have looked behind that curtain in the strangest, most startling way . . ." He had seen his years with Alice in the nursery, sharing the measles, setting up their little marriage compacts as "Henry" and "Mary" — "compacts which lasted their hours of innocence, but which after thirty-seven years come back to me today as the only innocent and living facts of life . . .

"Dear Alice's life didn't seem beautiful, but I doubt not it was interiorly beautiful. There is nothing beautiful in a life that has nothing to overcome. And she overcame more than any of us can ever know. How frustrated her life was seems almost appalling. Of course you and I do not know where she has gone. All that I *feel* I know is that she has gone where love is. When we have love with us, we know that love lives. I hope some part of my heart has gone with hers, away from the poor shams in which most of us have to live."

And from New York, William Dean Howells wrote to Henry:

> 241 East 17th St.
> March 25, 1892

My dear James:

I have been trying, on other sheets, to say something to you about your sister's death. But there seems nothing to say except that my wife and I feel it in itself and for you as I think you would wish us to feel it. Otherwise, it is inexpressible. I knew, from your brother, of her willingness, her eagerness to be gone, but I know that this is no measure of your bereavement. — I remember her as she used to be in Cambridge, sitting in the library, where your father used to write in the midst of his family, and how she looked and laughed; a clear, strong intelligence, housed in pain. Her memory is eternally dear to me for what she wrote us of Winny.

Perhaps you may sometime write me of her last days; that would be precious . . .

My wife and daughter join me in love to you.

> Yours ever,
> W. D. Howells

Henry's replies to all these letters repeat again and again how "rare and remarkable" his sister had been, and what a difference her absence would make in his own life. To his and Alice's old friend Francis Boott he confided his own "great sorrow . . . even with everything that made life an unspeakable weariness to her, she contributed constantly, infinitely to the interest, the consolation, as it were, in disappointment and depression, of my own existence . . . To me her death makes a great and sad personal difference — her talk, her company, her conversation and admirable acute mind and large spirit were so much the best thing I have, of late years, known here. But for her it is only blessed and bountiful." And he told his friend Henrietta Reubell, "She was not only my nearest and dearest relation, but she was a cherished social relation, as it were, as well, and a great — on the whole my greatest, social resource . . . But it is all over, utterly over, now."

•

Katharine sailed for America on the *Etruria* on April 9. Henry saw her off at Liverpool. She had closed up the Argyll Road house, spent several days with Annie Richards in London, and made a brief pilgrimage to some of Alice's favorite spots at Leamington. With her across the Atlantic she carried a box of white ash and two small, leather-bound, handwritten volumes. Two more years would pass before Henry or William would hear of the diary. The little box of ash was buried beside the graves of Henry and Mary James at the Cambridge Cemetery, facing out across the Charles River toward Soldiers Field. In Florence, the following year, William designed a small marble urn made to mark his sister's grave. On it, he had inscribed two lines from Dante's *Paradiso* in commemoration of Alice's life:

> . . . *ed essa da martiro*
> *e da essilio venne a questa pace.*

From martyrdom and exile to this peace.

Afterword

The Diary

KATHARINE LORING had four copies of Alice James's diary printed privately in 1894 (by John Wilson and Son, Cambridge) — one for herself and one for each of Alice's living brothers, William, Henry, and Rob. William, who received his copy in March, took it away to New Bedford for a twenty-four-hour vacation from his daily round of teaching, writing, and family life in Cambridge. There, alone, he read it through. "It sank into me with strange compunctions and solemnity," he wrote to Henry a few days later. "The diary produces a unique and tragic impression of personal power venting itself on no opportunity. And such really *deep* humor!" He went on, "Of course the whole thing is less new and odd to you than to me. It ought some day to be published. I am proud of it as a leaf in the family laurel crown, and your memory will be embalmed in a new way by her references to your person . . ."

But the whole thing *was* new and odd to Henry, who received William's letter in Italy. He had just heard of the diary's existence from Katharine, who had mailed his copy to London. He told William that news of the diary came as a " 'revelation' to me. — I mean a surprise and agitation. The agitation is a great and sacred impatience to see it — and above all, or also, to know if it was Alice's own design that it be printed, or a pious inspiration of KPL's. I can well believe that it is exceedingly remarkable — for I have never had occasion to express the full impression I received, in the last years of Alice's life, of the extraordinary energy and personality of her intellectual and moral being. There is almost no exhibition of it that would surprise me." He learned from

Katharine that the impetus to publish *had* come from Alice, but his anxiety about what the diary might contain remained high.

Finally his copy was forwarded from London to Venice, where he had come on a sad mission. Constance Fenimore Woolson had committed suicide there in January, and he was helping her sister dispose of Fenimore's belongings and literary remains. Of his own sister's literary remains he wrote at first that he found the diary "magnificent . . . rare — wondrous," but that he was preoccupied with Woolson affairs and "terribly scared and disconcerted — I mean alarmed — by the sight of so many private names and allusions in print." He wished Katharine had "sunk" a few names, "put initials — I mean in view of the danger of accidents, some catastrophe of publicity."

Henry James viewed personal publicity as a catastrophe. To thwart the curious future, he burned most of his letters and papers. His autobiography, a rich evocation of the growth of artistic consciousness, adroitly obscures many details of what actually happened. The novelist even seems to call attention to his own obscurantist tactics, as when mentioning, in "A Small Boy and Others," Edgar Allan Poe, "whom I cite not so much because he was personally present (the extremity of absence having just overtaken him) as by reason of that predominant lustre in him which our small opening minds themselves already recognised." He excoriated prying journalists in fiction. Matthias Pardon, in *The Bostonians,* is an "ingenuous son of his age" who views literary enterprise as "a state of intimacy with the newspapers, the cultivation of the great arts of publicity." To Pardon, "all distinction between the personal and the artist had ceased to exist; the writer was personal, the person food for newsboys, and everything and everyone were everyone's business." And in *The Aspern Papers,* the would-be biographer of poet Jeffrey Aspern, searching for precious documents in an illicit midnight trespass, is caught by the owner of the papers, Aspern's former mistress, whose "extraordinary eyes . . . glared at me . . . like the sudden drench, for a caught burglar, of a flood of gaslight . . . I shall never forget . . . the tone in which as I turned, looking at her, she hissed out passionately, furiously: 'Ah you publishing scoundrel!' "

In May of 1894, Henry described himself to William as "intensely nervous and almost sick with terror about possible publicity" resulting from the printing, even in private, of Alice's diary. He imagined Robertson and his wife showing their copy around Concord and discussing it "with the fearful American newspaper lying in wait for every whisper, every echo." And he was embarrassed at the thought of people reading what he had said about them in private to Alice, sometimes embroidering the truth for her entertainment: "When I see that I say that Augustine Birrell has a self-satisfied smirk after he speaks — and see that Katharine felt no prompting to exercise a discretion about the name I feel very unhappy, & wonder at the strangeness of destiny. I used to say everything to Alice (on system), that would *égayer* her bedside & many things in utter confidence. I didn't dream she wrote them down." But even that wouldn't have mattered, he said; it would, in fact, have interested him. "It is the printing of these precious *telles-quelles* that disturbs me when a very few merely superficial discriminations (leaving her *text* sacredly, really untouched) wd. have made all the difference."

Henry blamed Katharine, then, for what he did not like about the volume. He wrote her, he told William, "a letter which (discreet — on the subject of her editing — as it was) she may not have liked — perhaps." Apparently she did not, for she told Robertson's daughter almost forty years later that Henry had not wanted Alice's diary published, "although I know that she would have liked to have seen it printed," and that he had torn up his copy. Having registered his disapproval of Katharine's indiscretion, however, Henry went on to send William an appreciation of the diary itself that constitutes perhaps the best review their sister's book ever received:

As regards the life, the power, the temper, the humour and beauty and expressiveness of the Diary in itself — these things were partly 'discounted' to me in advance by so much of Alice's talk during her last years — my constant association with her — which led me often to reflect about her extraordinary way of taking life — and death — in very much the manner in which the book does. I find in its pages, for instance, many things I heard her say. Nonetheless I have been immensely impressed with the thing as a revelation of a moral and personal picture. It is heroic in its individuality, its independence — its face-to-face with the universe for and by herself — and the beauty and eloquence with which she often expresses this, let alone the rich irony and humour, constitute (I wholly agree with you) a new claim for the family renown. This last element — her style, her power to write — are indeed to me a delight — for I never had many letters from her. Also it brings back to me all sorts of things I am glad to keep — I mean things that happened, hours, occasions, conversations — brings them back with a strange, living rich-

ness. But it also puts before me what I was tremendously conscious of in her
lifetime — that . . . her tragic health was in a manner the only solution for her
of the practical problem of life.

He then turned to her anti-English sentiments and her political convictions:

The violence of her reactions against her British *ambiente,* against everything
English, engenders some of her most admirable and delightful passages — but
I feel in reading them, as I always felt in talking with her, that inevitably she
simplified too much, shut up in her sick room, exercised her wondrous vigour
of judgment on too small a scrap of what really surrounded her. It would have
been modified in many ways if she had *lived* with them (the English)
more — seen more of the men, etc. But doubtless it is fortunate for the fun
and humour of the thing that it wasn't modified — as surely the critical emotion (about them), the essence of much of their nature, was never more
beautifully expressed . . .
    I find an immense eloquence in her passionate "radicalism" — her most
distinguishing feature almost — which, in her, was absolutely direct and original (like everything that was in her); un-reflected, un-caught from entourage
or example. It would really have made her, had she lived in the world, a feminine "political force." But had she lived in the world and seen things nearer
she would have had disgusts and disillusions. However, what comes out in
the book — as it came out to me in fact — is that she was really an Irishwoman! — transplanted, transfigured — but none the less fundamentally national — in spite of her so much larger and finer than Irish intelligence. She
felt the Home Rule question absolutely as only an Irishwoman (not angli-
cized) could. It was a tremendous emotion with her — inexplicable in any
other way — and perfectly explicable by "atavism." What a pity she wasn't
born there — or had her health for it. She would have been (if, always, she
had not fallen a victim to disgust — a large "if") a national glory!

Her allusions to "H.," he told William, "fill me with tears and cover
me with blushes. What I should *like* to do *en temps et lieu* would be
(should no catastrophe meanwhile occur — or even if it should!) to *edit*
the volume with a few eliminations of text or dissimulations of names,
give it to the world and then carefully burn with fire our own four
copies." Meanwhile, he would bow his head and wait for the worst.
    The worst never came. Few people learned of the diary's existence.

Henry did destroy his copy — either in 1894 or in a later conflagration at the altar of privacy. William kept his, and his family eventually gave it to the Houghton Library at Harvard, along with a great many other family papers. Katharine, less than pleased with the diary's cool reception at the hands of Henry and William but perhaps sharing their concern about Bob's discretion, packed the whole thing — the original and the remaining two printed volumes — away in her house at Prides Crossing.

William and Robertson James died in 1910; Henry in 1916. Three decades after she first had the diary printed, Katharine gave one of the remaining copies to William's elder son, Harry, with the inscription, "Henry James from Katharine P. Loring. October 1923." That book is now in the Bancroft Library of the University of California, at Berkeley. The last copy, Katharine's own, was purchased from her family in 1964 by C. Waller Barrett and given by him to the University of Virginia's Alderman Library in 1967. Katharine died of pneumonia in August 1943, at the age of ninety-four. Louisa had died in 1924.

For almost forty years, Katharine kept the original handwritten volumes Alice had entrusted to her care. Then, in 1933, when Katharine was eighty-four and nearly totally blind, Robertson's daughter, Mary (Mrs. George Vaux of Bryn Mawr, Pennsylvania), wrote to her about publishing some of the diary in a book on the lesser-known members of the James family. Knowing that Alice had wanted the diary published, Katharine agreed. "Alice James, your Aunt," she wrote to Mrs. Vaux, "gave me her Diary before she died and I have given it to you, to use in anyway you see fit."

Mary Vaux hired a Philadelphia writer named Anna Robeson Burr, author of a biography of S. Weir Mitchell, to put together a volume they thought to call *The Gathering of the Family*. News of the project created a considerable flap among the James family descendants. Mrs. Vaux's brother, Ned (Edward Holton James), found the diary "one of the most important pieces of literature that has been produced by any James"; he thought it should be published intact rather than as part of something else, and had his doubts about Mrs. Burr. William's offspring did not like the idea of publication at all. Harry wrote to his sister, Peggy Porter, that he was trying to get Ned to help him "restrain" Mary Vaux: "I'm afraid she's all set to give what papers she has to a Philadelphian Mrs. Burr . . . with instructions to produce a book. The prospect does *not* fill me with joy."

Nevertheless, Mrs. Burr went ahead. She arranged with her publisher, Dodd, Mead and Company, to bring the book out in 1934 under the title *Alice James: Her Brothers — Her Journal.* The first third consists of an essay by Mrs. Burr called "Her Brothers." In it, Alice is once again relegated to the status of "mere" sister, only this time the limelight belongs not to her famous brothers but to Wilky and Rob, with whom she had a history of uneasy relations. Mrs. Burr's attempt to rescue these interesting and unhappy lives from obscurity is tantalizing but unsatisfactory; it oversimplifies the characters of all four brothers.

The remainder of the book, called "Her Journal," claims to present Alice's diary as written, with the single omission of the newspaper clippings Alice pasted into her pages. Mrs. Burr thought it best to leave out the clippings "not only because they concern events long past, relating often to minor Parliamentary debates and English local politics, but also because they dilute the rich flow of her own observation and feeling." On the contrary, the clippings convey important information about "events long past," and add dimension to the flow of Alice's observations, particularly since so many of her comments were about public or political issues. The omission is therefore a serious one. But more serious still is the "minor" editing Mrs. Burr did not even acknowledge: she freely changed original punctuation, sentence structure, and words, omitted whole days and passages — especially passages in French and comments on the missing newspaper clippings — and "sunk" proper names, so that, for example, Mrs. Sidgwick became "Mrs. S.," just as Henry would have had Katharine do in 1894, though by 1934 it was hardly necessary.

William's children, predictably, did not like the book. When the *Times Literary Supplement* printed a review that praised the diary ("The imprisoned light, thus set free, streams out with a singular brilliance") and criticized Mrs. Burr's editing ("It is irresistible to wish to hear the language that Alice would have launched upon her head. To speak plainly, Miss Burr would have been scorched"), Harry wrote to his sister that he "chuckled over it with malicious glee."

But for all Mrs. Burr's editorial errors, the diary was acclaimed by critics in England and the United States. "Here is a mind so direct and unshrinking, a humor so penetrating, a gift of words so accurate and uncompromising that the journal has the tonic effect of sunlight itself," wrote Harriet Fox Whicher in the New York *Herald Tribune.* "Alice

James's diary . . . is vigorous, frank and brilliant," said the daily *New York Times,* and C. Hartley Grattan in the Sunday *Times* called it "a supremely important addition to the literature about the James family . . . in character and intellect she was the equal of her distinguished brothers and a daughter, beyond all question, of her pungent and iconoclastic father." *The New Republic* applauded: "In some of her insights, some of her assessments of nineteenth-century humbug, Alice James went beyond either of her eminent brothers, and her judgments on the social history of her day have now the air of something like divinations." And Virginia Woolf's diary includes "Alice James" in a list of "Books read or in reading" on October 2, 1934.

Two public tributes to Alice as a writer and thinker in her own right appeared in the 1940s. Diana Trilling wrote a thoughtful appreciation in *The Nation* in 1943, based on the journal and using the James family as background to illuminate Alice's conflicts and achievement: "There is a common family store of perception, imagination, and, above all, gifts of style. Alice, too, can write that wonderful educated James prose with its incandescent accuracy and then its sudden flights of homeliness." She compared Alice with Emily Dickinson: "Both women . . . protested the life of public recognition too violently, just as each of them inevitably demanded, in what she sent into the world, too much attention for *herself;* but it is a common failing among women of talent. The essential difference between them is that in Emily Dickinson the writer was transcendent over the woman, and her poetry was the distillation of her first and best private emotions, whereas Alice James spent her first and best energies in ill health."

F. O. Matthiessen, who published his group biography, *The James Family,* in 1947, also brings in Emily Dickinson: "The quality that distinguishes Alice James's journal — . . . comparable to Emily Dickinson's quality — is her wealth of inner resources." *The James Family* concentrates on William, Henry, and Alice, and Matthiessen quotes at considerable length from Alice's journal and letters, treating her primarily as an intellectual and writer, and only secondarily as an invalid and sister: "Alice James, contemplating the world from her sanatorium, had come to a more incisive understanding of some of the forces in modern society than either of her brothers. She might take her lead from something one of them had said, but she then pursued her own reflections further. She often discussed English society with HJ. They agreed on many of the symptoms, but she pushed on to a diagnosis quite beyond his scope in its thoroughness."

Not until 1964 was the complete diary finally published, edited and with an introduction by Leon Edel. Edel restored the newspaper clippings from the original and annotated the text, identifying many of the people and events not immediately recognizable after seventy-five years. He made some stylistic corrections and changes in punctuation, and the publisher made a number of typographical errors. These details aside, the 1964 edition is a faithful reproduction of the original.

This version of the diary, too, met with critical acclaim. Gay Wilson Allen, in *The Saturday Review,* called it "one of the neglected masterpieces of American literature." And Marius Bewley took the publication of the diary as occasion to write an essay, entitled "Death and the James Family," in *The New York Review of Books.* He disliked Alice's tone and "aggressive shrillness" but admired her moral courage and the mind that "occasionally flashes through ... with a light so serene and fine that it sustains one across prickly pages until the signal lights again." In her dying, he observed, "the vanity of invalidism has been replaced by a courage and serenity that is [sic] wholly authentic and perfectly faultless." Like the hero of Tolstoy's *The Death of Ivan Ilyich,* she experienced a "stripping off from the mind and heart of the irrelevancies and distorted images of worldly life, of neurotic fears, and false values; and this brings a sense of release and purification." He described Alice's transfiguring acceptance of death as "peculiarly contemporary" and "a remarkable anticipation" of Heidegger. Bewley concluded by noting that Henry James, suffering his first stroke in December 1915 (he died two months later), heard a voice in his room say, "So here it is at last, the distinguished thing!" "The final effect of the diary on one's imagination," wrote Bewley, "is to make one believe it must have been the ghost of Alice, come back to reassure and congratulate her favorite brother on the threshold of his absolute moment."

The original handwritten volumes of the diary have been passed down through Robertson's descendants and now belong to his great-granddaughter, Alice James Vaux.

Illustrations

Following page 80

Alice James, 1870 (By permission of the Houghton Library, Harvard University)

Catharine Barber James (By permission of the Houghton Library, Harvard University)

William James of Albany (By permission of the Houghton Library, Harvard University)

Mary Walsh James (Courtesy of Henry James Vaux)

Henry James, Sr. (By permission of the Houghton Library, Harvard University)

Catharine Walsh (Courtesy of Henry James Vaux)

Alice James in Paris, about 1857 (By permission of the Houghton Library, Harvard University)

Alice at Newport, 1862 (By permission of the Houghton Library, Harvard University)

William James, about 1867 (By permission of the Houghton Library, Harvard University)

Henry James, Jr., about 1863 (Courtesy of Henry James Vaux)

Garth Wilkinson James, about 1861 or 1862 (Courtesy of Henry James Vaux)

Robertson James, Newport, 1862 (Courtesy of Henry James Vaux)

Alice James sketched by Henry, Jr., Chester, England, 1872 (By permission of the Houghton Library, Harvard University)

Sketches by William James (By permission of the Houghton Library, Harvard University)

Self-portrait by William James (By permission of the Houghton Library, Harvard University)

Henry James, Jr., 1859 or 1860 (Courtesy of Henry James Vaux)

Sara Sedgwick (Mrs. William Erasmus Darwin) (Courtesy of the Cambridge Historical Society)

Susan Sedgwick (Mrs. Charles Eliot Norton) (Courtesy of the Cambridge Historical Society)

Following page 272

Alice, about 1873 (By permission of the Houghton Library, Harvard University)

Henry James, Sr., about 1880 (Courtesy of Henry James Vaux)

Robertson James, about 1880 (Courtesy of Henry James Vaux)

Garth Wilkinson James in Milwaukee (Courtesy of Henry James Vaux)

Alice Howe Gibbens James with her son Henry, 1879 or 1880 (By permission of the Houghton Library, Harvard University)

The Bee or Banks Brigade, 1863 (Courtesy of the Cambridge Historical Society)

Adams House, the Adams Nervine Asylum, built about 1880 (Courtesy of the Boston *Globe*; photograph by Paul Connell)

Katharine Peabody Loring and friend (Courtesy of Mary Loring Clapp)

Study in Greens, 1917, by John Singer Sargent (Courtesy of Mary Loring Clapp)

Katharine Peabody Loring (Courtesy of Henry James Vaux)

The Manchester house and stables, 1884 (Courtesy of the Essex Institute, Salem, Massachusetts, and Dr. W. D. Sohier, Jr.)

Henry James at Aston Clinton, the de Rothschild country house in Buckinghamshire, 1888 (Collection of the author)

William James and his daughter, Margaret Mary, 1892 (By permission of the Houghton Library, Harvard University)

Henry and William James, about 1902 (By permission of the Houghton Library, Harvard University)

Alice James and Katharine Loring at Royal Leamington Spa, 1889–1890 (By permission of the Houghton Library, Harvard University)

Argyll Road, Kensington (Courtesy Kensington and Chelsea Borough Libraries, London)

Alice James in London, 1891 (Courtesy of Henry James Vaux)

Notes

All letters not otherwise identified are to be found in the Houghton Library, Harvard University. All references to the novels of Henry James, except as noted, are to the New York Edition. A bracketed date for a letter indicates that the date was not written on the letter. The following abbreviations are used throughout the notes:

AAR —Anne Ashburner Richards
AJ —Alice James
AHJ —Alice Howe Gibbens James (William's wife)
AK —Aunt Kate (Catharine Walsh)
CFW —Constance Fenimore Woolson
EHJ —Edward Holton James (Robertson's son)
ET —Edmund Tweedy
ETE —Ellen Tucker Emerson
FAK —Frances Anne Kemble
FB —Francis Boott
FRM —Frances Rollins Morse
GWJ —Garth Wilkinson James (brother)
HJ —Henry James (brother)
HJ Sr.—Henry James, Sr. (father)
HJ³ —Henry James (son of William and nephew of Alice)
KJP —Katharine Barber James Prince (cousin)
KPL —Katharine Peabody Loring
LB —Elizabeth Boott
MHJ —Mary Holton James (Robertson's wife)
MJ —Mary Walsh James (mother)
MJV —Mary James Vaux (Robertson's daughter)
MMJP—Margaret Mary James Porter (William's daughter)
RJ —Robertson James (brother)
RWE —Ralph Waldo Emerson
SSD —Sara Sedgwick Darwin
WDH—William Dean Howells

WJ —William James (brother)
Mrs. WJ of A.,—Mrs. William James of Albany (mother of HJ Sr.)

PRIVATE COLLECTIONS

Clapp—Private papers in the possession of Mary Loring Clapp.
Gregg—Papers from the Ralph Waldo Emerson Memorial Association, in the possession of Edith Gregg.
Vaux—Private papers in the possession of Professor Henry James Vaux (Robertson's grandson).

SELECTED BIBLIOGRAPHY

Allen, Gay Wilson. *William James.* New York: Viking Press, 1967.
Edel, Leon. *Henry James.* 5 vols. Philadelphia: J. B. Lippincott Company, 1953–1972.
James, Alice. *The Diary of Alice James.* Edited with an introduction by Leon Edel. New York: Dodd, Mead, and Company, 1964.
James, Henry. *The American Scene.* New York: Horizon Press, 1967.
———. *The Bostonians.* New York: Random House, Modern Library, 1956.
———. *Henry James Letters.* Edited by Leon Edel. 2 vols. Cambridge: Harvard University Press, 1974, 1975. Published in England by Macmillan London, Ltd.
———. *The Notebooks of Henry James.* Edited by F. O Matthiessen and Kenneth B. Murdock, New York: Oxford University Press, 1947.
———. "Notes of a Son and Brother," in *Henry James Autobiography.* Edited with an introduction by F. W. Dupee, New York: Criterion Books, 1956.
———. "A Small Boy and Others," in *Henry James Autobiography.* Edited with an introduction by F. W. Dupee, New York: Criterion Books, 1956.
James, Henry, Sr. *The Literary Remains of the Late Henry James.* Edited with an introduction by William James. Boston: James R. Osgood & Company, 1884.
James, William. *The Letters of William James.* Edited by Henry James [his son]. 2 vols. Boston: The Atlantic Monthly Press, 1920.
———. *The Principles of Psychology.* 2 vols. New York: Henry Holt and Company, 1907.
Matthiessen, F. O. *The James Family.* New York: Alfred A. Knopf, 1961.
Perry, Ralph Barton. *The Thought and Character of William James.* 2 vols. Boston: Little, Brown and Company, 1936.

Introduction

page
ix "When I am gone": AJ to WJ, July 31, 1891.
x "Try not to be ill": HJ to Grace Norton, July 28 [1883]; Henry James, *Letters,* vol. 2, p. 425, n.
x "a native of the James family": WJ to AJ, July 29, 1889.
xi "just to *be* something": Henry James, "Notes of a Son and Brother," p. 268.
xi "I am not sure": Ibid., p. 301.
xi "convert": Henry James, "A Small Boy," pp. 123–24.

page
xii "Greatest breach in nature": William James, *Principles,* vol. 1, p. 237.
xii "foundling": RJ, fragment of autobiography; Vaux.
xiii "In our family group": quoted in Leon Edel, *Henry James,* vol. 2, p. 49.
xiv Virginia Woolf, *A Room of One's Own* (New York: Harcourt, Brace, 1929), pp. 80–89.

Chapter One

3 "I asked how"; *Diary of Alice James,* p. 82.
5 "Not to me a 'liberal education' ": HJ Sr. to HJ, May 9 [1882?].
   "My heart melts": MJ to HJ Sr. [n.d.].
   "It is addressed": MJ to Mrs. WJ of A., January 14 [1854?].
6 "an ardent angler and gunner": Henry James, Sr., *Literary Remains,* p. 173.
   "I lived in every fibre": Ibid., p. 183.
   "My headlong eagerness": Ibid., pp. 160–61.
   "I doubt": Ibid., 185–86.
7 "for he was always": Ibid., pp. 146–47.
   "easy parent": Ibid., p. 188.
8 "I cannot imagine": Ibid., p. 182.
   "The parent": Ibid., pp. 159–60.
   "weakly, nay painfully": Ibid., p. 170.
   "Dear brother": Family Papers and Sermons of William James (1797–1868); Amherst College Library.
9 "showed itself so assiduous": Henry James, Sr., *Literary Remains,* p. 147.
10 "maternity itself ": Ibid., pp. 147–48.
   "soft flexibility": Ibid., p. 151.
   "She made her own": Ibid., p. 188.
11 "fond votary": Henry James, "A Small Boy," pp. 5–6.
   "the very air": Ibid., pp. 4–5.
   "gently-groaning": Ibid., p. 102.
   "hopelessly addicted": HJ Sr. to RJ [n.d.]; Vaux.
   "scarcely ever"; Ibid.
12 Last Will and Testament of William James of Albany; New-York Historical Society.
   "The rupture": Henry James, "A Small Boy," p. 109.
13 "envy, hatred, contempt": HJ Sr. to RJ, December 10 [1874]; Vaux.
   "run to the bosom": Ibid.
   "man without a handle": HJ Sr. to RWE, October 3, 1843; Perry, *William James,* vol. 1, p. 51.
   "You don't look upon Calvinism": HJ Sr. to RWE, May 11, 1843; Matthiessen, *James Family,* p. 43.
   "humanity seem more erect": H. D. Thoreau to RWE, June 8, 1843; Perry, *William James,* vol. 1, p. 48.
   "You say that you and Jesus are one": Matthiessen, *James Family,* p. 44.
   "still the same": HJ Sr. to RWE [1856].
   "Thomas Carlyle is incontestably dead": *Atlantic Monthly,* May 1881, p. 593.

page
14 "Suddenly in a lightning-flash": Henry James, Sr., *Literary Remains*, pp. 59–60.

"nothing in common except": J. J. Garth Wilkinson to HJ Sr., May 20, 1879; Perry, *William James*, vol. 1, pp. 26–27.

stood orthodox Calvinism on its head: Perry, *William James*, vol. 1, pp. 12–13.

15 Footnote: "native vigor": C. Hartley Grattan, *The Three Jameses* (London: Longmans, Green & Company, 1932), p. 42.

16 "literally the seminary": Henry James, Sr., *Literary Remains*, p. 175.

"demoralization": Ibid., pp. 169–70.

Footnote: "What Caskey": *New York Review of Books*, November 9, 1978, p. 39.

17 "With all the richness": William James, introduction to Henry James, Sr., *Literary Remains*, p. 9.

"*We had no note*": Henry James, "Notes of a Son and Brother," p. 278.

18 "I desire my child": Henry James, Sr., *The Nature of Evil* (New York: D. Appleton and Company, 1855), p. 99.

right to be unhappy: F. W. Dupee, *Henry James* (New York: William Sloane Associates, 1951), p. 92.

"Ah! those strange people": *Diary of Alice James*, p. 49.

"wished sometimes": RWE Notebooks; Perry, *William James*, vol. 1, p. 3.

"My paternal feeling": HJ Sr. to HJ, December 21 [1873?].

19 "How grateful": *Diary of Alice James*, p. 160.

Footnote: "My interest in life": RJ to WJ [n.d.].

20 "In a rash moment": *Diary of Alice James*, p. 84.

"The impish passion": Ibid., p. 120.

"A week before Father died": Ibid., p. 217.

Chapter Two

22 "unfortunate *mere* junior": HJ to WJ Jr., May 19, 1913.

23 "how feeble and diluted": *Diary of Alice James*, p. 32.

"This is No. 5": Ibid., p. 36.

24 "husband all his strength": MJ to RJ, September 27 [1874]; Vaux.

"If he has such broad": MJ to RJ, December 16 [1873]; Vaux.

"the less fine specimens": MJ to RJ, January 14, 1874; Vaux.

"come out for himself": MJ to Mrs. J. J. Garth Wilkinson, November 29, 1846.

"mandatory ways": RJ to AHJ, February 24, 1898.

"as little appreciated": RJ, fragment of autobiography; Vaux.

"the trouble": MJ to HJ, March 17 [1874].

Footnote: "full of indulgence": RJ to AHJ, February 24, 1898.

25 "morbidly hopeless": MJ to HJ, July 6 [1874].

"angelic patience": MJ to WJ, January 23 [1874].

"Mother is recovering": WJ to AJ, November 14, 1866.

"throw around you": MJ to HJ, May 18 [1874].

"If you will provide": HJ to MJ, June 3, 1874.

page

"Don't think I am meddling": MJ to RJ, September 27 [1874]; Vaux.
26   "heartily ashamed": MJ to RJ, November 1 [n.d.]; Vaux.
"Mother's words": *Diary of Alice James,* p. 79.
"Ever since the night": Ibid., p. 221.
"She was patience": Henry James, *Notebooks,* pp. 40–41.
27   fictional mothers: Edel, *Henry James,* vol. 3, p. 38.
28   "motor": William James, *Letters,* vol. 2, p. 163.
Footnote: Ellen Moers, *Literary Women* (New York: Doubleday, 1976), pp. 160–61.
29   "*I* play with boys": Henry James, "A Small Boy," p. 147.
"occupying a place": Ibid., p. 7.
"Humility": Ibid., p. 119.
"I never dreamed": Henry James, "A Small Boy," p. 101.
Footnote: Quoted in Leon Edel, *Henry James,* vol. 5, p. 298.
30   Dentist: Ibid., pp. 38–39.
Footnote: "I am not sure": Ibid., p. 94.
31   "vast caravansery": Ibid., pp. 18–19.
"upon our four stout boys": HJ Sr. to RWE, August 31, 1849.
32   "nothing but private sympathy": HJ Sr. to ET, February 24, 1852.
"the sort of sub-antagonism": WJ to RJ, May 23, 1870; Vaux.
33   Kate and "the Captain": HJ Sr. to ET, September 19 [1852].
"Capt. Marshall's assiduities": HJ Sr. to ET [fragment, probably 1853].
34   Wedding: New York *Evening Post,* February 19, 1853.
"frightful mistake": HJ Sr. to RWE, June 18, 1855.
Obituary: New York *Herald,* September 24, 1865.
36   "when in the golden": AJ to AHJ, May 5, 1889.

Chapter Three

37   "remarkably erect": Henry James, "A Small Boy," p. 173.
38   "without feeling": HJ Sr. to Mrs. WJ of A., September 25, 1855.
"We had fared": Henry James, "A Small Boy," p. 166.
"There's nothing like it": Ibid., p. 168.
39   "used to spoil": *Diary of Alice James,* p. 72.
"requirements of our small": Henry James, "A Small Boy," p. 173.
Millinery and theater: *Diary of Alice James,* p. 46.
40   "brother Bull": HJ Sr. to ET, May 23, 1856.
"l'ingénieux petit Robertson": Henry James, "A Small Boy," p. 185.
41   Rue d'Angoulême-St. Honoré: Ibid., pp. 189–190.
MJ on Paris: Letter to Mrs. WJ of A., August 25 [1856?].
"that wittiest": *Diary of Alice James,* p. 120.
42   "only ex-Fourierists": Henry James, "A Small Boy," p. 206.
43   "hotel children": Ibid., p. 19.
"What enrichment": AJ to WJ, November 4, 1888.
"girls": Henry James, "A Small Boy," p. 14.
"walking sedately": Ibid., pp. 376–77.

page
43 Footnote: *Letters of Mrs. Henry Adams,* edited by Ward Thoron (Boston: Little, Brown, 1936), pp. xi–xii; George Eliot, *The Mill on the Floss* (London: Complete Works, St. James Edition, 1907, vol 2), p. 222.

44 Lilla Cabot Perry: Van Wyck Brooks, *From the Shadow of the Mountain* (New York: E. P. Dutton, 1961), p. 45.

"There could not be": *Life and Letters of E. L. Godkin,* edited by Rollo Ogden (London: Macmillan, 1907), vol. 2, p. 218.

45 *Putnam's Monthly,* vol. 1, March 1853, pp. 279–88.

47 "But they are too dear": HJ Sr. to AJ [n.d.].

"heiress": HJ Sr. to AJ [n.d.].

"if I had had": *Diary of Alice James,* p. 66.

"delighting ever in the truth": Henry James, "A Small Boy," p. 126.

"literal played": Ibid., pp. 123–24.

48 "never had any": WJ diary, manuscript; Houghton Library, Harvard.

"first time": *Diary of Alice James,* pp. 128–29.

"adventuress": Henry James, "A Small Boy," p. 174.

49 "eldest superiority": HJ to RJ, October 1, 1909; Vaux.

"where Wilkie and I went": RJ to AHJ, February 24, 1898.

"Mother loves you more": HJ Sr. to HJ, August 8, 1873.

"I can't help feeling": HJ Sr. to HJ, May 8, 1882.

50 "spiritual transvestitism": Edel, *Henry James,* vol. 4, p. 265.

"In James's world": Ibid., p. 207.

"seemed to look at women": Edel, *Henry James,* vol. 2, p. 359.

"Millions of presumptuous girls": Preface to *The Portrait of a Lady,* vol. 1, p. xiii.

Footnote: Edel, Henry James, vol. 4, p. 259.

51 "I am not rebellious": *Diary of Alice James,* p. 119.

52 "Crinoline": Henry James, "A Small Boy," p. 52.

"Billy it seems": *Diary of Alice James,* p. 176.

"You lovely babe": WJ to AJ, September 14, 1861.

"Charmante Jeune Fille": WJ to AJ, March 6, 1862.

"Perfidious child!": WJ to AJ, June 15, 1862.

"Chérie Charmante": WJ to AJ, September 13, 1863.

"Alice the widow": WJ to parents, August 12, 1860.

"the sweet": Ibid.

"thousand thanks": WJ to parents [August 19, 1860?].

53 "sonnate": WJ to HJ Sr. [December 1859].

"excited a good deal": GWJ to HJ Sr. [December 1859].

54 "Love": William James, *Principles,* vol. 2, pp. 437–39.

55 "home pulling": HJ Sr. to Mrs. WJ of A., December 24 [1857].

"Young America": HJ Sr. to Mrs. C. P. Cranch, October 18, 1858.

56 "with Mother beside him": *Diary of Alice James,* p. 58.

"My dear Father": AJ to HJ Sr., March 11 [1860].

"Willy is very devoted": HJ Sr. to Mrs. WJ of A., October 15, 1857.

57 "Our Alice is still under discipline": Quoted in Leon Edel's Introduction to *Diary of Alice James,* p. 4.

"Father announces": AJ to WJ, March 16, 1890.

page
58   "Willy . . . felt": HJ Sr. to ET, July 24, 1860.
59   "Providential indication": Ibid.
     "they are getting": HJ Sr. to ET, July 18 [1860].
     "One chief disappointment": HJ Sr. to ET, July 24, 1860.

Chapter Four

60   "artificial and sophisticated": *Diary of Alice James,* p. 93.
     "witless dream": *The American Scene,* pp. 222–24.
61   "parentally bereft": Henry James, "A Small Boy," p. 10.
     "a thousand": *The American Scene,* p. 212.
     "Miss Hunter": Mary Powel, "Bowery Street," vol. 1B; Newport Historical Society.
62   "Tell me": AJ to WJ, December 11, 1889.
     Obituary: George H. Richardson Scrapbook; Newport Historical Society.
     Footnote: "My dear Mamma and papa"; Clapp.
63   "namby pamby tales": *Diary of Alice James,* p. 194.
     Godey's in 1860: Isabelle Webb Entrikin, *Sarah Josepha Hale and Godey's Lady's Book* (Philadelphia: [Lancaster, Printed by Lancaster Press, Inc.] 1946), p. 121.
     "decorous deviousness": Ann Douglas, *The Feminization of American Culture* (New York: Knopf, 1977), p. 71.
64   "I buried": Quoted in Henry James, "Notes of a Son and Brother," pp. 368–69.
     "And what sort of girl?": *Diary of Alice James,* p. 193.
     Footnote: "Dear old": Ibid., p. 84.
65   "I can hear": Ibid., p. 192.
     "the adipose": Edward W. Emerson, *The Early Years of the Saturday Club, 1855–1870* (Boston: Houghton Mifflin, 1918), p. 328.
66   Miss Peabody: Mark A. De Wolfe Howe, *The Later Years of the Saturday Club, 1870–1920* (Boston: Houghton Mifflin, 1927), pp. 156–57.
67   "Tell Alice": WJ to parents, December 15 [1861?].
     "gave the palpitating": HJ Sr. to RWE, December 22 [1861].
     Footnote 1: Louise Hall Tharp, *Adventurous Alliance* (Boston: Little, Brown, 1959), pp. 138–56.
     Footnote 2: HJ to AJ, April 25 [1873]; Henry James, *Letters,* vol. 1, p. 372.
68   "Charmante": WJ to AJ, March 6, 1862.
     Footnote: From ETE's manuscript biography of Lidian Emerson; Houghton Library, Harvard.
69   "full of intelligence": KJP to Julius Seelye, August 3, 1861; Amherst College Library.
     "its opera glass": Henry James, "Notes of a Son and Brother," p. 418.
70   "The Social Significance of Our Institutions" (Boston: Ticknor & Fields, 1861).
     "affectionate old papas": HJ Sr., fragment to unknown correspondent; Vaux.
71   "the best": WJ to KJP, September 12, 1863; William James, *Letters,* vol. 1, p. 44.
     "lightest of featherweights": WJ to HJ Sr., June 3, 1865.
72   "obscure hurt": Henry James, "Notes of a Son and Brother," pp. 114–15.

page
72 Back injury: Edel, *Henry James,* vol. 1, p. 164.
73 "romantic chances": Henry James, "Notes of a Son and Brother," p. 456.
    "seeing, sharing": Ibid., p. 461.
    "The water was warm": ETE to Haven Emerson, July 20, 1862.
74 "Everywhere soldiers": ETE to Lidian Emerson, July 5, 1862; Gregg.
75 "War feels to me": Richard B. Sewall, *The Life of Emily Dickinson* (New York: Farrar, Straus & Giroux, 1974), vol. 2, p. 536.
    "Alice is a dear": ETE to "Alice," an unidentified friend, August 26, 1862.
    liberal Northerners: George M. Fredrickson, *The Inner Civil War* (New York: Harper & Row, 1965), p. 152.
    "laughing, welcoming": Henry James, "Notes of a Son and Brother," p. 456.
    "cost me a heart-break": HJ Sr. to Elizabeth Peabody, July 22, 1863; Massachusetts Historical Society.
76 "knowing the fury": HJ Sr. to Elizabeth Peabody, July 30, 1863, Massachusetts Historical Society.
    "manly and exalted": HJ Sr. to Samuel G. Ward, August 1 [1863].
    "a temptation": HJ Sr. to RJ, August 29, 1864; Vaux.
77 "I hope you" HJ Sr. to RJ, August 31 [1864?].
    "My darling Bobbins": HJ Sr. to RJ, September 13 [1864]; Vaux.
78 "Have you got": WJ to AJ, June 15, 1862.
    "that idle and useless": WJ to MJ [September 1863?].
    "Dearest child": WJ to AJ, October 19, 1862.
79 Society work: Katherine Prescott Wormeley, "Reminiscences of Newport in the Fifties," *Newport History,* vol. 41, part 1, no. 129 (Winter 1968), pp. 8–9.
    "passionate fire": Mary Towle Palmer, *The Story of the Bee* (Cambridge: Riverside Press, 1924), pp. 3–7.
    Footnote: Ednah D. Cheney, *Louisa May Alcott, Her Life, Letters and Journals* (Boston: Little, Brown, 1911), p. 140–41.
80 "in America": *Diary of Alice James,* p. 97.
    "I am constrained": Ibid.
81 "ancient superstition": Ibid., p. 95.
    "low, grey Newport sky": Ibid.
82 "One feels": Edel, *Henry James,* vol. 2, p. 48.
    "the only thing": *Diary of Alice James,* p. 96.

Chapter Five

85 "chignons": HJ Sr. to AJ, July 1–2 [1872?].
86 "simmering": William Dean Howells, *Literary Friends and Acquaintances* (New York: Harper & Brothers, 1901), p. 267.
    "be carried home": *The American,* vol. 1, p. 41.
    "stupidity": MJ to HJ, January 21 [1873].
87 United States Census Bureau Reports for 1850, 1870, 1880 (Government Printing Office, Washington, D.C.).
    Unmarried women: Mary S. Hartman and Lois Banner, *Clio's Consciousness Raised* (New York: Harper & Row, Colophon, 1974), p. 120.

page
88 "I wish": AJ to AAR, April 12, 1876; National Library of Scotland.
    "glorious phalanx": Quoted in Van Wyck Brooks, *New England Indian Summer:
    1865–1915* (New York: E. P. Dutton, 1965), p. 102.
    Footnote: Lucy Washburn to FRM, December 26, 1876; Schlesinger Library,
    Radcliffe College.
89 Women's clubs: Eleanor Flexner, *Century of Struggle* (New York: Atheneum,
    1974), p. 180.
    "This generation": Charles Eliot Norton to Thomas Carlyle, in *Letters of Charles
    Eliot Norton* (Boston: Houghton Mifflin, 1913), vol. 2, p. 18.
90 "flatulent writing": Quoted in Van Wyck Brooks, *New England Indian Summer*,
    p. 104.
    "seemed to be": Ibid., p. 240.
91 "no one should": Helen Howe, *The Gentle Americans* (New York: Harper &
    Row, 1965), p. 173.
    "cocked": AJ to FRM, April 3, 1866.
    Footnote: Frances Rollins Morse, ed., *Henry and Mary Lee Letters and Journals:
    1802–1860* (Privately printed, Boston: Thomas Todd Co., 1926), p. 48.
92 "My dear Fanny": AJ to FRM [n.d.]
    "I intend": AJ to FRM, May 7 [1866].
    "You are the best": AJ to FRM, April 3, 1866.
93 "I have discovered": AJ to FRM, February 4, 1866.
94 "Marriage": HJ Sr. to RWE, March 9 [1865].
    "I suppose": AJ to FRM, July 22 [1866?].
95 "It gives": AJ to FRM [October 21, 1866].
    "I have been": AJ to FRM, February 4, 1866.
    "Now my dear": AJ to FRM, June 17 [1866].

Chapter Six

97   "good square house": Mrs. William G. Farlow, "Quincy Street in the Fifties,"
     Cambridge Historical Society Proceedings, vol. XVIII, 1925–26.
     "inner sepulchre": HJ to WJ, November 22 [1867].
98   "love to dear old": WJ to parents [September 18, 1865].
     "She is not able": HJ Sr. to AAR [n.d.]; National Library of Scotland.
     "Is it not": AJ to FRM, October 21 [1866].
     "with all those defunct": WJ to GWJ, March 13, 1867.
99   "I am glad": WJ to AJ, December 12, 1866.
     "Alas": WJ to AJ, Christmas, 1866.
     "I am charmed": HJ to AJ, January 4, 1867.
     " 'T is by": HJ to AJ, February 3, 1867.
     "looking as fat": MJ to AJ, December 1866.
     "quite disenchanted": MJ to AJ [January 1867?].
100 "Almost any": HJ Sr. to AJ [November 17], 1866.
     "My darling": HJ Sr. to AJ, December 21 [1866].
     Footnote: William Empson, *The Structure of Complex Words* (Ann Arbor: Uni-
     versity of Michigan Press, 1967), pp. 76–77.
101 "as if to be": Preface to *The Wings of the Dove*, p. vii.

page
101   Minny Temple: Henry James, "Notes of a Son and Brother," pp. 514-19.
        Footnote: Susan Sontag, *Illness as Metaphor* (New York: Farrar, Straus &
        Giroux, 1978), pp. 20-34.
103   George M. Beard, "Neurasthenia, or Nervous Exhaustion," *Boston Medical and
        Surgical Journal,* vol. III, no. 13 (April 29, 1869), pp. 217-19; Charles E. Ro-
        senberg, "The Place of George M. Beard in Nineteenth-Century Psychiatry,"
        Bulletin of the History of Medicine, 1962, p. 36.
        Footnote 1: Nathan G. Hale, Jr., *Freud and the Americans* (New York: Oxford
        University Press, 1971), p. 49.
        Footnote 2: Barbara Sicherman, "The Uses of Diagnosis: Doctors, Patients, and
        Neurasthenia," *Journal of the History of Medicine and Allied Sciences,* vol.
        XXXII, no. 1 (January 1977), pp. 39-40.
104   S. Weir Mitchell, "Rest in Nervous Disease: Its Use and Abuse," in E. C. Se-
        quin, ed., *A Series of American Clinical Lectures,* 1 (New York, 1875), quoted
        in Sicherman, "The Uses of Diagnosis," p. 41; Sigmund Freud and Josef
        Breuer, *Studies on Hysteria* (London: Penguin Freud Library, vol. 3, 1974),
        p. 202.
105   Footnote: S. Weir Mitchell, *Fat and Blood* (Philadelphia: J. B. Lippincott,
        1878), pp. 42-45; Ernest P. Earnest, *S. Weir Mitchell* (Philadelphia: University
        of Pennsylvania Press, 1950), pp. 85.
106   Hale, *Freud and the Americans,* p. 59.
        "a very original": WJ to AJ [December 12, 1866?].
        Charles Fayette Taylor, *Theory and Practice of the Movement Cure* (Philadelphia:
        Lindsay & Blakiston, 1861), pp. 255-91.
107   Charles Fayette Taylor, "Emotional Prodigality," read before the New York
        Odontological Society, March 18, 1879; reprinted in *The Dental Cosmos,* July
        1879, pp. 4-11.
109   "such fine accounts": MJ to AJ [January 1867?].
        "They gave": WJ to AJ, February 18 [1867?].
110   "on the continual verge": WJ to Thomas Ward, January 1868.
        "I wish you": WJ to AJ [February 18, 1867?].
        "There is no": MJ to AJ [April ?, 1867].
        "most remarkable": WJ to GWJ, March 13, 1867.
111   "Alice seems very bright": MJ to WJ, May 27 [1867].
        "He eats capitally": HJ Sr. to AJ, December 21 [1867].
        "to get a *corset*": HJ to WJ, May 21 [1867].
        "I am very doubtful": MJ to WJ, November 21 [1867].
        "I have invented": HJ to HJ Sr. [October 26, 1869].
112   "I somehow feel": WJ to AJ, May 14, 1868.
        "had the inclination": WJ to parents, October 5, 1868.
        "If I only had": GWJ to parents, December 31, 1868; Vaux.
113   "the admirable mother": AJ to WJ, June 8, 1867.
        "Alice I am sorry": MJ to WJ, June 10 [1867].
        "The other evening": AJ to WJ, August 6 [1867].
        Footnote: AJ to WJ, October 13, 1867.
114   The scene: AJ to WJ, October 13, 1867.
        "Have you the faintest": Ibid.
115   "My darling Willy": AJ to WJ, August 6 [1867].

Chapter Seven

page
118   "I have passed": *Diary of Alice James,* pp. 149–50.
119   "How far": William James, "The Hidden Self," *Scribner's* magazine, Jan-
       uary–June 1890, p. 371.
120   Footnote: Ernest Jones, *The Life and Work of Sigmund Freud,* abridged edition
       (New York: Basic Books, 1961), pp. 267–68.
122   *Daisy Miller,* p. 22.
       "The fortitude": RJ to AJ, February 28, 1868.
       "the sweetest": MJ to RJ, May 3, 1868; Vaux.
       "Alice says": MJ to GWJ, May 1 [1868]; Vaux.
       "We are as well": MJ to GWJ, May 8 [1868?]; Vaux.
       "All our time": MJ to GWJ, April 5 [1868]; Vaux.
123   "poor dear Alice": HJ Sr. to WJ, April 1 [1868].
       "I am excessively": WJ to AJ, March 16, 1868.
       Footnote: Freud and Breuer, *Studies on Hysteria,* p. 202.
124   "Let Alice": WJ to parents, January 22, 1868.
       "What pleases": WJ to AJ, June 23, 1868.
       "keep a stiff": WJ to AJ, June 4, 1868.
125   "a spark": *Diary of Alice James,* pp. 95–96.
       "dorsal infirmity": WJ to RJ, November 14, 1869; Vaux.
       Footnote: Henry James, "Notes of a Son and Brother," p. 541.
126   "Your case": WJ to RJ, June 22, 1872; Vaux.
       " 'I burn' ": HJ Sr. to RJ, December 10 [1874]; Vaux.
127   "Tonight": WJ diary, May 22, 1868.
       William James, *Varieties of Religious Experience* (New York: Longmans, Green &
       Company, 1925), pp. 160–61.
129   "so to sympathize": WJ diary, February 1, 1870.
       Stephen Spender, *New York Times Book Review,* March 12, 1944.
130   "His religious": WJ to RJ, July 25, 1870; Vaux.
       "obscene bird of night": Henry James, Sr., *Substance and Shadow* (Boston: Tick-
       nor & Fields, 1863), p. 75.
131   "What *is* living": *Diary of Alice James,* p. 38.

Chapter Eight

133   Palmer, *The Story of the Bee,* pp. 4–25.
135   "which is considered": AJ to WJ, June 8, 1867.
136   Female Humane Society work: "Secretary's Report for the Female Humane So-
       ciety of Cambridge," 1869; Cambridge Historical Society.
       Footnote: "It was the perennial freshness": *The Bostonians,* p. 183.
137   "I am amused": AJ to WJ, November 20 [1887].
       Footnote: Helen Howe, *The Gentle Americans,* p. 202.
138   "I hope": HJ to AJ, April 16 [1869].
       Ruskin: HJ to AJ, March 19, 1869; Henry James, *Letters,* vol. 1, p. 100.
       Tweedys: HJ to AJ, September 3 [1873].
       Arnold: HJ to AJ, April 25 [1873].
       Morrises: HJ to AJ, March 10 [1869]; Henry James, *Letters,* vol. 1, pp. 93–94.

page
138 George Eliot: HJ to HJ Sr., May 10 [1869]; Ibid., vol. 1, p. 116.
139 "I blush": WJ to HJ, June 12, 1869.
 "brings me such": HJ to AJ, June 19, 1869.
 "dropping": HJ to HJ Sr., May 10, 1869.
 "Father was loath": WJ to HJ, March 22, 1869.
 "I saw how": MJ to HJ Sr. [n.d.].
140 "lively all day": WJ to HJ, June 1, 1869.
 "Alice is busy": MJ to HJ, July 24, 1869.
 Footnote: HJ Sr. to Julia Kellogg, July 26 [1869].
141 "To prove": WJ to HJ, December 5, 1869.
 "telling of Alice's": HJ to MJ, December 21, 1869.
 "I don't know": WDH to HJ, January 2, 1870.
142 "taking notes": HJ Sr. to Theodora Sedgwick, March 9, 1871.
143 "Did Tom come": MJ to HJ and GWJ [July 10, 1871].

Chapter Nine

144 "It will do": FRM to "Aunt Lizzie" [Lowell?], April 25 [1872]; Schlesinger Library, Radcliffe College.
145 "I needn't have been": *Diary of Alice James,* p. 47.
 "genius of the house": HJ Sr. to AJ, June 27 [1872?].
 "Mme. de Sévigné": WJ to HJ, August 24, 1872.
 "ravished": HJ to Grace Norton, May 24 [1872].
146 "perfect feast": Henry James, *English Hours* (New York: Orion, 1960), p. 39.
 "Chester is": Ibid., p. 41.
 "too ovine": Ibid., pp. 53–54.
 "Alice enjoys": HJ to parents, June 4 [1872].
 "niched": HJ to parents, June 11, 1872.
147 "Alice's exploits": Ibid.
 "always at our door": AK to MJ, June 1, 1872.
 "an immense hit": HJ to parents, June 19 [1872].
148 "H. writes": *Diary of Alice James,* p. 46.
 "long enough": AJ to AAR, November 21, 1874; National Library of Scotland.
 "It was his first": *Diary of Alice James,* p. 47.
 "by its arranged": Ibid.
149 "still the perfection": HJ to parents, June 28 [1872].
 "like a new": HJ to parents, July 13 [1872].
 "My daughter": MJ to AJ, July 18 [1872].
150 "never fatiguing": HJ Sr. to AJ, June 27 [1872].
 "no little girl": MJ to HJ and AJ, July 26 [1872].
 "I am alone": HJ Sr. to AJ, May 21 [1872].
 "Father's account": HJ to parents, July 5 [1872].
151 "at all intellectual": MJ to AJ, July 18 [1872].
 "She will have": GWJ to AJ and HJ, August 28, 1872.
 "philosophical hypochondria": WJ to HJ, August 24, 1872.
 Footnote: GWJ to MJ, August 7, 1872.

page
152   "petticoat sway": HJ Sr. to AJ, August 6 [1872?].
      "Don't overdo": WJ to AJ, July 27-28, 1872.
      "sprung into": WJ to HJ, August 24, 1872.
      Footnote: "over-refinement": WJ to HJ, August 24, 1872; "as I thought": WJ
           to HJ, October 10, 1872; "constant use": WJ to HJ, November 24, 1872;
           "but let me say": HJ to WJ, quoted in Edel, *Henry James,* vol. 5, p. 300.
153   "nothing but comfort": HJ to parents, July 5 [1872].
      "one by one": HJ to parents, July 13 [1872].
      HJ on LB: Henry James, "Notes of a Son and Brother," pp. 520-22.
      Leon Edel on LB: *Henry James,* vol. 3, p. 198.
      "heavenly": AK to MJ, July 2 [1872].
154   "in spite of the fact": HJ to parents, August 11 [1872].
      "*unshared* society": HJ to parents, July 28 [1872].
      "if we could only": HJ to HJ Sr., August 11, 1872.
      "a person": HJ to parents, July 21 [1872].
      "Alice's own impulse": HJ to parents, August 11 [1872].
156   "not especially": HJ to parents, August 25 [1872].
      "I do hope": HJ Sr. to AJ, August 20 [1872].
      "Alice will give": HJ to parents, August 18 [1872].
157   "varies like a": Henry James, *Italian Hours* (Boston: Houghton Mifflin, 1909),
           pp. 9-10.
      "for the Riviera": HJ to parents, August 31 [1872].
      "nightmare": HJ to parents, September 15 [1872].
      "shaking": HJ to parents, September 19, 1872.
      "mutual monotony": HJ to parents, September 29, 1872; Henry James, *Letters,*
           vol. 1, p. 302.
      Footnote: HJ to WJ, September 22 [1872]; Ibid., p. 300.
158   "immense gain": HJ to parents, July 21 [1872].
      "very fruitful": HJ to parents, September 29 [1872]; Henry James, *Letters,* vol. 1,
           p. 303.
      "terrible murky Babylon": HJ to parents, October 10 [1872]; Ibid., p. 305.
      "I don't think": AJ to AAR, November 21, 1874; National Library of Scot-
           land.
159   "mind": HJ to parents, December 9, 1872.
      "elastic": WJ to HJ, November 24, 1872.
      "She continues": MJ to HJ, December 15 [1872].
160   "A. is full": MJ to HJ, April 27 [1873].
      "enjoy her husband's": HJ Sr. to HJ, July 1872.
      "I am frightened": AJ to AAR, February 28, 1877; National Library of Scot-
           land.

Chapter Ten

161   "even the fastidious": WJ to HJ, November 24, 1872.
      "Sargy and Lilla": AJ to SSD, February 1, 1874.
162   "If you don't": AJ to SSD, February 16, 1874.
      "struggling to like": AJ to SSD, March 25 [1874?].
      "wonder of wonders": AJ to AAR, February 13, 1875; National Library of Scot-
           land.

163   "Ellen Gurney": AJ to AAR, National Library of Scotland.

"Marny has": AJ to AAR, February 11, 1874; National Library of Scotland.

"We staid": AJ to SSD, September 23 [1876?].

164   "ardently matrimonial": AJ to AAR, May 10 [1876?]; National Library of Scotland.

"not eminently": AJ to AAR, March 14 [1875?]; National Library of Scotland.

Footnote: HJ to LB, October 30 [1878]; Henry James, *Letters,* vol. 2, p. 189.

165   "had I not been told": AJ to AAR, November 2, 1873; National Library of Scotland.

"only had word": AJ to AAR, December 21 [1873]; National Library of Scotland.

166   "where I shall see": AJ to AAR, March 14 [1875?]; National Library of Scotland.

"the former as uproarious": AJ to AAR, December 26, 1875; National Library of Scotland.

"seriously threatened": Ibid.

167   "I congratulate": WJ to AJ, December 11, 1873.

"I am so glad": AJ to AAR, October 11, 1874; National Library of Scotland.

"we have had": AJ to AAR, December 26, 1875; National Library of Scotland.

"greatest of all delights": AJ to AAR, July 12 [1874?]; National Library of Scotland.

old gentleman: AJ to AAR, October 11, 1874; National Library of Scotland.

168   "that you are growing": AJ to AAR, April 12, 1876; National Library of Scotland.

"some one": AJ to AAR, February 28, 1877; National Library of Scotland.

169   "My joy": AJ to SSD, March 25 [1874?].

"I have been": AJ to FRM [May 1875?].

"the most idiotic": AJ to AAR, April 12, 1876; National Library of Scotland.

171   "new sources": *The Society to Encourage Studies at Home* (Cambridge: Riverside Press, 1897), pp. 6–18.

"I am enjoying": Ibid., p. 71.

Health (Boston: Society to Encourage Studies at Home, 1894 edition).

173   "if it is": *The Society to Encourage Studies at Home,* p. 4.

174   "Lecky": HJ to parents, May 4, 1877.

175   "I am with": AJ to AAR, December 26, 1875; National Library of Scotland.

"I was deeply hurt": AJ to AAR, April 12, 1876; National Library of Scotland.

"Alice has got": WJ to HJ, December 12, 1875.

"I had a letter": AJ to AAR, September 23, 1876; National Library of Scotland.

176   "I wish that you": AJ to AAR, February 28, 1877; National Library of Scotland.

Chapter Eleven

177   "so well": AJ to SSD, September 23 [1876?].

"Your career": MJ to AJ [July 1874?].

page

"just come in": AK to RJ, June 9 [1876]; Vaux.

"an increase": AJ to AAR, May 4 [1873]; National Library of Scotland.

"Poor child!": MJ to HJ, March 21 [1873].

178   "So you have betaken": AJ to SSD, September 20 [1877?].

"gentle, kindly": HJ to WJ, January 28 [1878]; Henry James, *Letters,* vol. 2, p. 150.

"not rapturous": AJ to AAR [December 1877?]; National Library of Scotland.

179   "for not being able": AJ to FRM, November 25, 1878.

"I have always": AJ to AAR, November 14 [1878]; National Library of Scotland.

Footnote: "Annie A.": HJ to WJ, March 4 [1879]; Henry James, *Letters,* vol. 2, pp. 218-19.

180   "the affair": WJ to RJ, September 15, 1877; Vaux.

"Every Dr.": WJ to RJ, July 9, 1878; Vaux.

181   "the most simply": William James, *Principles,* vol. 2, p. 440.

"The great part": WJ to HJ, July 11, 1885.

"What *do* you": HJ to AJ, December 9, 1878.

"peerless specimen": HJ to AJ, June 5 [1878].

"Thou seemest": WJ to AJ, December 24, 1873.

"Beloved beautlet": WJ to AJ, February 13, 1874.

Footnote: HJ Sr. to Mrs. WJ of A., October 15, 1857.

182   "He is very sweet": MJ to HJ, April 3 [1874].

Footnote: "My beloved brother": GWJ to WJ, May 16, 1878.

183   "a nervous breakdown": MJ to RJ, May 23 [1878]; Vaux.

"and Alice much more": MJ to AHJ [May 1878?].

"share the cares": AK to MHJ, August 1 [1878?].

"periods of depression": MJ to RJ, June 1 [1878?]; Vaux.

"it seems rather": HJ to AJ, June 5 [1878].

"satisfaction": HJ to LB, June 15, 1878.

Footnote 1: "you started": AHJ to AJ [n.d.].

184   "Yes, I know": HJ to WJ, July 23 [1878]; Henry James, *Letters,* vol. 2, p. 179.

"I hope": HJ to MJ, July 15 [1878?].

"only, if she takes": HJ to HJ Sr., October 19 [1878].

"In the old days": *Diary of Alice James,* p. 201.

"vast and responsive": Ibid., p. 105.

"incredible": Ibid., p. 79.

185   William James, *Principles,* vol. 1, p. 294.

"The truth is": HJ Sr. to RJ, September 14 [1878]; Vaux.

Footnote: Sigmund Freud, "Mourning and Melancholia," *The Standard Edition of the Complete Psychological Works of Sigmund Freud* (London: The Hogarth Press, 1964), vol. 14, p. 246.

188   "No fiat": *Diary of Alice James,* p. 101.

189   "I am growing": AJ to FRM, October 7, 1879; Schlesinger Library, Radcliffe College.

"an object of compassion": AJ to FRM, November 25, 1878.

"savor of uncertainty": *Diary of Alice James,* p. 230.

Chapter Twelve

191   Meets KPL, 1873: KPL to HJ³, September 1 [1920].

"I wish you could know": AJ to SSD, August 9, 1879.

192   Louisa and Katharine Loring: From private conversation with members of the Loring family, and the Loring genealogy; New York Public Library.

"strength of wind": HJ to WJ, May 1 [1878]; Henry James, *Letters,* vol. 2, p. 172.

Footnote: A. Hunter Dupree, *Asa Gray* (Cambridge: Harvard University Press, 1959), p. 182.

194   "bosom of nature": AJ to SSD, August 9, 1879.

195   Footnote 1: Letter of September 16, 1909, quoted in Nathan G. Hale, Jr., ed., *James Jackson Putnam and Psychoanalysis* (Cambridge: Harvard University Press, 1971), pp. 23-24.

Footnote 2: Harriet Beecher Stowe, *The Minister's Wooing* (Boston: Houghton Mifflin, 1887), p. 3.

196   "celestial being": HJ to AJ, August 19, 1879.

"my sister Alice": WJ to FRM, Christmas, 1879.

Footnote: "I had a dream": AJ to FRM, October 7, 1879; Schlesinger Library, Radcliffe College.

197   "I confess": HJ to AJ, May 19 [1879]; Henry James, *Letters,* vol. 2, p. 233.

Footnote: "but it wouldn't": HJ to AJ, January 30, 1881; Ibid., p. 337; "so broken a reed": Preface to *The Portrait of a Lady,* pp. xvii-xix.

198   "From what you intimate": HJ to HJ Sr., June 5, 1881.

"the same delightful": AJ to MHJ [Wednesday, late October] 1881; Vaux.

"rather weaker": HJ to MJ, July 18, 1881.

"She appears to think": HJ to parents, July 31 [1881].

199   "a cool grey": Henry James, *Notebooks,* p. 36.

"I shall be": HJ to parents, September 9 [1881].

"Alice and Miss L.": HJ to parents, August 25 [1881].

200   "Dear Katharine and Alice": Sarah Orne Jewett to AJ and KPL, January 3, 1891; Loring Papers, Beverly Historical Society.

"their reach together": Quoted in Helen Howe, *The Gentle Americans,* p. 83.

201   "a dear little soul": AJ to FRM, October 7, 1879; Schlesinger Library, Radcliffe College.

AHJ on AJ and KPL: Allen, *William James,* p. 227.

"dear old Quincy Street": AHJ to HJ, March 22, 1892.

"it is absolutely": HJ to parents, August 25 [1881].

202   "Uncle Harry's": AK to MHJ, November 14, 1881; Vaux.

"thrive": RJ to HJ, January 28, 1882.

"one of those splendid": HJ to Mrs. Francis Mathews, February 13 [1882]; Henry James, *Letters,* vol. 2, pp. 378-79.

"taking up": AK to MHJ, February 9, 1882; Vaux.

"her Mother's": AK to MHJ, February 26, 1882; Vaux.

Footnote: CFW to HJ, February 12, 1882.

203   "how must she": AK to Mrs. C. P. Cranch, March 22 [1882].

"as a sublimation": *Diary of Alice James,* p. 231.

"a beautiful illumined": Ibid., p. 221.

"Instead of having": AJ to KJP, March 5 [1882]; Colby College Library.

"My father and Alice": HJ to Francis J. Child [February 1882]; Massachusetts Historical Society.

"very pleasant little house": AJ to MHJ, May 22 [1882]; Vaux.

204 "We moved": AJ to MHJ, July 3 [1882]; Vaux.

"very pretty": Henry James, *Notebooks*, p. 42.

205 "Our life": AJ to MHJ, July 9 [1882]; Vaux.

"selfish and tyrannical": MJ to GWJ, April 1, 1880; Vaux.

"the Asylum": MJ to MHJ [May 21, 1881].

"Poor boy!": AJ to HJ, October 2 [1882].

"I can never hope": AJ to MHJ, March 13, 1882; Vaux.

"How long": AJ to HJ, October 3 [1882].

Footnote: GWJ to MHJ [August 1882?]; Vaux.

206 "for the bricks": Ibid.

"Now that the moves": AJ to FRM, September 11 [1882?].

"distinctly widowed farewell": HJ Sr. to HJ, May 9 [1882].

207 "something lying": AK to HJ, December 2 [1882].

"It is weary work": Grace Ashburner to Mrs. Samuel G. Ward, December 28, 1882.

208 "and no wonder": AK to HJ, December 2 [1882].

"this disgusting world": AK to WJ, December 23, 1882.

"He gets over": KPL to RJ, December 11 [1882]; Vaux.

"yearned unspeakably": HJ to WJ, December 26 [1882].

"Oh, I have": HJ to WJ, December 28 [1882].

209 "My darling Harry": AJ to HJ, December 20 [1882].

"Most unfortunately": KPL to HJ[3], September 1 [1920].

"somewhere out of the depths": HJ to WJ, January 1883.

210 "Darling old father": WJ to HJ Sr., December 14 [1882?].

211 Money by 1979 standards: Bureau of Labor Statistics.

"unjust and damnable": GWJ to RJ, December 26, 1882; Vaux.

"sadly broken": HJ to WJ, January 23 [1883]; Henry James, *Letters*, vol. 2, p. 402.

212 "She assures me": HJ to WJ, August 17 [1883].

"For you": WJ to AJ, December 20, 1882.

"we were so glad": AJ to SSD, May 5 [1884].

213 "The sincerity": *Diary of Alice James*, p. 125.

"one of the most intense": Ibid., pp. 78–79.

Chapter Thirteen

214 "She would be utterly": Grace Ashburner to Mrs. Samuel G. Ward, January 10, 1883.

"I feel strangely": HJ to Macmillan, January 27 [1883]; British Library.

215 "set up a common": HJ to FAK, February 1, 1883.

"deluge of petticoats": Henry James, "A New England Winter," *The Complete Tales of Henry James,* edited by Leon Edel (Philadelphia: J. B. Lippincott, 1963), vol. 6 (1884–1888), p. 141.

Footnote: GWJ to HJ and AJ, February 6, 1883.

page
217 "but as she is": *Diary of Alice James*, p. 67.
"one of those longings": *Diary of Alice James*, p. 212.
" 'busy ineffectiveness' ": AJ to FRM, December 28 [1887?].
"I am sorry": AJ to AHJ [February 1884].
Footnote 1: Lucy Larcom to KPL, Saturday morning [n.d.]; Loring Papers, Beverly Historical Society.

218 "the happy news": AJ to AHJ [April 5, 1887].
"I am more": AJ to WJ, April 24 [1887?].
"towed my heart": AJ to AK, December 29, 1888.
"K. says": *Diary of Alice James*, p. 148.
Footnote: "little Israelite": Allen, *William James*, p. 272.

219 "subjection": AJ to SSD, April 1, 1889.
"ladies who": AJ to WJ, November 4, 1888.
"Why try": AJ to AHJ, May 5, 1889.
"Yes, I will": HJ Sr. to AHJ [July 1880].
"When will women": *Diary of Alice James*, p. 60.

220 "not a crown": AJ to AK, April 23 [1886].
"Her existence": AJ to AK, November 15 [1887?].

221 Adams Nervine Annual Reports, 1882 and 1883.

223 "Weir Mitchell": Quoted in Earnest, *S. Weir Mitchell*, p. 89.
"I dined": WJ to AJ, October 19, 1885.
Footnote: Van Wyck Brooks, *New England Indian Summer*, pp. 218–19; Kenneth Lynn, *William Dean Howells* (New York: Harcourt Brace Jovanovich, 1971); WDH to AJ, April 26, 1889.

224 "The value": Adams Nervine Annual Report, 1883.

225 "but there has been": HJ to FB, July 26 [1883].
"My sister": HJ to Macmillan, June 11, 1883; British Library.
"markedly and encouragingly": HJ to WJ, August 17 [1883].

226 "it looks": GWJ to WJ, September 25 [1883].
"my presence": WJ to AJ, October 2, 1883.
"I should like": AJ to MHJ, December 18 [1883]; Vaux.
"May they have been": HJ to WJ, November 24 [1883].
"She has always liked": AK to MHJ, February 2 [1884].

227 William B. Neftel, "Clinical Notes on Nervous Diseases of Women," *Archives of Scientific and Practical Medicine* (New York and Philadelphia, May 1873), vol. 1, no. 5.

228 "wonderfull change": AJ to FRM [Sunday, 1884].
"alien, odious": Ibid.
"I went": AJ to SSD, May 5 [1884].

229 "I have been anxious": Ibid.
"spirit enough": HJ to WJ, March 22 [1884].
"Those ghastly days": *Diary of Alice James*, p. 45.
"ways and means": AJ to SSD, May 5 [1884].
"tide of homesickness": *Diary of Alice James*, p. 119.

Chapter Fourteen

233 "so distinctly": *Diary of Alice James*, pp. 149–50.

"It's rather strange": *Diary of Alice James*, p. 36.

Footnote: ". . . I have": *Roderick Hudson*, p. 74.

234   "dear anxious": HJ to Grace Norton, November 3 [1884].

"in a *very*": HJ to AK, November 11, 1884.

235   "never nervous": HJ to AK, November 24, 1884.

"the only man": AJ to AHJ, December 8, 1884.

"a grim spectre": AJ to WJ, January 31 [1885].

"great distress": HJ to WJ, January 2, 1885.

236   "I asked": AJ to AK, January 31 [1885].

"It may seem": AJ to WJ, January 3–7 [1886?].

"I think the difficulty": Ibid.

237   "this seems highly": AJ to WJ, September 18, 1886.

"My doctor": AJ to AK, January 31 [1885].

238   "an outlet": *Diary of Alice James*, p. 25.

"an emotional volcano": AJ to WJ, August 21, 1888.

"What an indigestion": *Diary of Alice James*, p. 60.

"a pale fluid": Ibid., p. 96.

"congenital faith": Ibid., p. 131.

"Yesterday Nurse": Ibid., pp. 48–49.

239   "the sense of vitality": Ibid., p. 49.

"Kath. comes": AJ to AK, January 31 [1885].

"peculiar, nervous": MJ to AJ, November 18 [1884].

"regular boom": AJ to AHJ, November 8 [1886?].

"delicate and critical": HJ to LB, April 24, 1885.

240   "deadly consumptive": HJ to Grace Norton, May 8 [1885].

"having nervous fits": HJ to AK, May 19 [1885].

"We must": HJ to AK, May 12 [1885].

241   "in an acute": HJ to AK, May 19 [1885].

242   "quite as strongly": HJ to AK, May 12 [1885].

"She seems as large": *Diary of Alice James*, p. 56.

243   "Katharine is a most": Ibid., p. 164.

Rossetti's lines: Ibid., p. 140.

"A life lifted out": Ibid., p. 151.

244   "the situation of women": Henry James, *Notebooks*, pp. 46–47.

245   "full of rectitude": *The Bostonians*, pp. 3–7.

"very eloquent": Ibid., pp. 185–86.

246   "stilled herself": Ibid., p. 309.

"placed under the protection": Ibid., pp. 197–98.

247   John Bunyan's heaven: Quoted in Justin Kaplan, *Mr. Clemens and Mark Twain* (New York: Simon and Schuster, 1966), p. 139.

"The whole generation": *The Bostonians*, p. 343.

Footnote: F. R. Leavis, *The Great Tradition* (New York: George W. Steward, 1949), p. 138.

248   "we pity her": Dupee, *Henry James*, p. 153.

"Olive would never": *The Bostonians*, p. 398.

249   "a peculiar intense": Henry James, *Notebooks*, pp. 181–82.

Footnote: HJ to WJ, February 14, 1885.

252   "anchorages": AJ to WJ, January 31, 1885.

Chapter Fifteen

253 "vast sea of mews": AJ to AK, November 21 [1885].
"a few virtuous": AJ to WJ, January 3 [1886].
"How can you": AJ to SSD, February 5 [1886?].
"There are two": AJ to AK, April 23 [1886?].

254 "A great many people": HJ to WJ, May 9 [1886].
"she is the best": HJ to WJ, November 13, 1886.
"amiable ladies": AJ to FRM, April 11 [1886?].
"incredibly crude": AJ to AHJ, November 8 [1886].
"made memorable": AJ to WJ, May 19 [1886].
"came a few days": Ibid.

255 "Patriotism": AJ to AHJ, December 10 [1888].
"came suddenly": *Diary of Alice James*, p. 57.
"A moribund": AJ to WJ, September 10 [1886].
"all round": WJ to AJ, September 27, 1886.
"inferior in culture": WJ to AJ, October 16, 1887.
"our inferiority": AJ to WJ, November 20 [1887].

256 "played you a base trick": AJ to WJ, January 3 [1886?].
"to Heaven that": *Diary of Alice James*, p. 231.
"an artless": AJ to WJ, March 31, 1889.

257 "The light is shrieking": *Diary of Alice James*, p. 147.
"which reprobate": Ibid., p. 217.
"it evidently": HJ to WJ, January 2, 1885.
"Father and William's": *Diary of Alice James*, p. 57.
"expressed himself": Ibid., p. 68.

258 hereditary melancholy: HJ to LB, January 7 [1886].
"she so dreaded": AHJ to AJ, April 6 [1886].
"My heart is wrung": AJ to WJ, April 23 [1887?].
"bruised wings": AJ to AHJ, December 3 [1887].
"cruelly what paralytics": AJ to WJ, December 11 [1887].

259 "That *her*": AJ to FRM, December 28 [1887?].
"I am grieved": CFW to KPL, October 9, 1887; Loring Papers, Beverly Historical Society.
"Henry is somewhere": AJ to WJ, November 4, 1888.
"Henry has been galavanting": AJ to AK, December 9, 1888.

260 "I hope Mr. James": CFW to KPL, September 19 [1890]; Loring Papers, Beverly Historical Society.
"I am now going": Ibid.
"It opens a new field": Ibid.
"but as a link": AJ to SSD, February 5 [1886?].
"most delicious Philistine": AJ to SSD, December 9 [1888].

261 "absolutely nightmarish": AJ to SSD, February 5 [1886?].
"One day": *Diary of Alice James*, p. 66.
"refined mortal": Ibid., p. 173.
"Could anything": AJ to AHJ, January 9, 1890.

262 "What a devil": *Diary of Alice James*, p. 173.
"poor Harry": AJ to WJ, May 19 [1886].

page

"I have been reading": AJ to WJ, November 20, 1887.

263   "to have been morally": AJ to AHJ, December 10 [1888].

264   George Eliot, *The Mill on the Floss,* p. 181; George Eliot, *Daniel Deronda* (London: Penguin Books, 1967), p. 717; George Eliot, *The Mill on the Floss,* p. 20.

265   "Read the third volume": *Diary of Alice James,* pp. 40–42.

George Eliot: HJ, *Atlantic Monthly,* May 1885, pp. 668–78.

Footnote: Gordon Haight, ed., *The George Eliot Letters* (New Haven: Yale University Press, 1954–55), vol. 1, p. xiv.

266   Footnote: Quoted in HJ, *Atlantic Monthly,* May 1885, p. 669.

267   "loyalty to Lizzie": AJ to FRM, April 11 [1886?].

"You poor child": WJ to AJ, July 8, 1886.

"very fraternal": AJ to WJ, September 10 [1886].

268   "The weary journey": AJ to MHJ, March 12, 1888.

"To think": AJ to WJ and AHJ, November 20 [1887].

"Forgive all this": AJ to AK, October 8, 1888.

Leo Tolstoy, *War and Peace,* translated by Constance Garnett (New York: Random House, Modern Library), p. 256.

270   "The fact that": AJ to FRM, June 24, 1888.

"She didn't": AJ to WJ, November 4, 1888.

"What a pity": *Diary of Alice James,* p. 52.

271   "What an interest": AJ to WJ, August 21, 1888.

"I passed": AJ to FRM, April 11 [1886?].

"I'll not use that word": *Diary of Alice James,* p. 81.

"How picturesque": Ibid., pp. 166–67.

Chapter Sixteen

273   "pleasure the handmaid": *Royal Leamington Spa, Official Guide* (London: Published for the Leamington Town Council by Edward J. Burrow, Cheltenham, 1911).

"altogether too": AJ to SSD, October 4 [1887].

274   "Since Kath.": AJ to WJ, November 20 [1887].

"where the trees": AJ to Mrs. Samuel Morse, June 9 [1889?].

"I think": *Diary of Alice James,* p. 25.

275   "I am as much": *Diary of Alice James,* p. 166.

Footnote: Henry James, "Eugénie de Guérin's Journal" and "The Letters of Eugénie de Guérin," *Notes and Reviews* (Cambridge, Massachusetts: Dunster House, 1921), pp. 117–23 and 209–18.

276   "little rubbish heap": Ibid., p. 78.

"coral insect": Ibid., p. 109.

"friendless": Ibid., p. 130.

"mildewed toadstool": Ibid., p. 135.

"collection simply": Ibid., p. 152.

"cramp themselves": AJ to WJ and AHJ, August 21, 1888.

"I would give": AJ to WJ, January 29–31, 1889.

Footnote: Winifred Stephens Whale, *Madame Adam* (New York: E. P. Dutton, 1917), pp. 230–31.

277 " 'Noblesse oblige' ": *Diary of Alice James*, p. 155.
"I find myself": Ibid., pp. 87–88.
278 "heart sickening day": Ibid., pp. 158–59.
"Gladstone will": AJ to WJ, November 20 [1887].
279 KPL to W. E. Gladstone, September 20, 1890; British Library, Manuscripts Room, Gladstone Papers, vol. CCCXXVI.
"in at the fun": *Diary of Alice James*, p. 229.
"a curious nature": Ibid., p. 75.
"To an American": Ibid., pp. 175–76.
280 "How I wish": Ibid., p. 113.
"as if they were friends": Ibid., pp. 169–70.
281 "embodiment": Ibid., p. 119.
"I don't want": *The Princess Casamassima*, vol. 2, p. 146.
"magnificent": AJ to AHJ, November 8 [1886?].
"unaccountable": AJ to WJ, April 24 [1887?].
282 "perfect little": *The Princess Casamassima*, vol. 2, p. 199.
"strange, bedizened": Ibid., vol. 2, p. 165.
"small, odd, sharp": Ibid., vol. 1, p. 140.
"intensely individual": Ibid., vol. 2, p. 164.
"freakish inconsistency": Ibid., vol. 2, p. 289.
"the stoicism": Ibid., vol. 2, p. 204.
"and let their": Ibid., vol. 2, p. 164.
"Do I need": Ibid., vol. 2, p. 285.
283 "Oh, her health": Ibid., vol. 2, pp. 293–94.
"avail himself": Lionel Trilling, *The Liberal Imagination* (New York: Harcourt Brace Jovanovich, 1978), p. 85.
Footnote 1: WJ to Mary Tappan [1892].
Footnote 2: Ibid., p. 76.
284 "but it also puts": HJ to WJ, May 28, 1894.
"with a queer look": *Diary of Alice James*, pp. 51–52.
285 "it is quite": WJ to HJ, February 1, 1889.
"as usual lying": AJ to WJ, January 29–31, 1889.
286 "Poor Aunt Kate's life": AJ to WJ, March 22, 1889.
"A life interest in a shawl!": AJ to WJ, April 7, 1889.
"covered himself": WJ to AHJ, July 29, 1889; quoted in Allen, *William James*, p. 308.
"Beneath all the accretions": WJ to AJ, July 29, 1889.
"treasure beyond price": AJ to WJ, March 31, 1889.
"excellent H.": AJ to WJ, November 20, 1887.
287 "*bon comme le pain*": AJ to E. L. Godkin, June 20 [1890?].
"is the place for me": AJ to AHJ, January 9, 1890.
"crossed the water": *Diary of Alice James*, p. 104.
"Henry the patient": Ibid.
"as if there had been": HJ to AJ, June 6, 1890.
"The great family event": *Diary of Alice James*, p. 161.
288 "*The American* died": Ibid., pp. 224–25.
"I was surprised": Ibid., p. 198.

page
289 "has embedded": *Diary of Alice James,* p. 212.
     "inestimable": WJ to AJ, July 8, 1886.
     "splendid, noble": WJ to AJ, January 27, 1886.
     "I am entirely": WJ to AJ, August 13, 1890.
     "I do hope": WJ to AJ, August 23, 1891.
     "Imagine my entertainment": *Diary of Alice James,* pp. 139–40.
     Footnote: Henry James, *Letters,* vol. 3, pp. 291 and 340–45.
290 "In comparing": Ibid.
     "It is reassuring": Ibid.
291 "I answered": AJ to AHJ, March 7 [1886].
     "It occurred": *Diary of Alice James,* pp. 227–28.
292 "If I can get": Ibid., p. 113.
     "How it fills": Ibid., p. 146.
293 "But what of the success": Ibid., p. 87.
     "*experience* the pain": Ibid., p. 129.
     Footnote: CFW to KPL, October 9, 1887; Loring Papers, Beverly Historical Society.
294 "I used to wonder": Ibid., p. 160.
     "ministrant at the altar": Ibid., p. 202.
     "The other day": *Diary of Alice James,* p. 145.
295 "There has come": Ibid., p. 131.

                        Chapter Seventeen

296 "squalid indigestions": *Diary of Alice James,* p. 135.
     "I have never seen": KPL to FRM, September 23 [1890?].
     "I had to get a little": *Diary of Alice James,* p. 200.
     "unspeakable": Ibid., p. 210.
297 "present condition": HJ to WJ, November 7, 1890.
     "For a long time past": *Diary of Alice James,* p. 210.
     "When death": Ibid., p. 185.
     "Remaining here": Ibid., p. 150.
     "only to wave": Ibid., p. 181.
     "good scraplet": Ibid., p. 203.
298 "absurdly happy": Ibid.
     "seized the": Ibid., p. 218.
     "*Mes beaux restes*": Ibid., p. 219.
     "If K. knows": Ibid., p. 176.
     "It must be allowed": Ibid., p. 225.
299 "recital": Ibid., p. 169.
     "back into the": AJ to AHJ, February 5, 1890.
     "My soul will never": *Diary of Alice James,* p. 57.
     Footnote: Private conversation with Leon Edel; *The Wings of the Dove,* vol. I, pp. 235 and 246; Edmund Wilson, "The Ambiguity of Henry James," *The Triple Thinkers* (New York: Harcourt, Brace 1938), p. 131; Edmund Wilson, *Letters on Literature and Politics,* edited by Elena Wilson (New York: Farrar, Straus & Giroux, 1977), p. 239.
300 "Sir Andrew": Ibid., p. 226.

page

301 "To him who waits": *Diary of Alice James,* p. 207.
"To any one who has not": Ibid., pp. 207–208.
"I cannot make out": Ibid., p. 209.
"Having it to look": Ibid., p. 208.

303 ". . . So far from": WJ to AJ, July 6, 1891.

304 "My dearest William": AJ to WJ, July 30, 1891.

305 "some suggestion": HJ to William Wilberforce Baldwin, July 24, 1891; Pierpont Morgan Library.

306 "He appears": HJ to WJ, July 31, 1891.
"*yearns* to see you": HJ to William Wilberforce Baldwin, September 6, 1891; Pierpont Morgan Library.
"Your limp & shadowy": AJ to William Wilberforce Baldwin, November 16, 1891; Pierpont Morgan Library.
"condition of greater": HJ to WJ, July 31, 1891.
"altogether refused": WJ to Mary Tappan [1892].

307 "How *Harry*": WJ to AJ [October 1, 1891?].
"These long pauses": *Diary of Alice James,* p. 218.
"It is very gratifying": Ibid.
"Alice lives": CFW to William Wilberforce Baldwin, February 5, 1892; Pierpont Morgan Library.
"She breaks out with": WJ to AJ, November 22, 1891.

308 "the most remarkable": WJ to HJ, August 20, 1891.
"only brings out": HJ to RJ, September 8, 1891; Vaux.
"11th hour": *Diary of Alice James,* p. 135.
"published *The Tragic Muse*": Ibid., p. 211.
"disclosed its iniquities": Ibid., p. 222.
"very creditable book": WJ to AJ, November 26, 1890.
Charles Lloyd Tuckey, *Psychotherapeutics or Treatment by Hypnotism and Suggestion* (London: Balliere, Tindall & Cox, 1890).

309 "turned on the hypnotic Tuckey": *Diary of Alice James,* p. 222.
"supposing that your being": AJ to WJ, December 22 [1891].
"If it were possible": *Diary of Alice James,* pp. 222–23.

310 "It is curious": Ibid., p. 222.
"As the ugliest": Ibid., p. 225.
"It isn't in the sorrows": Ibid., 229.
"amusing episode": Ibid., p. 230.
"There *is* nothing": HJ to WJ, February 15 [1892].

311 "as it was so good": *Diary of Alice James,* p. 89.
"My wills": Deposition of Alice James, 72298; Commonwealth of Massachusetts, Essex County Probate, Salem, Massachusetts.
"K. told me": *Diary of Alice James,* p. 89.

312 "really a tragic": HJ to WJ, March 2, 1892.
"I am being ground": *Diary of Alice James,* p. 232.
Footnote: Edel, *Henry James,* vol. 3, pp. 317–18.

313 "Katharine can't help it": Ibid.
Dream: HJ to FB, March 6 [1892].
"Her lungs": HJ to WJ, March 5, 1892.
TENDEREST LOVE: HJ to WJ, March 5, 1892.

page
314 couldn't live another day: HJ to WJ, March 8, 1892.
"For about seven hours": Ibid.
"Her face": Ibid.
"first and last": *Diary of Alice James,* pp. 216–17.
315 "inoffensive, sweet-voiced": HJ to WJ, March 9, 1892.
"It was all somehow": HJ to FB, March 9, 1892.
"in this damp": HJ to WJ, March 8, 1892.
"Poor little Alice!": WJ to HJ, March 7, 1892.
"I cannot give you": KPL to FRM, March 12 [1892].
"a sort of lifting": RJ to FRM, March 14, 1892.
316 "My dear James": WDH to HJ, March 25, 1892.
"great sorrow": WJ to FB, March 9 [1892].
317 "She was not only": HJ to Henrietta Reubell, March 15, 1892.

Afterword

319 "It sank": WJ to HJ, March 24, 1894.
" 'revelation' ": HJ to WJ, April 8, 1894.
320 "magnificent . . . rare": HJ to WJ, May 25, 1894.
"whom I cite": Henry James, "A Small Boy," p. 36.
"ingenuous son": *The Bostonians,* p. 125.
"extraordinary eyes": *The Aspern Papers,* p. 118.
"with the fearful": HJ to WJ, May 28, 1894.
321 "When I see that I say": Ibid.
"a letter which": Ibid.
"although I know": KPL to MJV [1933?]; Vaux.
"As regards the life": HJ to WJ, May 28, 1894.
322 "fill me with tears": Ibid.
323 "Alice James, your Aunt": KPL to MJV, July 14 [1933?]; Vaux.
"one of the most": EHJ to MJV, November 16, 1933; Vaux.
"I'm afraid": HJ[3] to MMJP, November 20, 1933; Bancroft Library, University of California at Berkeley.
324 "not only because": Anna Robeson Burr, *Alice James: Her Brothers — Her Journal* (New York: Dodd, Mead, 1934), p. viii.
"The imprisoned light": *Times Literary Supplement,* October 11, 1934.
"chuckled over it": HJ[3] to MMJP, January 9, 1935; Bancroft Library, University of California at Berkeley.
"Here is a mind": New York *Herald Tribune,* May 20, 1934.
325 "vigorous, frank and brilliant": *New York Times,* May 17, 1934.
"a supremely important": *New York Times Book Review,* May 20, 1934.
"In some of her insights": *The New Republic,* June 27, 1934.
"There is a common": *The Nation,* January 9, 1943.
"The quality": Matthiessen, *James Family,* p. 275.
"Alice James": Ibid., p. 648.
326 "one of the neglected": *The Saturday Review,* September 5, 1964.
"aggressive shrillness": *New York Review of Books,* November 5, 1964.

Acknowledgments

MARK TWAIN once said that biographies are "but the clothes and buttons of the man — the biography of the man himself cannot be written." Many people and institutions have aided me in the search for Alice James's clothes and buttons. My editor, Jonathan Galassi, has been of inestimable help as friend and literary critic ever since the idea of writing about Alice James first occurred to me. Leon Edel told me early on about letters I might never otherwise have found, and very kindly answered batteries of questions throughout the course of my work. And I am greatly indebted to Alexander R. James for his permission, as literary executor, to quote from the James family archives all over the world.

By far the greatest collection of James letters and documents is at the Houghton Library, Harvard University, and I would like to thank the library for permission to quote from this essential material. I am particularly grateful to Rodney G. Dennis, Houghton's Curator of Manuscripts; Marte Shaw, Curator of the Reading Room; and the Reading Room staff, Deborah Kelley, Jessica Owaroff, and Dennis Marnon, for their invaluable assistance over the past five years. I owe special thanks to Henry James Vaux of Berkeley, California, for generously allowing me to make use of and quote from his extensive private archive, including the original handwritten volumes of Alice James's diary. And I am extremely grateful to Mary Loring Clapp for her ample and unflagging help with information about the Loring family and Prides Crossing, and for permission to quote from her family papers.

For their critical readings of the manuscript and insightful suggestions, I would like to thank Jean Block, Constance Brown, Stephanie Engel, Michael T. Gilmore, Nathan Leites, Jim Peck, and Louise Strouse. Frances L. Apt went way beyond the call of copy-editing duty in her close attention to the manuscript's final draft. Many others have assisted me over the past several years in various ways: I am especially grateful to Daniel Aaron, Gay Wilson Allen, Georges, Anne, and Valerie Borchardt, Frances L. Burnett, Amelia F. Emerson, Elliot and Kay Forbes, Edith Gregg, H. Montgomery Hyde, Justin Kaplan, John V. Kelleher, Augustus Peabody Loring, the Misses Pehrson — present owners of 41 Argyll Road — Malcolm and Sheila Perkins, Christopher Ricks, C. Nicholas Rostow, Janos and Helen Scholz, Joan Shurcliff, Dr. John P. Spiegel, Dr. W. Davies Sohier, Jr., and Dr. J. Martin Woodall.

In addition, I am indebted to the following individuals and libraries for access to, and in many cases permission to quote from, their collections: the Alderman Library, University of Virginia (the C. Waller Barrett Collection); the Trustees of Amherst College and the Amherst College Library; the Bancroft Library, University of California at Berkeley; Robert R. Perron and the Beverly Historical Society; the British Library; G. B. Warden and the Cambridge Historical Society; J. S. Bixler and the Special Collections department of the Miller Library, Colby College; the Countway Medical Library, Harvard University; the Kensington and Chelsea Borough Libraries, London; the Massachusetts Historical Society; the Pierpont Morgan Library; Alan S. Bell and the Trustees of the National Library of Scotland; the Newport Historical Society; the New-York Historical Society; the New York Public Library; the New York Society Library; the Redwood Library and Athenaeum, Newport; Barbara Haber, Eva Moseley, and the Arthur and Elizabeth Schlesinger Library on the History of Women in America; the Vassar College Library; the Warwickshire County Council, Leamington Spa.

I had an invaluable year, 1976–1977, at the Radcliffe Institute, which provided me with an office, the status of Fellow, and full access to Harvard's facilities.

And finally, for the financial support without which this biography could not have been written (Mark Twain notwithstanding), I want to thank the John Simon Guggenheim Memorial Foundation, the National Endowment for the Humanities, and the National Endowment for the Arts.

Index

Abolitionism. *See* Slavery
Academy of Arts and Letters, 29n
Adam, Juliette, 276
Adams, Abigail Brooks, 227
Adams, Henry, 43n, 95, 150, 227, 258
Adams, Mrs. Henry (Marian Hooper;
 "Clover"), 43n, 95, 150, 156, 163,
 257–58
Adams, Isaac, 221n
Adams, John Quincy, 135n
Adams, Seth, 221
Adams Nervine Asylum, 221–25
Agassiz, Louis, 67n, 86, 98
Agassiz, Mrs. Louis (Elizabeth Cary), 86,
 98, 136n, 173; schools founded by, 67,
 91, 170n, 220
Ahlborn, Dr. (Henry Sr.'s physician), 207
Alcott, Bronson, 13, 86, 89, 135
Alcott, Louisa May, 79n, 89, 109
Alice James: Her Brothers—Her Journal
 (Burr, ed.), 324
Allen, Gay Wilson, 326
Ambassadors, The (H. James, Jr.), 27, 54,
 90, 146, 197n
American, The (H. James Jr.), 27, 86; dra-
 matized, 287–89, 306–7, 308
American Equal Rights Association
 (1866), 88
American Scene, The (H. James Jr.), 60
American Women's Suffrage Association,
 215–16
Andrew, Governor John, 75
Andrew family, 142
Anthony, Susan B., 215

Appleton, Frances Elizabeth ("Fanny";
 Mrs. Charles Cabot Jackson), 165, 166,
 175
Appleton, Robert and Rebecca Went-
 worth, 165n
Apthorp, William, 165
Arnold, Matthew, *xiii*, 138, 235
Ashburner, Anne, 136
Ashburner, Annie. *See* Richards, Mrs.
 Francis
Ashburner, Grace, 136, 142, 214
Ashburner, Samuel, 179n
Aspern Papers, The (H. James Jr.), 320
Associated Charities of Boston, 92
Atkinson, Charles, 141, 164, 254
Atlantic Monthly, 13, 86, 99, 115n, 142,
 158, 174, 197n, 265
Austen, Jane, 10n, 109, 138, 162
Awkward Age, The (H. James Jr.), 27
Azeglio, Marchese d', Massimo Taparelli,
 80

Baldwin, Dr. William Wilberforce, 298,
 299n, 305–6, 307, 313
Bancroft, George, 60, 139
Bancroft, John, 139
Bancroft, Mr. (acquaintance), 165
Banks, General Nathaniel Prentiss, 133
"Banks Brigade." *See* "Bee"
Barber, John and Janet Rhea (great-
 grandparents), 10
Barker, Anna. *See* Ward, Mrs. Samuel
 Gray
Barlow, General Francis, 94
Barrett, C. Waller, 322

Beach, Dr. Henry Harris Aubrey, 207, 235
Beard, Dr. George M., 103-4, 105-6, 107
Bedford, Duke of, 271
"Bee" (sewing bee), 79, 114, 132-35, 136n, 141, 150, 161, 163
Beecher, Catharine, 16n
Beecher, Henry Ward, 16n
Beecher, Lyman and Roxana Foote, 16n
Bellows, Reverend Dr., 34
Bewley, Marius, 326
Birrell, Augustine, 321
Bismarck, Prince Otto von, 149, 276-77; as symbol, 238, 239
Boningue, Marie, 48
Boott, Elizabeth ("Lizzie"), 140, 142, 164, 165, 167, 183, 204, 259, 270, 313; AJ quoted on art of, 88, 267; AJ meets in Europe, 153-56
Boott, Francis, 140, 142, 153-56, 167, 204, 267; HJ Jr. letters to, 225, 315-16
Bostonians, The (H. James Jr.), 83, 86, 90, 136, 200, 244-51, 284, 320
Boston Symphony Orchestra, 91
Bowditch, Henry P., 194
Bradfield, Emily, 311, 315
Bradford, George Partridge, 64-65, 135
Bragg, Julia, 132
Breuer, Josef, 120n
Brook Farm, 42, 95n
Brooks, Phillips, 223
Brooks, Van Wyck, 44, 90, 223n
Brown, John, 64
Browning, Robert and Elizabeth Barrett, 135n
Bruce, Robert, king of Scotland, 3
Bryant, William Cullen, 30
Buchan, John, 250n
Bundle of Letters, A (H. James Jr.), 164n
Bunyan, John, 247
Burney, Fanny, 291
Burr, Anna Robeson, 323-24
Byron, George Gordon Lord, 249-50

Cabot, Frances (Mrs. Charles Jackson), 91n
Cabot, Lilla. See Perry, Mrs. Thomas
Calvinism. See Religion
Carlyle, Thomas, 13, 89, 137, 262, 267, 268
Cary, Caroline. See James, Mrs. Garth Wilkinson
Cary, Elizabeth. See Agassiz, Mrs. Louis
Caskey, Marie, 16n
Channing family, 86

Charcot, Jean-Martin, 103n, 123n, 256
Chichester, Mrs. (Englishwoman), 14
Child, Francis J., 67n, 85, 86, 203, 311
Child, Helen, 85
Child, Henrietta, 311
Child, Theodore, 164n
Christianity the Logic of Creation (H. James Sr.), 17
Church of Christ Not an Ecclesiasticism, The (H. James Sr.), 5
Civil War, 63; effects of, xv, 87-88, 103n, 193; James boys and, 70-73, 75-78, 80, 193n
Clapp, Miss (schoolmistress), 91
Clark, Sir Andrew, 298-301
Clark, Sir John and Lady, 199
Clarke, James Freeman, 73, 89
Clarke, Sarah Freeman, 73, 74
Cleveland, Elizabeth, 173n
Columbia College (New York), 4
Compton, Edward, 287, 288
Comte, Auguste, 266, 269
Cooper, James Fenimore, 259
Couture, Thomas, 88
Crocker, Lucretia, 173n
Cross, Florence, 254, 260, 264
Cross, John, 260, 265, 291
Cross, Mary, 254, 260, 264, 290, 300
Curtis, Lawrence, 166n
Cusin, Amélie, 37-38, 39
Cutts, Gertrude. See Story, Mrs. Moorfield

Daisy Miller (H. James Jr.), 27, 122
Daly, Augustin, 289n
Dana, Charles Henry, 30
Dana, Charlotte and Elizabeth, 132
Dana, Mrs. Richard Henry, 136n
Danse, Augustine, 40, 48
Dante Alighieri: quoted, 317
Darwin, Charles, 137, 291n
Darwin, Henrietta. See Litchfield, Mrs. R. B.
Darwin, William Erasmus, 178, 179
Darwin, Mrs. William (Sara Sedgwick), 138, 141n, 144, 149, 214, 219; AJ letters to, 83, 161-63, 169, 177, 178, 187, 191, 194, 212, 228, 229, 253, 260, 261, 273-74; AJ friendship with, 136-37, 179, 234, 254
Delacroix, Ferdinand, 36
Dial, The (periodical), 95n
Diary: AJ begins keeping, 272, 273-80, 284, 289, 292, 295; preserved, 317; published, 319-26
Dickens, Charles, 28n, 30, 39, 62n, 273

Dickinson, Emily, 291, 325; quoted, 75, 290

Disengaged (later *Mrs. Jasper's Way*) (H. James Jr.), 289n

Dixey, Mr. (Ellen Tappan's fiancé), 162, 164

Dixwell, Annie, 313

Dixwell, Fanny. *See* Holmes, Mrs. Oliver Wendell

Dixwell, Susan Hunt, 114, 132, 133, 150

Dodd, Mead and Company, 324

Dorr, Mr. and Mrs., 95

Douglas, Ann, 63, 90n, 105n

Dupee, F. W., 18, 248

Dupree, A. Hunter, 192n

Duveneck, Frank, 267, 270, 311

Dwight, John Sullivan, 95

Edel, Leon, xn, 27, 72, 101, 153, 259, 299n, 326; quoted, 50, 82

Edes, Richard, 222

Eliot, Charles W., 135n, 170n

Eliot, George, 44n, 50, 137, 138, 254, 260, 269-70, 275, 291n; writings, 174, 251, 262, 264-66, 272

Eliot, Samuel, 173n

Elliott, Maud Howe, 74n

Emerson, Edith (Mrs. William Hathaway Forbes), 66-67, 68n, 73-74, 94

Emerson, Edward, 65-66, 67, 68n

Emerson, Ellen, 66-67, 68n, 73-75 *passim*, 81, 82

Emerson, Ralph Waldo, 15n, 64, 73n, 89, 135, 135n, 136n, 142, 245, 254, 269; HJ Sr. as friend of, 13, 18, 30, 65, 86, 123; HJ Sr. letters to, 31, 67-68, 94

Emerson, Mrs. Ralph Waldo (Lydia Jackson; "Lidian"), 68n, 73n, 86

Emerson, William, 161

Empson, William; quoted, 100n

Equal Rights Association (E.R.A.), 215

Eugénie, empress of the French, 41

Europeans, The (H. James Jr.), 164n

Fechter, Charles Albert, 141

Felton, Cornelius, 67n

Female Humane Society of Cambridge, 136

Feminism, feminist movement. *See* Women

Ferenczi, Sandor, 195n

Fields, James T., 86

Fields, Mrs. James T. (Annie), 86, 200, 220, 245

FitzGerald, Edward, 268

Flaubert, Gustave, 262, 282

Foote, Roxana. *See* Beecher, Mrs. Lyman

Forbes, John Murray, 94

Forbes, William Hathaway, 94

Fourier, Charles, and Fourierism, 14n, 42

France, Anatole, 262, 269

Franco-Prussian War, 141-142

Franklin, Benjamin, 60

Fredrickson, George M., 87; quoted, 16n

Freud, Sigmund, 104, 120n, 123n, 185n, 195n

Froude, James Anthony, 137, 262

Fuller, Margaret, 73n, 109

Garrison, William Lloyd, 88-89

Garrod, Dr. (British physician), 235, 236, 237, 273

Gibbens, Alice Howe. *See* James, Mrs. William

Gilman, Arthur, 220

Gladstone, William Ewart, 265n, 278-79, 299

Godefroi, Annette, 35, 37

Godey's Lady's Book, 63-64

Godkin, E. L., 44-45, 142, 166, 169, 254, 289

Golden Bowl, The (H. James Jr.), 27n, 54, 153

Grant, General Ulysses S., 133n

Grattan, C. Hartley, 325

Gray, Alice, 311

Gray, Asa, 62n; 192, 198-99

Gray, Mrs. Asa (Jane Loring), 62n, 132, 136n, 192, 198-99

Greeley, Horace, 30

Green, John Richard, 174-75

Green, Mrs. John Richard, 235, 254, 261

Griffin, Louisa, 311

Gurney, Edmund, 270, 271

Gurney, Ephraim Whitman, 163, 258, 270

Gurney, Mrs. Ephraim (Ellen Hooper), 95-96, 136n, 163, 166, 173n, 220, 258

Hagen, Hermann, 217n

Hale, Nathan G., Jr.: quoted, 103n, 106

Hale, Sarah Josepha, 63

Haller, John S., Jr., and Robin, 105n

Halsted, Dr. William Stewart, 305n

Harbinger, The (periodical), 95n

Hardy, Thomas, 266

Harland, Marion (Mary V. Terhune), 63

Hartington, Lord, 278

Harvard "Annex," 170n, 193, 220

Harvard University, 79, 87, 95n, 170n, 175, 191, 208; William and Henry attend, 71, 78, 85, 200; AJ attends lectures at, 142; family papers at Houghton Library, 183n, 323

Hassett, Simon, 311

Hawthorne, Nathaniel, 30, 42, 66, 86, 89, 135, 135n, 273

Health (tract), 171–73

Henry James (Edel), 259

Henry James Letters (Edel, ed.), xn

Higginson, Henry Lee, 91

Higginson, Mrs. Henry (Ida Agassiz), 86

Higginson, Thomas Wentworth, 75, 89, 290

Holmes, Dr. Oliver Wendell, 99, 192

Holmes, Oliver Wendell, Jr., 99, 110, 132, 142, 143, 150

Holmes, Mrs. Oliver Wendell (Fanny Dixwell), 132, 150

Holton, Mary. *See* James, Mrs. Robertson

Hooper, Ellen. *See* Gurney, Mrs. Ephraim

Hooper, Marian ("Clover"). *See* Adams, Mrs. Henry

Hopkinson, Grace, 132

Horsford, Lilian, 220

Howe, Helen, 137n

Howe, Julia Ward, 60, 74, 88, 89, 136, 193, 216

Howe, Mark A. de Wolfe, 137n

Howells, William Dean, 86, 90, 99, 113, 142, 174; quoted, 17, 141, 224n, 269, 316

Howells, Mrs. William Dean (Elinor Mead), 141, 223, 249

Howells, Winifred, 223, 249

Hubback, Mrs. Catherine Austen, 10

Hugo, Victor, 36, 141

Hull, Florence Howe, 74n

Hunt, William Morris, 58, 59, 71, 138

Hunter, Rebecca, 61–62

Huxley, Thomas, 20

Hysteria, *ix, xv,* 103n, 104, 106; AJ attacks, 118, 120–21, 123, 183, 215, 225, 227, 235–36; and female sexuality, 236–39; Freud on, 104, 120, 123; HJ on, 306; WJ on, 117, 120, 303, 306; treatments of, 223–27. *See also* Neurasthenia *and* Women

Illness as Metaphor (Sontag), 101n

Illustrated News, The, 98

Ireland, Miss (instructor-friend of AJ), 91

Italian Hours (H. James Jr.), 157

Jackson, Judge Charles, 91n

Jackson, Mrs. Charles (Amelia Lee, first wife; Frances Cabot, second wife), 91n

Jackson, Charles Cabot, 165–67, 175

Jackson, Dr. J. Hughlings, 103n

Jackson, Patrick Tracy, 92

Jackson, General Thomas J. ("Stonewall"), 133n

James, Alice: state of health of, *ix–x, xv,* 19, 32, 67–69, 82, 97–100, 106–14, 116, 139–41, 143, 167n, 177–78, (first collapse, 1868) 117–25, 128–31 *passim,* 132, 187, (and trip abroad, 1872) 144–60, (second collapse, 1878) 183–90, 197, 201, 212, 220, 302, (and trip abroad, 1881) 198–200, (parents' death and) 202–3, 207–9, 212, 214, 226, (Adams Nervine treatment) 221–25, (Neftel treatment) 227–28, (in last years) 233, 234–43, 253, 257, 259, 265–66, 271, 273–74, 285–87, 291–93, (and ability to glean information) 282, 283n, (and impending death) 296–98, 201–14, (and use of hypnosis) 308–9, 312; HJ Jr. letters to, *x,* 99, 138–39, 181, 183; WJ letters to, *x,* 25, 68–69, 78, 99, 106, 109–10, 112, 123–24, 152, 167, 212, 223, 226, 255, 267, 303–4, 307; birth and early childhood of, 22, 23, 24, 27–28, 31, 32, 35–36, 37–49, 51–59; travels and life abroad, (with family in Europe, 1855–60) 35, 37–43, (European tour, 1872) 144–59, (visits England, 1881) 197–200, 202 (later years) 19, 86, 135, 148, 201, 214, 229, 233–35, 239–43, 253–61 *passim,* 268, 271, 273–81 *passim,* 284, 287, 293n, 296–301, 305, 306–8; education of, 35, 37–48 *passim,* 57, 59, 61–62, 64, 78, 120–21, (attends lectures at Harvard) 142; and family relationships, 46–55 *passim,* 64–68 *passim,* 99–100, 108, 110, 118–23 *passim,* 139, 151, 160, 177–78, 181–88 *passim,* 196–97, 199–201, 203, 205, 212, 214–15, 226–27, 241–42, 250–60 *passim,* 267–68, 281–82, 284, 287, 289, 306–8, 314, 317, 326; family teasing of, 51–55, 66, 99–100, 110, 175, 181–82; reading of, 63–64, 99, 141, 174–75, 262–70; friendships of, 73–75, 86, 90–96, 136–37, 168, 196, 254, 258, (with Katharine Loring, *see* Loring, Katharine Peabody); and Civil War, 78–80; joins sewing "Bee," 79, 114, 132–35;

and "renunciation of life," 81–82, 97,
121; and thoughts of marriage, 94–95,
161–68; joins Female Humane Society,
136; interest of, in politics, 142,
276–82, 322; joins Society to Encourage
Studies at Home, 170–76, 177, 179; or-
ganizes lunch club, 177, 183; reaction
of, to William's engagement, 183–90;
and death of parents, 202–14 passim;
builds house in Manchester, 204–6,
212, 311; and father's bequests, 207,
211–12; and ménage with Henry Jr.,
214–15; feminist sympathies of,
216–21; makes last trip abroad, 229,
233 (see also travels and life abroad,
above); begins keeping diary, 272,
273–80, 284, 289, 292, 295, (diary preserved, published) 317, 319–26; and
Aunt Kate's bequests, 286; anonymous
note published, 289–90; photographed,
298; will of, 311–12; death of, 314–17
James, Alice: QUOTED, 60, 64n, 201; on
parents/family life, 1, 3, 19–21, 23, 26,
39, 43, 55–56, 65, 114, 115, 135, 139,
203, 213; on education and upbringing, 1, 47–49 passim, 52, 57, 61–62, 65,
81; on unhappiness and "renunciation," 18, 51, 81, 189–90; on women
and female friends, 40, 88, 91–93,
95–96, 258, 260–61; on Civil War, 80;
on Katharine Loring, 83, 191, 194,
196, 206, 220, 242–44, 297, 298; on
Boston and Bostonians, 86, 212, 228;
on state of health, 98, 113, 117–20 passim, 125, 131, 177, 184, 189–91, 228,
229, 233–39 passim, 274, 291–96 passim,
(and impending death) ix, 297,
301–12 passim; on European tour
(1872), 145, 148, 158–59, 160; on marriage and male "superiority," 161–69
passim, 178, 179, 217–18, 219, 236, 267;
on work with home study society,
175–76; on original sin, 187, 263; on
"life in the wild," 194–95; on brothers
Henry and William, 198, 255, 257,
259, 262, 281, 285, 286–89, 302; on life
with father after mother's death,
203–4, 205–6; on brothers Rob and
Wilky, 205, 226; on father's death,
209, 212, 213; on homesickness, 228,
229–30; on life and politics in London,
253–55, 268, 277, 278, 279–80; on spiritualism, 256; on suicide, 258–59;
270–72; on "refinement," 261–62, 271;
on literature and literary criticism, 262,

265; on philosophical aims, 267–68,
276, 295; on Aunt Kate's death and
legacy, 285–86; on Henry's plays,
287–89; on own writing, 290–91. See
also letters to: Darwin, Mrs. William;
James, Henry, Jr.; James, Mrs. Robertson; James, William; James, Mrs.
William; Morse, Frances Rollins; Richards, Mrs. Francis; Walsh, Mrs. Catharine
James, Alice Gibbens (sister-in-law). See
James, Mrs. William
James, Alice (niece), 167, 311
James, Alice Runnells (nephew Billy's
wife). See James, Mrs. William
James, Augustus (uncle), 8, 9
James, Catharine Margaret (aunt). See
Temple, Mrs. Robert
James, Edward Holton ("Ned"; nephew),
167, 294, 323
James, Garth Wilkinson ("Wilky";
brother), xii, 22, 24, 29–30, 52, 73, 74,
115, 122, 142, 143, 202, 324; with family in Europe (1855–60), 38, 41, 48,
49, 57, 58, 59; letters quoted, 53, 151,
182n, 205n, 211, 214–15n; at school in
Concord, 64, 65, 67; and Civil War,
71, 73, 75–76; emotional problems, illness, and bankruptcy of, 97, 111, 112,
200, 207, 211, 226; WJ letter to, 98;
engagement, marriage, and children of,
150–51, 162, 167, 182n, 217, 311; relations of, with AJ, 151, 214; death of,
226
James, Mrs. Garth (Caroline Cary), 150,
162, 167, 226
James, Henry, Sr. (father), 73, 74, 85, 97,
109, 140, 200, 201, 219, 312, 317; writings of (see also individual titles), x, 5,
7, 9, 17, 45, 82n, 89, 205, 257; and
child-rearing/education, xi, 9, 10, 12,
16, 17–20, 23, 30, 31, 38–39, 42–47,
55–59 passim, 64–68 passim, 108, 130;
views of, on women, xiii, 10, 13,
45–47, 89, 94, 108, 246, 275; meets and
marries Mary Walsh, 4–6, 12, 32; reli-
gious/mystical experience and philosophy of, 6–9, 12–19 passim, 29, 30, 119,
126, 128–29, 130, 294–95, 303; alcohol
addiction of, 7, 11–12; loses leg, 8–9,
11, 72, 82n; with family abroad,
(1840s) 13, 144, (1855–60) 31, 35, 38;
as "student," 17, 121; relations of, with
AJ, 46–47, 64–68 passim, 99–100, 108,
118, 120, 121, 123, 139, 177, 184–88,

197, 203, 205, 212; relations of, with HJ Jr., 49, 206-7, 208, 211; children's letters to, 56, 198, 201-2, (William's "farewell") 209-11; frailty and death of, 202-3, 205-13, 286; bequests of, 207, 211-12

James, Henry, Sr.: QUOTED: on wife, family, education, 5, 13, 16, 18-19, 38, 45-49 *passim*, 55-59 *passim*, 76-78, 142, 160, 180n, 206-7; on religion and doubt, 6, 7, 8, 13, 17, 21, 130n, 140n; on parents, 7-8, 9, 10; on children's illnesses, 19, 67-68, 98, 111, 123, 126, 140n, 150, 156, 185-86, 188; on Captain Marshall and Kate, 33-34; on life in Europe, 38, 40; on "Jane Smith" (Elizabeth Peabody), 66, 135; on Civil War, 70-71, 75-76; on Bostonians, 86; on marriage, 94, 160

James, Mrs. Henry, Sr. (Mary Robertson Walsh), 4, 13, 17, 33, 74, 94n, 125, 128, 136, 141, 196, 201, 208-13 *passim*, 317; courtship and marriage of, 5-6, 12, 32; dominance of family by, 11, 23, 24, 26, 44, 89, 113; and child-rearing/education, 23-27, 31-32, 38-39, 41, 46, 63, 66, 68, 108; in Europe with family, 41, 55-56; letters to family, 152, 158, (quoted) 5, 24-26 *passim*, 41, 99, 109-13 *passim*, 122-23, 139, 140, 143, 149-51, 159-60, 177-78, 182-84; children's letters to, 184, 198 (*see also* James, Henry, Jr.); death of, 202-3, 205, 207, 227, 286

James, Henry, Jr. ("Harry"; brother), 82, 98, 135, 142, 143, 216, 261, 325; writings of (*see also individual titles*), x, xi, xii, 10, 27, 50, 54, 60, 83, 86, 90, 94, 101, 102, 115, 122, 129, 136, 142n, 146, 152n, 153, 157, 158, 164n, 193n, 197n, 200, 231, 233, 244-51, 265, 266, 275n, 281-84, 287-91 *passim*, 299, 300n, 306-7, 308, 320, (AJ quoted on) 262, 287-89; parents' letters to, 18-19, 24-25, 140, 158, 159, 177-78, 182, 201; ill health of, 19, 32, 37, 72-73, 97, 111-12, 115, 124, 137, 139, 158, 209; birth and childhood of, 22, 28-30, 65n, 67; and relations with William, 28-29, 152n, 248, 257, 281; elected to Academy of Arts and Letters, 29n; travels and life abroad, 35, 37-43, 111, 137-39, 144-60, 296, 305, 319, (life in England) 13, 85, 86, 174, 178, 197-99, 226-27, 234, 239-40, 242, 244, 253, 285, 286; education of, 37-48 *pas-*

sim, 55-59 *passim*, 78, 85, 121; relations of, with AJ, 48-49, 51, 139, 196-200 *passim*, 212, 226, 241-42, 250-52, 254-60 *passim*, 284, 287, 289, 306, 314, 317, 326; and Civil War, 70-73, 76; AJ letters to, 99, 205-6, 209; WJ correspondence with, 114, 139, 140, 141, 152n, 159, 161, 175, 181, 307-8, 315 (*see also* James, William); letters of, to "Quincy Street," 146-47, 149, 153-59 *passim*, 178, 184, 198, 199, 201-2 (*see also* James, Alice); return visits to America, 201-3, 204, 209, 214-15, 221, 225; Aunt Kate's letter to, 207; and father's bequests, 211-12; and friendship with Constance Woolson, 259-60; death of, 323, 326

James, Henry, Jr.: QUOTED: on AJ's state of health, x, 139, 184, 198, 202, 225, 226, 229, 234-36 *passim*, 240-42, 257, 284, 296, 297, (and impending death) 306, 308, 310-14 *passim*; on grandparents and parents, xi, 11, 12, 17, 26-27, 47, 202, 226; on girls and women, xiii, 11, 43, 83, 245-47; on marriage, 25; on William, 29, 183-84, 257; on theatergoing, 30n; on governesses and education, 37-38, 42, 43, 47, 48; on Paris, 41; on Newport, 60, 69-70; on cousins, 61, 99, 102; on injury, and Civil War, 72, 73, 75; on Cambridge house, 97; on life and people abroad, 138, 146-47, 157-58, 174-75, 178, 197; on AJ abroad, 146, 147, 149, 153-58, 254; on Katharine Loring, 192, 196, 198, 199, 239, 240-41, 243; on own writings, 197n, 244, 249-50; on female friendships and feminism, 200, 245-47 (*see also* on girls and women, *above*); on Wilky, 211, 226; on AJ after parents' death, 212, 214, 215; on AJ's death, 315, 316-17; on AJ's diary, 319-22

James, Henry ("Harry"; nephew), 22, 201, 202, 209, 294, 323, 324

James, Herman (nephew), 180-81, 217

James, Joseph Cary (nephew), 167

James, Katharine Barber ("Kitty"; cousin). *See* Prince, Mrs. William Henry

James, Margaret Mary (niece). *See* Porter, Mrs. Bruce

James, Mary Holton (sister-in-law). *See* James, Mrs. Robertson

James, Mary Robertson (mother). *See* James, Mrs. Henry, Sr.

James, Mary Walsh (niece). *See* Vaux, Mrs. George

James, Robertson ("Rob" or "Bob"; brother), *xii*, 22–28 *passim*, 32, 33, 52, 74, 111, 142, 177, 311, 319, 320, 324, 326; letters quoted, 19n, 24, 145, 202, 315–16; brothers' letters to, 32, 125–26, 130, 180, 308; with family in Europe (1855–60), 35, 38, 40, 41, 42, 48, 49, 57; at school in Concord, 64, 65, 67; and Civil War, 75–78 *passim*, 193n; parents' letters to, 77–78, 183–88 *passim*; emotional problems of, 77–78, 97, 122, 125–26, 130, 196, 200, 205, 268; engagement, marriage, and children of, 150, 151, 162, 167, 200, 294; and father's death, 208, 209, 211–12; death of, 323

James, Mrs. Robertson (Mary Holton), 150–51, 162, 167, 186, 205–6, 226, 320; AJ letters to, 204, 205, 226, 268

James, William (grandfather), 6, 7, 8, 9, 10, 11–12, 58

James, Mrs. William (Catharine Barber), 6, 9–11, 31

James, Reverend William (uncle), 8, 12, 31, 69

James, William (brother), 17, 20, 47, 66, 82n, 92, 102, 142, 143, 157, 164, 166, 206, 207, 224, 234, 235, 238, 254, 275, 308, 325; AJ letters to, *ix*, 1, 43, 57, 62, 98, 113, 114, 115, 135, 137, 218, 219, 231, 236–37, 252–59 *passim*, 262–71 *passim*, 274–78 *passim*, 285–86, 304–5, 309; and psychology, *x*, 103, 126, 291, 306; ill health and "crisis" of, *xiii*, 19, 24–25, 32, 71, 87, 99, 106, 110–15 *passim*, 124–30 *passim*, 137, 140, 151, 180, 200; writings of, *xiii*, 54, 117, 127, 181, 185n, 200, 257, 308; and life and travels abroad, 13, 35, 47–52 *passim*, 86, 112, 123–24, 137, 144, 208, 214, 255, 306; parents' letters to, 25, 111, 113, 123; childhood of, 28–29; interest of, in drawing and painting, 28, 57n, 58–59, 71; and relations with HJ Jr., 28–29, 152n, 248, 257, 281; refuses membership in Academy of Arts and Letters, 29n; education of, 37–49 *passim*, 55–59, 78, 85, 110, 121, 126; marriage and family of, 43, 85, 179–84, 194, 196, 200–201, 202, 208, 217–18, 226, 255, 294; relations of, with AJ, 49, 52–55, 99, 110, 123, 139, 160, 181–82, 184, 196, 255–57, 267–68, 281–82, 287, 289, 306, 307–8; and Civil

War, 70–72, 76; HJ Jr. correspondence with, 138, 141, 184, 212, 225–26, 249n, 254, 284, 296, 297, 306, 310–15 *passim*, 319–22 (*see also* James, Henry, Jr.); "farewell letter" of, to father, 209–11; and father's bequests, 211–12; visits AJ and HJ in England, 285–86, 306–7; designs AJ's grave marker, 317; death of, 323

James, William: QUOTED: on HJ Jr. and writings, *x*, 152n, 286; on parents, 17, 25, 32, 130, 210–11, 213; on Academy of Arts and Letters, 29n; on education, 48; on "anti-sexual instinct," 54; on Civil War, 71–72; on own health, 112, 120n, 124, 125–26, 139, 180; on "crisis," 127–29 *passim*, 185n; on "noble sex," 167; on wife, 180, 181; on Wilky, 226; on Americans, 255; on AJ, 283n, ("sonnate" in honor of) 53, 55, (on invitations to) 67, 68–69, (on state of health) 69, 98, 99, 106, 109–10, 119, 123, 124, 140, 141, 152, 159, 175, 196, 229, 267, (on inactivity) 78, 79, (on letters) 145, (on impending death) 303–4, 307, (on death) 315, (on diary) 319

James, Mrs. William (Alice Howe Gibbens; sister-in-law), 22, 179–83, 196, 201, 208, 226, 248, 258, 307; AJ letters to, 201, 217–18, 219, 255, 258, 261–62, 276, 281, 287, 291

James, William ("Billy"; nephew), 22, 52, 208, 294

James, Mrs. William (Alice Runnells; nephew's wife), 22

James Family, The (Matthiessen), 325

Janet, Pierre, 117, 119

Jewett, Sarah Orne, 200, 245

Johnson, Samuel, 63, 100n, 146

Jones, Ernest, 120n

Jung, Carl, 195n

Kean, Charles, 40

Kemble, Fanny, 40, 215, 254, 261, 262

Kidder, Henry P., 222

King, Charlotte, 234

Kossuth, Lajos, 32

La Farge, John, 58, 61

La Farge, Mrs. John (Margaret Perry), 61

Larcom, Lucy, 217

Leavis, F. R.: quoted, 247n

Lecky, William E. H., 174

Lee, Amelia (Mrs. Charles Jackson), 91n

Lee, Harriet Jackson. *See* Morse, Mrs. Samuel Torrey
Lee, Higginson & Company, 165
Lee family, 91, 156
Leigh, Augusta, 249–50
Leverett, William C., 58
Lewes, George Henry, 13, 137
Lincoln, Abraham, 70, 80
Ling, Dr. Peter Henrik, 106
Litchfield, Mrs. R. B. (Henrietta Darwin), 291
Literary Remains of the Late Henry James, The (W. James, ed.), 82n, 257
Lombard family, 142, 156
London Daily News, 289–90
London Life, A (H. James Jr.), 231, 266
Longfellow, Henry Wadsworth, 60, 89
Longfellow, Mrs. Henry Wadsworth (Frances Elizabeth Appleton), 165
Loring, Augustus Peabody, 191, 193
Loring, Caleb William, 191, 192, 229
Loring, Mrs. Caleb William (Elizabeth Peabody), 191, 192
Loring, Charles Greeley, 192
Loring, Frank, 164
Loring, Jane. *See* Gray, Mrs. Asa
Loring, Katharine Peabody, 164, 173n, 175, 222; letters quoted, 62n, 279, 315; as friend and companion of AJ, 83, 191–203 *passim*, 216–29 *passim*, 233–35, 238–44, 248–53 *passim*, 260–67 *passim*, 271–80 *passim*, 293n, 296–304 *passim*, 308–15 *passim*; and AJ's diary, 317, 319–21, 323
Loring, Louisa Putnam, 191, 192, 199, 222, 229, 234, 235, 249, 323; illness of, 226, 227, 239–40, 241
Loring, William Caleb, 191, 193
Lowell, Charles Russell, 87
Lowell, Mrs. Charles Russell (Josephine Shaw), 95, 136n
Lowell, James Russell, 86, 132, 135n, 137, 157, 234, 248–49, 254
Lowell, Mrs. James Russell, 136n, 157, 234
Lowell, Mabel, 132, 134
Lowell, Nina, 86
Lowell, Robert, 76
Lyman family, 91

Macaulay, Thomas B., 174
Mann, Horace, 135
Marshall, Captain Charles H., 32–35
Marshall, Mrs. Charles H. *See* Walsh, Mrs. Catharine

Mason, Ellen, 173n
Massachusetts Woman Suffrage Association, 89
Mather, Cotton, 269
Matthiessen, F. O., 250n, 325
Maud, Constance, 212, 217
Mead, Mary, 141
Melville, Herman, 89
Mérimée, Prosper, 174
Mestayer, Emily, 30n
Mill, John Stuart, 13
Mitchell, Maggie, 141
Mitchell, Dr. Silas Weir, 103, 104, 105–6, 223–24, 225, 227, 323
Moers, Ellen: quoted, 28n
Montaigne, Michel de, 261, 262, 269
Morris, William and Jane, 137, 138
Morse, Frances Rollins ("Fanny"), 144, 156, 165, 174, 217, 296, 297; AJ friendship with, 86, 91–92, 113, 137, 141, 166, 196n, 263, 315; AJ letters to, 92–98 *passim*, 141, 169, 179, 189, 191, 196, 201, 206, 228, 267, 270, 271
Morse, Mary, 92, 189
Morse, Samuel Torrey and Harriet Jackson Lee, 92
Mrs. Jasper's Way (H. James Jr.), 289n
Mrs. Vibert (H. James Jr.), 288–89, 308
Murdock, Kenneth B., 250n
Murray Street (New York) Presbyterian Church, 4, 5
Myers, Frederick, 291

Napoleon III, 35
Nation, The, 98, 142, 146, 152n, 275n, 289, 325
National Institute/Academy of Arts and Letters, 29n
National Women's Suffrage Association convention (Boston, 1881), 215, 216
Nature of Evil, The (H. James Sr.), 17
Neftel, Dr. William B., 227–28
Neurasthenia, ix, xv, 103–6, 222–24 *passim*, 224–25, 237, 303. *See also* Hysteria *and* Women
New England Women's Club, 89
Newport News, 75
New Republic, 325
New York *Herald*, 34–35
New York *Herald Tribune*, 324
New York Review of Books, 326
New York Times, 325
North American Review, 86, 137
Norton, Charles Eliot, 60, 86, 89–90, 137, 149, 157, 158, 178n

Norton, Mrs. Charles Eliot (Susan Sedgwick), 136–37, 149, 157, 158, 178n
Norton, Grace, 136n, 137, 138, 219, 234, 240, 242, 261, 262
Norton, Jane, 136n, 137, 169
Notebooks (H. James Jr.), 250n
Nouvelle Revue, La, 262, 276

Olmsted, Frederick Law, 79

Page, Dr. Frank, 222–25
Page, William and Sophia Hitchcock, 135n
Paine Webber Jackson and Curtis, 166n
Pall Mall Gazette, 80, 277
Palmer, Mary Towle, 133, 134
Parker, Theodore, 88
Parkman, Francis, 90
Parnell, Charles Stewart, 278
Parsons, Caroline, 132, 133
Parsons, Emily, 133
Parsons, Theophilus, 132
Peabody, Elizabeth. See Loring, Mrs. Caleb
Peabody, Elizabeth Palmer, 66, 135–36, 141, 249; HJ Sr. letter to, 75–76
Peabody, Joseph Augustus and Louisa Putnam, 191
Peirce, Benjamin, 67n
Peirce, Charles Sanders, 115n
Peirce, Mrs. Charles Sanders (Melusina Fay), 115, 136n
Perkins, Elizabeth, 173n
Perkins, Ned, 94
Perry, Margaret. See La Farge, Mrs. John
Perry, Thomas Sergeant ("Sargy"), 44, 60, 63, 67, 161, 162
Perry, Mrs. Thomas (Lilla Cabot), 44, 161, 162
Phillips, Wendell, 135n
Piper, Mrs. William J., 256
Poe, Edgar Allan, 30, 89, 320
Pollock, Sir Frederick, 254
Porter, Benjamin Curtis, 148
Porter, Mrs. Bruce (Margaret Mary James; niece), 52, 55, 311, 323
Portrait of a Lady, The (H. James Jr.), 27, 50, 153, 197n
Powel, Mary, 61
Presbyterianism. See Religion
Prince, Dr. William Henry, 69
Prince, Mrs. William Henry (Katharine Barber James, "Kitty"; cousin), 69, 81, 203, 249

Princess Casamassima, The (H. James Jr.), 27n, 281–84
Princeton Theological Seminary, 4, 12
Principles of Psychology, The (W. James), 54, 181, 185n, 257, 308
Putnam, Dr. Charles, 194, 195
Putnam, Mrs. Charles (Lucy Washburn), 88n
Putnam, Elizabeth, 91, 311
Putnam, Dr. James Jackson, 103, 194, 195n, 222, 223n, 228
Putnam, Louisa, 191
Putnam's Monthly magazine, 45

Quincy, Josiah, 135n
Quincy, Mabel, 261

Radcliffe College, 67n, 170n. See also Harvard "Annex"
Reade, Charles, 141
Religion: Presbyterianism, 4, 5, 7; HJ Sr. and philosophy of, 6–9, 12–19 passim, 29, 30, 119, 126, 128–29, 130, 294–95, 303; Calvinism, 7, 12–13, 15, 16n, 45n, 58, 294; "feminization" of, in U.S., 90n; AJ's view of, 294–95. See also Swedenborg and Swedenborgianism
Renouvier, Charles, 129
Reubell, Henrietta, 317
Richards, Francis Gardiner, 179
Richards, Mrs. Francis (Annie Ashburner), 151, 179, 298, 317; AJ friendship with, 98, 141, 142, 229, 254, 311, 314–15; AJ letters to, 148, 158–69 passim, 175–79 passim
Richardson, Henry Hobson, 258
Rimmer, Dr. William, 66
Ripley, George, 30
Robertson, Alexander (great-grandfather), 3, 22
Robertson, Mrs. Alexander (Mary Smith; great-grandmother), 3
Robson, Frederick, 40
Roderick Hudson (H. James Jr.), 233
Romanoff, Alexander, 80
Rosenberg, Charles E., 106n
Rossetti, Christina: quoted, 243
Rossetti, Dante Gabriel, 137, 138
Rubáiyát: quoted, 268
Ruskin, John, 137, 138, 260, 273

Sacred Fount, The (H. James Jr.), 112n
Sanborn, Franklin B., 64, 67, 86, 89
Sand, George, 262, 263–64, 265, 269, 276
Sargent, John Singer, 192

Sargent, Mrs. John Singer, 136n
Saturday Morning Club, 193
Saturday Review, The, 98, 326
Schönberg, Baron von, 162
Secret of Swedenborg, The (H. James Sr.), 17
Sedgwick, Arthur George, 86, 136, 151
Sedgwick, Mrs. Arthur, 86, 151
Sedgwick, Sara. *See* Darwin, Mrs. William
Sedgwick, Susan. *See* Norton, Mrs. Charles Eliot
Sedgwick, Theodora, 136, 141, 142, 178
Sedgwick, Theodore and Sara Ashburner, 136
Seelye, Julius, 69
Sewall, May Eliza Wright, 217
Sex, attitudes toward, 28n, 54–55, 72, 102, 109, 124, 126, 218–19, 263. *See also* Women
Shaw, Josephine. *See* Lowell, Mrs. Charles Russell
Shaw, Nelly, 95
Shaw, Colonel Robert Gould, 75, 76, 87, 95, 135n
Sheridan, Richard Brinsley, 40
Sicherman, Barbara, 105n, 106n; quoted, 103n
Sidgwick, Henry, 254
Sidgwick, Mrs. William, 254, 324
Sidney, Sir Philip, 178
Simmons, Lizzie, 133–34
Simmons School of Social Work, 92
Slavery, 70, 80; and abolitionism, 64, 70–71, 87, 88
Smith, Mary. *See* Robertson, Mrs. Alexander
Smith-Rosenberg, Caroll, 93n, 105n, 168n
Social Significance of Our Institutions, The (H. James Sr.), 17
Society the Redeemed Form of Man (H. James Sr.), 17
Society to Encourage Studies at Home, 170–76, 177, 191, 193
Sontag, Susan: quoted, 101n
Sparks, Florence, 132
Spectator, The (periodical), 98
Spencer, Herbert, 20
Spender, Stephen, 129–30
Staël, Mme. Germaine de, 174
Stanton, Elizabeth Cady, 215
Stephen, Leslie, 137
Stevenson, Robert Louis, 39, 101n, 240
Stone, Lucy, 216
Storer, Margaret Woodbury ("Marny"). *See* Warner, Mrs. Joseph
Story, Moorfield, 166

Story, Mrs. Moorfield (Gertrude Cutts), 166n
Stowe, Harriet Beecher, 16n, 30, 89, 109, 195n
Study in Greens (Sargent painting), 192
Substance and Shadow . . . (H. James Sr.), 17
Sumner, Charles, 135n, 166n
Swedenborg, Emanuel, and Swedenborgianism, 14–15, 17, 19n, 119, 129, 135n, 140n

Taft, William Howard, 192
Tappan, Ellen, 162–63, 164
Tappan family, 68
Taylor, Dr. Charles Fayette, 98, 100, 106–10, 111
Taylor, Tom, 40
Temple, Ellen (cousin), 61, 73, 99
Temple, Henrietta (cousin), 61, 99
Temple, Katharine ("Kitty"; cousin), 61, 99, 125–26
Temple, Mary ("Minny"; cousin), 61, 99, 101, 102, 115, 125n, 157
Temple, Mary. *See* Tweedy, Mrs. Edmund
Temple, Colonel Robert (uncle by marriage), 61
Temple, Mrs. Robert (Catharine Margaret James; aunt), 61
Temple, Robert (cousin), 61
Temple, William (cousin), 61
Tennyson, Alfred Lord, 13
Terhune, Mary V. *See* Harland, Marion
Thackeray, William Makepeace, 39, 51, 197, 269, 273
Thies, Clara Crowninshield, 132
Thomson, Robert, 39
Thoreau, Henry David, 13, 89, 101n, 245
Thurber, James, 300n
Ticknor, Anna Eliot, 170–73, 177, 193, 220
Ticknor, George, 170
Ticknor, Mrs. George (Anna Eliot), 170, 173n
Times Literary Supplement, 324
Toepffer, Rodolphe, 30
Townsend, Dr. (British physician), 237
Tragic Muse, The (H. James Jr.), 290, 308
Trevelyan, Sir George Otto, 174
Trilling, Diana, 325
Trilling, Lionel, 283
Trollope, Mrs. Frances, 10
Tuckey, Dr. Charles Lloyd, 308–9, 310, 312, 313–14
Tuke, Dr. Daniel Hack, 240

Turner, Joseph M. W., 148n
Turn of the Screw, The (H. James Jr.), 50, 300n
Twain, Mark, 247
Tweedy, Edmund, 57n, 58–59, 138, 157
Tweedy, Mrs. Edmund (Mary Temple), 61, 138, 157

Uncle Tom's Cabin (Stowe), 30, 89, 115
Union College (Schenectady), 7; Henry Sr. at, 11
Union Defence Committee, 34
United States Sanitary Commission, 79

Van Dyck, Sir Anthony, 146, 148
Varian, Isaac Leggett, 6
Varieties of Religious Experience, The (W. James), 127
Vaux, Alice James (great-grandniece), 326
Vaux, Mrs. George (Mary Walsh James; niece), 167, 311, 321, 323

Wallace, Mackenzie, 174
Walsh, Alexander Robertson (uncle), 4
Walsh, Mrs. Catharine ("Aunt Kate"), 4, 5, 23, 24, 28–32 *passim,* 44, 65, 114, 122, 139, 142, 167, 183, 196, 205, 218, 219, 226–27, 248; marriage of, 32–35; travels in Europe, 35, 39, 40, 56, 140, 144–60; with AJ in New York, 98, 99, 106, 110; quoted on AJ, 177, 202–3, 207, 208; destroys family papers, 209; AJ letters to, 220, 239, 253–54, 259, 268; HJ Jr. letters to, 234, 235–36, 240–41, 242; death of, 285–86
Walsh, Elizabeth Robertson (cousin), 311
Walsh, Hugh (great-grandfather), 4
Walsh, Mrs. Hugh (Catharine Armstrong), 4
Walsh, Hugh (uncle), 4–5, 12
Walsh, James (grandfather), 3–4
Walsh, Mrs. James (Elizabeth Robertson), 3–4, 5, 11, 30
Walsh, James (uncle), 4
Walsh, John (uncle), 4, 32
Walsh, Mary Robertson (mother). *See* James, Mrs. Henry, Sr.
War and Peace (Tolstoy), 262, 268
Ward, "Bet," "Bessy," 67, 73, 95, 162
Ward, Mrs. Humphry, 235, 262
Ward, Samuel Gray, 60, 67, 115
Ward, Mrs. Samuel Gray (Anna Barker), 67
Ward, Tom, 73, 110

Warner, Joseph B., 163, 207, 220, 312
Warner, Mrs. Joseph (Margaret Woodbury Storer; "Marny"), 132, 133, 163, 183n, 207, 312
Washburn, Lucy. *See* Putnam, Mrs. Charles
Washington Square (H. James Jr.), 27n, 94
Watch and Ward (H. James Jr.), 142n
Watson, Jenny, 94
Watson, Sylvia, 161
Wetmore, William, 60
What Maisie Knew (H. James Jr.), 27
Whicher, Harriet Fox, 324
Whitman, Walt, 89
Whitney, Mattie, 234, 235
Whittier, John Greenleaf, 89
Wigan, Alfred, 40
Wilkinson, Dr. J. J. Garth, and Wilkinson family, 14, 22, 35, 38, 148, 235
Wilkinson, Mary, 235
Wilson, Edmund, 300n
Wings of the Dove, The (H. James Jr.), 27n, 54, 101, 102, 299
Woman's Rights Convention (1848), 88
Women: HJ Jr.'s attitude toward and writings about, *xiii,* 43, 49–51, 90, 101–2, 122, 200, 215, 244–51, 259–60; HJ Sr.'s attitude toward, *xiii,* 10, 13, 45–47, 89, 94, 108, 246, 275; Victorian attitude toward, *xv,* 28n, 69, 83, 100–101, 104, 109, 134, 167, 263, 271; post–Civil War, in New England, *xv,* 87–90; education of, *xv,* 43–47, 61–64, 67, 108, 109, 121, 170–76, 193, 220, 260; as writers, 10, 89–90, 275; and women's rights/suffrage movements, 88–89, 115n, 215–16, 220, 244; friendships between, 93–94n, 200, 244, 245; nervous disorders of, 100–101, 102–9, 119, 121–22, 124–25, 172–73, 221, 222–25, 227, 235–38 *passim;* indigent, relief of, 136; and nineteenth-century fictional heroines, 195–96, 245–49; Boston as "city of," 215; "busy ineffectiveness" of, 217, 243
Wood, Ann Douglas. *See* Douglas, Ann
Woolf, Virginia, *xiv, xv,* 325
Woolson, Constance Fenimore, 101, 254, 259, 262, 305, 312, 313, 320; quoted, 202n, 260, 293n, 307
Wordsworth, William, 63, 138, 261
Wright, Chauncy, 157
Wyman, Morrill, 222

OTHER NEW YORK REVIEW CLASSICS*

J.R. ACKERLEY My Dog Tulip
J.R. ACKERLEY My Father and Myself
J.R. ACKERLEY We Think the World of You
HENRY ADAMS The Jeffersonian Transformation
CÉLESTE ALBARET Monsieur Proust
DANTE ALIGHIERI The Inferno
DANTE ALIGHIERI The New Life
WILLIAM ATTAWAY Blood on the Forge
W.H. AUDEN W.H. Auden's Book of Light Verse
ERICH AUERBACH Dante: Poet of the Secular World
DOROTHY BAKER Cassandra at the Wedding
J.A. BAKER The Peregrine
HONORÉ DE BALZAC The Unknown Masterpiece *and* Gambara
MAX BEERBOHM Seven Men
STEPHEN BENATAR Wish Her Safe at Home
FRANS G. BENGTSSON The Long Ships
ALEXANDER BERKMAN Prison Memoirs of an Anarchist
GEORGES BERNANOS Mouchette
ADOLFO BIOY CASARES Asleep in the Sun
ADOLFO BIOY CASARES The Invention of Morel
CAROLINE BLACKWOOD Corrigan
CAROLINE BLACKWOOD Great Granny Webster
NICOLAS BOUVIER The Way of the World
MALCOLM BRALY On the Yard
MILLEN BRAND The Outward Room
JOHN HORNE BURNS The Gallery
ROBERT BURTON The Anatomy of Melancholy
CAMARA LAYE The Radiance of the King
GIROLAMO CARDANO The Book of My Life
DON CARPENTER Hard Rain Falling
J.L. CARR A Month in the Country
BLAISE CENDRARS Moravagine
EILEEN CHANG Love in a Fallen City
UPAMANYU CHATTERJEE English, August: An Indian Story
NIRAD C. CHAUDHURI The Autobiography of an Unknown Indian
ANTON CHEKHOV Peasants and Other Stories
RICHARD COBB Paris and Elsewhere
COLETTE The Pure and the Impure
JOHN COLLIER Fancies and Goodnights
CARLO COLLODI The Adventures of Pinocchio
IVY COMPTON-BURNETT A House and Its Head
IVY COMPTON-BURNETT Manservant and Maidservant
BARBARA COMYNS The Vet's Daughter
EVAN S. CONNELL The Diary of a Rapist
ALBERT COSSERY The Jokers
HAROLD CRUSE The Crisis of the Negro Intellectual
ASTOLPHE DE CUSTINE Letters from Russia
LORENZO DA PONTE Memoirs
ELIZABETH DAVID A Book of Mediterranean Food
ELIZABETH DAVID Summer Cooking

* *For a complete list of titles, visit www.nyrb.com or write to:*
Catalog Requests, NYRB, 435 Hudson Street, New York, NY 10014

L.J. DAVIS A Meaningful Life
MARIA DERMOÛT The Ten Thousand Things
TIBOR DÉRY Niki: The Story of a Dog
ARTHUR CONAN DOYLE The Exploits and Adventures of Brigadier Gerard
CHARLES DUFF A Handbook on Hanging
BRUCE DUFFY The World As I Found It
DAPHNE DU MAURIER Don't Look Now: Stories
ELAINE DUNDY The Dud Avocado
ELAINE DUNDY The Old Man and Me
G.B. EDWARDS The Book of Ebenezer Le Page
MARCELLUS EMANTS A Posthumous Confession
EURIPIDES Grief Lessons: Four Plays; translated by Anne Carson
J.G. FARRELL Troubles
J.G. FARRELL The Siege of Krishnapur
J.G. FARRELL The Singapore Grip
ELIZA FAY Original Letters from India
KENNETH FEARING The Big Clock
KENNETH FEARING Clark Gifford's Body
FÉLIX FÉNÉON Novels in Three Lines
M.I. FINLEY The World of Odysseus
THEODOR FONTANE Irretrievable
MASANOBU FUKUOKA The One-Straw Revolution
MARC FUMAROLI When the World Spoke French
CARLO EMILIO GADDA That Awful Mess on the Via Merulana
MAVIS GALLANT The Cost of Living: Early and Uncollected Stories
MAVIS GALLANT Paris Stories
MAVIS GALLANT Varieties of Exile
GABRIEL GARCÍA MÁRQUEZ Clandestine in Chile: The Adventures of Miguel Littín
ALAN GARNER Red Shift
THÉOPHILE GAUTIER My Fantoms
JEAN GENET Prisoner of Love
ÉLISABETH GILLE The Mirador: Dreamed Memories of Irène Némirovsky by Her Daughter
JOHN GLASSCO Memoirs of Montparnasse
EDMOND AND JULES DE GONCOURT Pages from the Goncourt Journals
EDWARD GOREY (EDITOR) The Haunted Looking Glass
WILLIAM LINDSAY GRESHAM Nightmare Alley
EMMETT GROGAN Ringolevio: A Life Played for Keeps
VASILY GROSSMAN Everything Flows
VASILY GROSSMAN Life and Fate
VASILY GROSSMAN The Road
OAKLEY HALL Warlock
PATRICK HAMILTON The Slaves of Solitude
PATRICK HAMILTON Twenty Thousand Streets Under the Sky
PETER HANDKE Short Letter, Long Farewell
PETER HANDKE Slow Homecoming
PETER HANDKE A Sorrow Beyond Dreams
ELIZABETH HARDWICK The New York Stories of Elizabeth Hardwick
ELIZABETH HARDWICK Seduction and Betrayal
ELIZABETH HARDWICK Sleepless Nights
L.P. HARTLEY Eustace and Hilda: A Trilogy
L.P. HARTLEY The Go-Between
NATHANIEL HAWTHORNE Twenty Days with Julian & Little Bunny by Papa
GILBERT HIGHET Poets in a Landscape

JANET HOBHOUSE The Furies

ALISTAIR HORNE A Savage War of Peace: Algeria 1954–1962

WILLIAM DEAN HOWELLS Indian Summer

BOHUMIL HRABAL Dancing Lessons for the Advanced in Age

RICHARD HUGHES A High Wind in Jamaica

RICHARD HUGHES In Hazard

RICHARD HUGHES The Fox in the Attic (The Human Predicament, Vol. 1)

RICHARD HUGHES The Wooden Shepherdess (The Human Predicament, Vol. 2)

MAUDE HUTCHINS Victorine

YASUSHI INOUE Tun-huang

HENRY JAMES The Ivory Tower

HENRY JAMES The New York Stories of Henry James

HENRY JAMES The Other House

HENRY JAMES The Outcry

TOVE JANSSON Fair Play

TOVE JANSSON The Summer Book

TOVE JANSSON The True Deceiver

RANDALL JARRELL (EDITOR) Randall Jarrell's Book of Stories

KABIR Songs of Kabir; translated by Arvind Krishna Mehrotra

HELEN KELLER The World I Live In

YASHAR KEMAL Memed, My Hawk

YASHAR KEMAL They Burn the Thistles

MURRAY KEMPTON Part of Our Time: Some Ruins and Monuments of the Thirties

DAVID KIDD Peking Story

ROBERT KIRK The Secret Commonwealth of Elves, Fauns, and Fairies

ARUN KOLATKAR Jejuri

DEZSŐ KOSZTOLÁNYI Skylark

TÉTÉ-MICHEL KPOMASSIE An African in Greenland

SIGIZMUND KRZHIZHANOVSKY Memories of the Future

MARGARET LEECH Reveille in Washington: 1860–1865

PATRICK LEIGH FERMOR Between the Woods and the Water

PATRICK LEIGH FERMOR Mani: Travels in the Southern Peloponnese

PATRICK LEIGH FERMOR Roumeli: Travels in Northern Greece

PATRICK LEIGH FERMOR A Time of Gifts

PATRICK LEIGH FERMOR A Time to Keep Silence

PATRICK LEIGH FERMOR The Traveller's Tree

D.B. WYNDHAM LEWIS AND CHARLES LEE (EDITORS) The Stuffed Owl

GEORG CHRISTOPH LICHTENBERG The Waste Books

JAKOV LIND Soul of Wood and Other Stories

H.P. LOVECRAFT AND OTHERS The Colour Out of Space

ROSE MACAULAY The Towers of Trebizond

DWIGHT MACDONALD Masscult and Midcult: Essays Against the American Grain

NORMAN MAILER Miami and the Siege of Chicago

JANET MALCOLM In the Freud Archives

JEAN-PATRICK MANCHETTE Fatale

OLIVIA MANNING Fortunes of War: The Balkan Trilogy

GUY DE MAUPASSANT Afloat

GUY DE MAUPASSANT Alien Hearts

JAMES MCCOURT Mawrdew Czgowchwz

JESSICA MITFORD Hons and Rebels

JESSICA MITFORD Poison Penmanship

NANCY MITFORD Madame de Pompadour

BRIAN MOORE The Lonely Passion of Judith Hearne

GEORGES SIMENON Pedigree

GEORGES SIMENON Red Lights

GEORGES SIMENON The Strangers in the House

GEORGES SIMENON Tropic Moon

GEORGES SIMENON The Widow

CHARLES SIMIC Dime-Store Alchemy: The Art of Joseph Cornell

MAY SINCLAIR Mary Olivier: A Life

TESS SLESINGER The Unpossessed: A Novel of the Thirties

VLADIMIR SOROKIN Ice Trilogy

DAVID STACTON The Judges of the Secret Court

JEAN STAFFORD The Mountain Lion

CHRISTINA STEAD Letty Fox: Her Luck

GEORGE R. STEWART Names on the Land

STENDHAL The Life of Henry Brulard

THEODOR STORM The Rider on the White Horse

HOWARD STURGIS Belchamber

ITALO SVEVO As a Man Grows Older

HARVEY SWADOS Nights in the Gardens of Brooklyn

A.J.A. SYMONS The Quest for Corvo

HENRY DAVID THOREAU The Journal: 1837–1861

TATYANA TOLSTAYA The Slynx

TATYANA TOLSTAYA White Walls: Collected Stories

EDWARD JOHN TRELAWNY Records of Shelley, Byron, and the Author

LIONEL TRILLING The Liberal Imagination

LIONEL TRILLING The Middle of the Journey

IVAN TURGENEV Virgin Soil

JULES VALLÈS The Child

MARK VAN DOREN Shakespeare

CARL VAN VECHTEN The Tiger in the House

ELIZABETH VON ARNIM The Enchanted April

EDWARD LEWIS WALLANT The Tenants of Moonbloom

ROBERT WALSER Jakob von Gunten

SYLVIA TOWNSEND WARNER Lolly Willowes

SYLVIA TOWNSEND WARNER Mr. Fortune

SYLVIA TOWNSEND WARNER Summer Will Show

ALEKSANDER WAT My Century

C.V. WEDGWOOD The Thirty Years War

SIMONE WEIL AND RACHEL BESPALOFF War and the Iliad

GLENWAY WESCOTT Apartment in Athens

GLENWAY WESCOTT The Pilgrim Hawk

REBECCA WEST The Fountain Overflows

EDITH WHARTON The New York Stories of Edith Wharton

T.H. WHITE The Goshawk

JOHN WILLIAMS Butcher's Crossing

JOHN WILLIAMS Stoner

ANGUS WILSON Anglo-Saxon Attitudes

RUDOLF AND MARGARET WITTKOWER Born Under Saturn

GEOFFREY WOLFF Black Sun

FRANCIS WYNDHAM The Complete Fiction

STEFAN ZWEIG Beware of Pity

STEFAN ZWEIG Chess Story

STEFAN ZWEIG Journey Into the Past

STEFAN ZWEIG The Post-Office Girl

BRIAN MOORE The Mangan Inheritance

ALBERTO MORAVIA Boredom

ALBERTO MORAVIA Contempt

JAN MORRIS Conundrum

JAN MORRIS Hav

PENELOPE MORTIMER The Pumpkin Eater

ÁLVARO MUTIS The Adventures and Misadventures of Maqroll

L.H. MYERS The Root and the Flower

DARCY O'BRIEN A Way of Life, Like Any Other

IRIS OWENS After Claude

RUSSELL PAGE The Education of a Gardener

ALEXANDROS PAPADIAMANTIS The Murderess

BORIS PASTERNAK, MARINA TSVETAYEVA, AND RAINER MARIA RILKE Letters, Summer 1926

CESARE PAVESE The Moon and the Bonfires

CESARE PAVESE The Selected Works of Cesare Pavese

LUIGI PIRANDELLO The Late Mattia Pascal

ANDREY PLATONOV The Foundation Pit

ANDREY PLATONOV Soul and Other Stories

J.F. POWERS Morte d'Urban

J.F. POWERS The Stories of J.F. Powers

J.F. POWERS Wheat That Springeth Green

BOLESŁAW PRUS The Doll

RAYMOND QUENEAU We Always Treat Women Too Well

RAYMOND QUENEAU Witch Grass

RAYMOND RADIGUET Count d'Orgel's Ball

JULES RENARD Nature Stories

JEAN RENOIR Renoir, My Father

GREGOR VON REZZORI Memoirs of an Anti-Semite

GREGOR VON REZZORI The Snows of Yesteryear: Portraits for an Autobiography

TIM ROBINSON Stones of Aran: Labyrinth

TIM ROBINSON Stones of Aran: Pilgrimage

MILTON ROKEACH The Three Christs of Ypsilanti

FR. ROLFE Hadrian the Seventh

GILLIAN ROSE Love's Work

WILLIAM ROUGHEAD Classic Crimes

CONSTANCE ROURKE American Humor: A Study of the National Character

TAYEB SALIH Season of Migration to the North

TAYEB SALIH The Wedding of Zein

GERSHOM SCHOLEM Walter Benjamin: The Story of a Friendship

DANIEL PAUL SCHREBER Memoirs of My Nervous Illness

JAMES SCHUYLER Alfred and Guinevere

JAMES SCHUYLER What's for Dinner?

LEONARDO SCIASCIA The Day of the Owl

LEONARDO SCIASCIA Equal Danger

LEONARDO SCIASCIA The Moro Affair

LEONARDO SCIASCIA To Each His Own

LEONARDO SCIASCIA The Wine-Dark Sea

VICTOR SERGE The Case of Comrade Tulayev

VICTOR SERGE Conquered City

GEORGES SIMENON Act of Passion

GEORGES SIMENON Dirty Snow

GEORGES SIMENON The Man Who Watched Trains Go By

GEORGES SIMENON Monsieur Monde Vanishes